PEOPLE AND PROFESSIONS OF CHARLESTON, SOUTH CAROLINA, 1782-1802

JAMES W. HAGY

CLEARFIELD

Printed for
Clearfield Company by
Genealogical Publishing Co.
Baltimore, Maryland
1992

Reprinted for
Clearfield Company by
Genealogical Publishing Co.
Baltimore, Maryland
1995, 1999, 2008

ISBN-13: 978-0-8063-1323-8
ISBN-10: 0-8063-1323-4

Contents

INTRODUCTION

This volume is an attempt to identify people in Charleston, South Carolina from 1782 to 1802 by using the city directories and the federal censuses. These sources do not exist for earlier years as the first directory appeared in 1782 and the first federal census was taken in 1790.

City directories and censuses give the names of the heads of households or businesses. The directories, in addition, list the professions of the people and their addresses. The census reports record the number of free persons, broken down by age categories, and the number of slaves in the household. Not until 1850 did the census list all residents of a household giving their name, age, and place of birth. Examination of that census and later ones show that the figures cannot be trusted, in many cases, to determine family size. For example, non-related individuals often lived in households. Therefore, these numbers are not given here. Anyone who wants to find these can consult the original census reports.

Some names will appear more than once in the census reports and directories. At times, this results from more than one person having the same name; however, this more often happens when a person owns more than one piece of property. Occasionally it could be a duplicate entry.

The spelling of some names varies from source to source. Sometimes the enumerators give phonetic equivalents. At others times they just do not know how to spell a name properly, as in the case of French and German names. Generally, the spelling is approximate and can be recognized. Another problem with spellings arises with the census reports. These are handwritten lists and are often difficult to decipher. Sometimes the people who made the lists did not do so very carefully. In addition, the paper has often faded, or turned brown, or ink has come through from the opposite side. Vowels and initials can be the most difficult to discern. The spellings of names as they appear in the records have been retained even when it is known they are wrong, or appear to be incorrect. If a names does not appear where it should in a list, a scan of other names beginning with the same letter of the alphabet might be helpful. An examination of the original census report might show that the name has been transcribed incorrectly. Modern abbreviations for Senior and Junior have been substituted for those used in the records. Names have usually been spelled out when the abbreviations are understood, such as <u>Wm</u>. for <u>William</u>.

In addition to free whites, the city of Charleston had a considerable number of "free persons of color." They do not appear in the directories for these years, while the census of 1790 usually lists only a first name for them and the 1800 enumeration only has the word "free."

While the city directories furnish the professions of individuals, these should be used with some caution. Each editor tended to use his definitions. This is especially true for shopkeepers, storekeepers, and merchants. Apparently shopkeepers and storekeepers were the same but compilers of the directories use both. They might also call a shopkeeper a merchant although this term generally meant a large scale businessman in the wholesale or import/export business. If a person is listed in several directories the status becomes clearer. Looked at over a period of time, the directories show that little social or economic mobility existed. Families tend to occupy the same status over long periods of time, sometimes into the present. A number of people have two or more professions listed. Some abbreviations of professions are not understood and have been retained. The spelling of some professions has been changed to conform to present day use such as "tailor" for "taylor."

The directories also give the street addresses of people. In some cases street names have changed over the years, but older names can generally be identified with present ones. Street numbers present a much more difficult problem. The early nineteenth century city had no official numbering system. Therefore, some house numbers changed although others remain the same. The present system of numbering houses with odd numbers on one side of the street and even ones on the other was not necessarily followed. Also houses succumbed to rot, neglect, and fires from time to time. The area might be left vacant for a number of years and new houses on the site might have different numbers. A compiler of a directory in the 1830s indicated that many houses had no numbers. Therefore, he gave them numbers of his choice. This may have happened on other occasions as well. Therefore, to identify a particular house with any certainty one must consult other sources. The surest method would be to trace the deeds recorded in the office of the Register of Mesne Conveyance at the Charleston County Courthouse.

Many people had their place of business and residence at the same address. On occasion a separate residence is indicated or only the residence is given. As an example, a person working at the Custom House might have his home address given. The same might be true for an important political figure. On the other hand, some individuals have their places of business indicated, such as at a wharf, but have no indication of their residence. This could result if several members of a household were engaged in different businesses. Also the boarding houses of the city apparently contained many people who operated shops or engaged in professions. This certainly can be seen with the 1850 census. Occasionally, some people have two places of business given.

The listings have a number of abbreviations which cannot be deciphered. They have been left as they appear. Others have usually been spelled out.

Despite the limitations of the directories and the censuses both can be extremely useful in understanding Charleston and its people.

CHAPTER 1

THE 1782 CITY DIRECTORY

The first city directory for Charleston was published by John Tobler as a part of *The South-Carolina and Georgia Almanack, for the Year of Our Lord 1782: Being Second After Leap Year. Containing The Lunations; Eclipses; Rising and Setting of the Sun: Rising and Setting of the Moon and Stars; Aspects; Judgment of the Weather &tc, &tc, &tc.* (Charleston: R. Wells & Co., 1782).

The directory took up slightly more than 5½ pages and included entries for 258 individuals, 253 men and 5 women (1.94%). The British occupied the city at the time and the list reflects this. Many of the people listed were government officials.

The businesses and residences concentrated in the lower part of the peninsula especially on Broad Street, The Bay, Tradd Street, Church Street, and Meeting Street. Smaller numbers are found elsewhere.

Twenty-six locations are represented. They are: Bay 46, Bay Continued 2, Beaufain Street 1, Bedon's Alley 5, Beresford's Alley 1, Broad Street 59, Burn's Wharf 2, Chalmer's Street 1, Church Street 35, Cumberland Street 1, Ellery Street 2, Elliot Street 2, Friend Street 1, Gibbes Street 1, Greenwood's Wharf 3, King Street 8, Meeting Street 21, Moore Street 3, Orange Street 2, Pinckney Street 1, Queen Street 7, Short Street 1, Stoll's Alley 1, Tradd Street 38, Union Street 1, White Point 1.

As for professions, more people were listed as merchants (39%) than anything else. The group of British officials in the city was the second greatest in number (9.7%).

The professions were: attorney 11, baker 4, banker 1, barber 1, blacksmith 2, bookbinder & stationer 1, British official 25, broker 1, cabinet maker 1, carpenter 5, carver & gilder 1, cooper 1, engraver 1, esquire 13, factor 9, grocer 10, insurance broker 2, jeweller & goldsmith 1, leather dresser 1, merchant 98, milliner 2, physician 14, printer 4, rector 2, saddler 1, school master 1, ship chandler 3, ship carpenter 1, shoemaker 2, silversmith 5, surgeon 1, tailor 5, tavern keeper 6, tin man 1, turner 1, undertaker 1, upholsterer 1, vendue master 8, and wine merchant 2.

Alexander, Alexander. School Master. 25 Union St.
Alexander, William. Merchant. 51 Bay
Ancrum, William & George. Merchants. 1 Ellery St.
Arwin & Rugger. Merchants. 90 Broad St.
Askew, James. Silversmith. 30 Bay
Atkins & Weston. Merchants. 6 Legare St.
Atkinson, Joseph. Merchant. 30 Broad St.
Austin, Adam. Merchant. 41 Broad St.
Austin, Robert. Tailor. 24 Bay
Baird, Robert. Tin Man. 78 Broad St.
Balfour, -----, Lt. Col. Commandant of Charlestown. 94 King St.
Baron, Alexander. Physician. 73 Broad St.
Bay, Elihu Hall. Attorney at Law. 54 Broad St.
Bentham & Sutcliffe. Merchants. 104 Broad St.
Bethune, John. Merchant. 10 Elliot St.
Biddulph, Robert. Banker. 9 Legare St.
Binne, William. Baker. 76 Church St.
Blair, James & Co. Merchants. 27 Bay
Blakely, David. Grocer. 25 Broad St.
Bower, William. Watchmaker. 28 Broad St.
Boyce, Katherine. Milliner. 79 Broad St.
Brisbane, James. Sheriff. 57 Broad St.
Brown & Grant. Surgeons. 85 Church St.
Brown, Clarkson & Co. Merchants. 28 Broad St.
Brown, James. Carpenter. 27 Tradd St.
Bruce, David. Printer. 85 Church St.
Bryden & Allen. Merchants. 1 Tradd St.
Buchanans & Robb. Merchants. 4 Bay
Buckle & Trescot. Ship Chandlers. 35 Bay
Bull, -----. Lieutenant-Governor. 57 Meeting St.
Bull, William, Jr. Esquire. 67 Tradd St.
Burt, William. Factor. 1 Gibbes St.
Caldwell, Henry. Grocer. 80 Tradd St.
Cam, William. Merchant. 21 Broad St.
Cape, Brian. Merchant. 84 Church St.
Carne, Samuel. Merchant. 9 Orange St.
Carson, William & James. Merchant. 3 Tradd St.
Carter, George. Physician. 70 Broad St.
Chambers, John. Merchant. 23 Bay
Chisolm, Alexander. Factor. 56 Church St.
Clark, Francis Ruth. Commissary of Forage. 3 Queen St.
Clitherall, James. Physician. 51 Tradd St.
Cohen, Gershon. Merchant. 29 Bay
Colcock, John. Attorney at Law. 73 Church St.
Collins & Hayes. Merchants. 12 Broad St.
Cooke & Webb. Vendue Masters. Broad St.
Cooke, James. Carpenter. 3 St. Michael's Alley
Cooke, Jonathan. Grocer. 24 Bay
Cooper, -----. Town-Adjutant. 55 Broad St.
Cooper, Robert. Rector St. Philip's. 78 Church St.
Coram, John. Tavernkeeper. 82 Church St.
Coram, Thomas. Engraver. 28 Queen St.
Corbett, Edward. Merchant. 8 Tradd St.
Courtney, Thomas. Tailor. 89 Meeting St.
Creighton, Joseph. Barber. 71 Church St.
Crook & Beard. Merchants. 91 Church St.
Cruden, John. Merchant. 10 Bay
Currie & Norris. Vendue Masters. 1 Bay
Dart, Benjamin. Factor. 15 Tradd St.
Davie, William. Grocer. 59 Tradd St.
Dawson, Christian, Mrs. 92 Meeting St.

Deas, John. Esquire. 67 Meeting St.
Deveaux, Jacob. Powder Receiver. 10 Tradd St.
Donaldson, James. Carpenter. 9 Tradd St.
Doughty, Thomas. Carpenter. 109 Meeting St.
Dow, Alexander. Ship Chandler. 38 Bay
Downes, Arthur. 48 Tradd St.
Drysdale, Alexander. Merchant. 80 Church St.
Duncan, George. Wine Merchant. 9 Elliot St.
Duncan, James. Blacksmith. Beresford's Alley
Dupont, Gideon. Merchant. 77 King St.
Edward, James. Factor. 76 Tradd St.
Ewing, John. Baker. 74 Tradd St.
Fardo, James. Factor. 110 Meeting St.
Farquhar, Robert & Co. Merchants. Tradd St.
Fell, Thomas. Tailor. 93 Church St.
Fisher, John. Cabinet Maker. 29 Meeting St.
Foster, Thomas & Seth. Merchants. 99 Broad St.
Fraser, Charles. Town-Major. 87 King St.
Fraser, James. Acting Barrack-master. 3 Legare St.
Fyffe, Charles. Physician to the Refugees. 27 Broad St.
Gaillard, Theodore. Merchant. 9 Bay
Garden, Alexander. Physician. 77 Broad St.
Geyer, John. Merchant. 87 Church St.
Gickie, William. Ship Chandler. Bay
Glen, John. Attorney at Law. 30 Meeting St.
Glen, William & Co. Merchants. 8 Elliot St.
Gordon, James. Merchant. 90 King St.
Gordon, Thomas Knox. Hon. 1 Short St.
Gottier, Francis. Silversmith. 98 Broad St.
Granger, Thomas. Merchant. 81 Tradd St.
Grant, & Kemmel. Saddlers. 15 Tradd St.
Grant, John. Wine Merchant. 31 Bay
Grant, John. Shoemaker. 3 Chalmer's St.
Gratton, Daniel. Merchant. 24 Broad St.
Gray, -----, Col. Paymaster of Militia. 75 Tradd St.
Greenwood & Legge. Merchants. 44 Bay
Gregoire, Douglas & Co. Merchants. 26 Church St.
Halinbaum, George. Physician. 10 Moore St.
Harleston, John. Esquire. 68 Tradd St.
Harper, Thomas. Jeweller & Goldsmith. 9 Bay
Harris & Blachford. Merchants. 36 Bay
Harris, Charles. Silversmith. 24 Meeting St.
Harris, Tucker. Physician. 147 King St.
Hayes, -----, Dr. Physician to Army. 52 Tradd St.
Hepburn, James. Attorney at Law. 95 Church St.
Hinds, Patrick. Shoemaker. 20 Beaufain St.
Hooper, Thomas & Co. 91 Broad St.
Hopton, William. Esquire. 116 Meeting St.
Hornby, William. Brewer. 7 King St.
Inglis, Alexander. Merchant. 31 Queen St.
Inglis, Thomas. Merchant. 61 Meeting St.
Jacobs, Jacob. Vendue Master. 2 St. Michael's Alley
Jenkins, Edward. Rector of St. Michael's. 70 Meeting St.
Johnson, Charles. Merchant. White Point
Johnson, James. Attorney at Law. 2 St. Michael's Alley
Johnson, Robert. Attorney at Law. 2 St. Michael's Alley
Jones, Joseph. Grocer. 5 Tradd St.
Keith, William. Physician. 11 Queen St.
Kershaw, William. Factor. Greenwood's Wharf
Kingsley & Taylor. Merchants. 16 Broad St.

2

LaMotte, James. Merchant. 92 Broad St.
Lawson & Price. Merchants. 46 Bay
Lechmere, Anthony. Merchant. 7 Bedon's Alley
Legare, Samuel. Insurance Broker. 26 Church St.
Lightwood, Edward. Merchant. 46 Meeting St.
Lindsay, Robert & William. Merchants. 46 Bay
Lockwood, Joshua. Watchmaker. 1 Broad St.
Logan, George. Physician. 18 Tradd St.
Lorimer, Alexander. Merchant. 15 Broad St.
Lowndes, Rawlins. Esquire. 63 Broad St.
M'Call, John. Insurance Broker. 77 Church St.
M'Callum & Ewing. Merchant. 28 Church St.
M'Douall, James. Merchant. 109 Broad St.
M'Kimmey, Mackie & Cameron. Coopers. 3 Bedon's Alley
M'Kinnon, —, Capt. D. Q. M. G. 2 Bay
M'Lauchlan, Colin. Merchant. 38 Bay
M'Leilan & Wallace. Merchants. 40 Bay
M'Murray, James & Co. Merchants. 54 Queen St.
M'Nair & Maxwell. Grocers. Tradd St.
M'Whann, William. Merchant. Tradd St.
Macbeth, Alexander. Merchant. 6 Elliot St.
MacIver, John & Alexander. Merchants. 100 Broad St.
Mackenzie, Andrew & Co. Merchants. 41 Bay
Mansell & Corbett. Merchants. 8 Cumberland St.
Manson, John. Merchant. 4 Bay
Mayott, John. Merchant. 38 Bay
Mazyck, Isaac. Esquire. 86 Broad St.
Mazyck, Stephen. Esquire. 85 Broad St.
Milling & Oliver. Painters & Glaziers. 93 Meeting St.
Mills & Hicks. Printers & Stationers. 12 Broad St.
Montcreiffe, —, Lt. Col. Chief Engineer. 72 Broad St.
Morgan, Charles. Bookbinder & Stationer. 106 Broad St.
Morris, John. Vendue Master. 43 Bay
Morrison, —, Major. Commissary General. 103 Church St.
Mowatt, George & Co. Merchants. 71 Church St.
Munro, George. Grocer. 27 Bay
Myot, John. Silversmith. 32 Broad St.
Neufville, Edward. Merchant. Bay
Newcomen & Collet. Merchants. 8 Bedon's Alley
Newton, William. Deputy Paymaster. 42 Meeting St.
Nicholson, John. Grocer. 45 Bay
O'Hara, Daniel. Grocer. 109 Broad St.
O'Hear, James. Factor. 4 Cumberland St.
Ogilvie, Charles. Merchant. 10 Bay Continued
Oliphant, Alexander. Factor. Greenwood's Wharf
Parker & Co. Merchants. 6 Bedon's Alley
Parkinson, John. Carver & Gilder. Moore St.
Patterson, William. Carpenter. 63 King St.
Patton, Robert. Merchant. 4 Bay
Pearce, Abraham. Undertaker. 32 Broad St.
Penman, James & Edward. Merchants. 15 Bay
Peronneau, Henry. Esquire. 105 Meeting St.
Peronneau, Robert. Physician. 105 Meeting St.
Phepoe, Thomas. Attorney at Law. 74 Broad St.
Philip, Robert. Esquire. 25 Queen St.
Pinckney, Charles. Esquire. 2 Orange St.
Poinsett, Elisha. Physician. 4 Broad St.
Powell, Hopton & Co. Merchants. 5 Bedon's Alley
Prevost, —, Major. D. Insp. Gen. Prov. Forces. 14 Bay
Primrose, Nicol. Merchant. 3 Broad St.
Prince, D., Lieut. Commissary Naval Prisoners. 55 Bay
Print, William. Attorney at Law. 41 Broad St.
Prout, Robert & William. Merchants. 89 Church St.

Ramadge, —, Mrs. Tavernkeeper. 89 Broad St.
Richardson, John. Merchant. 6 Broad St.
Richardson, John, Jr. Merchant. 22 Broad St.
Risk, Hugh & Co. Vendue Masters. 19 Church St.
Robertson, James. Printer. 20 Broad St.
Robertson, John. Tavernkeeper. 28 Bay
Roper, William. 52 Bay.
Rose, Alexander. Merchant. 37 Tradd St.
Rose, Hugh. Physician. 56 Church St.
Rose, John. Esquire. 8 Bay Continued
Ross, William Kerr. Merchant. 2 Tradd St.
Roupell, George. Deputy Postmaster General. 45 Tradd St.
Rowand, Robert. Merchant. 2 Friend St.
Russel, William. Vendue Master. 2 Stoll's Alley
Russell, John & William. Ship Carpenters. 1 Pinckney St.
Rutherford & Ainslie. Merchants. 6 Elliot St.
Savage, Edward. Judge Court Vice-Admiralty. 69 Church St.
Scarborough & Cooke. Merchants. 6 Broad St.
Schume, Conrod. Baker. 27 Meeting St.
Scott, Robert. Merchant. 44 Bay
Shirras, Alexander. Grocer. 38 Bay
Shoolbred & Moodie. Merchants. 83 Tradd St.
Simons, Maurice. Merchant. 87 Broad St.
Simpson, John & Thomas. Merchants. 32 Bay
Simpson, Jonathan & William. Merchants. 27 Church St.
Skene, James. Physician. 65 Tradd St.
Skottowe, Thomas. Sectretary of Province. 16 Broad St.
Smith, John. Merchant. 13 Broad St.
Smith, John, Jr. Factor. Burn's Wharf
Smith, Julius. Merchant. 79 Church St.
Smith, Nicholas. Silversmith. 29 Bay
Smith, Roger. Merchant. 21 Broad St.
Smith, Solomon. Upholsterer. 8 Tradd St.
Smith, William. Merchant. 33 Bay
Smyth, John. Merchant. Ellery St.
Snead, James. Turner. 92 Church St.
Snodgrass, William. Merchant. 94 Church St.
Somersall, William. Merchant. 53 Bay
Somervill & Duguid. Merchants. 101 Broad St.
Spooner, George. Inspector of Refugees. 43 Tradd St.
Stent, Samuel. Tailor. 22 Church St.
Stewart, Jane. Tavernkeeper. 22 Bay
Stewart, Thomas & Co. Vendue Masters. 42 Bay
Strickland, James. Tavernkeeper. 92 Broad St.
Swanson, David. Blacksmith. Burn's Wharf
Teasdale, John. Merchant. 82 Tradd St.
Thompson, John & William. Merchants. Tradd St.
Thomson, George, Jr. Merchant. Greenwood's Wharf
Thomson, Jane. Milliner. 86 Church St.
Thorne, Philip. Tavernkeeper. 43 Queen St.
Traile, —, Major. Commanding Officer Artillery. 25 Church St.
Troup, John. Attorney at Law. 51 Tradd St.
Tufts & Ryan. Merchants. 26 Bay
Tunno, John & Adam. Merchants. 48 Bay
Turnbull, Andrew. Physician. 80 Broad St.
Valk, Jacob. Broker. 109 King St.
Vinyard, John. Leather Dresser. 1 Moore St.
Wagner, John. Merchant. 75 Broad St.
Walker & Maitland. Merchants. 92 Broad St.
Ward, Joshua. Attorney at Law. 11 Tradd St.
Warington, James. Merchant. 90 Meeting St.
Warington, Nicholas. Tailor. 90 Meeting St.

3

Warwick, Anthony & Co. Merchants. 90 Church St.
Watson & Denninson. Vendue Masters. 3 Broad St.
Wayne, Richard. Merchant. 81 Tradd St.
Wells, M. & Sons. Printers & Booksellers. 71 Tradd St.
White, Gideon. Merchant. 27 Church St.
Williams, Robert. Attorney at Law. 16 Tradd St.
Wilson, Robert. Physician. 96 Broad St.
Winstanley, Thomas. Clerk of Police. 12 Elliot St.
Wragg, John. Esquire. 55 Broad St.
Wray, George. Commissary of Artillery. 61 Church St.
Wright, Alexander. Esquire. 40 Meeting St.
Wright, James. Baker. 56 Church St.

CHAPTER 2

THE 1785 DIRECTORY

The 1785 Directory was published by John Tobler as the *South Carolina and Georgia Almanack for 1785* (Charleston: 1784). It contains only 172 entries of which 2 are women. No professions are listed for individuals.

The streets with the most people were Broad Street (23%), The Bay (20%), Church Street (13%), and Tradd Street (10%). Later The Bay was to be known as East Bay and still later East Bay Street. King Street which eventually became the chief commercial street had few businesses at this time.

The streets or other localities with the total number of entries were: Amen Corner 1, Archdale Street 1, Bay 34, Bedon's Alley 7, Broad Street 39, Church Street 22, Cumberland Street 1, East Bay Street 1, Elliot Street 10, Everleigh's Wharf 1, Exchange 1, George Street 1, Jervey & Water's Wharf 1, King Street 7, Meeting Street 8, On the Wharf 1, Pinckney Street 1, Queen Street 13, Roper's Wharf 1, Scott's Wharf 1, St. Michael's Alley 1, Tradd Street 17, Union Street Continued 1.

Listings in 1785 Directory.

Aitken, John. 7 Elliot St.
Alexander, Alexander. 25 Union St. Continued
Atkinson, Joseph. 103 Church St.
Audley, Erasmus. 5 Elliot St.
Austen & Moore. 24 Bay
Ball, Jennings & Co. 52 Bay
Ball, Joseph. 66 Church St.
Ballantine & Warham. 7 Tradd St.
Beard, Charles. 3 Broad St.
Bee, Thomas. 25 Church St.
Bethune, Alexander. 113 Broad St.
Blacklock & Tunno. 26½ Broad St.
Blakely, Samuel. 25 Broad St.
Bleakly, Archibald. Church St.
Boomer, John. 90 Church St.
Bounetheau, Peter. 1 George St.
Bourdeaux, Daniel & Co. 48 Bay
Bowen & Markland. 15 Meeting St.
Bower, Katharine. 28 Broad St.
Brailsford, William. 49 Bay
Brown, Jeremiah. 68 Church St.
Buckley, Thomas. 54 Broad St.
Budd, John, Dr. 43 Queen St.
Burd & Boden. 28 Amen Corner
Burgwin, Hooper & Alexander. 8 Bedon's Alley
Buyck, Augustinus. 2 Queen St.
Calvert, John. 9 Church St.
Cam, William. 28 Bay
Campbell, Laurence. Scott's Wharf
Cannon, Daniel. 5 Queen St.
Cantor & Co. 16 Meeting St.
Cart, John & Co. 24 King St.
Chandler, Isaac, Dr. 52 Broad St.
Childs, Nathan & Co. 85 Church St.
Chisolm, Alexander & Co. 11 Elliot St.
Cobham, George. 20 Broad St.
Cochran, Robert. 25 Bay
Cohen & Alexander. Exchange
Conyers, Holmes & Co. 51 Bay
Cooth, James. 1 Queen St.
Coram, Thomas. 28 Queen St.
Crafts, William & Co. 5 Bay
Cripps, John Splatt & Co. 94 Broad St.
Cudworth & Waller. 92 Broad St.
Cudworth, Benjamin. 2 Cumberland St.
Cunnington, William. 7 Bedon's Alley
Dawes, Ralph. 2 Elliot St.
Dillon & Chiffelle. 50 Queen St.
Doughty, Thomas. 108 Meeting St.
Doughty, William. 108 Meeting St.
Drayton & Stevens. 2 St. Michael's Alley
DuPre, Cornelius. 23 Church St.
Edwards, James. Tradd St.
Ellisnore, James. 30½ King St.
Ellison & Dupont. 3 Bedon's Alley
Eveleigh, Thomas & Co. 48 Bay
Farr, Thomas. 87 Broad St.
Ferguson, Charles. 80 Tradd St.
Fisher, Hughes & Edwards. 6 Tradd St.
Flagg, George. 23 King St.
Flagg, Henry Collins, Dr. 63 Tradd St.
Folker, John Casper. 12 Broad St.
Gaillard, Theodore. 9 Bay

Gibbes, William Hasell. 74 Broad St.
Gibbons, John. 48 Bay
Gibbs, John Walters. 11 Queen St.
Gibson, Robert, Jr. 50 Broad St.
Gillon, Alexander. 14 Bay
Gowdey, William. 106 Broad St.
Graaf, Sibells Brasselman & Co.
Grant & Simons. 41 Bay
Grattan, Francis. 22 Meeting St.
Gregoire, James. Bedon's Alley, corner Tradd
Grimke, John Faucheraud. 100 Meeting St.
Grimke, John Paul. 101 Meeting St.
Guerard, Benjamin, His Ex. 59 Queen St.
Hahnbaum, George, Dr. 52 King St.
Hall, Daniel & Co. 5 Tradd St.
Hall, Thomas. 30 Broad St.
Hane & Berk. 100 Broad St.
Harbison, John. 20 Bay
Harris & Blachford. 27 Tradd St.
Harris, Tucker, Dr. King St.
Harth, John. 46 Broad St.
Hatfield, John. 18 Bay
Hazelhurst, Robert & Co. 44 Bay
Hort & Warley. 39 Bay
Houckgeest, A. E. Van Braam. 42 Bay
Hutson, Richard. 59 Tradd St.
Huxham, Courtney & Eales. 80 Church St.
Jacks, James. Broad St.
Jervey & Walter. On the Wharf
Jones, Joseph. Tradd St.
Lamb, David. 90 Church St.
Lathrop & Snowdon. 29 Queen St.
Lawson & Price. 29 Broad St.
Legare, Samuel. 26 Church St.
Lesterjette & Cochran. 25 Bay
Ley, Francis. 6 Tradd St.
Lindsay, Robert and William. 46 Bay
Lockey, Bradford & Co. 19½ Bay
M'Callum & Ewing. Tradd St.
M'Caulay & Davis. 8 Church St.
M'Clure, Cochran & William. 40 Bay
M'Credie & Hamilton. 11 Broad St.
M'Leod, Angus. 8 Tradd St.
M'Leod, William & Co. 6 Elliot St.
M'Whann, William. 5½ Elliot St.
Manson, John & Thomas. 87 Church St.
Mathews, Benjamin & George. 26½ Church St.
Mauger, John. 9 Bedon's Alley
Merrick & Conrse. 7 Bedon's Alley
Mey, Florian Charles. 18 Pinckney St.
Midwood, Samuel. 5¼ Elliot St.
Miller, James. 21 Bay
Miller, John, Printer. 91 Church St.
Mitchell & Donnom. 23 Bay
Morgan, Charles. 12½ Broad St.
Morris, Thomas. 50 Bay
Nelson, George & Co. 19 Church St.
Newhouse, Lewis & Co. 13 Queen St.
Norris, Robert & Co. 5 Bedon's Alley
North & Blake. 43 Bay
O'Hara, Stewart & Co. 11 Elliot St.
O'Hear, Theus & Legare. Eveleigh's Wharf
Parker, John & William. 27 Church St.

Peace, Isaac & Co. 7 Elliot St.
Penman, James & Edward. 15 Bay
Pleym, Andrew. 38 Bay
Porter, John. 27 Queen St.
Primerose, Thomson & Co. Jervey & Walter's Wharf
Prioleau, Samuel, Jr. & Co. Broad St. & Bay
Rhodes, John. 3 Tradd St.
Roach, William. 9 Broad St.
Roberts, Thomas, Bookseller. 84 Church St.
Russell, Jenkins & Co. Bay
Russell, Thomas Commander. 37 King St.
Rutledge, Edward. 53 Broad St.
Rutledge, Hugh. 3 Queen St.
Rutledge, John. 72 Broad St.
Scarbrough & Cooke. 7 Broad St.
Shirras, Alexander & Co. 29 Bay
Simpson, John & William. 27 Tradd St.
Slann & Guignard. 81 Tradd St.
Smerdon, Henry. 99 Broad St.
Smith, Desaussure & Darrell. 83 Tradd St.
Smith, John & Archibald. 14 Broad St.
Smith, Roger & Peter. 101 Broad St.
Smith, William & Co. 10 Broad St.
Stevens, Daniel. 15 Archdale St.
Stevens, Ramsay & Co. 92½ Broad St.
Stewart, Hayes & Co. 11 Elliot St.
Stewart, Robert & Hall. 39 Bay
Teasdale, John & Co. 39 Bay
Thayer & Bartlet. King St., corner Queen
Thompson & Lennox. 110 Broad St.
Timothy, Ann. 89 Broad St.
Trescot, Edward. 117 Meeting St.
Tunno, Adam. 82 Tradd St.
Van Rhyn & Newman. 29 Bay
Villepontoux & Co. Roper's Wharf
Wadsworth & Porter. 91 Broad St.
Wakefield, James. 88 Broad St.
Walker & Maitland. 21 Church St.
Walker, Alexander. 88 Church St.
Ward, Samuel. 4 Queen St.
Webb & Doughty. 111 Broad St.
Wells & Bethune. 10½ Broad St.
Weyman, Edward. 98 Church St.
Wilkinson, Abraham & Co. 90 Broad St.
Wilson, John & Co. 24 East Bay St.
Winthrop, Todd & Winthrop. 46 Bay

CHAPTER 3

THE 1790 DIRECTORY

Jacob Milligan published *The Charleston Directory and Revenue System* (Charleston: T. B. Owen, 1790). This is the first available directory that has a substantial number of names, 1620 entries in all. It contains a map of the city, times of meetings of lodges and societies, a list of corporations, signals at the fort, a list of the harbor pilots, information on the revenue system of the United States, and "Abstracts of the Most Material of the New Collection of Laws."

Since the compiler of the Directory made an attempt to list a considerable portion of the city residents, this volume gives a good idea of the professions and places of residence or business of the city.

A total of 105 locations was given. The places with the most entries were King Street with 15%, East Bay 9%, Church Street 7%, Broad Street 6%, Meeting Street 6%, Tradd Street 6%, and Queen Street 6%.

The places and number of entries for each are Allen Street 3, Ansonborough 1, Archdale Street 20, Barracks 2, Beale's Wharf 10, Beaufain Street 14, Bedon's Alley 12, Beresford Street 16, Beresford's Alley 18, Boundary Street 4, Broad Street 102, Bull Street 3, Burn's Lane 3, Chalmer's Alley 11, Chalmer's Lane 1, Champney's Row 3, Champney's Wharf 4, Charles Street 8, Church Street 119, Clifford Street 7, Clifford's Alley 2, Cochran's Wharf 3, Cock Lane 4, Coming Street 5, Cumberland Street 8, Custom House 1, Dutch Church Alley 7, East Bay 141, Ellery Street 11, Elliot Street 40, Elliot's 1, Eveleigh's Wharf 2, Exchange 6, Federal Green 1, Fish Market Wharf 2, Friend Street 6, Front Street 5, Gadsden's Alley 1, Gadsden's Wharf 1, George Street 11, Gibbes Street 3, Gillon Street 2, Graeme's Wharf 1, Greenwood's Alley 2, Greenwood's Wharf 7, Guignard Street 18, Harleston's Green 2, Hasell Street 21, Henry Street 1, Jervey's Wharf 7, King Street 246, Kinloch Court 3, Lamboll's Lane 5, Legare Street 14, Liberty Street 4, Lodge Alley 1, Longitude Lane 3, Louisbourg Coffee House 1, Lynch's Lane 14, Magazine Street 8, Maiden Lane 8, Market Square 3, Mazyck Street 9, Meeting Street 162, Mey's Alley 5, Moore Street 13, Motte's Wharf 7, Near the Old Church 2, New Gaol 1, New Market 1, Orange Street 8, Pinckney Street 30, Pitt Street 2, Price's Alley 3, Queen Street 98, Quince's Street 2, Roper's Alley 1, Roper's Wharf 4, Savage's Green 3, Scarborough Street 2, Short Street 4, Smith's Lane 2, Snitter's Alley 2, Society Street 12, South Bay 12, St. Michael's Alley 3, St. Philip's Academy 1, St. Philip's Parsonage 1, St. Philip's Street 5, State House Square 3, State House Yard 1, Stoll's Alley 10, Sugar House Yard 1, Tradd Street 101, Trott Street 32, Union Street 26, Union Street Continued 24, Unity Alley 2, Vanderhorst's Wharf 1, Water Street 5, Wayne's Court 2, Wentworth Street 12, West Street 1, Wragg's Alley 9, and Wyatt's Lot 7.

The professions followed by most people were shop keeper or store keeper (17% of 1424), merchant (12%), planter (9%), carpenters of various types (6%), factor (4%), tailor (4%), mariner (3%), baker (2%), lawyer (2%), butcher (2%), and physician (2%). This shows the nature of the economy of the city which supplied the plantations of the Carolina Low Country. The fact that Charleston served as a seaport is also evident. In addition, the number of physicians in the community attest to the dangerously unhealthy climate.

The professions for men and women as listed in the directory were: academy 1, apothecary 3, assistant St. Philip's Church 1, associate judge 3, attorney at law 29, attorney general 1, auctioneer 16, auditor general 1, baker 31, band box maker 1, barber 1, barrister at law 1, beer house 1, billiard table 2, blacksmith 16, blockmaker 2, boarding house 22, boarding school 3, bookbinder 2, botanist 1, bottle seller 1, brass founder 1, brewer 2, brick layer 20, broker 7, butcher 29, button maker 1, canon St. Philip's Church 1, cabinet maker

8

15, carpenter 68, carter 9, carver 3, chair maker 3, chancellor 2, chocolate maker 1, cigar maker 5, city sheriff 1, city marshall 1, city treasurer 1, city intendant 1, clerk 14, coach maker 4, coffee house 1, colfbaunkeep 1, Colum. Academy 1, com. pub. rec. 1, commandant, Fort Johnson 1, commiss. f. est 1, commission loan 2, confectioner 1, constable 7, cont. statemeas. 1, cooper 10, counsellor at law 3, currier 1, custom house boat 3, dentist 1, deputy city sheriff 1, deputy sheriff 1, deputy secretary 1, distiller 5, district judge 1, district marshall 1, drayman 4, draymaster 1, dyer 1, engraver 3, esquire 1, factor 56, fisherman 3, fruit shop 1, gardener 5, gauger customs 1, jail keeper 1, goldsmith 2, governor 1, grocer 15, gunsmith 4, hair dresser 12, harness maker 1, hatter 4, horse dealer 1, house carpenter 4, indigo broker 1, innholder 6, inspector 8, intelligence office 1, ironmonger 1, Jewish priest 1, justice peace 1, land surveyor 1, librarian 1, lieutenant governor 1, limner 2, livery stables 1, lumber measurer 3, magistrate 1, mahogany sawyer 1, mantua maker 3, Marine Hospital 1, mariner 42, master chancery 1, master Poor House 1, merchant 164, mesen. h. rpr. 1, midwife 1, milliner 1, miniature painter 1, money collector 1, music master 1, music shop 1, musician 1, naval officer 1, notary public 2, ordinary 1, organist 1, overseer 1, p.m. 1, painter 12, pastor 3, perfumer 1, physician 23, pilot 9, planter 129, porter house 2, postmaster 1, powder receiver 1, printer 6, prod. music 1, rabbi 1, rector 4, register chan. 1, reverend 1, rope maker 1, saddler 10, sailmaker 5, school master 14, school mistress 16, scrivener 8, seaman 2, seamstress 3, seedman 1, sheriff 1, ship carpenter 8, ship chandler 3, ship joiner 2, shipwright 8, shoemaker 23, shop keeper 211, silversmith 10, state treasurer 1, state physician 1, state printer 1, stationer 1, stay maker 1, store keeper 27, stone cutter 1, sugar baker 1, surgeon 4, surveyor customs 1, surveyor general 2, tailor 49, tallow chandler 4, tanner 9, tax collector 2, tin man 6, tobacco inspector 2, tobacconist 1, turner 3, U. S. attorney 1, umbrella maker 1, upholsterer 1, V.C. of France 1, vintner 1, violin player 1, wagon yard 4, warden 3, watchmaker 11, watchman 6, wharfinger 3, wheelwright 2, widow 2, wine merchant 2, wood measurer

A large part of those who were listed without a profession were women. No doubt, many of them were widows, although only two are so noted. Women constituted almost 14% of the people listed (222 of 1620). The directory had professions for 73 of them. The largest group, 34%, were store or shop keepers, while 25% taught or ran schools, 22% operated boarding houses or inns, and 8% made their living by sewing. One women is listed as a cigar maker, one as the state printer, and two as planters. When women are listed in professions which were typically not followed by them, they usually are widows who are operating a business which their husbands ran before them. Other professions were baker, band box maker, midwife, and milliner.

Abendanon, Joseph. Broker. 40 King St.
Abernethie, Thomas. Engraver. 42 Queen St.
Abertie, Francis. Cigar Maker. Wayne's Court
Abrahams, Emanuel. Scrivener. 256 King St.
Abrahams, Jacob. Shop Keeper. 70 East Bay
Abrahams, Judah. 94 Tradd St.
Adams & English. Shop Keepers. 21 East Bay
Adams, William. Carpenter. Pinckney St.
Adamson, Jane. 28 Queen St.
Aertsen, Guilliem, Esq. City Sheriff. 259 King St.
Aguire, Gugelan. Tin Man. 220 Meeting St.
Akin, Thomas. Mariner. 97 East Bay
Alexander, Abraham. Scrivener. 224 King St.
Alexander, Alexander. School Master. 7 Union St. Continued
Alexander, David. Merchant. 3 Bedon's Alley
Alexander, Hector. Shop Keeper. Motte's Wharf
Alexander, Judah. Shop Keeper. 10 Clifford St.
Allen & Ewing. Merchants. 120 Tradd St.
Allison, James. Cooper. Beale's Wharf
Allston, William. Planter. 104 East Bay
Ancrum, William. Planter. 13 Ellery St.
Anderson, Alexander. Grocer. 53½ East Bay St.
Anderson, Ann. 19 Union St. Continued
Anderson, Robert. Shop Keeper. 240 King St.
Andrews, Jane. 243 Meeting St.
Anthony, Emanuel. Mariner. 24 Elliot St.
Anthony, John. Harness Maker. 51 Meeting St.
Archibald, George. Attorney at Law. 48 Broad St.
Armstrong, Fleetwood. Shop Keeper. 128 East Bay
Armstrong, William. Saddler. 90 King St.
Arnold, Jonathan. Wagon Yard. 157 King St.
Arnold, Matthew. Brick Layer. 118 King St.
Arnst, Mary. 61 Queen St.
Arnts, Margaret. 15 Dutch Church Alley
Ashton, Sarah. 5 Maiden Lane
Askew, James. Watchmaker. 96 Broad St.
Atkinson, William. Carpenter. 25 Beresford's Alley
Atmar, Ralph. Mesen. H. Repr. State House Yard
Audley, Martha. 23 King St.
Austen, Robert. Tailor. 51 East Bay
Avon, Solomon. Shop Keeper. 46 King St.
Axton, Elizabeth. 127 Church St.
Axton, William. Lumber Measurer. 17 King St.
Azabee, Abraham. Rabbi. 6 Beresford St.
Bacot, Thomas William. Tax Collector. 103 Broad St.
Badger, James. Painter. 93 Queen St.
Badger, Jonathan. Painter. 49 Meeting St.
Badger, Joseph. Painter. 118 Queen St.
Baker, Samuel. School Master. 10 Church St.
Balantine, James. Coroner. 46 Tradd St.
Ball & Minnott. Factors. Vanderhorst's Wharf
Ball, Ann. 17 Church St.
Ball, Elizabeth. 15 Church St.
Ball, John. Planter. 24 Hasell St.
Ball, Thomas. Factor. Lynch's Lane
Bampfield, Rebecca. 39 Church St.
Bampfield, William. Porter House. 183 Meeting St.
Barker, Isaac. Tailor. 11 Elliot St.
Barker, William. Brick Layer. 35 Guignard St.
Barnett, Ann. 2 St. Michael's Alley
Baron, John. Merchant. 120 Broad St.
Barron, Alexander. Physician. 248 Meeting St.
Bartlett, Isaac. Merchant. 8 Stoll's Alley

Baruck, Solomon. Shop Keeper. 246 King St.
Bass, John. Mariner. 10 Orange St.
Bay, Elihu Hall. Attorney at Law. 240 Meeting St.
Bayley, William, Esq. East Bay
Baylis, William. Carpenter. 253 Meeting St.
Beach, Samuel. Planter. 8 King St.
Beadon, William. Sailmaker. Water St.
Beale, John, Esq. 34 East Bay
Beard, Charles. Merchant. 22 Elliot St.
Beard, Robert. Tin Man. 88 Broad St.
Beatty, Robert. Store Keeper. 28 Broad St.
Beauffet, George. Barber. 5 Tradd St.
Bee, Joseph. Carpenter. 3 Wragg's Alley
Bee, Mary. 6 Wragg's Alley
Bee, Thomas, Esq. District Judge. 100 Church St.
Beekman, Bernard. Planter. 109 East Bay
Beekman, Samuel. Blockmaker. 50 East Bay
Beibliat, Peter. Mariner. 5 Price's Alley
Bell, John. Shop Keeper. 150 King St.
Bell, William. Shop Keeper. 248 King St.
Bellamy, Hester. 33 King St.
Bellenger, John. Planter. 65 Meeting St.
Below, Joakim. Shop Keeper. 119 King St.
Beltzer, Christian. Butcher. 161 Meeting St.
Benbridge, Henry. Limner. 30 Broad St.
Benjamin, Samuel. Shop Keeper. 195 King St.
Bennea, Peter. Ship Carpenter. Lynch's Lane
Bennett, John. Carpenter. 21 Trott St.
Bennett, Thomas. Carpenter. 74 Church St.
Bentham, James. Magistrate. 47 Church St.
Beresford, Richard. Planter. 75 Broad St.
Bering, John. Silversmith. 125 Broad St.
Berney, John. Merchant. 24 East Bay
Berwick, Ann. 16 South Bay
Besselleau, Lewis. Planter. 28 Beaufain St.
Bethune, Angus. Merchant. 22 Broad St. corner Church
Bethune, Hugh. Merchant. 269 King St.
Bibean, Francis. Merchant. 13 Union St. Continued
Bieller, Joseph. Butcher. 26 Archdale St.
Bird, Elizabeth. 13 Union St. Continued
Biverly, Frederick. Shop Keeper. 23 Union St. Continued
Black, John. Merchant. 12 Broad St.
Black, Nathaniel. Shop Keeper. 7 Ellery St.
Blackaller, Oliver. Shop Keeper. 10 Union St. Continued
Blacklock, William. Merchant. 8 Meeting St.
Blair, John. Shop Keeper. 25 Church St.
Blair, William. Constable. Near the Old Church
Blake, Edward. Factor. 1 Legare St.
Blake, Elizabeth. Plantress. 9 Church St.
Blake, John. Shop Keeper. 20 East Bay
Blake, John. Merchant. 213 King St.
Blake, John. Merchant. 29 Elliot St.
Blakely, Samuel. Store Keeper. 28½ Broad St.
Blamyer, William. Lumber Measurer. Magazine St.
Bocquet, Peter. Planter. Wentworth St.
Boddie, Sarah. Boarding House. 20 Tradd St.
Boderum, Joseph. Clerk. 7 Pinckney St.
Bogle, Agnes. 184 King St.
Bohm, Charles. Billiard Table. 38 King St.
Bold, Rhodes & Co. Merchants. 132 Tradd St.
Bolton, Martha. 1 Pinckney St.

Bonneau, Francis. Carpenter. 58 Broad St.
Bonsell, Samuel. Planter. 5 Wentworth St.
Booner, Christian. Shop Keeper. 11 Queen St.
Booner, Dolly. 106 King St.
Booth, Catherine. Boarding House. 84 East Bay
Bordeaux, Daniel. Merchant. 22 Beaufain St.
Boucheneau, Charles. Scrivener. 170 Meeting St.
Bounetheau, Peter. Esquire. 286 King St.
Bounnetheau, Peter. Clerk of Council. 30 Trott St.
Bowen, Thomas B. Printer. 38 East Bay
Bowing, George. 13 Moore St.
Bowman, John. Planter. 124 East Bay
Bradford and Co. P. M. 130 Tradd St.
Bradford, Charles. Porter House. 130 Broad St.
Bradford, Thomas. Prod. music. 14 Elliot St.
Bradford, William. Merchant. 43 Meeting St.
Brady, Mary. 82 Church St.
Brailsford, Samuel. 1 Friend St.
Brailsford, William. Planter. 45 Meeting St.
Braly, Thomas. Shop Keeper. 220 King St.
Brandford, Elizabeth. 34 Meeting St.
Bremar, Francis. Surveyor General. 132 King St.
Bricken, Sarah. School Mistress. 129 East Bay
Briendly, Stephen. Pilot. 2 Greenwood's Alley
Brodie, Thomas. Factor. 105½ Church St.
Brook, Mary. 14 Dutch Church Alley
Broughton, Ann. Plantress. 103 Tradd St.
Browelee, John. Merchant. 212 King St.
Brower, Jeremiah. 13 King St.
Brown & Hutchinson. Shop Keepers. 124 Church St.
Brown, James. 131 King St.
Brown, Jeremiah. Mariner. Lynch's Lane
Brown, Joseph. Planter. 66 Tradd St.
Brown, Roger. Mariner. 27 Pinckney St.
Brown, Samuel. Planter. 7 Cumberland St.
Brown, William. Wagon Yard. 192 King St.
Bryan, Arthur. Merchant. State House Square
Bryan, John. Planter. 39 Pinckney St.
Bryan, Samuel. Tailor. 185 Meeting St.
Buckerage, ——. Wheelwright. Union St. Continued
Buckle, Thomas. Merchant. 56 Broad St.
Buckmire, Charles. Butcher. 7 Burn's Lane
Buckmire, John. Butcher. 135 King St.
Budd, John. Physician. 45 Church St.
Bull, William. Planter. 282 King St.
Buller, Jacob. Butcher. 13 Beresford St.
Buntin, William. Shoemaker. 152 Meeting St.
Burger, David. Gunsmith. 31 Queen St.
Burn, James. Cabinet Maker. 285 King St.
Burnham, Sarah. 14 Maiden Lane
Burns, John. Shop Keeper. 5 Union St.
Buro, John. Fisherman. 3 Ellery St.
Burrill & Storum. Shop Keepers. 106 Church St.
Burt, William. Wood Meas. 116 Queen St.
Bury, Richard. Butcher. 14 Beresford's Alley
Bury, Susannah. Shop Keeper. 197 King St.
Butler, Charles P. Silversmith. 285 King St.
Butterton, Joseph. Pilot. 7 Maiden Lane
Buyck, Peter. Bottle Seller. 27 Elliot St.
Buyer, John Goodly. Shop Keeper. 177 Meeting St.
Byrd, Samuel. Tailor. 39 Union St.
Cahill, Daniel. Clerk. 35 King St.
Cain, Grace. 57 Queen St.
Calaghan, John. Tallow Chandler. 40 Tradd St.
Caldwell, Henry. Store Keeper. 123 Tradd St.
Caldwell, Joseph. Shop Keeper. 215 Meeting St.
Calhoun, John Ewing. Attorney at Law. 127 King St.
Calvert, John. Inspector. 86 Church St.

Calvert, Lawrence. Shop Keeper. 41 Elliot St.
Calwell, Henry. Shop Keeper. 24 Church St.
Cam, William. Merchant. 127 Queen St.
Cambridge, Tobias. Auctioneer. 7 Orange St.
Cameron, Alexander. Shop Keeper. 81 King St.
Cameron, Alexander. Dyer. 79 Church St.
Cameron, Andrews. Seaman. 37 Pinckney St.
Cameron, David. Butcher. 15 Trott St.
Cameron, Lewis. Store Keeper. 137 Tradd St.
Campbell, Archibald. Merchant. 17 Elliot St.
Campbell, John. Beale's Wharf
Campbell, Laurence. Auctioneer. 1 Roper's Alley
Campbell, McCartan. Planter. 105 East Bay
Cane, Conrad. Carter. 13 Hasell St.
Cannon, Daniel. Carpenter. 22 Queen St.
Cantor, Jacob. Merchant. 216 Meeting St.
Cantorson, Joshua. Limner. 104 King St.
Canty & Solomons. Shop Keepers. 135 Queen St.
Cap, Dominick. Mariner. Lamboll's Lane
Cape, Bryan. Factor. 91 East Bay
Carnes, John. Apothecary. 119 Queen St.
Carnes, Lawrence. Shop Keeper. 41 Elliot St.
Carnes, Susannah. 83 Tradd St.
Carpenter, James. Shop Keeper. 133 Queen St.
Carr, Wilder & Co. Store Keepers. 39 Tradd St.
Carrel, Daniel. Silversmith. 129 Broad St.
Carson, James. Printer. 136 Tradd St.
Cart, John, Jr. Clerk. George St.
Cart, John, Sr. 125 Queen St.
Carter, George. Surgeon. 111 King St.
Carter, John. Shop Keeper. 98 Tradd St.
Cartmell, William. Store Keeper. 53 East Bay
Carton, Elizabeth. 8 Wragg's Alley
Castine, John. Mahogony Sawyer. 19 Beresford St.
Cavaneau, James. Factor. 8 Union St. Continued
Caveneau, Elizabeth. Seamstress. 200 King St.
Cazaneau, Edward. Merchant. 134 Tradd St.
Chalmers, Elizabeth. 108 Queen St.
Chalmers, Gilbert. Carpenter. 23 Beaufain St.
Chalmers, Rebecca. 40 Trott St.
Champney, John. Wharfinger. 94 King St.
Chanler, Isaac. Physician. 54 Broad St.
Chapman, William. Sailmaker. 27 Archdale St.
Charles, James. Baker. 113 Tradd St.
Cheves, Alexander. Shop Keeper. 96 King St.
Chion, P. G. & Son. Merchants. 39 East Bay
Chisholm, Alexander. Planter. 307 King St.
Chisholm, Alexander, Jr. Factor. 18 South Bay
Chitty, Ann. 3 Moore St.
Christian, Robert. Boarding House. 136 Tradd St.
Christie, Alexander. Baker. 105 Queen St.
Christie, Edward. Shop Keeper. 93 Church St.
Chupein, Lewis. Hair Dresser. 37 Church St.
Clark, Jeremiah. Measurer of Lumber. Greenwood's Alley
Clark, John. Painter. 13 Hasell St.
Clark, John. Scrivener. 247 Meeting St.
Clark, Sarah. Shop Keeper. Roper's Wharf
Clark, William. Sailmaker. 36 Pinckney St.
Clarke & Latham. Watchmakers. 125 Broad St.
Clarke, James. Tailor. Jervey's Wharf
Clarke, John. Watchman. 1 Federal Green
Clarke, Mary. Shop Keeper. 170 King St.
Clarkson, Alexander. 3 Meeting St.
Clements, John. Carpenter. 49 Queen St.
Clementson, Alexander. Deputy City Sheriff. 2 Wentworth St.
Clifford, Elizabeth. 33 Wentworth St.

11

Clime, Mary. 138 King St.
Clitheral, James. Physician. 44 Broad St.
Coates, Thomas. Mariner. 97 East Bay
Cobia, Daniel. Butcher. 18 Beresford St.
Cobia, Francis. Butcher. 161 Meeting St.
Cobia, Nicholas. Butcher. 36 Archdale St.
Cochran, Bridget. Shop Keeper. 89 King St.
Cochran, Robert. 75 Meeting St.
Cochran, Thomas. Factor. 138 East Bay
Cogdale, Jane. 180 King St.
Coghlan, William. Shop Keeper. 8 Union St.
Cohen, Gershom. Merchant. 22 Church St.
Cohen, Gershom. Factor. 140 East Bay
Cohen, Jacob. Shop Keeper. 92 King St.
Cohen, Jacob. Auctioneer. South Side of Exchange
Cohen, Moses. Boarding House. 98 King St.
Coile, Margaret. 16 Pinckney St.
Colcock & Graham. Auctioneers. North Side of Exchange
Colcock, Job. Auctioneer. 109 Tradd St.
Colcock, —— Mrs. Boarding School. 101 Tradd St.
Cole, Richard. Factor. 213 Meeting St.
Collet, William. Ship Carpenter. 114 East Bay
Collins, Jonah. House Carpenter. Wyatt's Lot
Collins, Mary. Wyatt's Lot
Collis, Elizabeth. 99 Tradd St.
Colsman, Henry. Drayman. Coming St.
Condy & Bryan. Merchants. 4 Champney's Row
Connelly, Mary. School Mistress. 205 Meeting St.
Connor, Bryan. Shop Keeper. Motte's Wharf
Connor, Thomas. Shop Keeper. Greenwood's Wharf
Cook, Jonathan. Grocer. 57 East Bay
Cook, Lewis. Watchman. 14 Beresford's Alley
Cook, Thomas. Shop Keeper. 99 King St.
Cook, Thomas. Cabinet Maker. 12 Meeting St.
Cook, William. Merchant. 2 Gillon St.
Cookson & Williamson. Grocers. 69 East Bay
Cooper, James. 25 Union St.
Coram, Francis. Scrivener. 255 King St.
Coram, Thomas. Engraver. 81 Queen St.
Corbet, Samuel. City Marshall. 5½ Meeting St.
Corbett, Thomas. Merchant. 11 Cumberland St.
Cordes, John. Planter. 72 Broad St.
Corre, Charles Godfrey. Merchant. 43 Broad St.
Course, Isaac. Merchant. 98 Queen St.
Courtney, James. Tailor. 44 Meeting St.
Cowen, John. Overseer. 35 Pinckney St.
Cox, Ann. School Mistress. 10 Stoll's Alley
Cox, Henrietta Maria. 42 Trott St.
Cox, John. Planter. 128 Church St.
Cox, John. 3 Elliot St.
Cox, Susannah. Mantua Maker. 40 Church St.
Cozens, Matthew. Mariner. 3 Beresford's Alley
Crafts, William. Merchant. 16 East Bay
Crafts, William. Merchant, Dwelling. 12 Church St.
Cramer, Tobias. Shop Keeper. 2 Unity Alley
Crawford & Wallace. Painters & Glaziers. 18 East Bay
Crawford, William. Grocer. 121 Tradd St.
Creighton, Joseph. Hair Dresser. 28 Church St.
Creitner, Barbara. 23 Archdale St.
Cripps, John Splatt. Merchant. 102 Broad St.
Crocker & Sturgis. Merchants. 8 Champney's Wharf
Cromwell, Elizabeth. 34 Tradd St.
Crook, Shanks. Shoemaker. 14 Queen St.
Cross, George. Merchant. 52 King St.
Cross, Susannah. 10 Union St.
Crowe, Edward. Custom House Boat. 10 Chalmer's Alley

Crowley, Charles. Store Keeper. 71 King St.
Crowley, Michael. Store Keeper. 97 Queen St.
Cruger, Frederick D. Factor. 38 Meeting St.
Cudworth, Nathaniel. Clerk. 15 Hasell St.
Cughna, George. Shoemaker. 76 King St.
Cumin, Casper. Violin Player. 224 King St.
Cunningham, John. Shop Keeper. 146 King St.
Cuppage, Hugh. Mariner. 225 Meeting St.
Curling, Thomas. Shop Keeper. 2 Cock Lane
Curry, William. Shop Keeper. Beale's Wharf
Curry, William. Seaman. 24 Pinckney St.
Custer, James. Clerk. 26 Queen St.
DaCosta, Isaac. Store Keeper. 72 King St.
DaCosta, Samuel. Shop Keeper. Motte's Wharf
DaCosta, Sarah. 25 Archdale St.
Dallas, Angus. Store Keeper. 1½ Queen St.
Daniel, Elizabeth. 2 Scarborough St.
Darby, William. Silversmith. 20 Broad St.
Darrell, Benjamin. Mariner. 22 Meeting St.
Darrell, Edward. Merchant. 25 East Bay
Dart John Sanford. Clerk H.R. Custom House
Dart, John Sanford. Notary Pub. 2 Front St.
Davie, William. Money Collector. 5 Short St.
Davis, Jane. Band Box Maker. 9 Beresford's Alley
Davis, L. H. Attorney at Law. 93 Queen St.
Davis, Thomas. Shop Keeper. 207 King St.
Dawes, Margaret. 131 Church St.
Dawson, Christiana. Boarding House. 2 Kinloch Court
Dawson, John. Planter. 92½ East Bay
Dawson, Michael. Constable. 12½ Pinckney St.
Deady, Thomas. Shop Keeper. 12 Union St. Continued
Deas, John. Planter. 14 Meeting St.
Deas, John, Jr. Planter. Lamboll's Lane
Deas, William. Attorney at Law. 52 Meeting St.
Decker, William & Co. Merchants. 8 Elliot St.
Delcor, Peter. Shop Keeper. 24 Archdale St.
DeLyon, Isaac. Shop Keeper. 58 King St.
Dener, George. Tanner. 3 Mazyck St.
Dener, Peter. Tanner. 5 Dutch Church Alley
Dennis, Richard. Merchant. 11 Hasell St.
Denoon, David & Co. Auctioneers. Beale's Wharf
Denton, James. Fish Market Wharf
Desaussure, Daniel. Merchant. 249 Meeting St.
Desaussure, H. William. Attorney at Law. 30 Tradd St.
Desel, Charles. Cabinet Maker. 44 Church St.
Desel, Charles. Cabinet Maker. 15 Maiden Lane
Devernay, Peter F. Gunsmith. 96 Broad St.
Dewar, Robert. 93 Tradd St.
Dewees, Sarah. 10 Liberty St.
Dewees, William. Factor. 101 East Bay
Dickenson, Jeremiah. Mariner. 9 Cumberland St.
Dickson, Samuel. School Master. 72 Meeting St.
Dill, Joseph. House Carpenter. 295 King St.
Dimes, Ann. School Mistress. 31 Church St.
Disher, Mary. 1 Wragg's Alley
Ditchman, John. Mariner. 38 Hasell St.
Dodsworth, Ralph. Merchant. 228 King St.
Doggett, Henry. Auctioneer, Dwelling. 57 Church St.
Doggett, Henry. Auctioneer. Beale's Wharf
Dollaghan & Brannen. Shop Keepers. 21 East Bay
Donaldson, James. Carpenter. 22 Tradd St.
Donavan, James. Brick Layer. 6 Trott St.
Dorman, Robert. Shop Keeper. 26 King St.
Dougherty, Patrick. Sailmaker. 14 Wragg's Alley
Doughty, Abraham. 9 Dutch Church Alley
Doughty, Thomas. Factor. 59 Meeting St.
Doughty, William. Planter. 202 Meeting St.
Douglas, Joseph. Shop Keeper. 79 King St.

Douglas, Nathaniel. Shop Keeper. 97 Church St.
Douxfaint, Mary Esther. 84 Church St.
Downe, James. Wharfinger. 112 Church St.
Drayton, Jacob. Attorney at Law. 56 Meeting St.
Drayton, John. Attorney at Law. 42 Meeting St.
Drayton, Rebecca. Coming St.
Drayton, Stephen. Com. Pub. Rec. 26 Meeting St.
Dubuard, Peter. Hair Dresser. 235 Meeting St.
Duff, David. School Master. 4 Wentworth St.
Duff, John. Carter. Barracks
Duffy, Andrew. Shop Keeper. 238 Meeting St.
Dullas, Joseph. Shop Keeper. 35 East Bay
Duncan, Archibald. Blacksmith. 91 Church St.
Duncan James. Blacksmith. 18 Beresford's Alley
Duncan, Patrick. Shop Keeper. 80 King St.
Duncan, Thomas. Tailor. 117 Queen St.
Duntze, Gerard. Shop Keeper. 249 King St.
Duval, Catharine. 113 Church St.
Dwight, Isaac. Factor. Pitt St.
Eames, Martha. Shop Keeper. Greenwood's Wharf
Earnest, Jacob. Tailor. 276 King St.
Easton, Susannah. Barracks
Eberly, John. Baker. 17 Guignard St.
Eckhard, Jacob. Music Master. 33 Archdale St.
Eden, Joshua. Turner. 15 Beresford's Alley
Edgeworth, John. Drayman. Greenwood's Wharf
Edwards, Alexander. Attorney at Law. 6 Meeting St.
Edwards, Edward & Co. Grocers. 17 Tradd St.
Edwards, James. Factor. 118 Tradd St. & Eveleigh's
Edwards, John. Shop Keeper. 303 King St.
Edwards, John. 7 Meeting St.
Eldridge, Randall. Mariner. 117 East Bay
Elizabeth. Seamstress. 200 King St.
Elliott, Elizabeth. 306 King St.
Elliott, Thomas. Planter. 3 Gibbes St.
Elliott, Thomas O. Planter. 17 Legare St.
Ellis, John. Mariner. Wyatt's Lot
Elmore, Jeffe. Tailor. 14 Hasell St.
Elsinore, James. Clerk of Treasury. 12 King St.
Elsworth, Theophilus. Gauger Customs. 73 East Bay
Emanuel, Joseph. Cigar Maker. Lynch's Lane
Emmet, Charlotte. 7 Bedon's Alley
Evans, George. Planter. 44 Trott St.
Eveleigh, Thomas. Planter. 229 Meeting St.
Ewing, Adam. Merchant. 259 Meeting St.
Ewing, Robert. Merchant. 125 Tradd St.
Fabre & Price. Merchants. 23 East Bay
Fabre, John, Rev. C. Rector Lutheran Church. 31 Archdale St.
Fair, William. Shoemaker. 5 Elliot St.
Fair, William. Factor. 62 Meeting St.
Fardo, George. Factor. 90 East Bay
Farquahar, John. Scrivener. 2 Pitt St.
Farr, Joseph. Planter. 12 Orange St.
Fayssoux, Peter. Physician. 76 Tradd St.
Felix, Frederick. Hair Dresser. 26 Church St.
Fell, Thomas. Merchant. 23 Broad St.
Ferguson, Ann. 67 Tradd St.
Ferril, Anthony. Cigar Maker. 25½ Elliot St.
Fiddy, William. Store Keeper. 16 Broad St.
Fields, John. Tobacconist. 187 Meeting St.
Finlayson, John. Carpenter. 4 Trott St.
Finlayson, Mungo. Cabinet Maker. 32 Queen St.
Fishburne, William. Planter. 12 Hasell St.
Fisher & Berney. Merchants. 9 Tradd St.
Fisher, George. Butcher. 103 Meeting St.
Fitzhipps, John. Shop Keeper. 155 King St.
Fitzpatrick, John. Merchant. 14 Beresford St.

Fleming, John. Watchman. 11 Clifford St.
Fletcher, Phoebe. 5 Beresford's Alley
Flint, Joseph. Shop Keeper. 31 Union St.
Florine, Lucas. 34 Guignard St.
Fluitt, Samuel. Shop Keeper. 1 King St.
Fogartie, Mary. School Mistress. 280 King St.
Folker, Gasper. Tanner. 11 St. Philip's St.
Ford, Bartholomew. Shoemaker. 93 Queen St.
Ford, J. Attorney at Law. 30 Tradd St.
Ford, Mary. 294 King St.
Fordham, Richard. Ship Carpenter. 3 Cock Lane
Forrest, George. Merchant. 67 East Bay
Forrest, Michael. School Master. 4 Wentworth St.
Forrester, William. Mariner. 172 Wentworth St.
Foskey, Bryan. Shop Keeper. 16 Union St.
Foster, Thomas. Factor. 10 Meeting St.
Fowke, Chandler D. Attorney at Law. 104 Broad St.
Fraser, Alexander. Planter. 78 Tradd St.
Fraser, William. Attorney at Law. 89 Broad St.
Frazer, ——. Shop Keeper. 220 King St.
Freeman, William. Distiller. 34 Trott St.
Freer, Ann. 109 Church St.
Freer, Sarah. 31 Wentworth St.
Freer, Thomas. Price's Alley
Friend, George. Baker. 39 Union St.
Friend, Uldy. Baker. 276 King St.
Frink, Thomas & Co. Store Keepers. Beale's Wharf
Fripp, William. Planter. 305 King St.
Frish & Wesinger. Shop Keepers. 22 Union St.
Frish, Charles. Shop Keeper. 239 King St.
Frost, Thomas, Rev. Assistant St. Philip's Church 21 Archdale St.
Fullam, William. Shop Keeper. Jervey's Wharf
Fuller & Brodie. House Carpenters. 2 Longitude Lane
Fuller, Thomas. Planter. 91 Tradd St.
Fullerton, Elizabeth. School Mistress. 86 Queen St.
Furman, Richard, Rev. Pastor Baptist Church. 19 Church St.
Gabeau, Anthony. Tailor. 232 Meeting St.
Gabel & Corre. Merchants. 43 Broad St.
Gadsden, Christopher. Planter. 4 Front St.
Gadsden, Philip. Factor. 5 Front St.
Gadsden, Thomas. Factor. 6 Front St.
Gaillard, Theodore. Planter. 88 East Bay
Gaillard, Theodore, Jr. Attorney at Law. 45 Tradd St.
Galway, Michael. Shop Keeper. 206 King St.
Gardner, John. Merchant. 6 Tradd St.
Gardner, William. Carver & Gilder. 206 Meeting St.
Garner, Ann. 11 Orange St.
Garrett, Joshua. George St.
Gaultier, Joseph. Auctioneer. 92 Tradd St.
Geddes, Henry. Store Keeper. 86 King St.
Geiger, Henry. Distiller. Coming St.
Gennerick, John F. Grocer. 114 Tradd St.
Gensill, John. Marine Hospital. 167 King St.
George, Henry. Shop Keeper. 216 King St.
George, James. Ship Carpenter. 125 East Bay
Georghegan, Dominick. Sugar Baker. Church St.
Gerley, John. Tailor. 4 Mazyck St.
Gervais, John Lewis. Merchant. 71 Broad St.
Geyer, John. Planter. 11 Meeting St.
Gibbes, John. Planter. 5 Legare St.
Gibbes, Robert. Planter. 19 Meeting St.
Gibbes, William Hasell. Master Chancery. 57 Meeting St.
Gibbs, Amariatha. 30 Queen St.
Gibbs, George. Baker. 42 Union St.
Gibbs, Mary. 59 Queen St.

13

Gibson, Robert. Saddler. 242 King St.
Gilbert, Elizabeth. Shop Keeper. 125 Church St.
Gilchrist, Adam. Merchant. 43 East Bay
Gilchrist, Malcolm. Shop Keeper. Greenwood's Wharf
Gillon, Alexander. Planter. 89 Tradd St.
Gist, W. Henry. Shop Keeper. 206 King St.
Gist, William. Shop Keeper. 211 King St.
Given, Robert. Stone Cutter. 22 Beresford's Alley
Glaze, John. Planter. 3 Cumberland St.
Glover, Ann. 312 King St.
Glover, William. Fisherman. Union St. Continued
Godfrey, Thomas. Carpenter. 13 Liberty St.
Godfrey, Thomas. Shop Keeper. 154 King St.
Good, Sarah. School Mistress. 9 Stoll's Alley
Goodwin, Robert. Blacksmith. 13 Queen St.
Gordon, James. Merchant. 6 Hasell St.
Gordon, John. Pilot. 22 Guignard St.
Gordon, John. Factor. 6 Society St.
Gordon, Mary. 8 Ellery St.
Gorton, James. Shop Keeper. Motte's Wharf
Gottier, Isabella. 14 Mazyck St.
Graeme, Ann. 82 Queen St.
Graeser, Jacob Conrad. Merchant. 42 Broad St.
Graff & Co. Merchants. 206 3/4 King St.
Graham, Mary. 108 Tradd St.
Graham, Richard. Shop Keeper. 4 Union St.
Graham, Samuel. Blacksmith. 3 Longitude Lane
Grant, Alexander. Baker. 148 King St.
Grant, Hary. Merchant. 12 East Bay
Grant, John. Saddler. 88 King St.
Grant, Lewis. Shop Keeper. 13 Union St.
Gravenstine, Frederick. Tailor. 1 Mazyck St.
Graves, James. Brick Layer. 6 Stoll's Alley
Gray, Benjamin. Factor. 77 Meeting St.
Gready, James. Saddler. 85 King St.
Green, William. Shop Keeper. 71 East Bay
Greenhill, Hugh & Co. Carpenters. 20 Legare St.
Greenland, Daniel. Factor. 39 Meeting St.
Greenland, George. Factor. 142 East Bay
Greenville, James. Hair Dresser. 87 King St.
Greenwood, William. Merchant. 1 Gadsden's Alley
Greenwood, William. Merchant. 2 Ellery St.
Gregoire, Son & Davidson. Merchants. 129 Tradd St.
Gregson, Thomas. Brewer. Magazine St.
Gressel, George. Carpenter. 34 Trott St.
Griggs, John. Factor. 9 Eveleigh's Wharf
Griggs, John. Factor. 22 King St.
Grimball, C. Isaac. Planter. 273 Meeting St.
Grimes, Mary. Shop Keeper. 15 Union St.
Grimke, John F. Associate Judge. 2 Orange St.
Grimke, John Paul. 54 Meeting St.
Gross, Charles. Gardener. 152 King St.
Grott, Francis. Gardener. 18 Trott St.
Gruber, Charles. Cooper. 80 Queen St.
Gruly, Joseph. Carpenter. 4 Cock Lane
Guerard, Mary Ann. 130 Church St.
Guilleaud, Claudius. Baker. 8 Elliot St.
Gunn, William. Blacksmith. 6 Queen St.
Guy, James. Tailor. 194 King St.
Hahnbaum, Christian. Physician. 235 King St.
Haig & Dunn. Carpenters. 116 East Bay
Haig, Mary. 10 Ellery St.
Haindsdorff, Henry. Carver. 15 Hasell St.
Hains, Heath. Shoemaker. 32 Motte's Wharf
Hall, Daniel. Merchant. 3 State House Square
Hall, Mary Ann. 16 King St.
Hall, Thomas. Postmaster. 32 Broad St.
Hall, William. Mariner. 5 Cumberland St.

Halliday, George. Mariner. 106¼ East Bay
Ham, Richard. Inspector Customs. 8 Chalmer's Lane
Ham, Thomas. Inspector Customs. 24 Beresford's Alley
Hamilton & Harper. Merchants. 15 Elliot St.
Hamilton, David. Ship Carpenter. 27 Guignard St.
Hamilton, James. Planter. 53 Meeting St.
Hamilton, James. Merchant. 11 Broad St.
Hamilton, John. Carpenter. 33 Archdale St.
Hampton, William. Cabinet Maker. 13 Beresford's Alley
Hancock, Elizabeth. 6 Maiden Lane
Hand, Margaret. Boarding House. 18 Queen St.
Haney, John. Wagon Yard. 163 King St.
Harboroskie, Ann. Store Keeper. 46 Broad St.
Harden, Sarah. 27 Society St.
Hare, Edward. Shop Keeper. 106 King St.
Hargreaves, Josh. & Jos. Merchants. 21 Broad St.
Harleston, Ann. 20 Hasell St.
Harman, Michael. Butcher. George St.
Harmond, John. Carter. Wentworth St.
Harper, Robert. Shop Keeper. 88 King St.
Harris, Andrew. Merchant. 6 Clifford St.
Harris, John Hartley. Canon St. Philip's Church. 113 Queen St.
Harris, Thomas. Boarding House. 237 King St.
Harris, Tucker. Physician. 69 King St.
Harrison, Isaac. Shop Keeper. 132 Queen St.
Harrison, John. Shoemaker. 25 Broad St.
Hart, Christopher. Store Keeper. 43 Broad St.
Hart, Dorcas. Seamstress. 25 Union St. Continued
Hart, Philip. Broker. 136 Queen St.
Hart, Simon. Shop Keeper. 252 King St.
Harth, ——. Shop Keeper. 65 East Bay
Harth, John. Store Keeper. 16 Archdale St.
Hartley, Elizabeth. 9 Meeting St.
Harvey & Dill. Grocers. 9 Bedon's Alley
Harvey, Benjamin. Brick Layer. 31 Beaufain St.
Harvey, Elizabeth. Market Square
Harvey, Elizabeth. 10 Dutch Church Alley
Harvey, Thomas. Store Keeper. 39 Archdale St.
Haunbuam, George. Physician. 258 King St.
Hauser, Elias. Boarding House. 205 King St.
Hawes, Adoniah. Painter. 254 King St.
Hawkins, James. Carpenter. 273 King St.
Hayward, Hannah. 18 Church St.
Hazlehurst, Rob. & Co. Merchants. 13 East Bay
Hazlewood, John. Painter. 36 Pinckney St.
Heliger, Joseph. Engraver. 6 Elliot St.
Henderreckson, Belsha. Carpenter. 23 Society St.
Henning, John Fred. Store Keeper. 32 Church St.
Henri, Peter. Miniature Painter. 89 Church St.
Henry, Francis. Button Maker. 28 Archdale St.
Henry, Jacob. Shop Keeper. 53 King St.
Henry, John. Blacksmith. 91 Meeting St.
Hesseling, I. H. Colfbaunkeep. 137 King St.
Heyward, Nathaniel. Planter. 118 East Bay
Hilagers, George A. Shop Keeper. 54 Tradd St.
Hill, Duncan. Mariner. 96 Church St.
Hill, Eleanor. 14 Union St.
Hill, Joseph. Jervey's Wharf
Hill, Paul. Shop Keeper. 1 Beresford St.
Hillegas, Philip. Grocer. 96 Tradd St.
Hilligas, Jacob. Shop Keeper. 6 Moore St.
Himili, James. Watchmaker. 126 Broad St.
Hinds, Patrick. Shoemaker. 33 Beaufain St.
Hinlen, Thomas. Planter. Bull St.
Hinson, Thomas. Merchant. 26 Society St.

Hirreld, George. Tailor. 6 Beresford's Alley
Hislop & Snowden. Store Keepers. 134 Queen St.
Hodson, Margaret. Boarding House. 57 King St.
Hogan, David Henry. Mariner. 2 King St.
Hogarth, William. Shoemaker. 242 Meeting St.
Holbeck, John. Brick Layer. 8 Moore St.
Holland, Hugh. Carter. 112 East Bay
Hollaway & Thayer. Shop Keepers. 57 King St.
Hollingshead, William, Rev. Pastor Congregational Church. 93 Meeting St.
Holmes, Isaac. Lieutenant Governor. 15 Legare St.
Holmes, John B. Attorney at Law. 6 Meeting St.
Holmes, Thomas. Saddler. 264 King St.
Holmes, William. Auctioneer. North Side of Exchange
Holt, William. Shoemaker. 4 Unity Alley
Honeywood, Arthur. Blacksmith. 1 Moore St.
Hook, George. Carpenter. 12 Chamber's Alley
Hope, Mary. South Bay
Hope, Thomas. Cabinet Maker. 15 Friend St.
Hopton, Sarah. 81 Meeting St.
Hornley, Thomas. Distiller. 214 King St.
Horry, Thomas. Planter. 274 Meeting St.
Hort, William. State Treasurer. 28 Guignard St.
Horton, Thomas. Shop Keeper. 26 Queen St.
Hostige, Jehu. Shop Keeper. Greenwood's Wharf
House, Mary Ann. Shop Keeper. 251 King St.
House, Samuel. Clerk. 7 Chamber's Alley
Hover, John. Tailor. 7 King St.
Howard, Robert. Factor. Jervey's Wharf
Howard, Robert. Factor. 128 Queen St.
Howell, John. Hair Dresser. 223 King St.
Howell, John. Constable. 17 Beresford St.
Hoyland, Ann Maria. School Mistress. 86 Broad St.
Hubert, Barry. Shop Keeper. 7 Union St.
Hubert, Charles. Merchant. 27 Elliot St.
Hudson, Mary. Mantua Maker. 34 King St.
Hugeley, John. Shop Keeper. Smith's Lane
Huger, Isaac, Jr. Sheriff Charleston District. 59 Broad St.
Huger, Isaac, Sr. District Marshall. 59 Broad St.
Huger, John. Commission Loan Office. 73 Broad St.
Hughes, John. Ship Joiner. Wragg's Alley
Hume, John. Planter. 77 Queen St.
Hunt, Thomas. Brewer. 30 Elliot St.
Hunter, E. & Jacob. Shop Keepers. East Bay
Hutchings, William. School Master. 14 Hasell St.
Hutchinson, Jeremiah. Chair Maker. Meeting St.
Hutchinson, Thomas, Sr. Planter. East Bay
Hutchinson, Thos. Jr. Planter. 21 South Bay
Hutson, Richard. Chancellor. 102 Tradd St.
Hutton, James. Clerk. South Bay
Hymes, Solomon. Shop Keeper. 244 King St.
Inglesby, William. Tailor. 36 Church St.
Inglis, Alexander. Planter. 84 Queen St.
Irons, Berry. Tailor. 18 Clifford's Alley
Irving, Beaufain John. 10 Legare St.
Irving, James. Carpenter. Roper's Wharf
Izard, Charlotte. 1 Cumberland St.
Izard, Ralph. Planter. 83 Broad St.
Jacks, James. Watchmaker. 44 East Bay
Jackson, John. Planter. 26 Guignard St.
Jackson, John. Watchmaker. 129 Broad St.
Jackson, John. Butcher. 12 Liberty St.
Jacobs, Jacob. Shop Keeper. 82 King St.
Jacobs, Jacob. Auctioneer. Under the Exchange
Jacobs, Jacob Auctioneer. Dwelling 20 Meeting St.
Jamieson, Rebecca. Boarding School. 29 Church St.
Jean, Paul Costa. Jewish Priest. 83 Church St.

Jeffries, Mary. 65 Queen St.
Jenkins, Edward. Rev. 84 Tradd St.
Jennings & Woddrop. Merchants. 9 East Bay
Jermain, John. Shop Keeper. 275 King St.
Jervey, Thomas. Factor. 1 St. Michael's Alley
Jesse, Sarah. Shop Keeper. 50 Broad St.
Jessum, Matthew. Shop Keeper. 137 Queen St.
Johnson, John. Clerk. Near the Old Church
Johnson, William. Mariner. 16 Friend St.
Johnson, William. Blacksmith. 10 Charles St.
Johnston & Wallace. Brick Layers. 11 Union St. Continued
Johnston, Andrew. Planter. 3 St. Philip's St.
Johnston, Charles. Merchant. Lamboll's Lane
Johnston, David. Shop Keeper. Greenwood's Wharf
Johnston, Eliza. 3 Charles St.
Johnston, Hester. 1 Clifford's Alley
Johnston, Jacob. Carpenter. 2 Boundary St.
Johnston, John. Wagon Yard. 165 King St.
Johnston, William. Hair Dresser. 49 Church St.
Jolly, Maybury. Hatter. 111 Queen St.
Jones, Abraham. Shop Keeper. 41 Church St.
Jones, Alexander. Shop Keeper. 107 Church St.
Jones, Henry. Shop Keeper. Beale's Wharf
Jones, Jesse. Tanner. 25 King St.
Jones, Joseph. Shop Keeper. 15 Tradd St.
Jones, Samuel. Shop Keeper. 268 King St.
Jones, Sarah. Shop Keeper. 13 Beresford's Alley
Jones, Thomas. Planter. 4 Guignard St.
Jones, William. Cabinet Maker. 51 Broad St.
Jones, William. Clerk. Jervey's Wharf
Joseph, Israel. Indigo Broker. 56 King St.
Juhan, Alexander. Musician. 111 Tradd St.
Kaiser, John. Deputy Sheriff. 274 King St.
Kalcoffen, John. Constable. 78 Church St.
Kalteisen, Michael. Commandant Fort Johnson. 13 Maiden Lane
Kean, David. Coach Maker. 29 Archdale St.
Keeley, Sebastian. Merchant. 41 East Bay
Keen, Thomas. Mariner. 16 Union St. Continued
Keith & Wish. Shop Keepers. 131 Queen St.
Keith, Isaac S. Pastor Congregational Church. 76 Tradd St.
Kelder, Henry. 7 Clifford St.
Kelly, John. Shop Keeper. 116 King St.
Kemmell, John. Saddler. 46 Queen St.
Kemmell, Mary. Shop Keeper. 42 Queen St.
Kempton, Ann. Shop Keeper. 17 Chalmer's Alley
Kennan, Henry. Factor. 1 West St.
Kennear, Alexander. Shop Keeper. Greenwood's Wharf
Kennedy & Parker. Merchants. 9 Broad St.
Kennedy, Andrew. Merchant. 37 King St.
Kennedy, James. Planter. 100 Tradd St.
Kennedy, John. Shop Keeper. East Bay
Kern, Frederick John. Merchant. 193 King St.
Kerr, Andrew. Merchant. 135 Tradd St.
Kerr, John. Hatter. 14 Trott St.
Kersey, William. Shop Keeper. 184 Meeting St.
Kershaw, John. Silversmith. 97 Broad St.
Kevan & Powrie. Merchants. 14 Broad St.
King, Eleanor. Shop Keeper. 45 King St.
King, Timothy. Shop Keeper. 132 Queen St.
Kinloch, Cleland. Planter. Hasell St.
Kinloch, Francis. Planter. 123 Queen St.
Kirk, John. Shop Keeper. Boundary St.
Kirk, John. Merchant. 59 East Bay
Knight, Christopher. Attorney at Law. 225 Meeting St.
Know, Conrad. Butcher. 145 Meeting St.

15

Knox, Robert. Continued Statemeas. 17 Union St. Continued

Kosskey, Anthony Jan. Blacksmith. 23 Beresford St.
Kraps, Andrew. Baker. 49 King St.
Kriebel, Frederick. Surgeon. 15 Beresford St.
Kruger, John Frederick. Surgeon. 198 King St.
Ladson, James. Planter. Lamboll's Lane
Ladson, Jane. 49 Tradd St.
Ladson, Sarah. 28½ Broad St.
Lahiffe, Maurice. Shop Keeper. 76 King St.
Lamb & Montgomerie. Merchants. 17 Elliot St.
LaMotte, James. Factor. Graeme's Wharf
Lancaster, William. Printer. 14 Wragg's Alley
Lance, Ann. 10 Allen St.
Lance, Lambert. Attorney at Law. 90 Queen St.
Lanchester, Henry. Merchant. 4 Pinckney St.
Lang, Jane. 73 Church St.
Langford, Ann. 23 Guignard St.
Langstaff, John. Store Keeper. Beale's Wharf
Larrey, Robert. Carpenter. 62 Church St.
Latham, Daniel. Distiller. 2 Hasell St.
Latham, Eleanor. School Mistress. 32 Meeting St.
Lawrance, Estel. Shipwright. 15 Pinckney St.
Lawry, John. Shop Keeper. 14 Union St. Continued
Lawton, Winmal. Planter. Lynch's Lane
Lazarus, Mark. Shop Keeper. 101 King St.
Lebbey, Nathaniel. Blockmaker. 83 East Bay
Lee & Banks. Merchants. 47 King St.
Lee, Francis. Shop Keeper. 19 Tradd St.
Lee, Stephen. Watchmaker. 42 Broad St.
Lee, Thomas. Attorney at Law. 91 Broad St.
Lee, William. Watchmaker. 91 & 95 Broad St.
Legare & Theus. Merchants. 101 Church St.
Legare, Benjamin. Justice Peace. 11 Stoll's Alley
Legare, Daniel. Planter. Ansonborough
Legare, Daniel, Jr. Planter. 11 Mazyck St.
Legare, Samuel. Merchant. 101 Church St.
Legare, Solomon. Factor. 18 Friend St.
Legare, Thomas. Planter. 50 Tradd St.
Legge, Edward. Planter. 45 Trott St.
Legge, Samuel. Carpenter. 38 Archdale St.
Lehre, Mary. 11 Liberty St.
Lehre, Thomas. Planter. 293 King St.
Lenneau, Bazil. Tanner. 25 Beaufain St.
Lennox, William. 5 Orange St.
Lenud, Henry. Planter. 1 Hasell St.
Lepoole, Peter. Merchant. 82 Queen St.
Lesesne, Isaac. Planter. 111 East Bay
Lesesne, Sarah. 108 East Bay
Leslie, George. Shop Keeper. 94 Church St.
Levaux, John. Carpenter. 37 Trott St.
Levi, Hiram. Broker. 231 King St.
Levi, Moses. Shop Keeper. 113 King St.
Levi, Moses. Shop Keeper. 233 King St.
Levi, Solomon. Shop Keeper. 247 King St.
Lewie & Coulback. Fisherman. 3 Union St. Continued
Liber, John. Shoemaker. 164 King St.
Liblong, Henry. Shoemaker. 160 King St.
Lightwood, Edward. Planter. 266 Meeting St.
Limehouse, Thomas. Shop Keeper. 34 Broad St.
Lindsay, Robert. Merchant. 136 Church St.
Linguard, Mary. 72 Church St.
Lining, Charles. Ordinary & Attorney. 17 Friend St.
Little, Robert. Carpenter. 9 Wragg's Alley
Livingston, William. George St.
Lloyd, John. Planter. 8 Legare St.
Lloyd, John, Jr. Merchant. 110 Broad St.
Lloyd, Joseph. Shop Keeper. 15 Bedon's Alley

Lloyd, Joseph. Shop Keeper. 61 Meeting St.
Lane, Alice. 7 King St.
Lockey, George. Merchant. 79 East Bay
Lockwood, Joshua. Merchant. 42 East Bay
Lockwood, Thomas. Planter. 207 Meeting St.
Logan, George. State Physician. 32 Tradd St.
Logan, William. Factor. 292 King St.
Long, Edward. Tailor. 3 Queen St.
Long, Elizabeth. 178 King St.
Long, Lewis. Carter. 179 Meeting St.
Loocock, Aaron. Planter. 31 Tradd St.
Lopez, Aaron. Scrivener. 2 Clifford St.
Lord, Ann. 25 Beaufain St.
Lothrop, Seth. Merchant. 136 East Bay
Love, John. Fruit Shop. 8 Tradd St.
Loveday, John. Factor. 10 Moore St.
Lowndes, Rawlins. Planter. 74 Broad St.
Luckie, John. Saddler. 65 King St.
Lunt, William. Tallow Chandler. 16 Chalmer's Alley
Luyton, William. Shop Keeper. 133 Tradd St.
Lynah, James. Physician. 55 Meeting St.
Lynch, James. Coach Maker. 78 Meeting St.
Lyon, Abraham. Blacksmith. 6 Short St.
Lyon, Mordecai. Tailor. 231 King St.
M'Arthur, John. Shoemaker. 9 Union St. Continued
M'Bride, James. Shop Keeper. 58 East Bay
M'Bride, Thomas. Shop Keeper. 34 Queen St.
M'Call, Hext. Attorney at Law. 267 Meeting St.
M'Call, James. Auditor General. 88 Church St.
M'Call, John. City Treasurer. 110 Church St.
M'Call, John. Tailor. 78 East Bay
M'Calla, Thomas. Physician. 223 Meeting St.
M'Callister, Archibald. Planter. 23 Hasell St.
M'Callister, John. Stay Maker. 246 Meeting St.
M'Callum, James. Merchant. 6 Elliot St.
M'Cauly & Davis. Merchants. 13 Broad St.
M'Clure, Cochran & W. Merchants. 7 Tradd St.
M'Comb, James. Auctioneer. Behind the Exchange
M'Connell, William. Tailor. 2 Elliot St.
M'Corkel, Samuel. Carpenter. 132 Queen St.
M'Cormick, Sparks & Co. Store Keepers. 183 King St.
M'Crady, Edward. Vintner. 63 East Bay
M'Credie, David. Merchant. 8 Broad St.
M'Donald, Archibald. Tailor. 49 Church St.
M'Donald, Charles. Store Keeper. 186 Meeting St.
M'Donald, William. Shop Keeper. 22 East Bay
M'Dowell, John. Merchant. 4 Broad St.
M'Gee, John. Shop Keeper. 224 King St.
M'Hugo, Anthony. Shop Keeper. 63 Meeting St.
M'Intosh, Simon. Attorney at Law. 30 Beaufain St.
M'Iver, John. Printer. 23 Tradd St.
M'Kann, James. Beer House. 12 Beresford St.
M'Kee, Samuel. Shop Keeper. 47 King St.
M'Kenzie, Alexander. Shop Keeper. 12 Union St.
M'Kenzie, Andrew. Grocer. 108 Broad St.
M'Kenzie, John. Pilot. 2 Charles St.
M'Kenzie, Kennedy. Butcher. 29 Society St.
M'Kimmy, John. Brick Layer. 28 King St.
M'Kimmy, William. Cooper. Lynch's Lane
M'Lean, Evan. Tailor. 35 Church St.
M'Lean, Lachlan. Tailor. 40 Church St.
M'Leith, Agnes. Shop Keeper. 1 Elliot St.
M'Leod, William & Co. Merchants. 11 East Bay
M'Lish, Mary. School Mistress. 54 Church St.
M'Lane, John. Master Poor House. 1 Mazyck St.
M'Mahan, John. Shop Keeper. 39 Queen St.
M'Nab, Alexander. Watchman. 35 Meeting St.
M'Neal, Archibald. Shop Keeper. 205 Meeting St.

16

M'Neal, Archibald. Hatter. 36 Broad St.
M'Neil, Catharine. Shop Keeper. 37 Hasell St.
M'Pherson, Duncan. Shop Keeper. 74 King St.
M'Pherson, Jane. Shop Keeper. 32 King St.
M'Pherson, John. Planter. 23 Legare St.
M'Queen, John. Merchant. 17 Broad St.
M'Queen, Robert. Shop Keeper. 8 Queen St.
M'Whann, William. Merchant. 38 Church St.
Mackay, Crafts. Watchmaker. 129 Broad St.
Mackie, Ann. 6 Legare St.
Mackie, James. Cooper. 4 Bedon's Alley
Magood, Simon. Cochran's Wharf
Main, Thomas. Shipwright. 1 Mey's Alley
Main, William. Shop Keeper. 71 East Bay
Malcolm, Joseph. Shop Keeper. East Bay
Malland, Charles. Carpenter. 9 Clifford St.
Manigault, Gabriel. Planter. 89 East Bay
Manigault, Joseph. Planter. 82 Tradd St.
Mann & Foltz. Merchants. 3 East Bay
Mann, Margaret. School Mistress. 58 Meeting St.
Mann, Spencer. Merchant. 55 Church St.
Mannerg, Archibald. Boarding House. 8 Bedon's Alley
Manning, Hugh. Mariner. Market Square
Manson, George. Shipwright. 3 Ellery St.
Manson, John. Merchant. 38 Queen St.
Mapey, Catharine. 261 Meeting St.
Mark, Conrad. Cooper. 276 King St.
Markland & M'Iver. Printers. 47 East Bay
Markland, John. Printer. 40 Tradd St.
Markley, Abraham. Shop Keeper. 125 King St.
Marks, Anthony. Shop Keeper. 218 King St.
Marks, James. Shop Keeper. Beale's Wharf
Marks, Joseph. Ship Carpenter. 8 Pinckney St.
Marr, Ann. 132 Church St.
Marrow, Elizabeth. 5 Charles St.
Marshall, John. Cabinet Maker. 219 Meeting St.
Marshall, William. Factor & Wharf. Roper's Wharf
Marshall, William. Attorney at Law. 38 Tradd St.
Marston, Nathaniel. Mariner. 27 Pinckney St.
Martin, Chreshan. Tanner. 144 Meeting St.
Martin, Daniel. Watchman. 44 King St.
Martin, Edward. Brick Layer. 113 East Bay
Martin, Jacob. Merchant. 214 Meeting St.
Martin, John C. Innholder. 230 King St.
Martin, Rebecca. Boarding House. 14 Queen St.
Martin, Thomas. Factor & Grocer. 11 Tradd St.
Mason, William. Clerk Common Pleas. 49 Broad St.
Mathews, John. Chancellor. 85 East Bay
Matlack, William. Watchmaker. 20 Broad St.
Matthews, Benjamin. Planter. 108 Church St.
Matthews, Edith. State House Square
Matthews, George. Factor. 102 Church St.
Matthews, Peter. Mariner. 22 Trott St.
Matthews, William. Planter. 92 Meeting St.
May, George. Ship Joiner. 126 East Bay
Mayer, G. John. Grocer. 52 East Bay
Mazyck, Daniel. Deputy Secretary. 41 Trott St.
Mazyck, Stephen. Planter. 1 Short St.
Mazyck, William. 83 Queen St.
Mears, John. Brass Founder. 64 Meeting St.
Meckleswitz, Felix de. Mariner. 5 Magazine St.
Mey, Charles Florian. Merchant. 40 Pinckney St.
Michael, John. Distiller. 30 Pinckney St.
Middleton & Ramsey. Tailors. 43 Queen St.
Middleton, Mary. Widow. Front St.
Middleton, Thomas. Planter. 82 Tradd St.
Midford, George. Shipwright. 6 Chalmer's Alley
Milander, Adam. Shop Keeper. 64 King St.

Miller, Ann. 15 King St.
Miller, Benjamin. Butcher. 8 Burn's Lane
Miller, George. Shop Keeper. 22 Beresford St.
Miller, James. Merchant. 103 Church St.
Miller, James. Wine Merchant. 64 East Bay
Miller, John. Shop Keeper. 186 King St.
Miller, John David. Silversmith. 109 Broad St.
Miller, Nicholas. Baker. 3 Wentworth St.
Miller, Rence. 275 Meeting St.
Miller, Samuel. Carpenter. 27 Trott St.
Milligan & M'Kune. Carpenters. 85 Church St.
Milligan, Jacob. Intelligence Office. 3 Champney's Row
Milligan, James. Jail Keeper. New Goal
Milligan, John. Mariner. Lamboll's Lane
Milligan, John. Inspector Customs. 3 Lodge Alley
Mills, George. Shoemaker. 77 King St.
Mills, ——, Rev. Mr. Rector St. Andrew's Church. 47 Tradd St.
Mills, William. Tailor. 105 Church St.
Milner, Daniel. Chair Maker. 272 Meeting St.
Milner, George. Blacksmith. Cochran's Wharf
Milner, John. Gunsmith. Snitter's Alley
Minchin, John. Grocer. 10 Elliot St.
Minnick, John. Merchant. 32 East Bay
Minott, John. Factor. Lynch's Lane
Minott, William. Mariner. Lynch's Lane
Mintsing, Christian. Blacksmith. 78 King St.
Miott, John. Silversmith. 230 Meeting St.
Mitchell, Andrew. Shop Keeper. 103 Meeting St.
Mitchell, Elizabeth. 7 Trott St.
Mitchell, John. Warden, N.P. &c. 30 East Bay
Mitchell, John. Notary Public. 264 Meeting St.
Mitchell, Lazarus. Mariner. 20 Beresford St.
Mitchell, Mary. 5 Moore St.
Mitchell, William. Carpenter. 32 Guignard St.
Mitchell, Wm. Boone. Attorney at Law. 264 Meeting St.
Moer, William. Cooper. Gadsden's Wharf
Moncrief, John. Mariner. 34 Guignard St.
Moncrief, John. Carpenter. 102 East Bay
Moncrieff, John & Co. Merchants. 18 Elliot St.
Mood, Peter. Silversmith. 238 King St.
Moodie, Benjamin. Merchant. 3 Church St.
Moore & Denny. Saddlers. 202 King St.
Moore, John. Butcher. 19 Hasell St.
Moore, John. Shop Keeper. 190 King St.
Moore, John. Planter. 51 King St.
Moore, Joseph. Shop Keeper. 100 East Bay
Moore, Peter Joseph. Dentist. 42 King St.
Moore, Richard. Painter & Glazier. 102 King St.
Moore, Thomas. Butcher. 171 Meeting St.
Morgan, Ann. 39 King St.
Morgan, Charles. Shipwright. 36 Trott St.
Morgan, Edward. Custom House Boat. Cochran's Wharf
Morris, George. Painter & Glazier. Lynch's Lane
Morris, Lewis. Planter. 260 Meeting St.
Morris, Mary. 30 Wentworth St.
Morris, Thomas. Merchant. 14 East Bay
Morrison, Ann. Milliner. 105 3/4 Church St.
Morrower, Margaret. 12 Pinckney St.
Moses, Abraham. Shop Keeper. 55 East Bay
Moses, Barnet. 7 Moore St.
Moses, Henry. Shop Keeper. 55 East Bay
Moses, Isaac. Shop Keeper. 2 Beresford St.
Moses, Lyon. Shop Keeper. 83 King St.
Moses, Philip. Apothecary. 119 Tradd St.
Motte, Abraham. Factor. 18 Meeting St.

17

Motte, Francis. Factor. 60 East Bay
Motte, Isaac. Naval Officer. 262 Meeting St.
Motter, Isaac. 104 King St.
Moubray, William. Boarding House. 112 Tradd St.
Moultrie, Alexander. Attorney General. 17 South Bay
Moultrie, James. Physician. 17 South Bay
Moultrie, William. Planter. 60 Meeting St.
Muirhead, James. Bookbinder. 7 Elliot St.
Muller, Albert Arney. Powder Receiver. Wentworth St.
Mulligan, Francis. Shop Keeper. 127 East Bay
Munary, Robert. Shoemaker. 75 King St.
Muncreef, Richard. Planter. 5 Magazine St.
Muncreef, Susannah. 21 Queen St.
Munro, John. Wharfinger. 1 Pinckney St.
Murphy, James. Shop Keeper. 25 Meeting St.
Murphy, John. Gardener. 3 Boundary St.
Murray, Thomas. Cooper. 91 Church St.
Murset, Amelia. Shop Keeper. 27 Church St.
Myer, Philip. Baker. 272 King St.
Myers, Israel. 20 Union St. Continued
Myers, Joseph. Auctioneer. Back of Exchange
Myers, Samuel. Tailor. 233 King St.
Mylne, James. Baker. 20 Union St.
Neiser, Henry. Baker. 11 Beresford St.
Neiser, Philip. Baker. 84 King St.
Nelson, George. Merchant. 95 Church St.
Neufville, John. Commission Loan. 85 Queen St.
Neufville, John, Jr. Register Chancery. 33 Meeting St.
Neufville, William. Physician. 124 Broad St.
Newman, Fred. George. Broker. 11 Moore St.
Newton, Downham. Mariner. 21 Society St.
Nicholas, Christopher. Carter. 10 Burn's Lane
Nicholson, John Paul. Shop Keeper. 44 Union St.
Nielson, James. Merchant. 29 Beaufain St.
Nipper, David Henry. Bookbinder. 225 King St.
Nixon, William, Rev. Colum. Academy. New Market
Norris, Nicholas. Grocer. 50 Broad St.
Norris, Robert & Co. Factors. 1 Bedon's Alley
North & Vesey. Shipchandlers. 38 East Bay
North, Edward. Shipchandler. 7 Church St.
North Susannah. 37 Tradd St.
Nott, Isabella. 58 Church St.
O'Brian, Thomas. Shop Keeper. 130 Queen St.
O'Hara, Daniel. Merchant. 128 Broad St.
O'Hear, James. Factor. Eveleigh's Wharf
O'Hear, James. Factor. Dwelling 5 Church St.
Continued
Oakman, Henry. Merchant. 16 Elliot St.
Oats, Charles. 26 Trott St.
Oats, Edward. 1 Charles St.
Oldman, Joseph. Confectioner. 221 Meeting St.
Oliphant, Catharine. 6 Union St. Continued
Oliphant, David. Painter. 66 King St.
Oliver, James. School Master. 22 Trott St.
Osborne, Henry. Academy. 11 Pinckney St.
Osgood & Greenwood. Grocers. 123 Broad St.
Owen, John. Merchant. 27 Tradd St.
Paget, Thomas. School Master. 63 Church St.
Palmer, Job. Carpenter. 26 Trott St.
Palmer, John. Constable. 3 Water St.
Parker, Isaac. Planter. 11 Legare St.
Parker, John. Planter. 10 George St.
Parker, John & George. Brickmakers. 80 East Bay
Parker, John, Jr. Attorney at Law. 41 Meeting St.
Parker, Joseph. Butcher. 114 East Bay
Parker, Thomas. Attorney at Law. 41 Meeting St.
Parkinson, John. Carver & Gilder. 4 Moore St.
Parrie, Murraline. Baker. 20 Beresford's Alley

Parsons, Susannah. 20 Church St.
Patrick, Casimer. Shop Keeper. 185 King St.
Patterson, William. Carpenter. 271 King St.
Patton, Catharine. Midwife. 6 East Bay
Paul, Andrew. Shop Keeper. 51 Church St.
Payne, William. Merchant. 21 Elliot St.
Peace, Isaac. Merchant. 110 Tradd St.
Peak, John. Tailor. Magazine St.
Peckham, Benjamin. Store Keeper. Motte's Wharf
Pecton, Ruth. School Mistress. Wyatt's Lot
Pelton, Roderick. Shoemaker. 28 Queen St.
Pemble, David. Tailor. 58½ East Bay
Pencil, Emanuel. Tin Man. 48 Meeting St.
Penman, James & Ed. Merchants. 75 East Bay
Peppin, Joseph & Co. Merchants. 35 Elliot St.
Peppin, Matthew. Merchant. 106 Broad St.
Perry, Eleanor. Boarding House. 204 Meeting St.
Petrie, Elizabeth. 1 Orange St.
Petry, -----, Monsieur. V. C. of France. 279 King St.
Petsch, Adam. Physician & Apothecary. 241 King St.
Philips, Benjamin. Shop Keeper. 115 King St.
Philips, John Christian. Baker. 105 King St.
Philips, Thomas. Saddler. 62 King St.
Philips, Thomas. Coach Maker. 73 Meeting St.
Pierce, Benjamin. Painter. 35 Broad St.
Pierce, Robert. Brick Layer. 35 Meeting St.
Pillason, William. Billiard Table. 26 King St.
Pilsbury, Samuel. Inspector Customs. 43 Union St.
Pinckney, Charles. Governor. 270 Meeting St.
Pinckney, Charles C. Counsellor at Law. 92 East Bay
Pinckney, Frances S. 16 Legare St.
Pinckney, Frances. 270 Meeting St.
Pinckney, Thomas, Jr. Planter. 270 Meeting St.
Pinger, Lewis. Hair Dresser. 62 East Bay
Pitts, Frances. 1 South Bay
Plumb, Jacob. Baker. 169 King St.
Plunkett, Thomas. Shop Keeper. East Bay
Poinsett, Elisha. Physician. 5 Broad St.
Pollock, Solomon. Horsedealer. Bull & Rutledge Sts.
Pope, Alexander. Carpenter. 94 Queen St.
Pope, Samuel. Carpenter. 4 Pinckney St.
Porcher, Philip. Planter. 6 Archdale St.
Postell, Thomas. Planter. 179 King St.
Powell, Ruth. 2 Lynch's Lane
Poyas, John Earnest. Physician. 4 Orange St.
Poyas, John Lewis. House Carpenter. 38 Guignard St.
Poyas, Magdalene. 36 Meeting St.
Prentice, John. Coach Maker. 29 Archdale St.
Prestman & Calhoun. Merchants. 36 East Bay
Price, Ann. 52 Broad St.
Price, William. Merchant. 2 Bedon's Alley
Primrose, Nicol. Inspector Customs. St. Philip's St.
Prince, Ann. 98 Queen St.
Prince, Charles. Tin Man. 267 King St.
Prince, Charles. Pilot. 115 Tradd St.
Pringle, John Julius. U. S. Attorney. 105 Tradd St.
Pringle, Robert. Planter. South Bay
Prioleau, Philip. Librarian, Library Society. 21 East
Bay
Prioleau, Samuel. Planter. 21 Church St.
Prioleau, Samuel, Jr. Factor. 48 Church St.
Pritchard, John, Mrs. 4 Magazine St.
Pritchard, Paul. Shipwright. 88 East Bay
Purcell & Hoburne. Carpenters. 43 Trott St.
Purcell, Henry, Dr. Rector St. Michael's Church. 89
Tradd St.
Purcell, Joseph. Land Surveyor. 121 King St.
Purchess, Samuel. Seedsman. 39 Elliot St.

Purse, Elizabeth. Boarding House. 30 Broad St.
Purse, William. Watchmaker. 30 Broad St.
Pyott, Peter. Draymaster. St. Philip's St.
Quan, Robert. Hair Dresser. Queen St.
Quash, Robert. Planter. 76 Broad St.
Quin, James. Painter. 5 Chalmer's Alley
Quin, Robert. Constable. 12 Allen St.
Quinby, Henry. Carpenter. 78 Meeting St.
Quingin, David. Mariner. Roper's Wharf
Radcliffe, Elizabeth. 11 George St.
Radcliffe, Thomas. Planter. 6 George St.
Rader, Philip. Shoemaker. 118 Broad St.
Rainier, David. Pilot. 8 Maiden Lane
Ralph, John. Cabinet Maker. 52 Church St.
Ramage, Frances. Boarding House. 6 Cumberland St.
Ramsey, David. Physician. 90 Broad St.
Ramsey, Joseph. Physician. 80 Tradd St.
Ranger, Jacob. Shop Keeper. 226 King St.
Ransier, J. L. Gunsmith. 210 King St.
Ravenel, Daniel. Planter. 100 Broad St.
Ravenel, Elizabeth. 107 Queen St.
Read, Jacob. Barrister at Law. 131 East Bay
Read, John. Wheelwright. 210 Meeting St.
Read, William. Physician. 11 Church St.
Reader, George. Butcher. 10 Society St.
Rechon, David. Tailor. 110 King St.
Redmond, Andrew. Turner. 80 Church St.
Reed, George. Shop Keeper. 2 Tradd St.
Reese, John. Custon House Boat. 31 Pinckney St.
Reese, Martha. Boarding House. 95 Queen St.
Reeves, Enos. Goldsmith. 234 Meeting St.
Reid, George. Merchant. Meeting St.
Reil, John. Shop Keeper. 27 Henry St.
Rester, Henry. Watchman. 119 Meeting St.
Reyley, John. Blacksmith. 9 Ellery St.
Reynolds, George. Gardener. 42 George St.
Rhind, Elizabeth. Boarding School. 98 Church St.
Rice, Thomas. Pilot. 115 Queen St.
Richards, Gasper. Tailor. 64 Queen St.
Richardson, John. Planter. 120 King St.
Richardson, John. Factor. 36 Elliot St.
Ridfield, Christopher. Drayman. Sugar House Yard
Righton, Joseph. Cooper. 118 Church St.
Righton, M'Cully. Cooper. 120 Church St.
Rimoli, Martin. Carpenter. Coming St.
Ripley, Paul. Pilot. 23 Beresford's Alley
Rivers, Beulah. Widow. 7 Stoll's Alley
Rivers, Francis. Carpenter. 5 Wragg's Alley
Rivers, John. Planter. Stoll's Alley
Rivers, Samuel. Shipwright. 4 Water St.
Rivers, Thomas. Planter. Stoll's Alley
Rivers, Thomas. Butcher. 1 Water St.
Roberts, Ann. 16 Church St.
Roberts, Thomas. Carpenter. 24 Queen St.
Roberts, William. Shop Keeper. 4 Queen St.
Roberts, William. Chair Maker. 87 Queen St.
Robertson, Alexander. Shop Keeper. 95 King St.
Robertson, John. Warden. 128 King St.
Robinson, John. Brick Layer. 5 Cock Lane
Robinson, Joseph. Carpenter. 39½ Meeting St.
Robinson, William. Merchant. 26 Elliot St.
Roche, Jeremiah. Shop Keeper. East Bay
Rodamond, Rachel. Market Square
Rogers, Christopher. Tailor. 25 Tradd St.
Rogers, Lewis. Perfumer. 121 Broad St.
Rogers, Maria. School Mistress. St. Philip's St.
Rogers, Sarah. Shop Keeper. 126 Church St.
Roggaman, Anthony. Tailor. 85 Church St.

Rogley, Anthony. Shop Keeper. 20 Tradd St.
Rolinbury, Francis. Carpenter. 10 Trott St.
Roper, Joseph. Turner. 13 Pinckney St.
Roper, Thomas. Planter. 4 East Bay
Rose, Alexander. Planter. 2 Church St.
Rose, Jeremiah. Tailor. 40 Church St.
Rose, Rebecca. 5 Smith's Lane
Ross, Elizabeth. Shop Keeper. 16 Bedon's Alley
Ross, George. Tin Man. 115 Tradd St.
Ross, Kenneth. Shop Keeper. 15 Church St.
Ross, Malcolm. Carpenter. 29 Society St.
Ross, Thomas. Mariner. 95 Queen St.
Roupel, Daniel. Umbrellla Maker. 226 Meeting St.
Rouse, James. Currier. 87 King St.
Rouse, William. Shoemaker. 3 Tradd St.
Rout, George. School Master. 9 Moore St.
Rout, Michael. Carter. 1 Boundary St.
Rowand, Robert. 2 Friend St.
Royall, William. School Master. 35 Tradd St.
Ruberry, John. Tailor. 115 Queen St.
Rummey, Joseph. Chocolate Maker. 99 East Bay
Rush, Matthias. Tailor. 243 King St.
Russell, Ann. Lynch's Lane
Russell, Benjamin. Brick Layer. 31 Guignard St.
Russell, Nathaniel. Merchant. 16 East Bay
Rutledge, Edward. Counsellor at Law. 55 Broad St.
Rutledge, Hugh. Counsellor at Law. 3 Short St.
Rutledge, John, Sr. Associate Justice U.S. 82 Broad St.
Ryan, Peter. Shop Keeper. 54 East Bay
Rychbosch, Francis. Broker. 27 Elliot St.
Sailor, David. Cooper. 38 Elliot St.
Sanders, John. Planter. 8 Cumberland St.
Sandiford, James. Tailor. 4 Magazine St.
Sarrazin, Jonathan. 9 George St.
Sasportas, Abraham. Merchant. 45½ East Bay
Sass, Jacob. Cabinet Maker. 40 Queen St.
Saults, John. Mariner. 11 Chalmer's Alley
Saunders, Roger Parker. Planter. 22 South Bay
Savage, Martha. Savage's Green
Savage, Mary. 59 King St.
Schmidt & Molich. Merchants. 9 Champney's Wharf
Scott, David. Brick Layer. Quince's St.
Scott, James. Grocer. 49 East Bay
Scott, William. Planter. 85 Tradd St.
Scott, William & Samuel. Merchants. 213 King St.
Scottow, Samuel. Carpenter. 181 King St.
Screven, Thomas. Planter. 117 Church St.
Seavers, Abraham. Carpenter. 33 Pinckney St.
Seeress, Martin. Tailor. Lynch's Lane
Seiger, Charles Lewis. Physician. 208 Meeting St.
Seixas, Abraham. Tallow Chandler. 112 King St.
Selbey, George. Store Keeper. 229 King St.
Seller, Michael. Tanner. 11 Archdale St.
Seller, Philip. Baker. 172 Meeting St.
Serjeant & Cambridge. Auctioneers. Beale's Wharf
Seymour, Isaac. Mariner. 257 Meeting St.
Shaffer, Henry. Carter. 28 Beaufain St.
Shaw, Mary Elizabeth. 33 Tradd St.
Shead, George. School Master. 283 King St.
Shelback, Charles. Baker. 2 Union St.
Shepherd, Jane. 37 Meeting St.
Shields, Edward. Merchant. 16 Tradd St.
Shier, John. Carpenter. Coming St.
Shifflee, George. Shop Keeper. 18 Chalmer's Alley
Shirras, Alexander. Ironmonger. 48 East Bay
Shirtliff, Austin & Strobel. Merchants. 19 Broad St.
Shoolbred & Moddie. Merchants. 26 East Bay

Shrewsbury, Edward. Shipwright. 132 East Bay
Shrewsbury, Mary. 32 Pinckney St.
Shrewsbury, Stephen. Carpenter. 12 Guignard St.
Shultz, Casper C. Merchant. 87 Broad St.
Shultz, Daniel. Mariner. 20 Trott St.
Shum, Conrad. Baker. 244 Meeting St.
Sickels, Ethan. Shop Keeper. 37 East Bay
Sifley, Lewis. Baker. 2 Beresford St.
Simmons, Francis. Planter. Legare St.
Simmons, Thomas. Planter. 133 Church St.
Simmons, William. Planter. 104 Tradd St.
Simons, Anthony. Factor. 286 King St.
Simons, Blake & Vanderhorst. Factors. 51 East Bay
Simons, James. Planter. 2 Pinckney St.
Simons, Sampson. 6 Price's Alley
Simons, Samuel. Shop Keeper. 43 Tradd St.
Simons, Thomas. Planter. 130 East Bay
Simpson, Mary. Baker. 17 Union St. Continued
Singleton, Bracey. Innholder. Louisbourg Coffee House
Singleton, Daniel. Brick Layer. 25 Trott St.
Singleton, Thomas. 168 King St.
Sinkler, James. Planter. 32 Pinckney St.
Siser, Michael. Baker. 113 King St.
Sisk, Susannah. Boarding House. 22 Union St. Continued
Skirving, Charlotte. 8 Church St.
Skirving, William. Planter. South Bay St.
Skrine, William. Factor. 21 King St.
Slowman, Henry. Tailor. Wyatt's Lot
Slowman, John. Tailor. 36 Tradd St.
Smerdon, Elias. Merchant. 93 King St.
Smith, Andrew. Shop Keeper. 165 Meeting St.
Smith, Archibald. Shop Keeper. 218 Meeting St.
Smith, Daniel. Scriviner. 14 Society St.
Smith, Desaussure & Darrel. Merchants. 25 East Bay
Smith, George. Merchant. 2 Meeting St.
Smith, James. Attorney at Law. 30 Church St.
Smith, James. Shop Keeper. 27 King St.
Smith, John. Shop Keeper. 236 King St.
Smith, John. Shop Keeper. 19½ Union St.
Smith, John. Mariner. 42 Church St.
Smith, John. Baker. 42 Queen St.
Smith, John. Merchant. 15 Broad St.
Smith, John Press. Surgeon & Midwife. 68 East Bay
Smith, Josiah. Merchant. 2 Meeting St.
Smith, Morton. Innholder. Jervey's Wharf
Smith, O'Brien. Planter. 10 Guignard St.
Smith, Peter. Carpenter. 35 Archdale St.
Smith, Peter. Planter. 26 Beaufain St.
Smith, Robert, Rev. Dr. Rector St. Philip's Church. St. Philip's Parsonage
Smith, Roger. Merchant. 43 Church St.
Smith, Samuel. Merchant. 2 Meeting St.
Smith, Samuel. Carpenter. 21 Hasell St.
Smith, Thomas. Planter. Harleston's Green
Smith, Thomas. Mariner. 18 Pinckney St.
Smith, Whiteford. Shop Keeper. 1 Queen St.
Smith, William. Merchant. 3 Broad St.
Smith, William, Rev. St. Philip's Academy
Smyser, Hannah. 56 Church St.
Smyth, John. 11 Ellery St.
Smyth, Robert. Wine Merchant. 19 Queen St.
Snipes, William Clay. Planter. 208 King St.
Snitter, Charles. Rope Maker. Snitter's Alley
Snowden, Charles. Merchant. 61 East Bay
Snyder, Paul. Carpenter. 100 King St.
Sommers, John. Carpenter. 27 Hasell St.
Sommers, Martha. 1 East Bay

Sommersall, William. Merchant. 2 East Bay
Spaving, Patrick. Shop Keeper. 45 Queen St.
Spears, James. Carpenter. 7 Society St.
Speisegger, John, Jr. Music Shop. 97 Tradd St.
Spencer, George. Shop Keeper. 133 King St.
Spencer, Sebastian. Shoemaker. 203 Meeting St.
Spidle, George. Tanner. 6 Dutch Church Alley
Spinler, Jacob. Hair Dresser. 46 East Bay
Spitzer, Barend Moses. Broker. 2 Champney's Row
Sproul, Alexander. Shoemaker. 15 King St.
Squibb, Robert. Gardener. Savage's Green
St. John, Mary. 11 Allen St.
Steadman, Charles. Carpenter. 33 Trott St.
Steadman, James. Carpenter. 110 East Bay
Steel, William. Inspector Customs. 40 Elliot St.
Stent, Samuel. Tailor. 98 Church St.
Stevens, Cotton Mather. Warden Work House. Savage's Green
Stevens, Daniel. Planter. 41 George St.
Stevens, Jervis Henry. Organist. 256 Meeting St.
Stevens, Ramsey & Co. Apothecaries. 107 Broad St.
Stevens, William. Physician. 11 King St.
Stevens, William. Broker. 154 Tradd St.
Stevenson, John. Carpenter. 88 Queen St.
Stewart & Potter. Merchants. 131 Tradd St.
Stewart, Allan. Shop Keeper. 68 Meeting St.
Stewart, Ann. Shop Keeper. 29 King St.
Stewart, Jane. School Mistress. 20 Union St. Continued
Stewart, Margaret. Innholder. 66 East Bay
Stewart, Mary. 39 Hasell St.
Stewart, Thomas. Merchant. 29 East Bay
Stock, Margaret. 14 King St.
Stoll, Jacob. Tin Man. 189 King St.
Stoll, Sarah. 8 Dutch Church Alley
Stone, Love. 304 King St.
Stone, Samuel. Mariner. 2 Stoll's Alley
Stoops, Benjamin. Shoemaker. 9 Union St.
Strobel, Daniel. Tanner. 149 Meeting St.
Strobel, Jacob. Butcher. 3 Magazine St.
Stromer, H. M. Merchant. 20 Elliot St.
Stupitch, ----, Dr. Botanist. 16 Beresford St.
Sudor, Elizabeth. Cigar Maker. 35 Meeting St.
Sudor, Peter. Cigar Maker. 28 Union St.
Summers, Benjamin. Shop Keeper. 6 Ellery St.
Surtil, Martha. Shop Keeper. 6 Broad St.
Sutherland, Francis. Shop Keeper. 3 1/3 Queen St.
Sutton, John. Carpenter. 178 Meeting St.
Swain, Luke. Mariner. 3 Stoll's Alley
Swendler, Mary. 13 Mazyck St.
Swinton, Hugh. Factor. 3 Champney's Wharf
Switzer, John Randolph. Saddler. 234 King St.
Sykes, Thomas. 125 King St.
Symonds, Francis. Baker. 33 Union St.
Syms, John. Shop Keeper. 140 Queen St.
Taggart, Mary. 21 Meeting St.
Tart, Nathan. Planter. 96 Queen St.
Tash, Edward. Blacksmith. 12 Queen St.
Taylor, Bennett. Merchant. 18 Broad St.
Taylor, George. Attorney At Law. 228 Meeting St.
Taylor, James. Merchant. 40 East Bay
Taylor, John. Silversmith. 17 Beresford's Alley
Taylor, Paul. Carpenter. 38 Trott St.
Taylor, William. Brick Layer. 2 Charles St.
Teasdale, Isaac. Merchant. 122 Queen St.
Teasdale, John. Merchant. 46 Church St.
Teasdale, John. Merchant. 2 Champney's Wharf
Teibout, Sarah. Boarding House. 4 Kinloch Court
Tennent, Susannah. 81 Tradd St.

Tew, Charles. Grocer. 95 Tradd St.
Tew, Thomas. Brick Layer. 10 King St.
Thayer, Bartlett, & Co. Merchants. 31 East Bay
Theus, James. Merchant. 89 Church St.
Theus, Rosanna. Boarding House. 87 Church St.
Theus, Simeon. Planter. 277 King St.
Thomas, John. Hair Dresser. 25 Elliot St.
Thomas, John B. Shop Keeper. Motte's Wharf
Thomas, Mary Lamboll. 8 King St.
Thomas, Stephen. Tailor. 34 Elliot St.
Thompson, Daniel. Shop Keeper. South Bay
Thompson, Esther. Shop Keeper. 19 East Bay
Thompson, J. Hamden. School Master. 30 King St.
Thompson, James. Tailor. 120 Queen St.
Thompson, James. Carpenter. 2 Queen St.
Thompson, John. School Master. 66 Meeting St.
Thompson, John. Mariner. 24 Tradd St.
Thompson, Peter. Carpenter. 115 East Bay
Thorne, John G. Sailmaker. 21 Guignard St.
Threadcraft, Bethel. Watchmaker. 255 King St.
Timmons, Lewis. Auctioneer. 11 Guignard St.
Timothy, Ann. State Printer. 84 Broad St.
Tobias, Joseph. Store Keeper. 203 King St.
Todd, John. Planter. 271 Meeting St.
Todd, John. Innholder. 70 Meeting St.
Todd, Joseph. Merchant. 3 St. Michael's Alley
Tonge, Mark. Shop Keeper. 56 East Bay
Toole, John. Tailor. 41 Elliot St.
Toole, Michael. Tailor. 9 Queen St.
Toomer, Anthony. Brick Layer. 7 Legare St.
Torry, Elias. Pilot. 6 Maiden Lane
Toussiger, James. Carpenter. 2 Water St.
Tragg, Lawrence. Brick Layer. 253 Meeting St.
Trenas, George. Baker. 32 Beaufain St.
Trenholm, William. Merchant. 1 Tradd St.
Trescot, Edward. Tax Collector. 82 Meeting St.
Trezevant, Peter. Merchant. 3 Kinloch Court
Trezevant, Theodore. Tailor. 44 Church St.
Troup, John. Attorney at Law. 117 Tradd St.
Tucker, Benjamin. Mariner. 265 Meeting Street
Tucker, Mary. School Mistress. 9 Charles St.
Tunno, Adam & Willm. Merchants. 28 East Bay
Tunno, George. Merchant. 31 Broad St.
Turnbull, Andrew. Physician. 76 East Bay
Turpin, Hannah. Boarding House. 53 Church St.
Turpin, William. Store Keeper. 172 King St.
Tweed, Alexander. Planter. 112 Queen St.
Vale, John David. Merchant. 111 Broad St.
Vanderhorst, Arnoldus. City Intendant. 15 East Bay
Vanrynn, Emelina. Store Keeper. 33 Broad St.
Vardell, Elizabeth. 19 King St.
Vardell, Robert. Tailor. 10 Bedon's Alley
Velsing, John. Baker. Bull St.
VerCnocke, F. I. Merchant. 30 East Bay
Veree, Mary. 13 Church St.
Vesey, Joseph. Ship Chandler. 281 King St.
Veyong, George. Carter. George St.
Villepontoux, Benjamin. Factor. 5 East Bay
Virgin, George. Shop Keeper. 43 Tradd St.
Vos, Andrew. Merchant. 31 Broad St.
Wagner, Christopher. Drayman. 5 Trott St.
Wagner, George. 85 Broad St.
Wagner, John. Merchant. 85 Broad St.
Wainwright, Richard. Planter. 286 King St.
Walcot, Samuel. Shop Keeper. 60 King St.
Walker, Robert. Carpenter. 28 Society St.
Walker, Sylvanus. Tobacco Inspector. 2 Quince's St.
Walkman, Mark. Shop Keeper. Fish Market Wharf

Wallace, Elizabeth. Boarding House. 23 Union St.
Continued
Wallace, James. Merchant. 1 Longitude Lane
Wallace, Thomas. Cabinet Maker. 237 Meeting St.
Walters, William. Hatter. 224 King St.
Ward, John. Attorney at Law. 255 Meeting St.
Ward, Joshua. Attorney at Law. 255 Meeting St.
Ward, Love. 315 King St.
Ward, Theophilus. School Master. 24 Queen St.
Warham, Charles. Merchant. 1 Gibbes St.
Waring, Joseph. Planter. 69 Meeting St.
Waring, Thomas. Factor. Jervey's Wharf
Waring, Thomas. Commiss. F. Est. 40 Meeting St.
Warley, Foelix. Clerk of Senate. 22 Society St.
Warley, George. Brick Layer. 20 Beaufain St.
Washing, Gasper. Butcher. 136 King St.
Washing, George. Butcher. 146 Meeting St.
Washing, John. Butcher. Meeting St.
Washington, William. Planter. 1 Church St.
Waties, Thomas. Associate Judge. 87 East Bay
Watson, Alexander. Factor. 107 East Bay
Watson, John. Cabinet Maker. 21 Tradd St.
Watson, John & George. Upholsterers. 104 Church St.
Watts, Charles. Cabinet Maker. 237 Meeting St.
Watts, John. Carpenter. Wyatt's Lot
Wayne, Sarah. Mantua Maker. 16 Beresford's Alley
Weare, Peter. Shoemaker. 15 Clifford St.
Webb, John. Merchant. 14 Moore St.
Webb, William. 14 Moore St.
Welch, George. Baker. 21 Trott St.
Welch, John. Tobacco Inspector. 5 Union St.
Wells, Edgar. Merchant. 10 Broad St.
Wesner, Philip Henry. Innholder. 262 King St.
Westermyer, Henry. Goldsmith. 23 Church St.
Weston, Plowden. Planter. 37 Queen St.
Weyman, Edward. Surveyor Customs. 50 Church St.
Whieldon, Joseph. Tailor. 7 Elliot St.
White, Blakley. Planter. 36 King St.
White, Sims. 12 Ellery St.
White, Sims & Son. Factors. 1 Gillon St.
White, William. Factor. 1 Bedon's Alley
Whitefield & Brown. Merchants. 127 Broad St.
Whitesides, Edward. Shop Keeper. 28 Pinckney St.
Wightman, William. Silversmith. 236 Meeting St.
Wightman, William. Merchant. 227 Meeting St.
Wilcocks, John. Blacksmith. 9 Trott St.
Wilkie, William. Factor. 27 East Bay
Wilkie, William. Boarding House. 6 Bedon's Alley
Wilkins, James. Carpenter. 2 Gibbes St.
Wilkinson, Morton. Planter. 5 Church St.
Wilkinson, Richard. Livery Stables. 73 Meeting St.
Williams, Elizabeth. 17 Legare St.
Williams, Isham. 132 East Bay
Williams, John. Coffee House. 128 Tradd St.
Williams, Margaret. 60 Queen St.
Williams, Mort. John. Ship Carpenter. 6 Charles St.
Williamson, John. Blacksmith. 48 King St.
Williamson, John. Merchant. 141 East Bay
Williman, Christopher. Butcher. 227 King St.
Williman, Jacob. Butcher. Harleston's Green
Willingham, Mary. 27½ Beaufain St.
Willson, John & Co. Merchants. East Bay
Wilson & M'Kennean. Tailors. 105 Church St.
Wilson, Archibald. Shop Keeper. 253 Queen St.
Wilson, Daniel. Planter. Elliot's b. Meeting St.
Wilson, John. Cabinet Maker. 217 Meeting St.
Wilson, John, Mrs. 51 Tradd St.
Wilson, Joseph. Planter. 4 Church St.

Wilson, Robert. Physician & Apothecary. 105 Broad
St.
Wilson, Samuel. Physician. 101 Broad St.
Winstanley, Thomas. Attorney at Law. 2 Scarborough
St.
Wish, Benajamin. Carpenter. 12 Mazyck St.
Wisinger, John. Baker. 182 King St.
Withers, John. Factor. 29 Trott St.
Wood, William. Inspector Customs. 22 Archdale St.
Woodcock, Richard. Tallow Chandler. 241 Meeting St.
Woolf, Frederick. Shop Keeper. 8 Beresford's Alley
Woolf, Henry. Shop Keeper. 129 King St.
Woolf, Matthias. Butcher. 2 Mazyck St.
Woolf, Rachel. Shop Keeper. 41 King St.
Wragg, Henrietta. 86 East Bay
Wragg, John. Planter. 15 Union St. Continued
Wray, John. Merchant. 10 Tradd St.
Wrench, Richard. Shop Keeper. 50 King St.
Wright, James. Baker. 42 Tradd St.
Wyatt, Peter. Carpenter. Wyatt's Lot
Yates, Seth. Ship Carpenter. Wayne's Court
Yates, William. Constable. 35 Union St.
Young, George. Butcher. 25 Guignard St.
Young, Hugh. Merchant. 96 Church St.
Young, John. Hair Dresser. East Bay
Young, P. William. Stationer. 24 Broad St.
Young, Susannah. School Mistress. Lynch's Lane
Young, William. Planter. Lynch's Lane
Zealy, James. Shoemaker. 298 King St.
Zylitra, Peter. Shop Keeper. 31 Elliot St.

CHAPTER 4

1790 CENSUS

The 1790 census, the first taken by the United States government, listed 1873 households in Charleston with 334 of those headed by women. This census can be compared with the 1790 city directory which has 1620 entries. The census includes free persons of color when they occupy separate households although they often only have first names. Quite a number of people in the census were not listed in the directory of that year and many in the directory cannot be found in the census. This does not necessarily mean they were not counted. As noted in the introduction several business people could have lived at one address or in boarding houses.

This census has been printed by the Census Department as *Heads of Families at the First Census of the United States in the Year 1790: South Carolina* (Washington: 1908). That list differs little from the handwritten original enumeration. Neither the printed version nor the manuscript is alphabetized which makes them difficult to use. The list which appears in this work has been put in alphabetical order. A number of names in the printed list are wrong, but a comparison with the original enumeration reveals they were wrong there as well. The names apparently were transcribed onto a master list with errors being made by the copyist.

Both the census and the directory are limited to the parishes of St. Philip's and St. Michael's which constituted the city.

While many family names can be found, a limited number of first names were used. For women the most common were Mary 15%, Elizabeth 12%, Ann 11%, and Sarah 8%. For men they were John 17%, William 9%, Thomas 6%, James 5%, and George 4%.

----- (Free Moore's)
----- (Free Moore's)
Abendanon, Joseph
Abernethie, Thomas
Abertie, Francis
Abigal (Free)
Abigal (Free)
Abrahams, Emanuel
Abrahams, Jacob
Abrahams, Judit
Ackman, Henry
Acquire, Guyetan
Adam & Tunno, W.
Adams & English
Adams, Samuel
Adams, William
Addamson, Ann
Affee (Free)
Aiken, Thomas
Akin, Ann
Akin, John & Philip Rider
Akin, Sarah
Alexander, Abraham
Alexander, Alexander
Alexander, David
Alexander, Hector
Alexander, Judit
Allison, James
Alston, John
Alston, William
Ancrumo, William O.
Anderson, Alexander
Anderson, Ann
Anderson, Robert
Andrew, Jane
Ann (Free)
Antanna, Kiss
Anthony, Emanuel
Anthony, John
Archebald, George
Armstong, William
Armstrong, Fleetwood
Armstrong, Rebecca
Arnold Jonathan
Arnold, Mathew
Arnot, Mary
Arnst, Margaret
Aron, Solomon
Artson, Gulliam
Ashton, Sarah
Askew, James
Atkinson, William
Atmore, Ralph
Audly, Martha
Austin, Robert
Austin, Surtliff, & Stroble
Axton, Elizabeth
Axton, William
Azabee, Abraham
Bacot, Thomas Wm.
Badger, James
Badger, Jonathan

Badger, Joseph
Baily, William
Baker, Elizabeth
Baker, Joseph
Baker, Samuel
Baker, William
Balis, William
Ball, Ann
Ball, Elizabeth
Ball, John
Ball, Thomas
Ballintine, James
Bampfield, Rebecca
Bancks & Lee
Barker, Isaac
Barnett, Ann
Barrick, Solomon
Barron, Alexander
Barron, John
Bartlett, Isaac
Bass, John
Bathune, Hugh
Bay, Elihu Hall
Bazeleau, Philip A.
Bazleau, Lewis
Beale, John
Beard, Charles
Beard, Robert
Beatty, Robert
Bebvan, Francis
Becae (Free)
Beck (Free)
Beckman, Barnard
Bedon, George (Free)
Bee, Joseph
Bee, Mary
Bee, Thomas
Beedon, William
Beekman, Samuel
Beeller, Joseph
Bell, John
Bell, William
Bellamy, Hester
Bellinger, Edmond
Bellinger, John
Belsher, Christian
Benjamin, Samuel
Benna, Peter
Bennet, John
Bennett, Thomas
Bennolds, George
Bentham, James
Beresford, Richard
Bering, John
Berney, John & Co
Berwick, Ann
Bess (Free)
Bess (Free)
Betty (Free)
Betty & Lucy (Free)
Bieller, Jacob
Binah (Free)

Bishop, John
Black, George
Black, John
Black, Nathaniel
Blackally, Oliver
Blacklock, William
Blair, John
Blair, William
Blake, Edward
Blake, John
Blake, John
Blakly, Samuel
Blemyer, William
Bocquett, Peter
Boddie, Sarah
Boderum, Joseph
Bogie, Agnus
Bohn, Charles
Boillat, Peter
Bolton, Martha
Bonneau, Frances
Bonnell, Samuel
Bonneteale, Peter
Bonsel, John
Booner, Christian
Booner, Dolly
Booth, Catherine
Boston (Free)
Bourdeaux, Daniel
Bowen, George
Bowen, James
Bowen, John
Bowen, Thomas B.
Bowman, John
Boyer, Jacob
Bradford, Charles
Bradford, Thomas
Brady, Mary
Brailsford, Samuel
Brailsord, William
Braly, Thomas
Branfield, William
Branford, Elizabeth
Bremer, Francis
Brewer, Mary
Bricken, Sarah
Briely, Frederick
Brindley, Stephen
Brooks, Mary
Broughton, Ann, Miss
Brower, Jeremiah
Brown & Hutchinson
Brown, James
Brown, Jeremiah
Brown, John
Brown, Joseph
Brown, Roger
Brown, Samuel
Brown, William
Brownlee, John
Bryan, Authur
Bryan, -----, Capt.

Bryan, John
Bryan, Samuel
Buckel, Thomas
Buckmire, John
Buckmire, Charles
Buckrage, Richard
Budd, John
Bull, William
Bulow, Joachim
Bunting, William
Burd, Elizabeth
Burger, David
Burie, Richard
Burie, Susanah
Burk, Adenus
Burn, John
Burne, James
Burnham, Sarah
Buro, John
Burril & Slocum
Burt, William
Busheneau, Charles
Butler, Charles P.
Butterton, Joseph
Buyer, John Goody
Buyne, Peter
Byrd, Samuel
Cahill, Daniel
Cain, Gracy
Calahan, John
Caldwell, Henry
Caldwell, Joseph
Calla, Thomas
Calmbers, Elizabeth
Calvert, John
Calwell, Henry
Cam, William
Cambee, John
Cambple, McCarten
Cambridge, Tobias
Cameran, Alexander
Cameran, Alexander
Cameron, Andros
Cameron, David
Cameron, Lewis
Campbell, Lurence
Campble, John
Cane, Conroid
Cannon, Daniel
Canterson, Joshua
Cantor, Jacob
Canty & Solomons
Cap, Dominick
Cape, Bryan
Carfts, William
Carnes, John
Carnes, Lawrence
Carns, Susanah
Carpenter, James
Carr, Richard W. & Co.
Carrol, Daniel
Carson, Elizabeth
Carson, James
Cart, John, Jr.
Cart, John, Sr.
Carter, Freter
Carter, George
Carter, John

Cartmell, William
Castine, John
Cate (Free Moore's)
Cattle, Billy (Free)
Cavancau, James
Cavineau, Elizabeth
Cazeneau, Edward
Chalmbers, Gilbert
Chalmers, Rebecca
Champney, John
Chandler, Isaac
Chapman, William
Chetty, Ann
Chevers, Alexander
Chiltt, Casper & Co.
Chion, P. G. & Son
Chisolm, Alexander, Jr.
Chisolm, Alexander, Sr.
Chrithsburgh, Conrod
Cirus (Free)
Clarissa (Free)
Clark, John
Clark, John
Clark, William
Clarke, James
Clarke, Jeremiah
Clarke, John
Clarke, Mary
Clarke, Sarah
Clarkson, Alexander
Clemenson, Alexander
Clements, John
Clementson, John
Clifford, Elizabeth
Clime, Mary
Clitherall, James
Cloe (Free)
Closman, Henry
Coats, Thomas
Cobia, Daniel
Cobia, Francis
Cobia, Nicholas
Cobia, Nicholas
Cochran & Wm McClure
Cochran, Robert
Cochran, Robert
Cockcock, Job
Cockland, William
Cockran, Thomas
Cogdale, Jane
Cohen, Gerhsam
Cohen, Jacob
Cohen, Moses
Coil, Margaret
Colback, George
Colcock, Miliscent
Cole, Ricahrd
Cole, Ruth (Free)
Cole, Tom (Free)
Collet, William
Collins, Jonah
Collins, Mary
Collist, Elizabeth
Connelly, Mary
Conner, Bryan
Conner, Thomas
Cook, Jonathan
Cook, Levi

Cook, Thomas
Cook, Thomas
Cook, William
Cook, William
Cookson & Williamson
Cooper, James
Coram, Francis
Corbett, Samuel
Corbett, Thomas
Cordes, John
Cosom, Thomas
Costa, Jean Paul
Coulhoun, John E.
Course, Isaac
Courtney, James
Cowan, John
Cox, Ann
Cox, Henerita M.
Cox, John
Cox, John
Cox, Susanah
Cozzens, Mathew
Cranford & Wallace
Crawford, William
Crawley, Charles
Crawley, Michael
Creighton, John
Creighton, Joseph
Cripps, I. S.
Cristia, Alexander
Cristian, Robert
Cristie, Edward
Critner, Barbary
Crocker & Sturges
Cromwell, Elizabeth
Cross, Clarisa (Free)
Cross, George
Cross, Susanah
Crowe, Edward
Crueshanks, Daniel
Cruger, Frederick D.
Cubbage, Hugh
Cudworth, Nathaniel
Cughna, George
Cumine, Casper
Cunningham, John
Cunnington, William
Curling, Thomas
Curry, William
Curry, William
Custers, James
Dallas, Angus
Daniels, Elizabeth
Daniels, ——, Mrs. (Free)
Darby, James
Darby, William
Darrel, Edward
Darrell, Benjamin
Dart, Amelia
Dart, John Sandford
David (Free)
Davie, William
Davis, Harmon
Davis, Harmond
Davis, Jane
Davis, L. H.
Davis, Thomas
Dawes, Margaret

Dawson, Christian
Dawson, John
Dawson, Michael
Deady, Thomas
Deans, John
Deas, John, Jr.
Deas, William
Decker, William
DeCosta, Isaac
DeCosta, Samuel
DeCosta, Sarah
Delcare, Peter
Delcore, Peter
DeLyon, Isaac
deMicklaswietz, Felix
Dener, George
Dener, Peter
Dening, Elisha
Dennis, Richard
Denny & Moore
Denoon, David
Denton, James
Dervees, William
DeSaussure, William
Desil, Charles
Dessasure, Daniel
Desverness, Peter F.
Detcham, John
Devaull, Catherine
Dewar, Robert
Dewees, Sarah
Dickenson, Jeremiah
Dickenson, Samuel
Dill, Joseph, Sr.
Dimes, Ann, Miss
Dina (Free)
Dina (Free), &c
Disher, Mary
Dodsworth, Ralph
Dogget, Henry
Dohartee, Paterick
Dollaghan & Brennen
Donavan, James
Donnaldson, James
Dormond, Robert
Doughty, Thomas
Doughty, William
Douglass, Abraham
Douglass, Joseph
Douglass, Nathaniel
Doux, Saint, Mary H.
Downe, James
Drayton, Jacob
Drayton, John
Drayton, Rebecca
Drayton, Stephen
Dubard, Peter
Duff, David
Duff, John
Duffy, Andrew
Dullas, Joseph
Duncan, James
Duncan, Paterick
Duncan, Thomas
Dunce, Gerard
Dwight, Isaac
Eames, Martha
Earnest, Jacob

Easton, Susannah
Eayers, William
Eberley, John
Eckhart, Jacob
Eden, Joshua
Edgworth, John
Edwards, James
Edwards, John
Edwards, John
Edwards, Mary
Eldridge, Randle
Elliott, Elizabeth
Elliott, Thomas
Elliott, Thomas O.
Ellis, Henry
Ellis, John
Elmore, Jessy
Elsinore, James
Elsworth, Theophilus
Emanuel, Joseph
Emmitt, Charlotte
Evans, George
Eveleigh, Thomas
Ewen, Adam
Ewing, Robert
Faber, John C.
Fabria & Price
Fair, William
Fair, William
Falker, J. Jasper
Fanny (Free)
Fardo, George
Farquer, John
Farr, Joseph
Fash, Sarah (Free)
Faysoux, Peter
Fells, Thomas
Ferguson, Ann
Ferril, Anthony
Fiddy, William
Fields, John
Findlayson, John
Findlayson, Mungo
Finton (Free)
Fiphipps, Thomas
Fisher & Burney
Fisher, George
Fitzpaterick, John
Fitzsimons, Chrs.
Flagg, George
Flemming, John
Fletcher, Phebe
Flint, Joseph
Flix, Frederick
Fllis (Free)
Fluitt, Samuel
Fogartie, Mary
Ford, Bartholime
Ford, Mary
Fordham, Richard
Forest, Michael
Forrest, George
Forrest, William
Foshie, Bryan
Foster, Thomas
Frances (Free)
Fraser, William
Frazer, Alexander

Frazer, Christian
Freaer, Rebecca
Freear, Sarah
Freeman (Free)
Freeman, William
Freer, Ann
Frezvant, Peter
Friend, George
Friend, Uly
Frinch, Thomas
Frish & Wisinger
Frish, Charles
Frost, Thomas
Fullam, William
Fuller & Brodie
Fuller, Thomas
Fullerton, Elizabeth
Furman, Richard
Gabeau, Anthony
Gable & Corrie
Gaddes, Henry
Gadsden, Christopher
Gadsden, Philip
Gadsden, Thomas
Gaillard, Theodore
Gaillard, Theodore
Gailliard, Samuel
Galway, Michael
Gamble, John
Gansell, John
Gardner, Ann
Gardner, George (Free)
Gardner, John
Gardner, William
Garret, Joshua
Gasper, Richard
Gennerick, John F.
George (Free)
George, Henry
George, James
George's, James (City house)
Georghagan, Domenick
Gervis, John L.
Geskin, Henry
Geurard, Maryan
Geyer, John
Gibbs, Armarietta
Gibbs, George
Gibbs, John
Gibbs, Mary
Gibbs, Robert
Gibbs, William H.
Gibson, Robert
Gilbert, Elizabeth
Gilcrist, Adam
Gilcrist, Malcom
Gillion, Alexander
Gist, Mordica
Gist, William
Gitsinger, George
Given, Robert
Glaze, John
Glenn, John
Glover, Ann
Glover, Saunders
Glover, William
Godderd, John
Godderd, John

Godfree, Elizabeth
Godfree, Thomas
Godfry, Thomas
Goffe (Free)
Good, Sarah
Goodwin, Robert
Gordon, James
Gordon, John
Gordon, John
Gordon, Mary
Gordon, Penelope (Free)
Gottier, Issabellah
Gouber, Samuel
Gourley, John
Grace (Free)
Graffe & Co.
Graham, Mary
Graham, Richard
Graham, Samuel
Graham, William
Gram, Ann
Grant, Alexander
Grant, Hary
Grant, John
Grant, Lewis
Granville, James
Graves, James
Gray, Benjamin
Greecly, Joseph
Greedy, James
Green, William
Greenhill, Hugh & Co.
Greenland, Daniel
Greenwood, William
Gregory Son & Davidson
Gregson, James
Grenwood, William
Grevenstine, Frederick
Griarson, James
Grigg, John
Grimball, Isaac
Grimes, Mary
Grimkie, John F.
Grimkie, John F. (Returned)
Grimkie, John Paul
Grissel, George
Gross, Charles
Grott, Francis
Gruber, Charles
Guiger, Henry
Guillio, Claud
Guirley, John
Guitter, Joseph
Gunn, William
Guy, James
Hagan, David H.
Hahnbaum, Christian
Hahnbaum, George
Haig & Don
Hainsdorf, Henry
Hall, Daniel
Hall, George A.
Hall, Marian
Hall, Thomas
Hall, William
Ham, Richard
Ham, Thomas
Hamilton, David

Hamilton, James
Hamilton, John
Hamilton, John
Hand, Margaret
Haney, John
Hannah (Free)
Hannah (Free)
Harding, Sarah
Hare, Edward
Hargraves, J & J.
Harleston, Ann
Harlewood, John
Harmond, John
Harmond, Michael
Harper & Hamilton
Harper, Robert
Harris, Andrew
Harris, John H.
Harris, Thomas
Harris, Thomas
Harris, Tucker
Harrison, Isaac
Harrison, John
Harry (Free)
Hart, Doricus
Hart, Simon
Harth & Decosta
Harth, Christopher
Harth, John
Harth, Philip
Hartley, Elizabeth
Harvey, Elizabeth
Harvey, Elizabeth
Harvey, Thomas
Harvy, Benjamin
Hatter, John, Mrs. (Returned)
Hauser, Elias
Hawes, Anina P.
Hawkins, James
Hayward, Nathaniel
Hayward, William
Hazard & Robinson
Hazelhurst, Robert
Heains, Heath
Hear, James O.
Hencock, Elizabeth
Henderrickson, Betsha
Henling, Thomas
Henning, John F.
Henri, Peter
Henry, Francis
Henry, Jacob
Henry, John
Herreld, George
Hetseling, L. H.
Heyleger, Joseph
Hilagers, George A.
Hilages, Jacob
Hill, Duncan
Hill, Elenour
Hill, Joseph
Hill, Paul
Hilladay, George
Hillegas, Peter
Himley, James
Hinds, Paterick
Hindson, Thomas
Hislop & Snowden

Hodson, Margaret
Hogart, William
Hoit, William
Holland, Hugh
Hollingshead, William
Holloway & Thayer
Holmes, Isaac
Holms, John B.
Holms, Thomas
Holt, William
Homan, John
Honawood, Auther
Hook, George
Hope, John
Hope, May
Hope, Thomas
Hopton, Sarah
Horlback, John
Hornbey, Thomas
Horry, Harriot
Horry, Thomas
Horton, Thomas
Hostige, Joshua
House, Samuel
Hover, John
How, Marian
Howard, Mary
Howard, Robert
Howell, John
Howell, P.
Hoyland, Maria A.
Hrabowshie, Ann
Hubert, Berry
Hubert, Charles
Hudson, Mary
Hudson, Richard
Huger, John
Hugers, Isaac, Sr.
Hughly, John
Hughs, John
Hughs, Mary
Hughs, Paterick
Hume, John
Hunbum's, Chr. (place)
Hunt, Thomas
Hunter, Abraham
Hutchings, William
Hutchingson, Jeremiah
Hutchingson, Jeremiah
Hutchingson, Thomas, Jr.
Hutchingson, Thomas, Jr.
Hutton, James
Inglesbey, William
Inglis, Alexander
Irons, Berry
Irvin, James
Irvin, John
Izard, Charlott
Izard, Ralph, Jr.
Izard, Ralph, Sr.
Jacks, James
Jackson, John
Jackson, John
Jackson, John
Jacobs, Jacob
Jacobs, Jacob
James, Charles
Jeffries, Mary

Jemmison, Rebecca
Jenkins, Edward
Jennings & Woodrope
Jermin, John
Jervy, Thomas (Property of Thos. Hall)
Jessy, Sarah
Jesum, Matthew
Jinney (Free)
Jinnings, William
Joe (Free: a Moore)
Joe & Tom (Free)
John (Free)
Johnson (Free)
Johnson & Wallace
Johnson, Charles
Johnson, Elizabeth
Johnson, Jacob
Johnson, Jacob
Johnson, John
Johnson, John
Johnson, William
Johnson, William
Johnson, William
Johnson, William, Jr.
Johnston, Andrew
Johnston, David
Johnston, Hester
Jolly, Mabury
Jones, Abraham
Jones, Alexander
Jones, Henry
Jones, Jessy
Jones, Joseph
Jones, Samuel
Jones, Sarah
Jones, Thomas
Jones, William
Jones, William
Joseph (Free)
Joseph, Israel
Judit (Free)
Juhan, Alexander
Julet (Free)
Kaiser, John
Kane (Free)
Keaf, Ann
Keckley, Henry
Keckley, Margaret
Keeley, Sabastine
Keen, Thomas
Keith & Wish
Keith, Isaac
Kelcoffin, John
Kelder, Henry
Kellizan, Michael
Kelly, James
Kelly, Johanna
Keltizen, Elizabeth
Kemmel, John
Kemmel, Mary
Kempton, Ann
Kempton, William
Kendle,Mary
Keneday & McKinzie
Kennaday, John
Kennan, Henry
Kennear, Alexander

Kenneday & Parker
Kenneday, Andrew
Kenneday, James
Kern, John F.
Kerr, Andrew
Kerr, John
Kersey, William
Kershaw, John
Kiel, John
King, Benjamin
King, Elenour
King, Timothy
Kinloch, Francis
Kirk, John
Kirk, John
Kister, Henry
Kitty (Free)
Kitty (Free)
Knew, Chonrod
Knights, Christopher
Knights, David
Knox, Robert
Knox, Sarah
Kosskey, Anthony J.
Kraps, Andrew
Krible, Frederick
Kruger, Charles
Lachiffe, Maurice
Ladson, James
Ladson, Jane
Lagare, Daniel
Lahery, Mary
Lake, William
Lamb & Montgomery
Lambold (Free)
Lampton, Sarah (Free)
Lancaster, William
Lance, Ann
Lance, Lambert
Lanchester, Henry
Lander (Free)
Lane, Alica
Lang, Jane
Lang, William
Langford, Ann
Langstaff, John
Larry, Robert
Latham, Daniel
Latham, Eleanour
Laurence, Etsal
Lavingston, William
Lawry, Andrew
Lawson, Mary
Lawton, Winmal
Lazarine, Jonathan
Lazurus, Mark
Leavey, Moses
Lebbey, Nathaniel
Lee, Francis
Lee, Stephen
Lee, William
Lefoy, Daniel
Legare, Benjamin
Legare, Daniel
Legare, Samuel
Legare, Solomon
Legare, Thomas
Legash, Margaret

Legg, Edward
Legg, Mary
Legg, Samuel
Lehrea, Thomas
Lemott's Counting house
Lenced, Henry
Leneau, Bazell
Lennox, William
Lepool, Peter
Lereaux, John
Leria (Free)
LeRoach, Elizabeth
Leslie, George
Lessesne, Sarah
Lessessne, Isaac
Levey, Hyman
Levey, Moses
Levy, Solomon
Libert, John
Liblong, Henry
Lights, Mary
Lightwood, Edward
Lindal, Joannis
Lindsey, Robert
Linneau, Charles
Little, Robert
Livbley, Joseph
Lloyd, John, Jr. & Co.
Lloyde, John, Sr.
Lloyde, Joseph
Lockey, George
Lockwood, Joshua
Lockwood, Thomas
Locock, Aron
Logan, George
Logan, William
Long, Edward
Long, Elizabeth
Long, Elizabeth, Jr.
Long, Lewis
Lopus, Aron
Lord, Ann
Lorthrop, Seth
Lothrop's, Seth (Store)
Love, John
Loveday, John
Lownes, Rolins
Lowrey, John
Luckey, John
Lucus, Florine
Lucy (Free)
Ludson, Sarah
Lunehouse, Thomas
Lunt, William
Luyton, William
Lynah, James
Lynch, James
Lyon, Abraham
Lyon, Mordica
Mackey, Ann
Mackey, Crafts
Mackey, James
MackLish, Mary
Magwood, Simon
Mahana, John
Main, Thomas
Main, William
Malcom, Joseph

Mallond, Charles
Malloney, Elizabeth
Manary, Robert
Manigault, Gabrial
Manigault, Gabrial
Mann, Margaret
Mann, Spencer
Manners, Archibald
Manning, Elenour
Manning, Hugh
Manro, Margaret
Manson, George
Manson, John
Marckland, John
Marckley, Abraham
Margaret (Free)
Maria (Free)
Marian (Free)
Marian (Free)
Mark, Conrod
Marks, Anthony
Marks, James
Martin, Edward
Marr, Ann
Marranty, Susa
Marsh, Joseph
Marshall, John
Marshall, William
Marshall, William
Martin & Robin (Free)
Martin, Christian
Martin, Daniel
Martin, Jacob
Martin, John C.
Martin, Nicholas
Martin, Rebecca
Martin, Thomas
Marton, Nathaniel
Mary (Free)
Mary (Free)
Mason, William
Massay, Catherine
Mathew (Free)
Mathew (Free)
Mathews, Benjamin
Mathews, George
Mathews, John
Mathews, Peter (Free)
Matlack, William
Matthew & Peppin
Matthews, Edit
Matthews, Peter
May, George
May, Jenny (Free)
Mayer, John G.
Mazyck, Daniel
Mazyck, Dick (Free)
Mazyck, Stephen
Mazyck, William
McAllister, Archebald
McAllister, John
McAuther, John
McBride, James
McBride, Thomas
McCall, Hext
McCall, James
McCall, John
McCall, John

McCally & Davis
McCan, James
McCarty, John
McClish, Angus
McComb, James
McComick, Sparks & Co.
McConnell, William
McCorkel, Samuel
McCrady, Edward
McCredie, David
McCuen, Peter
McCullum, James
McDonald, William
McDonnald, Archebald
McDonnald, Charles
McDowell, John
McFarson, Duncan
McGee, John
McHugo, Anthony
McIntosh, Samuel
McIver, John
McIver, Unis
McKee, Samuel
McKemmy, William
McKensie, Andrew
McKensie, John
McKimmy, John
McKinzie, Alexander
McKnabb, Alexander
McLane, Evan
McLane, John
McLane, Lauchlin
McLoad, William
McMahan, John
McMillian, Duncan
McNeal, Archebald
McNeil, Cathrine
McNiel, Archebald
McPherson, Jane
McPherson, John
McPherson, Peter
McQueen, John
McQueen Robert
McWann, William
Mears, John
Melander, Adam
Message, John
Methewis, William
Mey, Florine C.
Meyers, John G. (Store)
Michaels, John
Michin, John
Middleton, Mary
Middleton, Mary
Middleton, Ramsey
Middleton, Thomas
Midford, George
Millegan, John
Millegan, To.
Miller, Albert A.
Miller, Ann
Miller, Benjamin
Miller, George
Miller, George
Miller, Jacob
Miller, James
Miller, James
Miller, John

Miller, John David
Miller, Nelly (Free)
Miller, Nicholas
Miller, Ranee
Miller, Samuel
Milligan & McKune
Milligan, Jacob
Milligan, James
Milligan, John
Mills, George
Mills, A., Rev.
Mills, Robert
Mills, William
Milner, Daniel
Milner, G.
Milner, George
Minnick, John
Minott, John
Minott, William
Mintzeng, Christian
Miott, John
Mitchel, Andrew
Mitchel (Free)
Mitchell, Elizabeth
Mitchell, John
Mitchell, John, Sr.
Mitchell, Lazarus
Mitchell, Mary
Mitchell, William
Mobly, William
Moffett, Terrissa
Moires, Mary
Molly (Free)
Monro, Elizabeth
Monro, John
Moodie, Benjamin
Moodie, Peter
Moore (Free)
Moore, John
Moore, John
Moore, Peter J.
Moore, Richard
Moore, Thomas
More, John
Morgan, Ann
Morgan, Charles
Morgan, Edward
Morison, Ann
Morre, Joseph
Morris, George
Morris, Lewis
Morris, Thomas
Morrisson, Mathew
Moses, Abraham
Moses, Barnet
Moses, Henry
Moses, Isaac
Moses, Lyon
Moses, Philip
Moses, Sarah
Mosonyell, ----, Madam
Mott, Abraham
Mott, Francis & Co.
Mott, Isaac
Motter, Isaac
Moubray, William
Moulton, William
Moultrie, Alexander

Moultrie, William
Mulligan, Francis
Muncrief, Richard
Muncrief, Susannah
Muncriffe, John
Muncriffe, John
Muncriffe, John
Murehead, James
Murphy, James
Murphy, John
Murril, James
Murry, Thomas
Mursett, Amelia
Myer, Philip
Myers, Israel
Myers, Joseph
Myers, Samuel
Mylne, James
Naiser, Henry
Naiser, Philip
Nancy (Free)
Nancy (Free)
Nancy (Free)
Neilson, James
Nelly (Free)
Nelson, George
Nepper, David H.
Neuffvielle, William
Neuffville, John
Neufville, John
Newhouse, Lewis
Newman, George F.
Newton, Downham
Nicholas, Christopher
Nicholson, John P.
Nixon, William
Norris, Nicholas
North, Edward
North, Susanah
North's, Edward (place)
Nott, Isabellah
O'Brian, Thomas
O'Connor, John
O'Hara, Daniel
Oats, Charles
Oats, Edward
Oldman, Joseph
Oliphant, Catherine
Oliphant, David
Oliver, James
Orday, George
Osburne, Henry
Osgood & Greenwood
Otto, John
Overton, Daniel
Owen, John
Pagget, Thomas
Pahley, Elizabeth
Pallason, William
Palmer, Job
Palmer, John
Parkenson, John
Parker, Isaac
Parker, John
Parker, John
Parker, John, Jr.
Parker, Joseph
Parsons, Susannah

Paterick Casamare
Patterson, William
Patton, Catherine
Patty (Free)
Paul, Andrew
Payne, William
Peace, Isaac
Peack, John
Peak, John
Peckman & King
Peggy (Free)
Pencil, Emanuel
Penman, James & E.
Penny (Free)
Pepson, Benjamin
Perry, Eleanour
Perry, Helening
Perry, Marsaline
Perry, Susanah
Peter (Free)
Peter (Free)
Petrie, Elizabeth
Petry, John B.
Petsch, Adam
Philips, Benjamin
Philips, Elezer
Philips, John C.
Phillips, Thomas
Pierce, Robert
Pieton, Ruth
Pilips, Thomas
Pilsberry, Samuel
Pimble, David
Pinckney, Charles
Pinckney, Charles C.
Pinckney, Francis S.
Pinyea, Lewis
Pitt, Frances
Pitt, Mathew
Platt, Mary
Plumb, Jacob
Plunckett, Thomas
Poinsett, Elisha
Pollock, Solloman
Pope, Alexander
Pope, Samuel
Porcher, Philip
Postell, Thomas
Pourie & Kevan
Powell, Ruth
Poyas, John E.
Poyas, Magdalane
Poyass, John L.
Prentice, John
Pressman & Culhoun
Price, Ann
Price, William
Prileau, Samuel, Jr.
Prileau, Samuel, Sr.
Primrose, Nicol
Prince, Ann
Prince, Charles
Prince, Charles
Pringle, John Julis
Pringle, Robert
Prioleau, Philip
Prior, John
Prisgie, Kitty

Pritchard, I., Mrs.
Pritchard, Paul
Proby, Elenour
Prout, Joseph
Prudence (Free)
Purce, Benjamin
Purcell & Hoburn
Purcell, Henry
Purcell, Joseph
Purchase, Samuel
Purse, Elizabeth
Pyatt, Peter
Quash (Free)
Quash, Robert
Quigin, David
Quinby, Henry
Quinn, James
Quinn, Robert
Radcliffe, Elizabeth
Radcliffe, Thomas
Raen, David
Ragbush, H
Rainer, David
Ralph, John
Rammage, Frances
Ramsey, Joseph
Ramsy, David
Ransier, John L.
Rasdale, David
Ravenelle, Elizabeth
Read, Jacob
Read, William
Reader, George
Rechon, David
Redman, Andrew
Reed, George
Rees, Martha
Reese, John
Reeves, Enos
Reid, George
Reid, John
Reinger, Jacob
Rennolds, John
Resselback, J., Dr.
Revenell, Samuel
Rice, Thomas
Richardson, John
Richardson, John
Righton, Joseph
Righton, McCulla
Riley, John
Ripley, Paul
Rittfield, Christopher
Rivers, Bulah
Rivers, Francis
Rivers, John
Rivers, Samuel
Rivers, Thomas
Rivers, Thomas
Roach, Jeremiah
Roach, Michael
Roads, Bolds, & Co.
Roberts, Alexander
Roberts, Ann
Roberts, Thomas
Roberts, Thomas
Roberts, William
Roberts, William

Robertson, Alexander
Robertson, John
Robin (Free)
Robinson, Elizabeth
Robinson, Jane
Robinson, John
Robinson, Joseph
Robinson, Margaret
Robinson, Septimus
Robinson, William
Robinson, William
Roderick, Peter
Rodman, Rachel
Rogers, Christopher
Rogers, James
Rogers, Lewis
Rogers, Maria, Miss
Rogers, Sarah
Roggaman, Anthony
Rogly, Anthony
Rolmburgh, Francis
Roper, Hannah
Roper, Joseph
Roper, Thomas
Roper, Thomas (Returned)
Rose, Alexander
Rose, Jeremiah
Rose, Rebecca
Ross, Elizabeth
Ross, George
Ross, Kenneth
Ross, Malcom
Ross, Thomas
Roswell, Thomas
Rouse, James
Rouse, William
Rout, George
Rout, Michael
Rowand, Robert
Royall, William
Ruaffet, George
Ruberry, John
Rudy, John
Rumley, Martin
Rumney, Joseph
Rush, Mathias
Rush, Peter
Russell, Ann
Russell, Benjamin
Russell, Nathaniel
Rutchledge, Hugh
Rutledge, Edward
Rutledge, John
Rutledge, John (Returned)
Ryan, Elizabeth
Ryan, Peter S.
Ryley, John
Ryppel, Daniel
Sailor, David
Sally (Free)
Sam & Moll (Free)
Sandford, James
Sarah (Free)
Sarah (Free)
Sarah (Free)
Sarjent, William
Sary (Free)
Sasportas, Abraham

Sass, Jacob
Saults, John
Saunders, John
Saunders, John
Saunders, Rogers
Saunders, Thomas
Savage, Martha
Savage, Mary
Sawyer, Mary
Scharborough, William
Schepang, Lewis
Scott, James
Scott, Samuel & Wm.
Scott, William
Scotto, Samuel
Screven, Thomas
Scrine, William
Seamour, Isaac
Seavers, Abraham
Sebben, John
Seckway, Caroline
Secriss, Martin
Seeger, Charles L.
Segaler, William
Seixas, Abraham
Self, John
Self, Samuel
Seller, Philip
Seller, Thomas
Seward, John
Shafer, Henry
Shand, Robert
Shaw, Mary E.
Sheed, George
Sheilds, Edward
Sheir, John
Shelback, Charles
Shelpher, Christopher
Shephard, Jane
Shettlewinck, Catherine
Shifflee, George
Shifley, Lewis
Shirras, Alexander
Shirvin, William
Shrewsberry, Edward
Shrewsberry, Mary
Shrewsbury, Stephen
Shrivin, Charlotte
Shuan, Philip
Shubrick's, Thomas (place)
Shull, Catherine
Shultz, Daniel
Shum, Canrod
Sickels, Eathan
Sicler, Michel
Silbey, George
Simmons, Anthony
Simmons, Thomas
Simmons, William
Simons, James
Simons, Sampson
Simons, Samuel
Simons, Thomas
Simpson, Mary
Sinclier, Jame
Singletary, Thomas
Singleton, Bracy
Singleton, Daniel

Singleton, Thomas
Siser, Michael
Sisk, Susanah
Slade, Ann
Sloman, Henry
Slutterling, Mary
Smallwood, Richard
Smerdon, Elias
Smidth & Molich
Smith, Andrew
Smith, Ann
Smith, Annanias
Smith, Archebald
Smith, Benjamin
Smith, Christianna
Smith, Daniel
Smith, Elizabeth
Smith, Elizabeth
Smith, James
Smith, Jane
Smith, John
Smith, John
Smith, John
Smith, John
Smith, John
Smith, John
Smith, John P.
Smith, Josiah
Smith, O'Bryan
Smith, Peter
Smith, Peter
Smith, Robert
Smith, Robert
Smith, Robert
Smith, Samuel
Smith, Solomon
Smith, Thomas
Smith, Thomas
Smith, Thomas
Smith, Whitford
Smith, William
Smith, William
Smithers, Robert
Snetter, Charles
Snider, Pail
Snips, William E.
Snowden, Charles
Snowden's, Charles (store)
Soctt, David
Soctt, David
Solomons, Hymen
Somersell, William
Sommers, John
Sparing, Paterick
Spear, James
Speiseger, John
Spencer, George
Spencer, Sebastine
Spidle, Abraham
Spinler, Jacob
Spitzer, Barend M.
Sproul, Alexander
Squibb, Robert
St. John, Mary
Standly, Peter
Stannard, Thomas
Starns, Daniel
Steadman, James

31

Steedman, Charles
Steel, William
Stent, Samuel
Stevens, Cotton M.
Stevens, Daniel
Stevens, Jarvis H
Stevens, William
Stevens, William
Stevenson, John
Steward, John
Stewart & Potter
Stewart, Allen
Stewart, Ann
Stewart, Jane
Stewart, Margaret
Stewart, Mary
Stewart, Thomas
Stock, Margaret
Stoll, Jacob
Stoll, Sarah
Stone, Barbary
Stone, Love
Stone, Samuel
Stone, Thomas
Stopps, Benjamin
Strable, Jacob
Stroble, Daniel
Stroble, Margaret
Stromer, H. M.
Stupit, ----, Dr.
Suckey (Free)
Suckey (Free)
Suder, Elizabeth
Suder Peter
Summ, Martha
Summer's, Humphry, Negroes
Summers, Benjamin
Sumner, Eleanour
Surtill, Martha
Surtlif, John
Sutherland, Francis
Sutton, John
Swadler, Mary
Swain, Luke
Swinton, Hugh
Switzer, John R.
Syckes, Thomas
Sykes, ----, Rev.
Sym, John
Symes, John
Symonds, Francis
Symser, Hannah
Taggart, Mary
Tart, Nathan
Tash, Edward
Tayer & Bartlett & Co.
Taylor, Bennet
Taylor, George
Taylor, James
Taylor, John
Taylor, John
Taylor, Paul
Taylor, William M.
Teabout, Sarah
Teasdale, Isaac
Teasdale, John
Tennent, John
Tennent, Susanah

Tepio (Free)
Tew, Charles
Tew, Thomas
Theus, James
Theus, Rosennah
Theus, Simeon
Theyar, Zekekiah
Thomas, John
Thomas, John B.
Thomas, Mary L, and Samuel Beach
Thomas, Stephen
Thomas, Williams
Thompson, Easter
Thompson, James
Thompson, James
Thompson, John
Thompson, John
Thompson, Peter
Thomson, James
Thopson, Daniel
Threatcraft, Bethel
Thron, John
Timmons, Lewis
Timothy, Ann
Tisbourne, William
Toamer, Anthony
Tobias, Cramer
Tobias, Joseph
Toby (Free)
Todd, John
Todd, John
Todd, Joseph
Tom (Free)
Tom (Free)
Tom & Jim (Free)
Tonge, Mark
Tool, John
Tool, Michael
Torrens, Samuel
Torry, Elias
Tousiger, James
Towk, Chandeller D.
Tragg, Laurence
Trazvant, Theodore
Trencis, George
Trenholm, William
Trescott, Edward
Tripp, William
Troup, John
Tucker, Benjamin
Tucker, Mary
Tunno, George
Turnbull, Andrew
Turner, Thomas
Turpin, Hanah
Turpin, William
Tweed, Alexander
Vale, John David
Vanderhorst, Arnoldus
Vanryne, Annelena
Vardell, Elizabeth
Vardell, Robert
Varence, Adam
Veasey, Joseph
Verner, Harriott
Verrie, Mary
Veyoung, George
Vicors, John

Vilaret, Mary
Villaponteaux, Benjm.
Virgin, George
Vos, Andrew
Waggoner, George
Wagner, Christopher
Wainwright, Richd
Waldren, Sam (Free)
Walker, Robert
Walker, Sylvence
Walkman, Mark
Wallace, Elizabeth
Wallace, James
Wallace, Thomas
Walter, William
Ward, Joshua
Ward, Love
Ward, Theophilus
Warham, Charles
Waring, Joseph
Waring, Thomas
Waring's, Thomas (store)
Warley, Christian
Warley, Felix
Warley, George
Washing, Gasper
Washing, George
Washing, John
Washington, Thomas
Washington, William
Wassels, Catherine
Watson, Alexander
Watson, Benjamin
Watson, J. & George
Watson, James
Watson, John
Watson, Lidia (Free)
Watson, Sally (Free)
Watt, Ously
Wattes, Thomas
Watts, Charles
Way, Mary
Wayne, Sarah
Weackley, Nancy
Weathers, John
Weaver, Bett (Free)
Weaver, Peter
Webb, John
Welch, John
Wells, Edgar
Welsh, George
Wesner, Philip H.
Westermer, Andrew
Weston, Plowden
Weyly, Ann
Weyman, Edward
Whielden, Joseph
White, Blakely
White, Symes
White, William
Whitefield & Brown
Whiteside, Edward
Wight, William
Wightman, William
Wightman's, William (Store)
Wilcock, Samuel
Wilcock's, John
Wilfing, John

32

Wilkie, William
Wilkins, James
Wilkinson, Morton
Wilkinson, Richard
William (Free)
Williams, Elizabeth
Williams, Ishain
Williams, John
Williams, John M.
Williams, Margret
Williamson, John
Williamson, John
Williman, Jacob
Williman's, Jacob (Place)
Willingham, Mary
Willisnan, Jacob
Willson, John
Willson, Robert
Willson, William
Wilson & McKennon
Wilson, Archebald
Wilson, James
Wilson, John (store)
Wilson, Joseph
Wilson, John, Mrs.
Wilson, Samuel
Wintstanly, Thomas
Wish, Benjamin
Wisinger, John
Wood, William
Wood, William
Woodcock, Richard
Woodman, John
Woolf, Frederick
Woolf, Henry
Woolf, Rachel
Woolfe, Matthew
Wrag, Henerietta
Wragg, John
Wray, John
Wrench, Richard
Wright, James
Wyatt, John
Wyatt, Peter
Yeats, Seth
Yeats, William
Young, Archebald
Young, George, Jr.
Young, George Sr.
Young, Hugh
Young, John
Young, Susanah
Young, William
Young, William
Zealey, James
Zelstra, Peter

CHAPTER 5

THE 1794 DIRECTORY

The 1794 directory was compiled by Jacob Milligan as *The Charleston Directory* (Charleston: W. P. Young, 1794). It has 1525 entries.

Locations are given for 1517 of these with the most important being King Street 15%, Meeting Street, 10%, East Bay 9%, Church Street 8%, Broad Street 8%, Tradd Street 7%, and Queen Street 6% The most notable change from 1790 was the fact that Meeting Street had considerably more businesses than previously.

The total for each location is Allen Street 10, Amen Street 8, Anson Street 2, Ansonborough 2, Archdale Street 14, Bay 2, Beal's Wharf 1, Beaufain Street 10, Bedon's Alley 10, Bennett's Mills 1, Beresford Street 24, Beresford's Alley 5, Boundary Street 1, Broad Street 117, Bull Street 2, Burn's Lane 3, Champney's Row 1, Chalmers' Alley 8, Champney's Row 4, Champney's Wharf 1, Charles Street 7, Church Street 122, Clifford's Alley 6, Cochran's Wharf 1, Cock Lane 3, Craft's Wharf 5, Cumberland Street 11, Cumming Street 5, East Bay 130, Ellery Street 9, Elliott Street 41, Elliott Street Continued 1, Exchange 3, Federal Street 6, Friend Street 13, Front Street 4, George Street 12, Geyer's New Buildings 1, Geyer's Wharf 1, Gibbes Street 2, Gillon Street 1, Good Bye Alley 1, Graehm's Street 1, Graeme's Wharf 1, Guignard Street 20, Harleston's Green 1, Hasell Street 19, Hopkins Lane 1, Hopton's Alley 1, Hopton's Lane 2, Jail 1, King Street 224, Kinloch Court 4, Lamboll Street 5, Legare Street 14, Liberty Street 4, Lodge Alley 3, Longitude Lane 2, Lynch's Lane 13, Magazine Street 7, Maiden Lane 6, Market Square 6, Mazyck Street 4, Meeting Street 151, Montague Street 2, Moore Street 12, Orange Street 9, Pinckney Street 32, Pitt Street 3, Price's Alley 3, Pritchard's Wharf 1, Queen Street 91, Quince Street 5, Rhett Street 1, Rope Makers Lane 1, Scarborough 3, Short Street 3, Smith's Lane 2, Society Street 8, South Bay 10, St. Michael's Alley 3, St. Philip's Street 6, State House 1, State House Square 3, Stoll's Alley 9, Tradd Street 99, Trott Street 36, Union Street 28, Union St. Continued 17, Unity Alley 2, Up the Path Three Miles 1, Vanderhorst's Wharf 1, Water Street 3, Wentworth Street 1, West Street 1, Whim's Court 1, Wragg's Alley 2, Wyatt's Lot 3, Wyatt's Square 3.

Professions were listed for 1244 people. The most significant of these were: shop and store keepers 15%, merchants 13%, planters 7%, various types of carpenters 6%, tailors 4%, factors 4%, and lawyers 3%. Compared with 1790 this remained fairly stable. While planters abound in the Charleston directories, this volume contains one person who claimed to be a farmer, the only one noted in all the directories before the Civil War.

The positions held by people with the number for each are: advocate 1, agent to commission merchant 1, apothecary 7, associate judge 4, attorney at law 43, auctioneer 1, baker 22, barber 10, barrister at law 2, billiard table 2, blacksmith 13, block maker 2, boarding house 29, boarding school 4, book binder 2, book maker 1, bottle seller 1, brass founder 1, brick maker 2, brick layer 12, British consul 1, broker 10, butcher 22, c. Fort Johnson 1, c.p. accounts 1, cabinet maker 16, cake maker 1, carpenter 69, carter 6, carver 3, cashier 2, chair maker 1, chancellor 2, chief justice 1, cigar maker 1, city clerk 1, city guard 1, city marshall 2, city sheriff 1, city treasurer 1, clergyman 1, clerk 16, coach maker 6, coffee house 1, collector of customs 1, com. of loans 1, com. revenue cutter 1, comedian 1, commissioner p. accts 1, constable 3, cooper 13, counsellor 1, currier 1, custom house boat 1, cutler 1, dancing academy 1, dancing master 1, dentist 1, deputy sheriff 2, distiller 4, dray master 2, drayman 1, engraver 2, express rider 1, F. coffee house 1, F. district judge 1, F. teacher 1, factor 48, farmer 1, federal marshall 1, French consul 1, fruit shop 1, gauger for customs 1, general 1, governor 1, grocer 26, gunsmith 5, hackney coach 1, hair dresser 7, harbor master 1, harness maker 1, hatter 3, horse dealer 1, hotel 1, house carpenter 2, indigo broker 1, indigo factor 2, inn keeper 1, inspector of customs, insurance broker 2, intendant 1, ironmonger 1, jail 1, Jew butcher 1, jeweller 1, joiner 2, justice of peace 3, lamp lighter 1, librarian 1, lieutenant governor 1, lieutenant revenue cutter 1, limner 3, lumber measurer 1, mantua maker 2, marine hospital 1, mariner 5, master in chancery 1, merchant 167, meslenger H.R 1, midwife 4, milliner 2, money collector 1, money dunner 1, music master 2, music store 1, naval officer 1, notary public 2, ordinary 1, organ builder 1, painter 13, pastor 5, perfumer 1, physician 25, pilot 8, planter 96, porter house 1, powder receiver 1, president S.C. Bank 1, printer 6, public house 1, r. court equity 1, rector 3, register mesne conveyance 1, retailer lumber 1, reverend 4, rope maker 1, runner Branch Bank 1, saddler 10, sail maker 4, school master 14, school mistress 6, scrivener 12, secretary of state 1, senator to U.S. 1, sheriff C. T. D. 1, ship carpenter 11, ship chandler 1, ship joiner 1, ship master 25, ship wright 2, shoemaker 18, shop keeper 181, shrub w. house 1, silversmith 16, starch maker 2, state printer 1, state treasurer 1, states attorney 1, stay maker 1, stock jobber 1, stone cutter 1, store keeper 17, supervisor 1, surgeon 1, surveyor 5, surveyor customs 1, surveyor general 1, tailor 50, tallow chandler 6, tanner 10, tavern keeper 5, tax receiver 1, teller 2, tin man 6, tobacconist 4, tobacco inspector 2, turner 3, umbrella maker 1, upholsterer 2, vendue cryer 1, vendue master 16, vintner 2, wagon yard 3, watch maker 11, watchman 1, wheelwright 1, widow 3, wine merchant 1, wood measurer 1.

Women who constitute almost 13% of the entries in the directory (192) usually have no profession listed; however, those who do appear were mostly boarding house operators (35%), shop or store keepers (26%), or taught or operated schools (16%).

Their professions were: baker 1; blacksmith 1, boarding house 22, boarding school 4, cabinet maker 1, cake maker 1, carpenter 1, mantua maker 2, midwife 4, milliner 2, school mistress 6, shop keeper 14, store keeper 2, and tallow chandler 1. Two were listed as widows.

The women who are shown to be a blacksmith, a cabinet maker, and a carpenter are apparently widows. Elizabeth Honeywood, blacksmith in 1794, is probably the wife of Arthur Honeywood, blacksmith in 1790, Mrs. Finlayson, cabinet maker in 1794, is apparently the widow of Mungo Finlayson, cabinet maker in 1790, and Betye Henrichsen, carpenter, is possibly the widow of Besha Henderreckson, carpenter in 1790. In this case, however, the person may be the same and could be male.

Aaron, Solomon. Shop Keeper. 46 King St.
Abendanone, Joseph. Factor. 263 King St.
Abernethie, Thomas. Engraver. 42 Queen St.
Abrahams, Emanuel. Scrivener. 112 King St.
Abrahams, Jacob. Shop Keeper. 70 East Bay
Abrahams, Moses. Shop Keeper. 44 Queen St.
Adams, Samuel. Surveyor. 236 King St.
Adams, William. Ship Joiner. 90 East Bay
Addison, Joseph. 18 Hasell St.
Aertson, Guilliam. City Sheriff. 15 Friend St.
Aiguire, Gayton. Tin Man. 221 Meeting St.
Akin, Ann. Boarding School. 76 Church St.
Akin, Thomas. Shop Keeper. 30 Pinckney St.
Alexander & Price. Merchants. 9 Broad St.
Alexander, Abraham. Clerk State Treasury. 24 Beresford St.
Alexander, Alexander. School Master. 4 Union St. Continued
Alexander, David & Co. Merchants. 9 Broad St.
Alexander, Hector. Shop Keeper. 19 East Bay
Alexander, William. Shop Keeper. 76 King St.
Allen & Ewing. Merchants. 120 Tradd St.
Allen, Thomas. Ship Carpenter. 5 Charles St.
Allison, James. Cooper. 5 Union St. Continued
Allston, William. Planter. 9 King St.
Ancrum, William. Merchant. Ellery St.
Anderson, ----. Stay Maker. Elliott St.
Anderson, Ann. 14 Union St. Continued
Anderson, John. Clergyman. 183 King St.
Anderson, Robert. Shop Keeper. 19 Tradd St.
Andrews & Pendergrass. School Masters. 48 Meeting St.
Anthony, John. Harness Maker. 51 Meeting St.
Anthony, John. Tobacconist. 68 King St.
Appelton, John. Carpenter. 25 Meeting St.
Armstrong, Fleetwood. Shop Keeper. East Bay Continued
Armstrong, William. Saddler. 75 King St.
Ash, John, Sr. Planter. 17 South Bay
Ashton, Catherine. 5 Maiden Lane
Atmar, Ralph, Jr. Silversmith. 49 Meeting St.
Atmar, Ralph, Sr. Messenger H. R. State House, Back
Atwell, Ichabod. Wood Measurer. 62 Church St.
Audley, Martha. 23 King St.
Austin, Robert. Tailor. 50 East Bay
Axson, William, Jr. Carpenter. 127 Church St.
Axson, William, Sr. Lumber Measurer. 17 King St.
Bacot, ----, Mrs. 103 Broad St.
Bacot, Thomas Wright. Cashier, S.C. Bank. 13 Broad St.
Badger, James. Painter. 56 King St.
Badger, John. Painter. 38 Broad St.
Badger, Joseph. Painter. 17 Pinckney St.
Baiker, Joseph. Carpenter. 12 Hasell St.
Bailey, Henry. Attorney at Law. 6 Meeting St.
Baill, John. Shop Keeper. 24 Union St.
Baird, Thomas. Shop Keeper. 91 East Bay
Baist, George, Rev. Pastor Presbyterian Church. 28 Meeting St.
Baker, Ann. 10 Church St.
Baker, Francis. Brick Layer. 33 King St.
Baker, Samuel. Grocer. 18 Tradd St.
Bald, Rhodes & Co. Merchants. 132 Tradd St.

Balion, Andrew. Barber. 137 Queen St.
Ball, Ann. 17 Church St.
Ball, Elizabeth. 18 Church St.
Ball, John. Planter. 24 Hasell St.
Ball, Thomas. Factor. 14 Lynch's Lane
Bampfield, George. 93 Meeting St.
Banks, Charles & Co. Merchants. 129 Tradd St.
Banks, Charles & Co. Merchants. 22 Elliott St.
Baron, Alexander. Physician. 124 Queen St.
Barr, Jacob. Wagon Yard. 219 King St.
Barre, Solomon. Shop Keeper. 65 King St.
Bass, John. Ship Master. 88 East Bay
Bats, Thomas. Book Maker. 8 Bedon's Alley
Bay, Elihu Hall. Associate Judge. 239 Meeting St.
Bayer, J. G. Shop Keeper. 179 Meeting St.
Bayerle, Frederick. Shop Keeper. 40 Union St.
Baylis, William. Carpenter. 253 Meeting St.
Bayly, Benjamin. Planter. 21 South Bay
Beale, John. 34 East Bay
Beard, Jonas. Powder Receiver. Magazine St.
Beard, Robert. Tin Man. 88 Broad St.
Beatty, Robert. Store Keeper. 27 Broad St.
Beaufort, Charles. Billiard Table. 32 King St.
Bedon, George. Carpenter. 8 Hopton's Lane
Bee, Elizabeth. 8 Trott St.
Bee, Thomas, Jr. Attorney at Law. 100 Church St.
Bee, Thomas, Sr. Federal District Judge. 100 Church St.
Beedom, William. Sail Maker. 7 Water St.
Beekman, Bernard. Surveyor. 109 East Bay
Beekman, Samuel. Block Maker. 112 Queen St.
Bell, David & George. Merchants. 20 Elliott St.
Bell, William. Grocer. 248 King St.
Belser, Christian. Butcher. 151 Meeting St.
Bennett, Ather. Carpenter. 58 Queen St.
Bennett, John. Carpenter. Bennett's Mills
Bennett, Thomas. Carpenter. Harleston's Green
Bennett, William. Boarding House. 172 Meeting St.
Bennica, Peter. Ship Carpenter. Lynch's Lane
Bentham, James. Justice of Peace. 47 Church St.
Bering, John. Silversmith. 125 Broad St.
Bernes, Christian. Shop Keeper. 45 King St.
Berney, John & Co. Merchants. 24 East Bay
Berry, Francis H. Shop Keeper. Union St.
Bevin, Francis. Carpenter. 11 Union St. Continued
Bird, Reading. Butcher. 103½ Meeting St.
Bithouse, John. Shop Keeper. 156 King St.
Black, John. Merchant. 12 Broad St.
Black, Nathaniel. Inspector Customs. 7 Ellery St.
Blackaller, Oliver. Shop Keeper. 6 Union St. Continued
Blackie, Elizabeth. 14 Church St.
Blacklock, William. Merchant. 106 Broad St.
Blair, James. Clerk Branch Bank. 1 Stoll's Alley
Blake, Edward. Factor. 10 Legare St.
Blake, John. Grocer. 37 East Bay
Blake, John. Factor. Legare St.
Blakeley, Samuel. Store Keeper. 28 Broad St.
Blamyer, William. Librarian, Charleston Library Society. 77 Church St.
Bocher & Co. French Coffee House. Anson St., Corner
Bodie, Sarah. Boarding House. 26 Tradd St.

Boiler, Joseph. Butcher. 26 Archdale St.
Bollough, Mary. Pinckney St.
Bonetheau, Peter. City Clerk. 20 Trott St.
Bonneau, Francis. House Carpenter. 58 Broad St.
Bonsall, Samuel. Blacksmith. 5 Wentworth St.
Bonterle, Jean. Ship Master. 10 Queen St.
Booner, Christian. Shop Keeper. 11 Queen St.
Boothe, Thomas. Carpenter. 7 Stoll's Alley
Border, Mary. Shop Keeper. 15 Clifford's Alley
Bouchenneau, Charles. Waiter Branch Bank. 170 Meeting St.
Boulliat, Peter. Ship Master. 10 St. Philip's St.
Bourdeaux, Daniel. Merchant. 22 Beaufain St.
Bouth, Catherine. Boarding House. 84 East Bay
Bowen & Elliott. Painters. 9 Queen St.
Bowen & Harrison. Printers. 38 East Bay
Bowman, John. Planter. 33 Wentworth St.
Boyd, Elizabeth. 43 Trott St.
Bradford & Co. Music Store. 31 Church St.
Bradford, Charles & Co. Grocers. 120 Queen St.
Bradford, Thomas. Cabinet Maker. 30 Broad St.
Brailsford, John. Factor. Wentworth St.
Brailsford, Samuel. Merchant. 1 Friend St.
Brally, Thomas. Wagon Yard. 221 King St.
Branford, Elizabeth. 34 Meeting St.
Bremar, Francis. Surveyor General. 23 Trott St.
Bricken, Sarah. Boarding House. 6 Tradd St.
Brindley, Stephen. Pilot. 17 Maiden Lane
Brodie, Robert. Carpenter. 16 Lynch's Lane
Brodie, Thomas. Factor. Pritchard's Wharf
Brooke, Charles. Shop Keeper. 58 Union St. Continued
Broughton, Ann. 103 Tradd St.
Browell, James. Painter. 11 Clifford's Alley
Brower, Jeremiah. Scrivener. 22 Beresford St.
Brown, ——, Mrs. Midwife. 46 Tradd St.
Brown, Daniel. Mariner. 3 Pinckney St.
Brown, James. Grocer. 242 King St.
Brown, Joseph. 66 Tradd St.
Brown, Mary. 38 Archdale St.
Brown, Roger. Mariner. 27 Pinckney St.
Brown, Squire. Barber. 20 Tradd St.
Brownlee, John. Merchant. 208 King St.
Bruce, Daniel. Store Keeper. 25 Church St.
Bryan, Arthur. Merchant. 17 Elliott St.
Bryan, John. Planter. 39 Pinckney St.
Buckham, Jacob. Gunsmith. 9 Queen St.
Buckle, Thomas. Scrivener. 56 Broad St.
Budd, Abigail. Boarding House. 46 Church St.
Bulgin, James. Merchant. 11 Tradd St.
Bull, John. Planter. 316 King St.
Bulow, Joachim. Store Keeper. 119 King St.
Burckart, John. Express Rider. 13 Chalmers' Alley
Burger, David. Gunsmith. 21 Queen St.
Burgess, James & Co. Merchants. 23 Bay
Burke, Aedanus. Associate Judge. 138 Church St.
Burkmeyer, Charles. Butcher. 7 Burn's Lane
Burkmeyer, John. Butcher. Pitt St.
Burn, John. Shop Keeper. 36 Union St.
Burns, James. Cabinet Maker. 204 King St.
Burrell, Ebenezer. Shop Keeper. Craft's Wharf
Burrows, Frederick. Pilot. 5 Trott St.
Butler, Charles P. Silversmith. 255 King St.
Butterton, Joseph. Pilot. 2 Rhett St.
Buyck, Peter. Bottle Seller. 27 Elliott St.
Byrne, Patrick. Clerk to Supervisor. 129 Queen St.
Byrne, Robert. Shop Keeper. 103 Queen St.

Cain, Conrad. Carter. 34½ Trott St.
Caldwell & Lander. Grocers. 215 Meeting St.
Calhoun, William. Merchant. 99 Meeting St.
Callaghan, John. Tallow Chandler. 39 Tradd St.
Calvert, Elizabeth. Boarding House. 110 Queen St.
Calwell, Henry, Jr. Shop Keeper. 20 Tradd St.
Calwell, Henry, Sr. Grocer. 107 Church St.
Cam, ——. Widow. 127 Queen St.
Cambridge, Tobias. Vendue Master. 7 Orange St.
Cameron, Alexander. Shop Keeper. 81 King St.
Cameron, Lewis. Merchant. 137 Tradd St.
Camnon, David. Butcher. 260 King St.
Campbell, David. Planter. 5 Legare St.
Campbell, Laurence. Vendue Master. 13 Ellery St.
Cannon, Daniel. Carpenter. 22 Queen St.
Canter, Jacob & Emanuel. Shop Keepers. 18 King St.
Canter, Joshua. Limner. 260 King St.
Cantor & Co. Brokers. 57 Church St.
Canty, Henry & Co. Merchants. 36 East Bay
Cape, Brian. Factor. 80 East Bay
Carolan, Philip. Apothecary. 20 Broad St.
Carpenter, James. Shop Keeper. Union St. Continued
Carr & Firby. Shop Keepers. 42 East Bay
Carradeaux, ——. General. Wentworth St.
Carrell, Daniel. Silversmith. 124 Broad St.
Carson, James. Shop Keeper. 62 East Bay
Carson, William. Planter. 9 Meeting St.
Cart, John. Factor. 1 George St.
Cart, Joseph. Silversmith. 33 Guignard St.
Cart, Sarah. 125 Queen St.
Carter, George. Physician. 81 Church St.
Cartwright, Paul. 9 Lynch's Lane
Casey, Benjamin. Coach Maker. 46 Meeting St.
Casey, James. Coach Maker. 47 Meeting St.
Caveneau, James. Carter. Pinckney St.
Chalmers, Eliza. 108 Queen St.
Chambers, Gilbert. Carpenter. 23 Beaufain St.
Champneys, John. Planter. 24 King St.
Chandler & Marshall. Physicians. 54 Broad St.
Charles, Andrew. Grocer. 130 Broad St.
Charles, Henry. Carpenter. Wyatt's Lot
Charles, James. Baker. 113 Tradd St.
Chevers, Alexander. Shop Keeper. 96 King St.
Chion, Peter G. & Son. Merchants. 39 East Bay
Chisolm, Alexander. Planter. 307 King St.
Chitty, Ann. Shop Keeper. 114 King St.
Chouler, Joseph. Apothecary. 123 Broad St.
Chrietzburgh, Michael. Tailor. Hopton's Lane
Christian, Elizabeth. 14 Trott St.
Christie, Alexander. Baker. 106 Queen St.
Christie, Edward. Inspector Customs. 8 Chambers' Alley
Christie, Edward. Store Keeper. 93 Church St.
Chupein, Lewis. Hair Dresser. 37 Church St.
Clarke, Benjamin. Cutler. 33 Beaufain St.
Clarke, David. Watch Maker. 5 Price's Alley
Clarke, James. Tailor. 11 Elliott St.
Clarke, Jeremiah. Clerk of Markets. 15 Chambers' Alley
Clarke, John. Shop Keeper. 122 Church St.
Clarke, John. Butcher. 22 Trott St.
Clarke, Mary. 180 Meeting St.
Clarke, William. Sail Maker. 7 Pinckney St.
Clastier, Maxemellian. Starch Maker. 15 Beresford St.
Cleary, John R. School Master. 12 Liberty St.
Clement, John. Carpenter. 47 Queen St.
Clitherall, James. Physician. 45 Broad St.
Coats, Thomas. Tavern Keeper. 40 East Bay

37

Cobia, Elizabeth. 14 Beresford St.
Cobia, Margaret. 18 Beresford St.
Cochran, Robert. Com. Revenue Cutter. 74 Meeting St.
Cochran, Robert. Shop Keeper. 250 King St.
Cochran, Thomas. Factor. Cochran's Wharf
Coffin, Ebenezer. Merchant. 14 Tradd St.
Cohen, Gershon. Factor, &c. 12 Orange St.
Cohen, Isaac. Vendue Master. 227 King St.
Cohen, Jacob. Vendue Master. 267 King St.
Cohen, Jacob, Jr. Shop Keeper. 91 King St.
Cohen, Mordecai. Shop Keeper. 226 King St.
Cohen, Moses. Shop Keeper. 191 King St.
Coiles, Margaret. 16 Pinckney St.
Colcock, Melescent. Boarding School. 101 Tradd St.
Cole, Thomas. Brick Layer. 2 Trott St.
Collins, Mary. 11 Hasell St.
Condy, Jeremiah. Merchant. 217 Meeting St.
Condy, Jeremiah & Co. Merchants. 217 Meeting St.
Connelly, John. Ship Master. 21 Meeting St.
Conner, Bryan. Butcher. 156 King St.
Conyers, John. Vendue Master. 2 Stoll's Alley
Cook, Florence. 16 Bedon's Alley
Cook, Jonathan. Shop Keeper. 122 King St.
Cook, Thomas. Carpenter. 12 Meeting St.
Coram, Thomas. Engraver. 81 Queen St.
Corbett, Samuel. City Marshall. 232 Meeting St.
Corbett, Samuel. City Marshall.
Corbett, Thomas. Merchant. 11 Cumberland St.
Corbett, Thomas & Son. Merchants. East Bay
Corre & Schepler. Merchants. 76 East Bay
Couis, John. Grocer. 126 Broad St.
Courtney, Edward. Shop Keeper. 173 Meeting St.
Courtney, Humphrey. Merchant. 44 Meeting St.
Courtney, James. Tailor. 42 Meeting St.
Cowin, John. Hatter. 16 Chambers' Alley
Cox, John. Planter. 128 Church St.
Cox, Susannah. Mantua Maker. Federal St.
Cozins, Mathew. Inspector Customs. 5 Lodge Alley
Crafts, William. Merchant. 23 Hasell St.
Crafts, William & Ebenezer. Merchants. East Bay
Crawford, Alexander. Painter. 258 Meeting St.
Crawley, George S. Shop Keeper. 256 King St.
Crawley, Michael. Shop Keeper. 235 King St.
Creighton, Samuel. Barber. Amen St.
Cripps, John Splatt. Merchant. 102 Broad St.
Crocker & Sturges. Merchants. 99 Church St.
Crolan, Philip. Apothecary. 20 Broad St.
Cromwell, Elizabeth. 34 Tradd St.
Crookshanks, Daniel. Shoemaker. 17 Clifford's Alley
Crookshanks, Daniel. Shoemaker. 2 Broad St.
Crookshanks, William. Starch Maker. Bull St.
Cross & Crawley. Merchants. 41 East Bay
Cross, George. Merchant. 38 Tradd St.
Cross, James. Surveyor. 11 Guignard St.
Crowe, Edward. Custom House Boat. Pinckney St.
Cruger, David Frederick. Factor. 38 Meeting St.
Cudworth, Nathaniel. Scrivener. 225 Meeting St.
Cummings, Janet. Midwife. 282 King St.
Cunaghar, Thomas. Shop Keeper. Church St. & Water
Cunningham, John. Shop Keeper. 145 King St.
Cunnington, William. Justice of Peace. North of Exchange
Curling, Thomas. Shop Keeper. 199 King St.
Curtis, ----. Saddler. Society St.
Custer, James. Scrivener. 25 Queen St.
Cyples, Margaret. 7 Trott St.
D'Oyley, Ann. 82 Queen St.

DaCosta, Isaac. Merchant. 91 King St.
DaCosta, Joseph. Broker. 122 Broad St.
Daniel, Elizabeth. 63 George St.
Darrell, Benjamin. Ship Master. 23 Meeting St.
Darrell, Edward. Merchant. 24 East Bay
Darrell, Edward, Jr. Attorney at Law. 42 Broad St.
Dart, ----, Mrs. 28 Tradd St.
Dart, Isaac Motte. Attorney at Law. Ansonborough
Dart, John Sandford. Notary Public & Clerk H.R. 2 Front St. Ansonborough
Dater, Frederick. Reverend. 25 King St.
Davidson, Gilbert & J. Merchants. 8 Broad St.
Davie, William. Money Collector. 9 Friend St.
Davis, Jane. Shop Keeper. 308 King St.
Davis, John Maynard. Insurance Broker. 16 Elliott St.
Davis, Lighfoot H. Attorney at Law. 93 Queen St.
Davis, Thomas. Shop Keeper. 11 Tradd St.
Dawson, Christiana. Boarding House. 2 Kinloch Court
Dawson, John. Shop Keeper. 109 King St.
Dawson, John. Planter. 94 East Bay
Day, George. Silversmith. 10 Trott St.
Dazivido, Isaac. Shop Keeper. 71 King St.
Deady, Thomas. Shop Keeper. 18 East Bay
Dearlon, Martin. Shop Keeper. 45 Union St.
Deas, Elizabeth. 55 Church St.
Debow, John. Silversmith. 118 Queen St.
Delavergene, ----. 12 Moore St.
Delorme, Francis. Upholsterer. 115 Tradd St.
DeLyon, Isaac. 61 King St.
Dener, George. Tanner. Magazine St.
Dener, Peter. Currier. 5 Allen St.
Denny, Samuel. Saddler. 111 King St.
Denoor, David & Co. Vendue Masters. South Side of Exchange
Denton, James. Tavern Keeper. 87 King St.
DePass, Ralph. Vendue Master. 10 Union St. Continued
Depeyster, ----. 7 Hasell St.
Derverneys, Anthony P. Gunsmith. 97 Broad St.
Desaussure & Ford. Attorneys at Law. 29 Tradd St.
Desaussure & Greaves. Factors. Craft's Wharf
Desaussure, Daniel. Merchant. 249 Meeting St.
Desaussure, Henry Wm. Attorney at Law. 30 Tradd St.
Desell, Charles. Cabinet Maker. 51 Broad St.
Deveaux, Jacob. Factor. 2 St. Michael's Alley
Deveaux, Jacob & Son. Factors. Graehm's Wharf
Devona, ----. Wentworth St.
Dewar, Robert. Planter. 93 Tradd St.
Dewees, William. Factor. 65 Meeting St.
Dickenson, Francis. Attorney at Law. 10 Cumberland St.
Dickenson, Jeremiah. Ship Master. 10 Cumberland St.
Dickenson, Joseph. Carpenter. 40 King St.
Dickson, Samuel. School Master. 72 Meeting St.
Dill, Joseph, Jr. Merchant. 97 Church St.
Dill, Joseph, Sr. Carpenter. 295 King St.
Disher, Mary. 117 East Bay
Dodge, Joseph. Ship Carpenter. 1 Lodge Alley
Dodsworth, Ralph. Merchant. 15 Elliott St.
Donaldson, James. Carpenter. 116 Tradd St.
Donaldson, Mary. 22 Tradd St.
Dorrill, Robert. Shop Keeper. 6 Pinckney St.
Dougharty, Patrick. Sail Maker. 13 Amen St.
Doughty, Thomas. Factor. 59 Meeting St.
Doughty, William. Planter. 202 Meeting St.
Douglass, Nat. & John. Store Keepers. 94 Church St.
Douxsaint, William. Planter. 84 Church St.

Down, James. Factor. 16 East Bay
Downey, ——, Mrs. Good Bye Alley
Drayton, Jacob. Attorney at Law. 49 Broad St.
Drayton, John. Attorney at Law. 42 Meeting St.
Drayton, Thomas. Planter. 91 Queen St.
Drummond, Ann. 22 Guignard St.
Drummond, John. Shoemaker. 40 Elliott St.
Dubald, Frederick. 243 King St.
Dubuard, Peter. Barber. 99 Tradd St.
Duffy, Andrew. Shop Keeper. 238 Meeting St.
Duffy, James. Shop Keeper. Market Square
Dulles, Joseph. Store Keeper. 35 East Bay
Duncan, ——. Baker. 42½ Queen St.
Duncan & Murdock. Blacksmiths. Church St.
Duncan, James. Blacksmith. 18 Beresford St.
Dunn, Alexander. Carpenter. Federal St.
Dupre, Benjamin. Tailor. 90 Church St.
Durang, ——. 3 Cumming St.
Durffe, John. 178 King St.
Duvall, Catherine. 113 Church St.
Ebberly, John. Baker. 17 Guignard St.
Echlar, Christopher. Tailor. 50 King St.
Eckhart, Jacob. Music Master. 4 Beresford St.
Edean, Joshua. Turner. 15 Beresford St.
Edwards, Alexander. Attorney at Law. 249 Meeting St.
Edwards, James. Factor. 109 Tradd St.
Edwards, John. Auctioneer. 7 Meeting St.
Ehny, Catharine. 14 Magazine St.
Ehrick & Reynolds. Grocers. 118 Tradd St.
Elfe, Thomas. Cabinet Maker. 116 Queen St.
Elliott, Thomas. Planter. Gibbes St.
Elliott, Thomas Odinsell. Planter. 18 Legare St.
Ellmore, Jeffy. Tailor. 35 Church St.
Elsworth, Theophilus. Guager for Customs. 135 Queen St.
English, Thomas. Shop Keeper. 4 Tradd St.
Ewing, Adam. Merchant. 259 Meeting St.
Ewing, Robert & Adam. Merchants. 125 Tradd St.
Eyers, Thomas. Tailor. 7 Maiden Lane
Eyers, William. Pilot. 8 Pinckney St.
Fabert, Joseph. Grocer. 134 Queen St.
Fabre, John, Rev. Rector Lutheran Church. 31 Archdale St.
Fair, William. Factor. 62 Meeting St.
Fair, William. Tanner. Montague St.
Fair, William. Shoemaker. 26 Broad St.
Fairchild, Aaron. Blacksmith. 17 Pinckney St.
Fayssoux, Peter. Physician. 76 Tradd St.
Fell, Elizabeth. Milliner. 23 Broad St.
Fereaud, Alexander. 220 Meeting St.
Ferguson, ——, Mrs. Liberty St.
Fiddy, William. Store Keeper. 121 Broad St.
Fields, John. Tobacconist. 186 Meeting St.
Fields, William Brown. Tobacconist. 184 Meeting St.
Fife, James. Cooper. Whim's Court
Filbin, Charles. Planter. 9 Friend St.
Finlayson, ——, Mrs. Cabinet Maker. 32 Queen St.
Fisher, James. Merchant. 16 South Bay
Flagg, George. Planter. Federal St.
Flagg, Henry Collins. Physician. 9 Cumberland St.
Flagg, Samuel Hort. Dentist. Church St.
Flemming, John. City Guard. 44 King St.
Flemming, Robert. Shop Keeper. 117 King St.
Flint, Joseph. Grocer. 31 Union St.
Florin, Lucas. Clerk. 34 Guignard St.
Fogartie, Mary. School Mistress. 12 King St.
Folker, John Casper. Shoemaker. 11 St. Philip's St.

Fonspertius, ——, Citizen. French Consul. 127 King St.
Forbes, Elizabeth. 104 East Bay
Ford, Timothy. Attorney at Law. 284 Meeting St.
Fordham, Richard. Ship Carpenter. Cock Lane
Forrest, George. Merchant. 114 Broad St.
Forrest, Michael. 96 Queen St.
Foster, Thomas. Runner Branch Bank. 50 Church St.
Fowke, Chandler Din. Attorney at Law. 51 Tradd St.
Fowler & Brodie. Carpenters. 5 Longitude Lane
Fowler, Richard. Carpenter. Wyatt's Lot
Fraser, ——. Widow. 22 King St.
Fraser, John. Inspector Customs. 9 Bedon's Alley
Fraser, William. Attorney at Law. 89 Broad St.
Freeman, William. Factor. 6 South Bay
Freer, Ann. 109 Church St.
Freer, Sarah. Boarding House. 107 Queen St.
Freneau, Peter. Secretary of the State. Society St.
Friend, Ulrick. Baker. ½ Trott St.
Frink, Thomas & Co. Grocers. Beal's Wharf
Fripp, William. Planter. 8 Meeting St.
Frish, Charles. Shop Keeper. 188 King St.
Frist, John. Carter. 44 King St.
Frost, Thomas. Rev. 20 Archdale St.
Fry, Thomas. Tailor. 98 Tradd St.
Fuller, Thomas. Planter. 91 Tradd St.
Fullerton, Elizabeth. Boarding School. 86 Queen St.
Furman, Richard. Pastor Baptist Church. 19 Church St.
Gabeau, Anthony. Tailor. 232 Meeting St.
Gadsden, Christopher. Planter. 4 Front St., Ansonb.
Gadsden, Philip. Factor. 5 Front St., Ansonb.
Gadsden, Thomas, Mrs. 6 Front St., Ansonb.
Gaillard, John. Attorney at Law. East Bay
Gaillard, Theodore. Attorney at Law. 82 East Bay
Gaillard, Theodore. Factor. 87 East Bay
Gaillard, Theodore. Planter. 81 East Bay
Galloway, John. Tavern Keeper. 10 Union St.
Gamble, John. Inn Keeper. 97 King St.
Garden, Alexander. Planter. 3 Church St.
Gardner, William. Carver & Gilder. 47 Broad St.
Gare, Rebecca. 9 Allen St.
Gates, Thomas. Rev. 98 Meeting St.
Gaultier, Isabella. 15 Mazyck St.
Gaultier, Joseph. Vendue Cryer. 92 Tradd St.
Geddis, Henry. Shop Keeper. 86 King St.
Geddis, Robert & Co. Store Keepers. 53 East Bay
Gennerick, John Fred. Shop Keeper. 40 Tradd St.
Gensell, John. Marine Hospital. 167 King St.
George, James. Ship Wright. Up the Path 3 Miles
George, Mary. Shop Keeper. 216 King St.
Gerley, John. Tailor. Mazyck St.
Gervais, John Lewis. Commissioner P. Accounts. 70 Broad St.
Gesken, Henry. Cabinet Maker. 205 King St.
Geyer, John. Factor. 11 Meeting St.
Gibbes, John. Planter. 67 Tradd St.
Gibbes, Mary. Gibbes St.
Gibbes, William Hasell. Master in Chancery. 57 Meeting St.
Gibbs, George. Baker. 28 Elliott St.
Gibson, Ann Maria. School Mistress. Pinckney St.
Gibson, Robert. Saddler. 249 King St.
Gift, ——, Mrs. Widow Gen. Gift. 1 Wentworth St.
Gift, William. Shop Keeper. 209 King St.
Gilchrist, Adam. Merchant. 21 Church St.
Gitsenger, George. Shoemaker. 77 King St.
Given, Robert. Stone Cutter. Federal St.

Glover, Ann. 312 King St.
Goddard & Sturges. Surveyors. 92 Meeting St.
Godfrey, Thomas. House Carpenter. 14 Allen St.
Gomez, Elias. 10 Allen St.
Gondeville, ----. Shop Keeper. 3 Union St.
Good, Sarah. Boarding House. 37 King St.
Gordon, Andrew. Brick Layer. 13 Moore St.
Gordon, James. Shoemaker.
Gordon, James. Merchant. 26 East Bay
Gordon, James. Brick Layer. 11 Moore St.
Gordon, John. Factor. Quince St.
Gordon, Thomas. Grocer. 68 Meeting St.
Gordon, Thomas. Clerk S.C. Society. 12 East Bay
Gould, John. Shop Keeper. 192 King St.
Gourlay, John. Shoemaker. 185 Meeting St.
Gourlay, John. Shoemaker. 50 Meeting St.
Graeser, Conrad Jacob. Merchant. 71 Meeting St.
Graff, Seibels & Co. Merchants. 206 King St.
Graham, Mary. Midwife. 107 Tradd St.
Graham, Samuel. Blacksmith. 6 Longitude Lane
Graham, Samuel. Merchant.
Graham, William. Clerk Branch Bank. 35 Tradd St.
Grainger, James. Chair Maker. 15 Guignard St.
Grant, Alexander. Baker. 148 King St.
Grant, Hary. Agent to Commission Merchant. East Bay
Granville, James. Hair Dresser. 85 King St.
Grassell, George. Carpenter. Quince St.
Grattan, Daniel. 19 Beresford St.
Gravenstine, Frederick. Tailor. 2 Mazyck St.
Graves, Charles. Factor. 79 Tradd St.
Gray, Benjamin. Planter. 22 Trott St.
Green, William. Shop Keeper. 73 East Bay
Greenland, George. Factor. 39 Meeting St.
Greenwood, Robert. Shop Keeper. 3 Beresford St.
Greenwood, William., Jr. Merchant. 2 Ellery St.
Greenwood, William., Sr. Merchant. 28 Meeting St.
Greerly, Joseph. Carpenter. Cock Lane
Gregorie, James & Son. Merchants. 116 Broad St.
Grierson, James. Shop Keeper. 67 King St.
Grimbal, Mary M. 9 Church St.
Grimke, John F. Associate Judge. 29 Church St.
Grimke, Mary. 54 Meeting St.
Grossman, Francis. 64 Queen St.
Gruber, Charles, Jr. 253 King St.
Gruber, Charles, Sr. Cooper. 79 Queen St.
Gruber, Samuel. Cooper. St. Philip's St.
Guerard, Mary Ann. 137 Church St.
Guillaud, Claudius. Baker. 9 Elliott St.
Guirey, Elizabeth. Shop Keeper. 40 Church St.
Gunn, William. Gunsmith. 6 Queen St.
Gury, Charles F. 7 Burn's Lane
Guy, James. Tailor. 193 Meeting St.
Hadden, Gardner. Tailor. 85 Church St.
Haig, ----, Mrs. 21 Hasell St.
Haig & Dunn. Carpenters. 101 Meeting St.
Haig & Murray. Coopers. 90 Church St.
Haig, David. Cooper. 112 East Bay
Hainsdorf, Henry. Carver. 14 Hasell St.
Hair, Edward. 106 King St.
Hall, Daniel. Factor. 3 State House Square
Hall, Dominick A. Attorney at Law. 279 King St.
Hall, Mary Ann. 15 Magazine St.
Hall, Thomas. Clerk Federal Court. 32 Broad St.
Hall, Walter. Justice of Peace. 14 King St.
Hall, William. Ship Master. 5 Cumberland St.
Ham, ----, Mrs. Boarding House. 24 Beresford's Alley
Hambord, Godfrey. Carpenter. 13 Lynch's Lane

Hamilton, David. Ship Wright. 27 Guignard St.
Hamilton, James. Merchant. 11 Broad St.
Hamlin & Clessey. Saddlers. 33 Church St.
Hammett, Charlotte. 7 Bedon's Alley
Hammett, William, Rev. Pastor Trinity Church. Maiden Lane
Hammilon, John. Shop Keeper. 29 Union St.
Handy, Thomas. Constable. 6 Beresford's Alley
Hargreaves, Joshua & J. Merchants. 21 Broad St.
Harleston, Elizabeth. 20 Hasell St.
Harleston, John, Mrs. 106 Tradd St.
Harley, William. Butcher. Society St.
Harman, John. Carter. Cumming St.
Harper, Robert G. Attorney at Law. 52 King St.
Harris, Andrew. Broker. 44 Tradd St.
Harris, John Hartley. Hotel. 63 East Bay
Harris, Thomas. Boarding House. 237 King St.
Harris, Tucker. Physician. 69 King St.
Harrison, Isaac. 205 Meeting St.
Hart, Christian. Store Keeper. 204 King St.
Hart, Daniel. Store Keeper. 56 East Bay
Hart, Philip. Stock Jobber. 136 Queen St.
Harth, John. Shop Keeper. 1 Archdale St.
Harvey, Benjamin. Brick Layer. 35 Beaufain St.
Harvey, Elizabeth. 11 Allen St.
Harvey, Elizabeth. School Mistress. 3 Orange St.
Harvey, Robert. Merchant. 35 Elliott St.
Harvey, Thomas. Boarding House. 3 Market Square
Hatter, Elizabeth. 38 Queen St.
Haunbaum, Christian. Physician. 7 Moore St.
Haunbaum, George. Physician. 258 King St.
Hawkins, James. Cabinet Maker. 94 Tradd St.
Hawser, Elias. Shop Keeper. 203 King St.
Hayes, James. Constable. Union St. Continued
Hazard & Robinson. Merchants. 6 Champney's Row
Hazard, Rowland. Merchant. 1 Pinckney St.
Hazelwood, ----. Painter. 15 Queen St.
Hazlehurst, Robert. Merchant. 14 East Bay
Henrichsen, Betye. Carpenter. Society St.
Henry, George. Shoemaker. 1 Elliott St.
Henry, Jacob. Shop Keeper. 211 King St.
Heyneman, Valentine. Watchman. 20 George St.
Heyward, Hannah. 12 Legare St.
Heyward, Nathaniel. Planter. 118 East Bay
Heyward, Thomas, Jr. Planter. Church St.
Heyward, Thomas, Sr. Planter. 88 Tradd St.
Hill, Charles. Scrivener. 14 Chalmers' Alley
Hill, Duncan. Ship Master. 106 East Bay
Hill, Jonathan. Baker.
Hill, Paul. Distiller. 1 Beresford St.
Hill, Thomas. Grocer. 9 Tradd St.
Hillegas, George. Shop Keeper. 52 Tradd St.
Hillegas, Joseph. Billiard Table. 244 Meeting St.
Hillegas, Philip. Shop Keeper. 96 Tradd St.
Himelie, John James. Watch Maker. 119 Broad St.
Hinds, Patrick. Shoemaker. 37 Beaufain St.
Hinds, Thomas. Attorney at Law. 30 Broad St.
Hobart, John. Tailor. 1 Beresford St.
Hogsden, Mary. Mantau Maker. 36 King St.
Holinshead, William. Pastor Indepent. Church. 94 Meeting St.
Holmes, Isaac. Collector of Customs. 16 Legare St.
Holmes, John Bee. Intendant. 6 Meeting St.
Holmes, Thomas. Saddler. 28 Archdale St.
Holmes, William. Vendue Master. 314 King St.
Honeywood, Elizabeth. Blacksmith. 1 Moore St.
Horlbeck, John. Brick Layer. 8 Moore St.
Hornby, Thomas. Distiller. 214 King St.

Horry, Thomas. Planter. 274 Meeting St.
Horsey, Thomas. Scrivener. 6 Charles St.
Hort, William. State Treasurer. East Bay
Houlton, James. Money Dunner. 3 Water St.
House, Samuel. Broker. 7 Chambers' Alley
Howard, Ann. 183 Meeting St.
Howard, John. Hair Dresser. 225 King St.
Hoyland, Ann Maria. School Mistress. 86 Broad St.
Hrabowski, Ann. Store Keeper. 45 Broad St.
Huck, Michael. Hackney Coach. 264 King St.
Huger, Daniel Lionel. Federal Marshall. 59 Broad St.
Huger, Isaac. Planter. 59 Broad St.
Huger, John. Planter. 73 Broad St.
Hughes, John. Carpenter. 2 Wragg's Alley
Humphreys, Benjamin. 9 Orange St.
Hunt, ----. Ship Master. 23 Beresford St.
Hunt, ----, Mrs. Elliott St.
Hunter, Thomas. Ship Master. 67 Church St.
Hunter, William. Tailor. 2 Elliott St.
Hunter, William. Shop Keeper. 169 King St.
Hurst, Charles. Tailor. 49 Church St.
Hutchings, William B. School Master. 14 Hasell St.
Hutchinson, John. Shop Keeper. 65 East Bay
Hutson, Abel. Shop Keeper. 131 Queen St.
Hyams, Solomon. Shop Keeper. 190 King St.
Hyslop, Robert. Shop Keeper. 63 Church St.
Ingles, Alexander. 12 Short St.
Inglesby, Henry. Tailor. 23 Tradd St.
Inglesby, William. Tailor. 24 Tradd St.
Irvine, Matthew. Physician. Bay
Izard, Charlotte. 3 Cumberland St.
Izard, Ralph, Jr. Planter. 83 Broad St.
Izard, Ralph, Sr. Senator to U.S.
Jacks, James. Jeweller. 112 Broad St.
Jacks, Victor. Boarding House. 128 Queen St.
Jacobs, Jacob. Vendue Master. 20 Meeting St.
Jacobs, Jacob, Jr. Vendue Master. 35 King St.
Jacobs, Samuel. Shop Keeper. 168 King St.
Jaffray, James. Merchant. 135 Tradd St.
Jamieson, Rebecca. Boarding School. 105 East Bay
Jarman, John. Shop Keeper. 275 King St.
Jeffords, John. Tailor. 18 Pinckney St.
Jenkins, Edward. Rev. 6 Lamboll St.
Jennings & Woddrop. Merchants. 9 East Bay
Jenny, John. Baker. 2 Beresford St.
Jervey, Thomas. 16 King St.
Jessey, Sarah. Shop Keeper. 50 Broad St.
Johnson, Elizabeth. 3 Charles St.
Johnson, Isaac. Tailor. 14 Friend St.
Johnson, John. Store Keeper. 165 King St.
Johnson, W. I. Watch Maker. 93 King St.
Johnson, William. Blacksmith. 7 Charles St.
Johnson, William, Jr. Attorney at Law.
Johnston, Charles. Planter. 3 Lamboll St.
Johnston, Hester. 1 Clifford's Alley
Johnston, James. Shop Keeper. 220 King St.
Johnston, John. Clerk. 3 Ellery St.
Johnston, Robert. Tailor. 128 Broad St.
Johnston, William. School Master. Stoll's Alley
Jones & Clarke. Merchants. East Bay
Jones, Abraham. Shop Keeper. 201 King St.
Jones, Alexander. Grocer. 106½ Church St.
Jones, Henry. Carpenter. 3 Lodge Alley
Jones, Joseph. Shop Keeper. 15 Tradd St.
Jones, Samuel. Shop Keeper. 268 King St.
Jones, Thomas. President S. C. Bank. 4 Guignard St.
Josephs, Israel. Indigo Broker. 262 King St.
Juvignes, Dominick. Shop Keeper. 18 Queen St.

Kalckoffin, John. Shop Keeper. 88 King St.
Kaltielen, Michael. Commandant Fort Johnson. Maiden Lane
Karr, James. Boarding House. 1 St. Michael's Alley
Kasll, John. Shop Keeper. 27 King St.
Kay & M'Cawly. Grocers. 2 Tradd St.
Kay, James. Brick Layer. 291 King St.
Kay, Joseph. Butcher. 9 Trott St.
Keen, Thomas. Ship Master. 12 Union St. Continued
Keith, ----, Mrs. Boarding House. 119 Queen St.
Keith, Isaac S., Rev. Pastor Independent Ch. 59 Queen St.
Keller, John Jacob. Tavern Keeper. 57 King St.
Kelly, Mary. Shop Keeper. 116 King St.
Kelly, Tarence. Shop Keeper. 44 Union St.
Kelsall, John. 306 King St.
Kelse, John. 12 Trott St.
Kemmeil, ----, Mrs. 46 Queen St.
Kempton, Ann. Shop Keeper. 218 King St.
Kennedy, Andrew. Shop Keeper. 3 Union St. Continued
Kennedy, James. Planter. 32 Wentworth St.
Kennedy, John. Shop Keeper. 20 East Bay
Kennedy, William. Shop Keeper. 4 Broad St.
Kern, John Frederick. Merchant. 193 King St.
Kerr, Andrew. Merchant. 8½ Broad St.
Kerr, John. Hatter. 111 Queen St.
Kershaw, Charles. Merchant. 113 Queen St.
Kershaw, Joseph. Silversmith. 6 Market St.
Kevan, William. Merchant. 136 Tradd St.
King, Charles. Tailor. 91 King St.
King, Eleanor. Shop Keeper. 6 Charles St.
Kingman, Eliab. Hair Dresser. 4 Elliott St.
Kipps, Andrew. Shop Keeper. King St.
Kirk & Larkens. Merchants. 59 East Bay
Knoff, Conrad. Butcher. 146 Meeting St.
Kohne, John Frederick. Merchant. Craft's Wharf
Labbe, Anthony. Music Master. 23 Beresford St.
Ladson, ----, Mrs. Boarding House. 5 Orange St.
Ladson, James. Lieut. Governor. 14 Meeting St.
Lafar, Joseph. Dancing Master. Church St. & Lynch's Lane
Lahogue, Feret. 309 King St.
Lamb & Montgomery. Merchants. 23 East Bay
Lamotte & Chisonn. Factors. Vanderhorst's Wharf
Lamotte, James. Factor. 12 Church St.
Lampe, John. Watch Maker. 118 Tradd St.
Lance, Ann. 12 Friend St.
Lance, Lambert. Attorney at Law. 111 Friend St.
Lanchester, Henry. Grocer. 3 Pinckney St.
Lange, J. H. Merchant. 133 Tradd St.
Langford, Ann. 171 Meeting St.
Langstaff, John. 6 Elliott St. Continued
Lanneau, Bazil. Tanner. Pitt St.
Larabert, Frederick. Tallow Chandler. Cumming St.
Larry, Robert. Carpenter. 62 Church St.
Lasaver, ----, Miss. 66 Meeting St.
Latham, Daniel. Distiller. 2 Hasell St.
Lathuson & Co. Shop Keepers. 23 Union St.
Laughton, Winborn. Planter. 5 Lynch's Lane
Laval, Jacint. French Teacher. 1 Kinloch Court
Lazarus, Mark. Shop Keeper. 101 King St.
Leblanc, Henry. Shoemaker. 115 King St.
Lee & Miles. Factors. Geyer's Wharf
Lee, John & William. Merchants. 47 King St.
Lee, Stephen. Factor. 42 Broad St.
Lee, Thomas. Attorney at Law. 208 Meeting St.
Lee, William. Watch Maker. 91 Broad St.

41

Legare, Elizabeth. Society St.
Legare, Frances. Anson St.
Legare, Samuel. Merchant. 101 Church St.
Legare, Solomon. Factor. 5 East Bay
Legare, Theus & Prioleau. Merchants. 131 Broad St.
Legare, Thomas. Planter. 50 Tradd St.
Legge, Edward. Vendue Master. 45 Trott St.
Legge, James. Shop Keeper. 198 King St.
Lehre, Thomas. Planter. 293 King St.
Lehre, William. Physician. 11 Liberty St.
Lenox, William & Co. Merchants. 120 Broad St.
Lesesne, ----, Mrs. 1 Hasell St.
Lesesne, ----, Mrs. 108 East Bay
Leslie & Campbell. Shop Keepers. 96 Church St.
Levoux, John. Carpenter. 37 Trott St.
Levy, Hart. Shop Keeper. 184 King St.
Levy, Lyon. Shop Keeper. 204 King St.
Levy, Moses C. Shop Keeper. 283 King St.
Levy, Nathan. Shop Keeper. 222 King St.
Levy, Samuel. Shop Keeper. 182 King St.
Levy, Solomon. Shop Keeper. 247 King St.
Lewers, Thomas. Shop Keeper. 200 King St.
Lewis, Henry. Tailor. 300 King St.
Ley, Francis. Shop Keeper. Elliott St.
Libby, Nathaniel. Block Maker. 7 Wragg's Alley
Liddle, John. Shop Keeper. South Bay
Liedenhall, Johannes. 2 Gillon St.
Lightwood, Edward. Planter. 266 Meeting St.
Limehouse, Robert. Shop Keeper. 34½ Broad St.
Lindsay, Robert. Merchant. South Bay Point
Linguard, Mary. 74 Church St.
Linning, Charles. Ordinary. 10 Legare St.
Little, Robert. Carpenter. 12 Amen St.
Littlejohn, Duncan. Merchant. 140 Church St.
Livingston, Eleanor. 62 George St.
Lloyd & Paterson. Merchants. 31 Broad St.
Lloyd, John. Planter. 6 Lamboll St.
Lloyd, Joseph. Shop Keeper. 13 Elliott St.
Lane, Samuel. Carpenter. Maiden Lane
Lockwood, Joshua. 1 Smith's Lane
Logan, George, Mrs. 32 Tradd St.
Logan, William. Planter. 292 King St.
Loocock, Aaron, Mrs. 31 Tradd St.
Lopez, David & Aaron. Vendue Masters. 86 Tradd St.
Lord, Andrew, Mrs. 25 Beaufain St.
Lord, Richard. Clerk S.C. Bank. 43 Church St.
Lothrop, Seth & Co. Merchants. East Bay
Love, John. Fruit Shop. 8 Tradd St.
Loveday, John. Factor. 10 Moore St.
Lowndes, Rawlins. Planter. 74 Broad St.
Luckie, John. Saddler. 246 King St.
Lunt, Mary. Tallow Chandler. 13 Union St.
Luyton, William. Store Keeper. 8 Elliott St.
Lynah, James. Physician. 55 Meeting St.
Lyon, Mordecai. Shop Keeper. 53 East Bay
Lyon, Moses. Shop Keeper. 153 King St.
M'Beath & Ross. Merchants. 121 Tradd St.
M'Beath, Alexander. Merchant. 105 Broad St.
M'Bride & Forsyth. Shop Keepers. 225 Meeting St.
M'Bridge, James. Shop Keeper. 58 East Bay
M'Call, James. Planter. 88 Church St.
M'Call, John. City Treasurer. 110 Church St.
M'Call, John. Tailor. 78 East Bay
M'Calla, Thomas H. Physician. 10 Elliott St.
M'Cann, Edward. Porter House. 4 Market Square
M'Carty, William. Constable. 22 Beresford St.
M'Clary, Jane. Boarding House. 3 Union St.
M'Clish, ----, Mrs. Boarding House. 54 Church St.

M'Clish, Alexander. Brass Founder. 64 Meeting St.
M'Clure, Cochran & W. Merchants. 7 Tradd St.
M'Credie, David & Co. Merchants. 8 Broad St.
M'Donald, Patrick. Shop Keeper. 125 Church St.
M'Donald, William. Grocer. 22 East Bay
M'Dowall, James. Shop Keeper. 58 King St.
M'Dowall, John. Shop Keeper. 39 Queen St.
M'Dowall, John. Merchant. 104 Broad St.
M'Gee, John. Shop Keeper. 223 King St.
M'Intosh, Simon. Attorney at Law. 16 Friend St.
M'Iver, John. Printer. 111 Tradd St.
M'Kenny, George. Tailor. 3 Elliott St.
M'Kenzie & Hinson. Merchants. 29 Broad St.
M'Kenzie, Andrew. Grocer. 108 Broad St.
M'Khugo, Anthony. Inspector Customs. 63 Meeting St.
M'Kimmy, John. Brick Layer. 28 King St.
M'Koy, Abraham F. Clerk St. Philips.
M'Laren, James. Shop Keeper. 6 Union St.
M'Lean, Evan. Tailor. 230 Meeting St.
M'Mullen, Richard. Wagon Yard. 158 King St.
M'Neale, Ralph. Planter. 73 Church St.
M'Pherson, Duncan. Shop Keeper. 74 King St.
M'Pherson, John. Planter. 27 Trott St.
M'Queen, John. Merchant. 19 Broad St.
M'Whann, William. Merchant. 38 Church St.
Macauley, George. Merchant. 17 Broad St.
Mackey, Crafts. Watch Maker. 61 East Bay
Mackie & Williams. Coach Makers. 1 Federal St.
Macleod, William. Merchant. 10 East Bay
Macomb, James. Vendue Master. 52 Meeting St.
Maden & Woodworth. Hatters. 12 Elliott St.
Magan, Patrick. Watch Maker. 45 East Bay
Mailone, James. Shop Keeper. 97 Queen St.
Maine, William. Grocer. 71 East Bay
Makkay, John. Carpenter. 33 Trott St.
Managault, Joseph. Planter. 89 East Bay
Mann & Foltz. Merchants. 13 East Bay
Mann, Margaret. 56 George St.
Manning, Hugh. Carpenter. 9 Amen St.
Manson, John. Merchant. 32 Pinckney St.
Markland, John. Printer. 5 Union St. Continued
Markland, M'Iver & Co. Printers. 47 East Bay
Markley, Abraham. Merchant. 124 King St.
Marks, Humphry. Shop Keeper. 217 King St.
Marr, Ann. 139 Church St.
Marshall, ----, Mrs. 32 Guignard St.
Marshall, Barbary. Shop Keeper. 194 King St.
Marshall, John. Cabinet Maker. 219 Meeting St.
Marshall, William. Factor. 6 East Bay
Marshall, William. Attorney at Law. 43 Meeting St.
Martin, Christian. Tanner. 145 Meeting St.
Martin, Daniel. Lamp Lighter. 269 King St.
Martin, Davis & Martin. Merchants. 21 East Bay
Martin, Hawkins. 21 King St.
Martin, Jacob. Tanner. 214 Meeting St.
Martin, John Christopher. Tavern Keeper. 230 King St.
Martin, Thomas. Merchant. 1 Tradd St.
Mason, William. Clerk Court Common Pleas. 52 Broad St.
Mathews, George. Merchant. 102 Church St.
Matthews, Edeth. State House Square
Matthews, John. Chancellor. 86 East Bay
Matthews, William. Planter. Kinloch Court
Mattuce, John. Butcher. 13 Magazine St.
Mayer, John George. Insurance Broker. 129 Broad St.
Mazier, Francis. Barber. 1 Champney's Row
Mazyck, Daniel. Register Mesne Conveyance. 1 West St.

Mazyck, Mary. 101 Broad St.
Mazyck, Stephen, Sr. Planter. Short St.
Mazyck, William. Planter. 75 Broad St.
Meiks, Joseph. Shop Keeper. 15 Union St.
Merrell, Benjamin. Tailor. 45 Church St.
Mey, Florian Charles. Merchant. 40 Pinckney St.
Meyer, Philip. Baker. 42 Union St.
Meyers, Thomas. Shop Keeper. 66 King St.
Michael, John. Distiller. 29 Pinckney St.
Middleton & Ramsay. Tailors. 19 Elliott St.
Middleton, Arthur. Ansonborough
Miles, Robert. Planter. 10 Pinckney St.
Miller & Robinson. Store Keepers. 17 Tradd St.
Miller, James. Wine Merchant. 64 East Bay
Miller, James. Merchant. 103 Church St.
Miller, John. Carpenter. 288 King St.
Miller, John. Shop Keeper. 186 King St.
Miller, John David. Silversmith. 109 Broad St.
Miller, John James. Carpenter. 73 Meeting St.
Miller, Nicholas. Baker. 4 Wentworth St.
Miller, William. Tailor. 58½ East Bay
Milligan, Jacob. Harbor Master. N. E. of Exchange
Milligan, James. Jail. Jail
Milligan, John. Retailer Lumber. 6 Bedon's Alley
Milligan, John. Ship Master. 34 Archdale St.
Milligan, Joseph. Tallow Chandler. 72 King St.
Millin, John. 13 Beresford St.
Mills, William. Tailor. 105 Church St.
Milner, Daniel. Coach Maker. 251 Meeting St.
Milner, George. Blacksmith. 26 Guignard St.
Minnick, John. Merchant. Craft's Wharf
Minott, William. Mariner. 301 King St.
Mintzing, Philip. Blacksmith. 78 King St.
Miott, ——, Mrs. 126 Queen St.
Miott, John. Silversmith. 39 Trott St.
Mitchell, Andrew. Shop Keeper. 105 Queen St.
Mitchell, Andrew. Shop Keeper. 224 Meeting St.
Mitchell, Florine. Painter. 27 Hasell St.
Mitchell, James. 19 Pinckney St.
Mitchell, John. Notary Public. 30 East Bay
Mitchell, John Hinckley. Grocer. 51 East Bay
Mitchell, John Hinckley. Merchant. 10 Lynch's Lane
Mitchell, William Boone. Attorney at Law. 264 Meeting St.
Montgomery, Thomas. Merchant. 23 East Bay
Mood, Peter. Silversmith. 238 King St.
Moodie, Benjamin. British Consul. 120 Broad St.
Moore, John. Butcher. 58 George St.
Moore, John. Ship Master. East Bay
Moore, John. Shop Keeper. 189 King St.
Moore, John. Lieutenant R. Cutter. 3 Unity Alley
Moore, Joseph. Dray Master. 100 East Bay
Moore, Joseph Pitt. Surgeon. 42 King St.
Moore, Philip. Cabinet Maker. 246 Meeting St.
Morgan, Charles. Ship Carpenter. 1 Pinckney St.
Morris, George, Mrs. 21 Archdale St.
Morris, Lewis. Planter. 260 Meeting St.
Morris, Thomas. Merchant. 46 Trott St.
Mortimer, John. Carpenter. 3 Moore St.
Morton, William. Butcher. 102 Meeting St.
Moses, Abraham & H. Shop Keepers. 245 King St.
Moses, Henry. Shop Keeper. 55 East Bay
Moses, Isaac. Shop Keeper. 228 King St.
Moses, Lyon. Shop Keeper. 15 Allen St.
Moses, Philip. Broker. 14 Friend St.
Moses, Philip. Apothecary. 119 Tradd St.
Mota, Isaac. Shop Keeper. 18 King St.
Motte, Abraham. Planter. 18 Meeting St.

Motte, Francis. Merchant. 18 South Bay
Motte, Isaac. Naval Officer. 262 Meeting St.
Mouat, John, Mrs. 15 King St.
Moultrie, Alexander. Advocate. 4 Cumberland St.
Moultrie, James. Physician. 4 Cumberland St.
Moultrie, William. Governor. 60 Meeting St.
Muir & Boyd. Merchants. 111 Broad St.
Muirhead, James. Book Binder. 7 Elliott St.
Muller, Magdalen. Wentworth St.
Mulligan, Francis. Shrub W. House. 98 East Bay
Muncrieff, John. Carpenter. 12 East Bay
Muncrieff, John & Co. Merchants. 105 Broad St.
Muncrieff, Mary. 20 Queen St.
Munro, John. Watch Maker. 7 Elliott St.
Murphy, James. Shop Keeper. 27 Meeting St.
Murray, Thomas. Cooper. 91 Church St.
Myers, ——. Baker. Union St.
Myers, Israel. Jew Butcher. 15 Union St. Continued
Myers, Mary. State House Square
Myers, Samuel. Tailor. 232½ King St.
Mylne, James. Baker. 20 Union St.
Nann, Mary. Shop Keeper. 3 Meeting St.
Naser, Henry, Mrs. Baker. 11 Beresford St.
Naser, Philip. Baker. 34 King St.
Nathans, Moses B. Broker. 45 Queen St.
Nelson, ——. Silversmith. 21 Trott St.
Nelson, Andrew. Baker. 90 King St.
Nelson, Francis. Ship Carpenter. 116 East Bay
Nelson, James. 34 Beaufain St.
Neufville, Edward. Planter. 22 Legare St.
Neufville, John, Jr. Register Court Equity. 32 Meeting St.
Neufville, John, Sr. Com. of Loans. 85 Queen St.
Neufville, William. Physician. 85 Tradd St.
Nevil, Joshua. Cabinet Maker. 6 Clifford's Alley
Newton, Downham. Ship Master. Society St.
Nicks, William. Butcher. 24 Trott St.
Nickson, John. Shop Keeper. 6 Ellery St.
Niel, Rebecca. 90 Queen St.
Nipper, David. Book Binder. 99 King St.
Nixon, William. School Master. 95 Tradd St.
Nobbs, Samuel. Barber. 56 King St.
Norris, Andrew. Attorney at Law. 120 King St.
Norris, George. Saddler. 90 King St.
Norris, James. Painter. 26 Queen St.
Norris, Nicholas. Broker. 264 King St.
North & Vesey. Ship Chandlers. 38 East Bay
North, Edward. Merchant. 7 Church St.
North, Susannah. 37 Tradd St.
Notherman, Harman. Blacksmith. 187 King St.
Nott, Isabella. Boarding House. 58 Church St.
O'Donnald, James. Cooper. Pinckney St.
O'Hara, Charles. Merchant. 128 Broad St.
O'Hara, Daniel. Merchant. 128 Broad St.
O'Hear, James. Factor. 8 Meeting St.
Odin, Anthony. Limner. 2 Market Square
Ogier, Thomas. Factor. Geyer's New Buildings
Oliphant, David. Limner. 8 South Bay
Osborne, Henry. School Master. 78 Queen St.
Osborne, Thomas. Sheriff C. T. D. Lamboll St.
Owen, John. Merchant. 27 Tradd St.
Pagett, Thomas. School Master. 6 Cumberland St.
Pain & Bridgham. Merchants. 6 Champney's Wharf
Palmer, Job. Carpenter. 26 Trott St.
Parker, George. Brick Maker. Scarborough
Parker, John. Butcher. 115 East Bay
Parker, John. Brick Maker. Scarborough
Parker, John. Planter. 30 Trott St.

Parker, Samuel. 110 Queen St.
Parker, Sarah. 11 Legare St.
Parker, Thomas. Attorney at Law. 41 Meeting St.
Parker, William. M'Kenzie. Attorney at Law. 41 Meeting St.
Parkinson, John. Carver. 5 Moore St.
Parks, John. Shoemaker. 26 Union St.
Parris, Francis. Shop Keeper. 69 East Bay
Parsons, Susannah. 20 Church St.
Patricks, Casimere. Shop Keeper. 187 King St.
Patterson, William. Carpenter. 271 King St.
Patton, Alexander. Shop Keeper. 207 King St.
Patton, Catharine. Midwife. 117 Queen St.
Payne, William. Merchant. 115 Broad St.
Payton, Richard Henry. Attorney at Law. 47 Tradd St.
Peace, Isaac. Merchant. 110 Tradd St.
Peace, Joseph. Attorney at Law. 110 Tradd St.
Pearce, Robert, Mrs. 19 Hasell St.
Pearse, John. Painter. 8 Elliott St.
Peebles, James. Carpenter. 41 Trott St.
Peignea, Lewis. Hair Dresser. 62 East Bay
Peirson, James. Merchant. 42 Broad St.
Pelleson, Guilliam. Tallow Chandler. 24 Beresford St.
Pelsberry, Samuel. Inspector Customs. 20 Guignard St.
Pencill, Emanuel. Tin Man. 47 Meeting St.
Pendarvis, Josiah. Planter. 49 Tradd St.
Penman, J. & E. & Co. Merchants. 75 East Bay
Pepoon, Otis & Co. Merchants. East Bay
Peppin, Joseph & Co. Merchants. 32 East Bay
Peronneau, Mary. 102 Tradd St.
Peronneau, William. Planter. 266 Meeting St.
Perry, Edward. Planter. 1 Pinckney St.
Pestch, Adam. Physician. 241 King St.
Peter, Henry. Shop Keeper. 21 Elliott St.
Petrie, Edmund. Planter. 82 Church St.
Petrie, Elizabeth. 1 Orange St.
Philips, Benjamin, Jr. Shop Keeper. 196 King St.
Philips, John C. Baker. 105 King St.
Pickens, Ezekiel. Attorney at Law. 100 Meeting St.
Pierson, James. Merchant. 42 Broad St.
Pinckney, Charles. Planter. 268 Meeting St.
Pinckney, Charles C. Attorney at Law. 92 East Bay
Pinckney, Frances S. 17 Legare St.
Pinckney, Thomas. Planter. 4 Price's Alley
Piott, Peter. Dray Master. 9 St. Philip's St.
Plumb, Jacob. Baker. 147 King St.
Pointset, Elisha. Physician. 5 Broad St.
Pollock, Solomon. Horse Dealer. 7 Bull St.
Porcher, Philip. Planter. 6 Archdale St.
Postell, Susannah. 4 Hopton's Alley
Postell, Thomas. Planter. 8 Friend St.
Potter, John. Merchant. 131 Tradd St.
Pourie, Bazil. Merchant. 14 Broad St.
Poyas & Foster. Merchants. 126 Tradd St.
Poyas, Daniel. Carpenter. Wyatt's Lot
Poyas, John Ernest. Physician. 4 Orange St.
Poyas, John Lewis. Carpenter. 6 Guignard St.
Poyas, Magdalen. 36 Meeting St.
Prentice, John. Coach Maker. Archdale St.
Prestman, William. Merchant. 10 East Bay
Price, John. Merchant. 108 Church St.
Price, Sarah. Milliner. 34 Broad St.
Price, William. Merchant. 17 Elliott St.
Primrose, Nichol. Inspector Customs. St. Philip's St.
Prince, Ann. 114 Queen St.
Prince, Charles. Pilot. 13 King St.
Prince, Charles. Tin Man. 265 King St.
Pringle, John Julius. States Attorney. 105 Tradd St.

Prioleau, Edith. 21 Guignard St.
Prioleau, John. Factor. 15 Pinckney St.
Prioleau, Samuel. Factor. 48 Church St.
Pritchard, William. Ship Carpenter. 2 Charles St.
Purce, William. Watch Maker. 236 Meeting St.
Purcell, Henry, Rev. Rector St. Michael's Church. 89 Tradd St.
Purcell, Joseph. Surveyor. 1 Liberty St.
Quash, Robert. Planter. 76 Broad St.
Quin, James. Painter. 16 Chambers' Alley
Quinby, Henry. Carpenter. Quince St.
Quinby, Joseph. Carpenter. 5 Pinckney St.
Quince, Susannah. 30 Hasell St.
Ralph & Silberg. Cabinet Makers. 52 Church St.
Ramage, Charles, Mrs. Boarding House. 223 Meeting St.
Ramsay, David. Physician. 90 Broad St.
Ransier, ----. 9 Hasell St.
Ransier, Lambert. Gunsmith. 210 King St.
Ratcliffe, Elizabeth. 9 George St.
Ratcliffe, Thomas. Planter. 6 George St.
Ravenel, Daniel. Planter. 100 Broad St.
Ravenel, Elizabeth Jane. 57 George St.
Ravenel, Stephen. 43 Church St.
Read & King. Tin Men. 90 Church St.
Read, Jacob. Barrister at Law. 121 East Bay
Read, William. Physician. 11 Church St.
Redlech, William. Broker. 4 Champney's Row
Reeves, Enos. Silversmith. 234 Meeting St.
Regley, Anthony. Shop Keeper. 24 Elliott St.
Reid, George. Teller, S.C. Bank. 24 Meeting St.
Reid, John. Wheelwright. 213 Meeting St.
Reid, Walter. Blacksmith. 48 King St.
Revel, John. Planter. 80 Church St.
Revell, John. Ship Master. 20 Guignard St.
Reyley, John. Blacksmith. 77 Meeting St.
Reynolds, George. Carpenter. 42 George St.
Richards, Gasper. Tailor. 16 Clifford's Alley
Richardson, Barney. Carpenter. Wyatt's Square
Richardson, James. Planter. 121 King St.
Richardson, John. Merchant. 36 Elliott St.
Richon, David. Tailor. 110 King St.
Righton, Joseph. Cooper. 10 Stoll's Alley
Righton, M'Cully. Cooper. 120 Church St.
Rivers, Beulah. Cake Maker. St. Michael's Alley
Rivers, Francis. Planter. 8 Amen St.
Rivers, James. Carpenter. 53 Church St.
Rivers, Samuel. Carpenter. 4 Water St.
Rivers, Thomas. Butcher. 40 Trott St.
Roach, William. Clerk Branch Bank. Quince St.
Roanholm, Francis. Carpenter. 11 Trott St.
Robb, Michael. Shoemaker. 6 Elliott St.
Roberts, Ann. 16 Church St.
Roberts, John. Tailor. 34 Church St.
Roberts, William. Coach Maker. 88 Queen St.
Roberts William. Shop Keeper. 6 Queen St.
Robertson, Alexander. Shop Keeper. 95 King St.
Robertson, James. Shop Keeper. 197 King St.
Robertson, William. Attorney at Law. Church St. & Broad
Robinett, Francis. Cooper. 1 Unity Alley
Robinson, John. Brick Layer. Cock Lane
Robinson, Joseph. Carpenter. 277 King St.
Robinson, William. Shop Keeper. 26 Elliott St.
Rogers, Christopher. Tailor. 25 Tradd St.
Rogers, Lewis. Perfumer. 24 Broad St.
Rogers, Sarah. Shop Keeper. 126 Church St.
Rolander, Henry. Ship Master. 16 Tradd St.

Roper, Hannah. 4 East Bay
Roper, Joseph. Turner. 13 Pinckney St.
Rose, Alexander. Merchant. 2 Church St.
Rose, Hugh. Planter. 1 East Bay
Ross, Alexander. Scrivener. 14 Church St.
Ross, Elizabeth. Shop Keeper. 244 King St.
Ross, Kenneth. Shop Keeper. 15 Church St.
Ross, Thomas. Ship Master. 101 Queen St.
Roston, Lewis. Watch Maker. 133 King St.
Roupell, Daniel. Umbrella Maker. 226 Meeting St.
Roupell, George. 18 Tradd St.
Rouse, William. Tanner. 75 Meeting St.
Rousleau, Peter. Tailor. 133 Queen St.
Rout, George. School Master. 9 Moore St.
Rowand, Robert. Merchant. 2 Friend St.
Rowe, Michael. Carter. 21 George St.
Royall, William. School Master. 48 Tradd St.
Ruberry, John. Tailor. 115 Queen St.
Rumney, Joseph. Grocer. 99 East Bay
Rush, Mathias. Tailor. 243 King St.
Russell, Benjamin. Brick Layer. 31 Guignard St.
Russell, George. Ship Carpenter. 19 Lynch's Lane
Russell, John. Turner. 85 Meeting St.
Russell, Mary. 1 Lynch's Lane
Russell, Nathaniel. Merchant. 16 East Bay
Rutledge, Edward. Barrister at Law. 55 Broad St.
Rutledge, Edward, Jr. Attorney at Law. 106 Tradd St.
Rutledge, Hugh. Chancellor. 14 Short St.
Rutledge, John. Chief Justice. 82 Broad St.
Rutledge, John, Jr. Planter. 56 Meeting St.
Ryan, Peter Saul. Shop Keeper. 54 East Bay
Sader, Peter, Jr. Cigar Maker. 28 Union St.
Sansellery, Peter. Barber. 24 Elliott St.
Sarazin, Jonathan. Merchant. 3 St. Philip's St.
Sarzedas, David. Apothecary. 2 Beresford St.
Sarzedas, Moses. Merchant. 127 Broad St.
Sasportas, Abraham. Merchant. 16 Queen St.
Sass, Jacob. Cabinet Maker. 40 Queen St.
Saunders, Roger Parker. Planter. 18½ Friend St.
Sawyer, George. Shoemaker. 14 Beresford St.
Sayler, Elizabeth. 38 Elliott St.
Schaffer, Frederick. Shop Keeper. 8 Beresford St.
Schmidth & Molich. Merchants. 79 East Bay
Schultz, Daniel. Carpenter. 27½ Hasell St.
Schutt, Casper C. Merchant. 87 Broad St.
Scott, James. Grocer. 48 East Bay
Scott, William. Planter. 17 Lynch's Lane
Scotton, Susanna. 179 King St.
Scrivan, Thomas. Planter. 117 Church St.
Scrivener, James. Clerk. 130 King St.
Seabrook, Joseph. Planter. 304 King St.
Seavers, Abraham. Carpenter. 35 Pinckney St.
Secrists, Martin. Mariner. 11 Amen St.
Seilar, Michael. Tanner. Archdale St.
Selby, George. Merchant. 229 King St.
Sergeant, William. Vendue Master. 6 Church St.
Seymour, Isaac. Ship Master. 20 Lynch's Lane
Seymour, Stephen. Ship Master. 116 Church St.
Shaffer, Henry. Carter. 32 Beaufain St.
Shallier, Martin. Tailor. 19 Beresford St.
Shand, Robert. Inspector Customs. 5 Union St.
Shanks, Joseph. Mariner. 35 Meeting St.
Shapple, M. Planter. 21 Tradd St.
Shaw & Ewing. Carpenters. 59 King St.
Shaw, Elizabeth. Boarding House. 16 Elliott St.
Sheed, George. School Master. 283 King St.
Sheed, William. Apothecary. 106 King St.
Sheppard, Jane. Shop Keeper. 37 Meeting St.

Sheriff's Office. 2 Smith's Lane
Sherry, Arthur. Cooper. 13 Bedon's Alley
Shields, Edward. Store Keeper. 16 Tradd St.
Shireliff & Austin. Merchants. 45 Meeting St.
Shirer, John. Carpenter. Cumming St.
Shoolbread, James. Planter. 15 Meeting St.
Shrewsberry, Rebecca. East Bay
Shrewsberry, Stephen. Carpenter. 33 Archdale St.
Sibbins, Sisbe. Shop Keeper. 225 Meeting St.
Sibley, Lewis. Shop Keeper. 6 Moore St.
Simmons, Anthony. Factor. 285 King St.
Simmons, Charles H. Broker. 216 Meeting St.
Simmons, Vanderhorst & Co. Factors. 15 East Bay
Simmons, William. Tailor. 224 King St.
Simons, Francis. Boarding House. 9 Union St.
  Continued
Simons, Keating. Factor. 2 Pinckney St.
Simons, Samuel. 6 Price's Alley
Simons, Thomas. Factor. 70 Meeting St.
Singleton, Richard. Planter. Pitt St.
Singleton, Thomas. Tobacco Inspector. 175 King St.
Sisk, Susanna. Boarding House. 3 Union St. Continued
Skirving, Charlotte. 8 Church St.
Skirving, William. Planter. 1 South Bay
Skrine, William. Scrivener. 303 King St.
Smiser, Hannah. 56 Church St.
Smith, ——, Mrs. 83 Queen St.
Smith, ——, Mrs. Boarding House. 15 Broad St.
Smith, Archibald. Grocer. 24 Queen St.
Smith, Caleb. Shop Keeper. 51 Church St.
Smith, Christiana. School Mistress. 10 Amen St.
Smith, Daniel. Scrivener. 12 Guignard St.
Smith, James. Attorney at Law. 53 Meeting St.
Smith, James. Shop Keeper. 43 Union St.
Smith, John. Planter. 36 Church St.
Smith, John Christian. Factor. 53 King St.
Smith, John Holmes. Shop Keeper. 35 Broad St.
Smith, Josiah. Cashier, Branch Bank. 2 Meeting St.
Smith, Julius. Merchant. East Bay & Gillon
Smith, Morton. Insp. of Customs. 78 Church St.
Smith, O'Brian. Planter. 105 Queen St.
Smith, Peter. Planter. 26 Beaufain St.
Smith, Peter. Carpenter. 35 Archdale St.
Smith, Richard. 18 Hasell St.
Smith, Robert, Rev. Rector St. Philip's Church.
  Wentworth St.
Smith, Roger. Planter. 2 Orange St.
Smith, Samuel. Teller, Branch Bank. 98 Church St.
Smith, Samuel. Carpenter. 174 Meeting St.
Smith, Thomas. Ship Master. 20 Guignard St.
Smith, Thomas, Mrs. 19 Friend St.
Smith, Thomas Rhett. Attorney at Law. 30 Church St.
Smith, Whitford. Shop Keeper. 1 Queen St.
Smith, William. Tailor. 240 King St.
Smith, William. Ironmonger. 3 Broad St.
Smith, William. Merchant. East Bay
Smyth, John. Merchant. Ellery St.
Smyth, John. Shop Keeper. 239 King St.
Smyth, Robert. Planter. 19 Queen St.
Snitter, Charles. Rope Maker. 2 Rope Makers Lane
Snowden, Charles. Merchant. 67 East Bay
Solomons, Hyam. Shop Keeper. 130 Queen St.
Somersall, Thomas A. Merchant.
Somersall, William. Merchant. 2 East Bay
Somersall, William & Son. Merchants. 3 East Bay
Spears, James. Carpenter. 6 Society St.
Spering, Patrick. Shop Keeper. 212 King St.
Spiddle, Elizabeth. 6 Allen St.

45

Spiessiger, John. Organ Builder. 6 Legare St.
Spinler, Joseph. Hair Dresser. 46 East Bay
Spitzer, Bernard Moses. Broker. 2 Champney's Row
Stacker, Christopher. Butcher. 4 Allen St.
Steadman, James. Carpenter. 167 Meeting St.
Stent, Samuel. Tailor. 42 Church St.
Stephens & Ramsay. Physicians. 110 Broad St.
Stephens, William S. Physician. 11 King St.
Stevens, Cotten Mather. 256 King St.
Stevens, Daniel. Supervisor. 41 George St.
Stevens, Jarvis Henry. Deputy Sheriff. 256 Meeting St.
Stevens, William. Indigo Factor. 124 Tradd St.
Stevenson, John. Carpenter. 89 Queen St.
Stewart, Alexander. 29 King St.
Stewart, John. Tallow Chandler. 21 Union St.
Stewart, Thomas. Merchant. 29 East Bay
Stewart, William. Shop Keeper. Graehms St.
Stewarts, ——, Miss. School Mistress. 2 Kinloch Court
Stoll, Jacob. Tin Man. 129 King St.
Stoll, Sarah. 8 Allen St.
Stone & Purcell. Saddlers. 82 King St.
Stone, Barbary. 141 Meeting St.
Stone, Charles. 294 King St.
Stone, Isabella. 35 Trott St.
Stone, Love. 11 Orange St.
Stone, Samuel. Ship Master. 4 Stoll's Alley
Stoops, Benjamin T. Shoemaker. 103 Meeting St.
Stroble, Daniel. Tanner. 148 Meeting St.
Stroble, Jacob. Butcher. Magazine St.
Stromer, Henry Maine. Merchant. 49 East Bay
Sutherland, Francis. Shop Keeper. 4 Queen St.
Sutherland, George. Shop Keeper. 40 Church St.
Sutton, John. Shop Keeper. 180 Meeting St.
Sutton, Richard. Cooper. 19 Union St. Continued
Swadler, Mary. 13 Magazine St.
Swain, Joseph. Pilot. 2 Stoll's Alley
Swain, Luke. Pilot. 3 Stoll's Alley
Swinton, Hugh. Indigo Factor. 84 Meeting St.
Switzer, John Rodolph. Saddler. 234 King St.
Sylvester, Christian. Shop Keeper. Craft's Wharf
Syme, John. Shop Keeper. 139 Queen St.
Taggart, Mary. 21 Meeting St.
Tarver, John. School Master. Archdale St.
Tash, Edward. Blacksmith. 12 Queen St.
Taylor, Bennet. Merchant. 18 Broad St.
Taylor, George. Attorney at Law. 227 Meeting St.
Taylor, Joseph G. Vendue Master. 7 Cumberland St.
Taylor, Margaret. Store Keeper. 29 Elliott St.
Taylor, Paul. Carpenter. 38 Trott St.
Teasdale & Kindell. Merchants. 121 Queen St.
Teasdale, John. Merchant. 43 East Bay
Tennant, Susannah. 82 Tradd St.
Tew, Charles. Scrivener. 10 Lynch's Lane
Tew, John. Tailor. 41 Elliott St.
Tew, Thomas. Brick Layer. 19 King St.
Thayer, Ebenezer. Merchant. 52 Meeting St.
Thayer, William & J. Merchants. 31 East Bay
Therie, John Francis. Merchant. 68 East Bay
Theus, James. Merchant. 89 Church St.
Theus, Rosanna. 87 Church St.
Theus, Samuel. Vintner. 25 East Bay
Theus, Simeon. C.P. Accounts. 271 Meeting St.
Thomas, Elizabeth. Boarding House. 10 Beresford's Alley
Thomas, Francis. Grocer. 60 King St.
Thomas, James. Merchant. 31 Church St.
Thomas, John. Barber. 25 Elliott St.
Thomas, John David. Shop Keeper. 26 Union St.

Thomas, Mary Lamboll. 8 King St.
Thomas, Stephen. Tailor. 32 Elliott St.
Thompson, Daniel. Shop Keeper. South Bay
Thomson, Archibald. Ship Master. 66 East Bay
Thomson, Elizabeth. Boarding House. 28 Church St.
Thomson, James H. School Master. 30 King St.
Thomson, John. Planter. 9 Pinckney St.
Thomson, John. Ship Master. 22 Church St.
Thorn, John G. Sail Maker. 23 Guignard St.
Threadcraft, Bethel. Watch Maker. 254 King St.
Timmons, Lewis. Vendue Master. 102 Queen St.
Timothy & Mason. State Printers. 44 East Bay
Timothy, Benjamin F. Printer. 84 Broad St.
Tobias, Joseph. Shop Keeper. 202 King St.
Tonge, Mark. Shop Keeper. 60 East Bay
Tool, Michael. Tailor. 34 Union St.
Toomer, Anthony. Brick Layer. 7 Legare St.
Torrance, William H. Attorney at Law. 112 East Bay
Trenholm, William. Merchant. 18 Elliott St.
Trescot, Edward. Tax Receiver. 83 Meeting St.
Trezevant, Lewis. Attorney at Law. 43 Church St.
Trezevant, Peter. Merchant. 30 Queen St.
Trezevant, Theodore. Tailor. 43 Church St.
Troup, John. Attorney at Law. 117 Tradd St.
Tucker, Benjamin. Ship Master. 114 Church St.
Tullock, Peter. Shop Keeper. 2 Queen St.
Tunno, Adam. Merchant. 28 East Bay
Tunno, Thomas. Merchant. 22 Broad St.
Tunno, William. Merchant. East Bay
Tunnos & Cox. Merchants. 28 East Bay
Turner, Daniel Watson. Deputy Sheriff. Quince St.
Turner, Thomas. Dancing Academy. 94 Queen St.
Turpin, Hannah. Boarding House. 21 Beresford's Alley
Turpin, William. Merchant. 172 King St.
Tweed, Alexander. Planter. 111 East Bay
Tydeman, ——, Mrs. 84 Queen St.
Vacanna, ——. Joiner. Trott St.
Vale, John David. Farmer. Cumming St.
Van Ryan, & Savage. Shop Keepers. 33 Broad St.
Vanassendelft, William. Shipmaster. 23 Trott St.
Vanderhorst, Anoldus. Planter. 15 East Bay
Vansilver, ——. Physician. 113 King St.
Vardell, Elizabeth. 19 King St.
Vardell, Robert. Tailor. 10 Bedon's Alley
Vercnocke & Cockle. Merchants. 4 Bedon's Alley
Veree, Joseph. Scrivener. 13 Church St.
Vesey, Joseph. Merchant. 280 King St.
Vesier, M. 16 Beresford St.
Villepontoux, Jane. 5 East Bay
Villeret, Mary. 13 Allen St.
Virgin, George. Shop Keeper. 43 Tradd St.
Vliex, Frederick. Barber. 25 Church St.
Vos & Graves. Merchants. Society St.
Vos, Andrew. Merchant. 17 East Bay
Wadsworth & Turpin. Merchants. 171 King St.
Wagner, Christopher. Drayman. 6 Trott St.
Wagner, George. Merchant. 85 Broad St.
Wagner, John. Planter. 85 Broad St.
Wainwright, Richard. Planter. 286 King St.
Wall, Richard Gilbert. Vintner. 36 Queen St.
Wallis, Hugh. Painter. 33 Tradd St.
Wallis, James. Custon House Boat. Champney's Row
Wallis, Thomas. Cabinet Maker. 231 Meeting St.
Wallis, William. Cabinet Maker. 175 Meeting St.
Ward, John. Attorney at Law. Lamboll St.
Ward, Joshua. Counsellor. 255 Meeting St.
Ward, Love. 12 Church St.
Warham, Charles. Planter. 100 Tradd St.

Waring, John. Planter. Federal St.
Waring, Mary. 69 Meeting St.
Waring, Thomas. Factor. 40 Meeting St.
Warley, Elizabeth. 30 Beaufain St.
Warley, Feliz. Clerk the Senate. 44 Trott St.
Warnock, Joseph. Boarding House. 74½ East Bay
Warson, Thomas. Carpenter. 5 Stoll's Alley
Washington, William. Planter. 1 Church St.
Waties, Thomas. Associate Judge. 20 Legare St.
Watson, Alexander. Factor. 107 East Bay
Watson, Isaac. Shop Keeper. 274 King St.
Watson, John. Upholsterer. 104 Church St.
Watson, Joseph. Hair Dresser. 98 Broad St.
Watts, Charles. Cabinet Maker. 5 Market Square
Weaver, Peter. Shoemaker. 151 King St.
Webb, John. Merchant. 14 Moore St.
Webster, Thomas. Pilot. Wyatt's Square
Welch, George. Tobacconist. 19 Trott St.
Welch, John. Tobacco Inspector. Boundary St.
Welch, Mary. Boarding House. 61 Meeting St.
Welch, Thomas. Baker. 2 Union St.
Wells, Edgar & Son. Merchants. 10 Broad St.
Wells, Richard. Pinckney St.
Werthing, John. Butcher. 8 Burn's Lane
Weslinger, John. Baker. 181 King St.
Wesner, Philip. Public House. 261 King St.
West, Thomas Wade. Comedian. 78 Tradd St.
Westermyer, Andrew. Silversmith. 23 Church St.
Weston, John Holybush. Attorney at Law. 37 Queen St.
Weston, Plowden. Planter. 37 Queen St.
Weyman, Edward. Surveyor Customs. 8 Chambers' Alley
White, Blake Leay. Carpenter. 41 King St.
White, James. Shop Keeper. 136 Church St.
White, John. Factor. 12 Ellery St.
White, Sims. Factor. 12 Ellery St.
White, William & Co. Merchants. 1 Bedon's Alley
Whiteman, William. Silversmith. 226 Meeting St.
Whitfield & Brown. Merchants. 2 Bedon's Alley
Whitley, Moses. 35 Guignard St.
Whittimore, Reteen. Joiner. 44 Church St.
Wileseks, Jeremiah. Painter. 5 Beresford's Alley
Wilki, William. Factor. 11 East Bay
Wilkins, James. Carpenter. Wentworth St.
Willeman, Christopher. Tanner. 247 King St.
Williams, Elizabeth. 13 Legare St.
Williams, Isham. Ship Carpenter. 103 East Bay
Williams, John. Coffee House. 128 Tradd St.
Williams, John M. Ship Carpenter. 4 Charles St.
Williams, Joseph. Tailor. Hasell St.
Williams, Margaret. 60 Queen St.
Williman, Jacob. Tanner. Montague St.
Wilson & M'Kinnon. Tailors. 105½ Church St.
Wilson, John. Cabinet Maker. 95 Meeting St.
Wilson, Robert. Apothecary. 13 Broad St.
Wilson, Samuel. Physician. 101 Broad St.
Wilson, Sarah. 4 Church St.
Winstanley, Thomas. Attorney at Law. Scarborough
Winthrop, Joseph. Merchant. East Bay
Winthrop, Joseph. Merchant. 90 Tradd St.
Wish, Benjamin. Carpenter. 61 Queen St.
Withers, Rebecca. 8 Cumberland St.
Wittick, Charles. Silversmith. 237 Meeting St.
Wood, Thomas. Physician. 84 East Bay
Wood, William. Inspector Customs. 5 Hopkins Lane
Woolf, Frederick. Shop Keeper. 17 Union St.
Woolf, Henry. Shop Keeper. 232 King St.

Woolf, Matthias. Butcher. Mazyck St.
Wragg, John. Planter. 12 Union St. Continued
Wragg, William. Planter. 86 East Bay
Wrainch, John. Clerk to Commis. 52 King St.
Wrainch, Richard. Shop Keeper. 51 King St.
Wright, James. Baker. 42 Tradd St.
Wyatt, John. Carpenter. Wyatt's Square
Wyatt, Richard. Carpenter. 6 Amen St.
Yates, Seth. Ship Carpenter. 21 Lynch's Lane
Yates, William. Shop Keeper. 179 Union St.
Yoer, G. & S. Shoemakers. 97 Queen St.
Young, George. Butcher. 5 Guignard St.
Young, Hugh. Shop Keeper. 96½ Church St.
Young, Sarah. 81 Tradd St.
Young, Susannah. 257 Meeting St.
Young, William Price. Printer, Bookseller. 43 Broad St.
Zealy, ——, Mrs. Shop Keeper. 297 King St.
Zylestra, Peter. Shop Keeper. 31 Elliott St.

CHAPTER 6

THE 1796 DIRECTORY

The 1796 directory was published as *Clarke's Charleston Directory; With, a Large and Elegant Plan of the City, Engraved by Ralph, One of the First American Artists* (Charleston: S. J. Elliott, 1796). While Elliott can be found listed as a printer in the directory, Clarke is not there. Therefore, his full name is not known. Also, the map listed in the title has not survived.

The directory for 1796 has 1255 entries or 270 less than the 1794 volume. It also has only 200 women and for these only 79 have their first names listed. Obviously, the compiler did a less thorough canvass than had the previous ones in 1790 and 1794.

Business locations tended to be concentrated on King Street 18% (223 of 1249), Meeting Street 12%, Church Street 7%, Tradd Street 6%, and Broad Street 6%. The number for each location: Amen Street 3, Anson Street 1, Archdale Street 4, Beale's Wharf 5, Beaufain Street 12, Bedon's Alley 3, Beresford Street 9, Beresford's Alley 3, Blake's Wharf 1, Broad Street 75, Burchmyer's Alley 3, Chambers Alley 2, Champney's Row 3, Champney's Way 1, Champney's Wharf 2, Charles Street 1, Church Alley 2, Church Street 92, Church Street Continued 1, Coats' Row 4, Common Street 1, Crafts 4th Range 3, Crafts North Range 2, Crafts Range 1, Charts Row 1, Crafts South Range 4, Crafts Wharf 3, Cumberland Street 2, Cumming's Street 2, East Bay 129, Ellery Street 12, Elliot Street 28, Exchange 2, Federal Street 12, Fiddy's Row 3, Fish Market 1, Fort Mechanic 1, Friend Street 8, Gaillard's Wharf 2, George Street 15, Geyer's Range 2, Geyer's Wharf 2, Gibbes Street 2, Gillon Street 3, Guignard Street 20, Harleston's Green 2, Hasell Street 24, King Street 223, Legare Street 6, Liberty Street 11, Lodge Alley 3, Longitude Lane 4, Lynch's Lane 5, Magazine Street 1, Maiden Lane 10, Market Square 1, Mazyck Street 6, Meeting Street 145, Montague Street 4, Moore Street 7, Nichols Wharf 1, Orange Street 6, Parsonage Alley 3, Pinckney Street 33, Pitt Street 3, Price's Alley 1, Pritchard's Wharf 1, Prioleau's Wharf 1, Queen Street 45, Quince Street 5, Shevers Alley 1, Short Street 3, Smith Street 1, Smith's Lane 1, Society Street 8, South Bay 8, St. Philip's Street 9, Stoll's Alley 7, Tradd Street 80, Trott Street 36, Union Street 21, Union Street Continued 11, Unity Alley 2, Vanderhorst's Wharf, Water Street 1, Wentworth Street 14, White's Alley 1, Wragg's Alley 1, Wyatt's Lot 2.

The directory gives professions for 1177 people including 121 as widows, 1 as madam, and 35 as gentlemen. Discounting theses, merchants were 20% of those listed with a profession, grocers 10%, carpenter 6%, shops and stores 5/%, planters 5%, factor 4%, and attorneys 3%. This is an instance where the definitions of the compiler of the directory are different from the previous one. Merchants and grocers make up a considerably higher percentage than before while shop or store keepers are less.

The number for each profession is: accountant 2, attorney 32, attorney general 1, attorney S.C. District 1, auctioneer 19, baker 13, bishop 1, blacksmith 4, block maker 3, boarding house 17, book binder 1, bookkeeper 3, booksellers 1, brass founder 1, brick layer 12, British consul 1, broker 6, butcher 12, cabinet maker 14, captain 25, carpenter 46, carter 5, cashier 1, chair maker 2, chancellor 1, chancellor French consulate 1, cigar maker 1, city scavenger 1, city treasurer 1, clerk 14, clock maker 6, coach maker 6, coffee house 2, collector of customs 1, collector of revenue 2, colonel 3, confectioner 5, constable 1, consul of France 1, conveyancer 1, cooper 2, custom house officer 4, D.D 1, dancing master 1, dentist 1, deputy sheriff 1, distiller 3, doctor 7, drawing master 1, drayman 2, druggist 4, dry goods store 1, engraver 2, factor 39, federal marshall 1, fisherman 1, fruit shop 2, general 1, gentleman 35, glazier 1, goldsmith 3, governor 1, grocer 99, gauger 1, gunsmith 3, hair dresser 7, harness maker 2, hatter 2, high priest Jewish synagogue 1, inspector 4, insurance broker 1, intendant 1, ironmonger 2, jailer 1, jeweller 6, judge 5, keeper of Poor

House 1, laborer 1, last maker 1, late chief justice 1, librarian 1, limner 1, livery stable 3, loan office 1, lumber measurer 4, madam 1, magistrate 4, major 2, mantua maker 1, mariner 9, master in chancery 1, measurer 1, merchant 207, merchant tailor 1, midwife 3, milliner 3, minister 6, music instrument maker 1, musician 1, notary public 2, nurse 2, organist 1, painter 14, physician 23, pilot 3, planter 46, portrait painter, powder receiver 1, preceptor 4, president of S.C. Bank 1, president of S.C. Senate 1, printer 6, professor of music 1, pump maker 1, revenue officer 1, rigger 1, saddler 6, sail maker 2, school master 2, school mistress 2, senior commission loan office 1, senior shipwright 1, ship bread baker 1, ship carpenter 11, ship chandler 3, ship joiner 2, ship rigger 1, shipwright 1, shoe Warehouse 1, shoemaker 20, shop keeper 27, silversmith 4, Spanish consul 1, starch manufacturer 1, state treasurer 1, stay maker 1, store keeper 19, surgeon 1, surveyor 2, tailor 26, tanner 8, tavern keeper 4, tax collector 1, teacher 4, tide waiter 2, tin plate worker 3, tobacconist 4, upholsterer 2, usher 1, vendue master 1, watch maker 5, watchman 1, wharfinger 1, wheelwright, widow 121, wine merchant 1.

Listings follow the names of only 166 women. When the 121 widows and 1 madam are substracted, this leaves only 44 women with actual occupations. They are: baker 1, boarding house 9, butcher 1, cigar maker 1, coffee house 1, confectioner 1, dry goods store 1, grocer 2, midwife 3, millinter 3, nurse 1, saddler 1, school mistress 2, shopkeeper 10, store keeper 4, and tavern keeper 2.

Abrahams, Jacob. Grocer. 5 Queen St.
Abrahams, Moses. Gentleman. 46 Queen St.
Adams, Ann. Store Keeper. 90 East Bay
Aers, Charles. Painter. 30 Queen St.
Aertsen & Co. Auctioneers. Under the Exchange
Akeen, Thomas. Grocer. 26 Pinckney St.
Akin, Ann. Widow. 108 Church St.
Alexander, Alexander. Silversmith. Liberty St.
Alexander, David. Merchant. 9 Broad St.
Alexander, James. Grocer. 9 East Bay St.
Alexander, James. Grocer. 1 Queen St.
Alexander, William. Grocer. 10 Pinckney St.
Allen & Ewing. Merchants. 120 Tradd St.
Allston, William. Planter. 9 King St.
Allwright, James. Grocer. 176 Meeting St.
Ancrum, William. Gentleman. 13 Ellery St.
Anderson, Robert. Store Keeper. 19 Tradd St.
Anderson, William. Stay-Maker. 247 Meeting St.
Andrews & Pendergrast. Teachers. 49 Meeting St.
Anthony, John. Harness Maker. 234 Meeting St.
Appleton, John. Carpenter. 26 Meeting St.
Armstrong, Fleetwood. Gentleman. 172 Meeting St.
Armstrong, William. Saddler. 189 King St.
Ash, ——, Mrs. Widow. Guignard St.
Ash, ——, Mrs. Widow. 15 King St.
Ash, John. Planter. South Bay
Ashton, ——. Widow. 5 Maiden Lane
Atmar, Ralph. Silversmith. 50 Meeting St.
Audley, Mary. 9 Tradd St.
Austen, Robert. Tailor. 50 East Bay
Austin, William. Merchant. George St.
Axson, William. Lumber Measurer. 17 King St.
Azebi, Abraham. High Priest Jewish Synagogue. 207 King St.
Azuley, Isaac. Gentleman. 4 King St.
Baas, John. Captain. 88 East Bay
Baas, Thomas. Block Maker. 22 Hasell St.
Badger, James. Painter. Beresford's Alley
Badger, Jonathan. Painter. 8 St. Phillip's St.
Badger, Joseph. Painter. 17 Pinckney St.
Bailey & Waller. Booksellers. 27 Elliot St.
Bailey, Henry. Attorney at Law. 2 Moore St.
Baker, ——. Widow. 10 Church St.
Baker, Joseph. Carpenter. 13 Hasell St.
Ball, ——. Widow. 15 Church St.
Ball, Ann. Widow. 17 Church St.
Ball, John. Planter. Hasell St.
Ball, Thomas. 14 Lynch's Lane
Ball, Thomas. Factor. Vanderhorst's Wharf
Ballentine, ——. Widow. 114 Church St.
Ballentine, James. Brick Layer. 114 Church St.
Ballon, Andrew. Hair Dresser. 137 Queen St.
Banks, Charles & Co. Merchants. 128 Tradd St.
Baptist, ——. Madam. 6 Elliot St.
Barratt, Solomon. Merchant. 65 King St.
Barre, David. Grocer. 12 Church St.
Barron, Alexander. Physician. 82 East Bay
Bartet, ——. Widow. 11 Hasell St.
Bateman, Bernard. Block Maker. 109 East Bay
Bay, ——. Judge. 239 Meeting St.
Beale, John. Gentleman. 33 East Bay
Beard, ——, Mrs. Widow. 88 Broad St.
Beareau, James. Boarding House. 27 Queen St.

Beattie, William. Store Keeper. 169 King St.
Beaufort, Charles. 38 King St.
Beckman, Adam. Glazier. 189 Meeting St.
Bee, ——. Judge. 100 Church St.
Bee, ——. Widow. 7 Trott St.
Bee, William. Merchant. 7 Trott St.
Beekman, ——. Colonel. East Bay, corner Hasell St.
Beekman, Samuel. Pump Maker. 112 Queen St.
Belemy, ——. Widow. 35 King St.
Beleugey, ——. Printer. 100 Queen St.
Bell & Co. Grocers. 121 East Bay
Bell, David & George. Merchants. 25 Church St.
Bell, William. Grocer. 248 King St.
Benneis, Francis. Carpenter. 57 Meeting St.
Bennett, ——. Widow. 21 Trott St.
Bennett, Peter. Captain. 12 Lynch's Lane
Bentham, James. Magistrate. 39 East Bay
Beresford, Richard. Gentleman. 14 Friend St.
Bering, John. Jeweller. 125 Broad St.
Berney, John & Co. Merchants. 88 East Bay
Berry, Alexander. Shoemaker. 35 King St.
Bezlewtue, Lewis. Cabinet Maker. 30 Beaufain St.
Binoist, ——. Widow, Fruit Shop. 33 Church St.
Bissiere, Anthony. Tailor. 35 Church St.
Black, John. Merchant. 12 Broad St.
Black, Nathaniel. Carpenter. 7 Ellery St.
Blackford, Edward. Merchant. 99 Church St.
Blackie, Elizabeth. 14 Church St.
Blacklock, William. Merchant. 1 Crafts' South Range
Blacklock, William. Merchant. 31 Tradd St.
Blair, John. Ship Carpenter. 111 East Bay
Blair, William. Grocer. 121 King St.
Blake, John. Factor. South Bay
Blakely, Samuel. Merchant. 28 Broad St.
Blamyer, William. Librarian. 108 Church St.
Blandel, Peter. Attorney at Law. 19 Society St.
Bocquet, ——. Widow. 178 King St.
Bold & Rhodes. Merchants. 132 Tradd St.
Bollough, Elias. Beresford's Alley
Boone, Thomas. Carpenter. 5 Ellery St.
Booth, ——. Widow. 61 Meeting St.
Booth & Co. Merchants. 18 Elliot St.
Bougneuf, John. Gentleman. 21 Society St.
Boulinger, ——. Widow, Baker. 133 Queen St.
Bourdeaux, Daniel. Merchant. 23 Beaufain St.
Bowman, John. Planter. Wentworth St.
Boyd, Benjamin. Merchant. 139 King St.
Bozman, Ralph. Tailor. 98 King St.
Bradford, ——, Mrs. Store Keeper. 30 Broad St.
Bradford, Thomas. Musician. 31 Church St.
Brailsford, Samuel. 1 Friend St.
Brash, Charles. Inspector. 5 Gillon St.
Breant, John. Planter. 39 Pinckney St.
Bremar, Francis. Bookkeeper. 6 Wentworth St.
Brenford, ——, Mrs. 35 Meeting St.
Bridie, ——, Mrs. School Mistress. 15 Meeting St.
Brightman, George & Co. Blacksmiths. Ellery St.
Brindley, Stephen. Pilot. Maiden Lane
Brockway, Jeffe. Boarding House. 180 King St.
Brodie, Thomas. Factor. Cummings St.
Brooker, Anthony. Shoemaker. 32 Queen St.
Broughton, ——, Miss. 103 Tradd St.
Broughton, Peter. Planter. 122 East Bay

Brown, ——, Mrs. 99 Tradd St.
Brown & Mair. Merchants. 24 East Bay
Brown, Archibald. Factor. 22 Hasell St.
Brown, Codington & Co. Merchants. 8 Crafts' South Range
Brown, Daniel. Captain. 131 Church St.
Brown, George. Tailor. 1 Elliot St.
Brown, James. Merchant. 242 King St.
Brown, Jeremiah. Hasell St.
Brown, John. Merchant. 15 Broad St.
Brown, Joshua. Grocer. 297 King St.
Brown, Samuel. Merchant. 26 Elliot St.
Brown, Samuel. Shop Keeper. 152 King St.
Brown, Susannah. Midwife. 197 King St.
Brownlee, John. Merchant. 208 King St.
Bruckner, Daniel. Merchant. 49 King St.
Buchanan, Jacob. Gunsmith. 26 Queen St.
Buckle, ——, Mrs. 56 Broad St.
Bueld, ——, Mrs. Widow. 77 East Bay
Buist, George Rev. D.D. 3 Church St.
Bulet, ——, Mrs. Widow. 34 King St.
Bulgin, John. Merchant. 3 Crafts' South Range
Bulow, Charles. Merchant. 183 King St.
Bulow, John. Merchant. 183 King St.
Bunten, William. Shoemaker. 5 King St.
Burckmyer, John. Butcher. Wentworth St.
Burdenare, B. Peter. Tailor. 34 King St.
Burger, David. Gunsmith. 106 Queen St.
Burke, ——. Judge. 135 Church St.
Burn, James. Planter. 77 East Bay
Burns, James. Cabinet Maker. 136 Church St.
Buttler, Charles P. Jeweller. 225 King St.
Byre, John B. Shop Keeper. 147 Meeting St.
Byrne, Patrick. Hasell St.
Bythewood, Daniel D. 8 Pinckney St.
Bythewood, Thomas G. Captain. 26 Hasell St.
Cairoche, ——, Mr. Chancllor French Consulate. St. Philip's St.
Calder, Alex. Cabinet Maker. 248 Meeting St.
Caldwell, Henry, Jr. Grocer. 107 Church St.
Caldwell, Henry, Sr. Grocer. 106 Church St.
Caldwell, Joseph. Grocer. 215 Meeting St.
Calhoun, William. Merchant. East Bay
Callaghen, John. Merchant. 39 Tradd St.
Calvert, Elizabeth. Boarding House. 110 Queen St.
Cambridge, Tobias. Auctioneer. 5 Beale's Wharf
Cameron, Alexander. Grocer. 77 King St.
Cameron, Robert & Co. Merchants. 137 Tradd St.
Campbell, David. Planter. 6 Legare St.
Campbell, Denoon & Co. Auctioneers. 4 Gillon St., cr
Campbell, Douglas. Ship Rigger. 48 Hasell St.
Campbell, Henry & Co. Merchants. 7 Tradd St.
Campbell, Laurence. Auctioneer. St. Philip's St.
Camsen, Harman. Carpenter. Mazyck St.
Cannon, Daniel. Carpenter. 23 Queen St.
Cantee, ——, Mrs. Widow. 172 Meeting St.
Cantey, ——. Widow. 93 Tradd St.
Cantey, Henry & Co. Merchants. 36 East Bay
Cantor, Gasua. Limner. 260 King St.
Cantor, Jacob & Co. Brokers. Crafts' Wharf
Cape, Brian & Son. Factors & Insurance. 80 East Bay
Capwielle, Peter. Clerk. 110 Church St.
Cardoz, David. Measurer. Federal St.
Carey, ——, Mr. Teacher. 36 Trott St.
Carne, John. 32 Guignard St.
Carpenter, Hannah. Shop Keeper. 277 King St.
Carr, Wilder Richard. Merchant. 42 East Bay
Carrell, Daniel. Jeweller. 124 Broad St.

Carren, John B. Captain. 104 Tradd St.
Carson, ——, Mr. Planter. 9 Meeting St.
Cart, John. Factor. George St.
Carter, George. Physician. 118 Tradd St.
Casey, Benjamin. Coach Maker. 147 Meeting St.
Cattell, Frances. Widow. 10 Beresford St.
Caveneo, James. Carter. 12 Pinckney St.
Chalmers, B. John. Federal St.
Chalmers, Gilbert. Carpenter. 24 Beaufain St.
Champneys, John. Gentleman. 94 King St.
Chanler, ——. Physician. 54 Broad St.
Charles, James. Baker. 35 Tradd St.
Chevas, Alexander. Merchant. 96 King St.
Chicester, ——. Physician. Meeting St.
Chisolm, Alexander. Planter. 307 King St.
Chitty, Ann. 114 King St.
Chitty, John William. Grocer. 114 King St.
Chouler, Joseph. Druggist. 131 Broad St.
Christian, ——, Mrs. Widow. 13 Trott St.
Christian, William. Ship Carpenter. 6 Maiden Lane
Christie, Alexander. Baker. 104 Queen St.
Christie, Edward. Merchant. 14 Broad St.
Claret, James. Confectioner. 28 Church St.
Clark, ——, Mrs. Widow. 7 Pinckney St.
Clark, David. Watch Maker. 3 Price's Alley
Clark, John. Grocer. 123 Church St.
Clark, Mary. Shop Keeper. 146 Meeting St.
Clarkson, Alexander. Baker. 113 Tradd St.
Clarkson, William. Planter. 71 King St.
Claude, Delcol. 8 Cumberland St.
Cleapor, Charles. Sail Maker. 146 East Bay
Cleffey, Raimond. Saddler & Harness. 37 Church St.
Clime, Mary. Widow. 138 King St.
Clitheral, James. Planter. 17 Legare St.
Coats, ——, Mrs. Tavern Keeper. 63 East Bay
Cochran, ——. Captain Revenue Cutter. 75 Meeting St.
Cochran, Charles. Federal Marshall. 75 Meeting St.
Cochran, Margrot. Store Keeper. 267 King St.
Cochran, Robert. Grocer. 86 King St.
Cochran, Thomas. Planter. 140 East Bay
Coetoes, ——. Madam. Store Keeper. 10 Queen St.
Cohen, Gershom. Merchant. 105 King St.
Cohen, Jacob. Merchant. 132 King St.
Cohen, Jacob. Auctioneer. 1 Fiddy's Row
Cohen, Moses. Store Keeper. 191 King St.
Coiles, Margaret. Widow. 16 Pinckney St.
Colcock, ——, Mrs. Widow. 104 Queen St.
Colcock & Paterson. Auctioneers. Back of Exchange
Cole, Ruth. Widow. Federal St.
Collins, Mary. Widow. 12 Hasell St.
Condy, Jeremiah. Merchant. 218 Meeting St.
Connolly, ——. Captain. 22 Meeting St.
Conquereau, Charles. Cabinet Maker. 284 King St.
Consider, John. Store Keeper. 200 King St.
Conte, Signeret. Grocer. 104 King St.
Conyers, John. Auctioneer. 285 King St.
Cook, Eleanor. Shop Keeper. 57 East Bay
Cooper, Sarah. Widow. 2 Short St.
Coram, ——. Engraver. 81 Queen St.
Corbet, Samuel. Tavern Keeper. 233 Meeting St.
Corbett & Son. Merchants. 1 Crafts' Range
Corbie, ——, Mrs. Boarding House. 237 King St.
Corcoran, ——, Mrs. Shop Keeper. 56 King St.
Corre & Schepeler. Merchants. 76 East Bay
Cote, John. Ship Carpenter. 111 East Bay
Cotton & Statler. Carvers & Guilders. 20 Trott St.
Countee, Thomas. Factor. Gaillard's Wharf

Courtney, Edward. Merchant. 58 East Bay
Courtney, Humphrey. Merchant. 44 Meeting St.
Courtney, James. Merchant Tailor. 44 Meeting St.
Covie, ----, Mrs. Widow. 14 Beresford St.
Covie, Daniel, Mrs. Widow. 18 Beresford St.
Cowan, Abraham. Store Keeper. 199 King St.
Cowan, Mordecai. Merchant. 225 King St.
Cowie, John. Grocer. 40 Tradd St.
Cox, James. Merchant. 10 Lynch's Lane
Cox, Martha. 128 Church St.
Cox, Susannah. Widow. 11 & 12 Federal St.
Crafts, Ralph. Grocer. 5 King St.
Crafts, William. Merchant. 23 Hasell St.
Cranten, William. Grocer. 24 Church St.
Crater, Jane. Widow. Parsonage Alley
Cripps, John S. Merchant. 31 Broad St.
Crocker, Hichborn & Wright. Merchants. 8 Champney's Wharf
Cross & Crowley. Merchants. 41 East Bay
Cross, George. Merchant. 5 Society St.
Cross, John. Carpenter. Pitt St.
Cross, Matthew William. Brick Layer. 231 King St.
Crow, Edward. Inspector Customs. Longitude Lane
Crowley, Michael. Merchant. 235 King St.
Cruger, ----, Mrs. Widow. 14 Maiden Lane
Cruger, David. Factor. Prioleau's Wharf
Crukshank, Daniel. Shoemaker. 126 Queen St.
Crukshank, William. Shoemaker. 3 Elliot St.
Cudworth, Benjamin. Revenue Officer. 16 Trott St.
Cudworth, Nathaniel. Inspector Customs. 16 King St.
Culliatt, James. Coach maker. 11 Church Alley
Cultisen, Elizabeth. Church Alley
Cunningham, Charles. Merchant. 161 King St.
Cunningham, John. Merchant. 146 King St.
Cunnington, William. Magistrate. 40 East Bay
Currie, John. Grocer. 68 Meeting St.
Curtis, ----, Mrs. Widow. 3 Beresford St.
Custer, James. Accountant. 7 Maiden Lane
D'Aquilar, ----, Madam. 138 King St.
D'Azevedo, Isaac. Merchant. 74 King St.
DaCosta, Isaac. Planter. 204 King St.
DaCosta, Isaac. Merchant. 16 Hasell St., corner King
Daniel, Margaret. Widow. 115 Church St.
Daray & Fowavet. Carpenters. 9 Guignard St.
Darby, John. Goldsmith. 6 Pinckney St.
Darrell, Edward & Co. Merchants. 25 East Bay
Darrell, Edward, Jr. N.P., Attorney. Broad St.
Dart, Benjamin. Merchant. 28 Tradd St.
Dart, John. Attorney at Law. 28 Tradd St.
Dart, John Sandford. Gentleman. 23 Trott St.
Daulton, Peter. Captain. Lodge Alley
Davidson, Gilbert & John. Merchants. 16 Broad St.
Davis & Reid. Insurance Brokers. 21 East Bay
Davis, John M. Broker. 13 Guignard St.
Davis, Thomas. Store Keeper. 11 Tradd St.
Dawson, ----, Mrs. 85 Tradd St.
Dawson, John, Jr. Merchant. 14 Broad St.
Dawson, John, Sr. Gentleman. 93 East Bay
Deas, ----, Mrs. 104 East Bay
Deas, David. Attorney at Law. 104 East Bay
Debarre, James. 41 Trott St.
DeBowe, John. 119 King St.
Delaire, James. 10 Orange St.
DeLajenchere, ----, Mr. Brick Maker. 22 Society St.
DelaLane, ----. Wyatt's Lot
DelaLasane, ----, Mrs. Widow. 108 East Bay
Deleon, Israel. Auctioneer. 131 King St.
Deleon, Jacob. Auctioneer. Mazyck Street

Deleon, Jacob, Jr. Auctioneer. Fiddy's Row
Delie, ----, Mrs. Widow. 34 Trott St.
Delser, Christian. Butcher. 160 Meeting St.
Dener, George. Tanner & Currier. 6 Mazyck St.
Dennis, Richard. Merchant. 1 Hasell St.
Denny, ----. Physician. 113 King St.
Denny, James. Tobacconist. 18 Guignard St.
Denny, Samuel. Saddler. 111 King St.
Deoagar, Moses. 101 King St.
Depestre, Hector. Gentleman. Cummings St.
Depetievilie, Anthony. Drawing Master. Longitude Lane
Desaussure & Graves. Factors. 2 Crafts' Row
Desaussure, Daniel. Factor. 249 Meeting St.
Desaussure, Henry William. Attorney at Law. 29 Tradd St.
Deschamps, Joseph & Co. Merchants. 25 Broad St.
Desel, Charles. Cabinet Maker. 45 King St.
Desel, Charles. Cabinet Maker. 51 Broad St.
Deveaux, B. Attorney at Law. 24 Meeting St.
Deveaux, Israel. Physician. 126 Tradd St.
Deveaux, Jacob. Factor. 24 Meeting St.
Deveaux, Jacob & Son. Factors. Vanderhorst's Wharf
Dewar, Robert. Merchant. 93 Tradd St.
Dickens, Edward. Merchant. 115 East Bay
Dickenson, Jeremiah. Captain. 9 Cumberland St.
Dickenson, Joseph. Carpenter. Magazine St.
Dickson, Samuel. Preceptor. 150 King St.
Dierson, Martin. Carpenter. 5 Union St.
Dill, ----, Mrs. 295 King St.
Dill, Joseph. 294 King St.
Disher, Mary. Widow. 115 East Bay
Dodsworth, Ralph. Merchant. 15 Elliot St.
Dollane, ----, Mrs. Widow. 1 Union St. Continued
Donald, Robert. Attorney at Law. George St.
Donaldson, James. Carpenter. 116 Tradd St.
Donaldson, Mary. 22 Tradd St.
Donnall, Patrick. Grocer. 124 Church St.
Doughty, Thomas. Factor. 59 Meeting St.
Doughty, William. Merchant. 203 Meeting St.
Douglas, Nathaniel. Merchant. 94 Church St.
Douglass, Archibald. Grocer. 100 King St.
Downs, Jeremiah. Mariner. 6 Pinckney St.
Doyley, ----, Mrs. Widow. 82 Queen St.
Drayton, Jacob. Clerk Court Common Pleas. 49 Broad St.
Drayton, John. Attorney at Law. 84 Queen St.
Drennis, George. Baker. 34 Beaufain St.
Drummond, Ann. Widow. 9 Guignard St.
Drummond, John. Shoemaker. 2 Broad St.
Dryburgh, James. Carpenter. 9 Guignard St.
Dubert, Frederick. Tailor. 181 King St.
Duffy, Bernard. Grocer. 19 East Bay
Dulles, Joseph. Ironmonger. 35 East Bay
Dumont, William. Physician. George St.
Duncan, John. Merchant. 4 Champney's Row
Dupre, Benjamin. Tailor. 78 East Bay
Durat, Estradier. Madam. 226 King St.
Dursse & Menute. Grocers. 120 King St.
Eames, ----, Mrs. Boarding House. 4 Gillon St.
Easton, Susannah. Widow. Montague St.
Eberley, John. Baker. 27 Guignard St.
Eckhard, Jacob. Prof. of Music. 6 Beresford St.
Eddings, William. Planter. 4 Stoll's Alley
Edwards, James. Store Keeper. 108 Tradd St.
Edwards, John. Intendant. 7 Meeting St.
Egliston, John. Store Keeper. 157 King St.
Egner, Mary. Widow. 11 Beresford St.

Ehney, Catharine. Widow. Magazine St.
Ehrick, John. Grocer. 52 East Bay
Elf, Thomas. Cabinet Maker. 116 Queen St.
Elizer, Isaac. Merchant. 206 King St.
Elliot, Charles R. Painter & Glazier. 16 Queen St.
Elliot, Thomas. Planter. 2 Gibb's St.
Elliott, Samuel John. Printer. 47 East Bay
Ellison, Henry. Merchant. 1 Coats' Row
Ellsworth, Theophilus. Gauger. 132 East Bay
English, Dominick. Grocer. 127 Church St.
Erambert, August. Shop Keeper. 6 Union St.
Ernest, Jacob. Tailor. 26 Queen St.
Ewing, Alexander. Merchant. 103 Church St.
Ewing, Robert & Adam. Merchants. 125 Tradd St.
Eyre, Daniel. Pilot. 2 King St.
Eyre, Rebecca. Widow. 7 Pinckney St.
Fabre, Christopher John Rev. Minister. 28 Archdale St.
Fabre, Francis. Mariner. 3 Hasell St.
Faesch, ——, Mrs. Widow. 167 King St.
Fair, Robert. Shoemaker. 93 King St.
Fair, William. Shoe Warehouse. 26 Broad St.
Fair, William. Factor. 62 Meeting St.
Fairchild, Aaron. Blacksmith. 117 Pinckney St.
Fallait, Balanal. Widow. 27 Wentworth St.
Farrath, Sinerth. Gentleman. 109 King St.
February, Margaret. Widow. Federal St.
Fell, Eliza. Milliner. 23 Broad St.
Ferguson, Ann. Widow. Liberty St.
Ferotain, ——, Mr. Hatter. 14 Queen St.
Ferrice, Joseph. Shoemaker. 278 King St.
Ferulahegue, Keevi. Gentleman. 134 King St.
Fey, Charles. Boarding House. 32 King St.
Fiddy, William. Auctioneer. 1 Fiddy's Row
Fields, William B. Tobacconist. 7 Ellery St.
Fisher, Edward. Clerk. 16 South Bay
Fitsimons, Mary. Widow. 27 King St.
Flagg, George. Painter & Glazier. 4 Queen St.
Flagg, George, Jr. Carpenter. Maiden Lane
Flagg, Samuel H. Dentist. 30 Elliot St.
Fleming, Robert. Grocer. 117 King St.
Fletcher, John. Painter & Glazier. 250 Meeting St.
Flint, Joseph. Grocer. 31 Union St.
Flint, Joseph. Grocer. 5 Champneys' Row
Florin, Lucas. 33 Guignard St.
Flotto & Knapping. Merchants. 17 Elliot St.
Floyd, Thomas. Physician. 60 King St.
Fogartie, James. Merchant. 20 Broad St.
Folker, John C. Shoemaker. St. Philip's St.
Ford, Timothy. Attorney at Law. 30 King St.
Forest, ——. 17 Friend St.
Forrest, George. Merchant. 4 Hasell St.
Forrest, Joanna. Widow. 97 Queen St.
Forsyth, Thomas. Grocer. 225 Queen St., corner Meeting
Foster, Thomas. Gentleman. 305 King St.
Fowke, ——, Mrs. Widow. 16 Church St.
Fowler & Brodie. Carpenters. 4 Longitude Lane
Fowler, Mathias. Hair Dresser. 4 Coats' Row
Fowler, Samuel. Rigger. 2 King St.
Francis, David. Captain. Federal St.
Fraser, Alexander, Mrs. Widow. 22 King St.
Fraser, Thomas. Merchant. Pitt St.
Fraser, William. Attorney at Law. 89 Broad St.
Frederick, John. Shop Keeper. 5 Meeting St.
Freeman, ——, Mr. Gentleman. 102 Tradd St.
Freneau & Paine. Printers. 46 East Bay
Freneau, Peter. Printer. George St.

Friend, George. Baker. 39 Union St.
Friend, Ulrick. Baker. 1½ Trott St.
Frink, Thomas & Co. Grocers. Beale's Wharf
Frish, Charles. Merchant. 88 King St.
Fronte, ——. Physician. 2 Moore St.
Frost, Thomas, Rev. Minister. 16 Archdale St.
Fullterton, ——, Mrs. 86 Queen St.
Gabeau, Anthony. Tailor. 232 Meeting St.
Gabriel, Benjamin. Mariner. 6 Union St.
Gadsden, ——, Mrs. Widow. 25 East Bay
Gadsden, Christopher. Gentleman. 23 East Bay
Gadsden, Philip. Merchant. 124 East Bay
Gaillard, Edward. Planter. 8 East Bay
Gaillard, Theodore. Factor. 43 East Bay
Gaillard, Theodore. Attorney at Law. 53 Meeting St.
Gairdner, James & Co. East Bay
Gallagher, Felix, Rev. Minister. Wentworth St., corner St. Philips
Galler, ——, Mrs. Boarding House. 150 Tradd St.
Gamble, John. Grocer. 97 King St.
Gandovin, Eredorre. Hair Dresser. 2 Unity Alley
Gardiner, George. Brick Layer. 199 Meeting St.
Gardiner, William. Carver and Guilder. 47 Broad St.
Gaskin, Henry. Butcher. 206 King St.
Gates, ——, Rev. Minister. 100 Meeting St.
Gaultier, Isabella. Widow. Mazyck St.
Gaultier, Joseph. Auctioneer. 92 Tradd St.
Gauteveaux, ——, Mrs. Widow. 117 Queen St.
Geddes, Henry. Merchant. 54 East Bay
Geddes, Robert. Merchant. 54 East Bay
Geer, John. Merchant. 12 East Bay
Gennerick, John Frederick. Grocer. 216 King St.
George, Mary. Shop Keeper. 216 King St.
Gerley, John. Gentleman. 5 Mazyck St.
Gervais, John Lewis. Gentleman. 71 Broad St.
Gessendenner, John. Carpenter. 29 Beaufain St.
Gibbes, W. Hasell. Master Chancery. 57 Meeting St.
Gibbs, ——, Mrs. Widow. 1 Gibbs' St.
Gibbs, ——, Mrs. 20 Meeting St.
Gibbs, George. Baker. 28 Elliot St.
Gibbs, John. 91 Tradd St.
Gibson, Robert. Saddler. 249 King St.
Gilbert, Elizabeth. Shop Keeper. 125 Church St.
Gilchrist, Adam. Merchant. 21 Church St.
Gilchrist, Malcom. Grocer. 178 Meeting St.
Gilliland, David. Butcher. 103 Meeting St.
Girardon, Anthony. Shop Keeper. 141 Meeting St.
Gist, William. Merchant. 209 King St.
Given, David. Grocer. 103 Queen St.
Glen, John. Planter. 53 Tradd St.
Glover, Charles. Planter. 3 Pinckney St.
Glover, Wilson. Planter. 4 Ellery St.
Gmbert, John. Tailor. 41 Union St. Continued
Goddard, John. Surveyor. 173 Meeting St.
Godfrey, Elizabeth. Widow. 289 King St.
Gomez, Jacob. Merchant. 59 King St.
Goodtown, Peter. Mariner. 107 Meeting St.
Gordon, Andrew. Brick Layer. 181 Meeting St.
Gordon, Elizabeth. Widow. 9 Guignard St.
Gordon, James. Merchant. 28 East Bay
Gordon, John. Store Keeper. 31 Queen St.
Gordon, John. Grocer & Factor. Union St. Continued
Gordon, Thomas. Grocer. 98 Meeting St.
Gordon, William. Grocer. 87 King St.
Gorlieur, Francis. Gentleman. 204 Meeting St.
Gourdau, Joseph. Shoemaker. 99 Queen St.
Gourlay, John. Shoemaker. 186 Meeting St.
Grabenstein, Frederick. Shop Keeper. 4 Beresford St.

Graff, Peter C. Merchant. 206 King St.
Graham, John & Co. Merchants. 126 Broad St.
Graham, Richard. Deputy Sheriff. 13 Hasell St.
Graham, William. Clerk Branch Bank.
Granger, James. Coach Maker. 104 Meeting St.
Grant, Ann. Widow. 148 King St.
Grant, William. Captain. 207 Meeting St.
Granville, James. Hair Dresser. 274 King St.
Grassel, Sarah. Widow. 4 Quince St.
Gray, Benjamin. Planter. 22 Trott St.
Gray, William. Inspector. 2 White's Alley
Greaves, Charles. Factor. 54 Tradd St.
Green, C. James. Grocer. 104 Church St.
Green, William. Grocer. 8 Union St.
Greenhill, Hume. Carpenter. 94 Tradd St.
Greenwood, William. Merchant. 25 Beaufain St.
Greenwood, William, Jr. Gentleman. 2 Ellery St.
Gregory, James & Son. Merchants. 117 Broad St.
[two pages with approximately 60 names missing]
Harvey, Archibald. 18 Tradd St.
Haslett, John & Co. Merchants. 1 Champney's Wharf
Haslin, John. Gentleman. 137 King St.
Hatch, Robert. Mariner. 8 Union St.
Hatfield, -----, Mrs. Widow. 33 Trott St.
Hattier, -----, Mr. Grocer. 34 Tradd St.
Hattier, -----, Mr. Confectioner. 1 Broad St.
Hausen, Elias. Last Maker. 205 King St.
Hays, William. Butcher. Pitt St.
Haywood, Nathaniel. Planter. 117 East Bay
Haywood, Thomas. Judge. 18 Church St.
Hazard & Co. Merchants. Crafts' 4th Range
Hazlehurst, Robert. Merchant. 14 East Bay
Hazlewood, Joseph. Painter & Glazier. Union St.
Hendrickson, Beze. Carpenter. 3 Society St.
Henry, -----, Mrs. Milliner. 21 Elliot St.
Henry, Bennet & Co. Merchants. 19 Elliot St.
Henry, Jacob. Merchant. 211 King St.
Hewett, James. Captain. 12 Guignard St.
Heyliger, Joseph. Engraver & Printer. 243 Meeting St.
Hichborn, John. Merchant. 101 Meeting St.
Hickey, James. Grocer. 57 King St.
Hildrath, Benjamin. Sail Maker. 7 Pinckney St.
Hill, Charles. Clerk. 6 Wyatt's Lot
Hill, Duncan. Captain. 83 East Bay
Hill, Jonathan. Ship Bread Baker. 117 East Bay
Hill, Paul. Clerk German Church. 29 Archdale St.
Hilligas, Philip. Grocer. 96 Tradd St.
Hinds, Patrick. Shoemaker. 36 Beaufain St.
Hinds, Thomas. Attorney at Law. 32 Broad St.
Hippers, Peter. Grocer. 180 Meeting St.
Hislop, Robert. Lumber Measurer. 61 Church St.
Hoggson, -----, Mrs. Boarding House. 36 King St.
Hollingshead, William, Rev. Minister. 94 Meeting St.
Holloway, Daniel. Merchant. Crafts' 4th Range
Holmes, Isaac. Collector Customs. 14 Friend St.
Holmes, John Bee. Attorney at Law. 6 Meeting St.
Holmes, William & Co. Auctioneers.
Honeywood, -----, Mrs. 67 Meeting St.
Hook, Conrad. Carpenter. 19 Hasell St.
Hopeton, -----, Mrs. 81 Meeting St.
Horace, John. Planter. 119 East Bay
Hornby, Thomas. Distiller. 214 King St.
Horry, Thomas. Planter. 271 Meeting St.
Hort, William. Planter. 126 East Bay
House, Samuel. Clerk Sheriff Office. Union St. Continued
Howard, -----, Mrs. Widow. 166 Meeting St.
Howard, John. Grocer. 115 King St.

Hubberd, -----, Mrs. Widow. 29 King St.
Huck & Veronee. Livery Stables. 64 King St.
Huger, Isaac. General. 59 Broad St.
Hughes, James. Ship Joiner. 7 Amen St.
Humbert, Godfrey. Carpenter. 13 Lynch's Lane
Hunt, -----, Mrs. Boarding House. 27 Church St.
Hunter, James. Grocer. 28 Meeting St.
Hunter, Thomas. Captain. 106 Church St.
Hunter, William. Tailor. 2 Elliot St.
Hurst, Charles. Tailor. 49 Church St.
Hussy, Bryan. Mariner. 3 Stoll's Alley
Hutchins, William B. Teacher. 14 Hasell St.
Hutchinson, Ann. Widow. Fort Mechanic
Hutchinson, James. Baker. 91 King St.
Huxham, -----, Miss. Milliner. 10 Tradd St.
Hyams, Samuel. Merchant. 195 King St.
Irvine, Mathew, Dr. Physician. 105 East Bay
Irving, Jacob. Gentleman. 306 King St.
Irving, James. Carpenter. 7 East Bay
Jackson, John. Silversmith. 18 Pinckney St.
Jacobs, Jacob. Auctioneer. 27 Trott St.
Jacobs, Samuel. Gentleman. 95 Queen St.
Jacques, Victor. Fisherman. Blake's Wharf
Jaffaries, -----, Miss. Burckmyer's Alley
Jafferies, -----, Mrs. Widow. 65 Queen St.
Jameison, -----, Mrs. Widow. 70 Meeting St.
James, John. Carpenter. 5 Wentworth St.
Jarmain, John. Livery Stables. 4 Meeting St.
Jeantet, Gabriel. Merchant. 69 East Bay
Jearden, Lewis. Merchant. 8 Trott St.
Jeffords, John. Tailor. 18 Pinckney St.
Jenkins, Isaac Mrs. Widow. 8 Stoll's Alley
Jennings & Woddrop. Merchants. 9 East Bay
Jeume, Cabos. Merchant. 115 Tradd St.
Jeune, D. C. Boarding House. 32 Union St.
John, -----. Carpenter. 42 Trott St.
Johnson, Jacob. Carpenter. 17 Trott St.
Johnson, John. Wharfinger. 1 Ellery St.
Johnson, John. Magistrate. 165 King St.
Johnson, Thomas. Grocer. 25 Meeting St., corner Tradd
Johnson, William. Preceptor. Liberty St.
Johnson, William, Jr. Attorney at Law. 33 Broad St.
Johnson, William P. 165 King St.
Johnson, William. & Son. Blacksmiths. Charles St.
Johnston, Gaspar. Merchant. 149 King Stret
Johnston, Jabez W. Clock, Watch Maker. 29 Broad St.
Jones, Alexander. Gentleman. Longitude Lane
Jones, -----, Dr. Physician. 70 Meeting St.
Jones, Edward. Factor. 7 Church St.
Jones, Henry. Ship Carpenter. 3 Lodge Alley
Jones, Israel. Planter. 262 King St.
Jones, Jeffe. Planter. 25 King St.
Jones, Jehu. Tailor. 303 King St.
Jones, Joseph. Store Keeper. 15 Tradd St.
Jones, Nathaniel. Grocer. 9 Tradd St.
Jones, Samuel. Merchant. 268 King St.
Jones, Thomas. Tailor. 78 Meeting St.
Jones, Thomas. Pres. S.C. Bank. 4 Guignard St.
Jones, William. Constable. 288 King St.
Josephs, Israel. Merchant. 262 King St.
Joy, Abraham. Ship Joiner. 8 Amen St.
Joy, Daniel. Carpenter. Burckmyer's Alley
Keel, -----, Mrs. Widow. St. Philip's St.
Keen, Thomas. Captain. 12 Union St. Continued
Keister, Henry. Watchman. 8 Meeting St.
Keith, Isaac, Rev. Minister. 59 Queen St.
Keith, Sylvanus. Grocer. 136 East Bay

Kelly, Mary. Grocer. 116 King St.
Kelly, William. Butcher. 111 East Bay
Kemp & Fraser. Merchants. 16 Tradd St.
Kempton, Ann. Widow. 104 Church St.
Kennedy, John. Grocer. 20 East Bay
Kern, J. Frederick. Merchant. 193 King St.
Kernan, James. Grocer. 275 King St.
Kerr, Andrew. 9 Broad St.
Kevan, William. Merchant. 136 Tradd St.
Khone, Frederick. Merchant. 39 East Bay
Kirk & Lukens. Merchants. 59 East Bay
Kirkland, Joseph, Dr. Physician. Federal St.
Kissick, Francis. Mariner. 2 Lodge Alley
Knox, Mathew. Grocer. 309 King St.
Knox, Thomas. Grocer. 6 Beale's Wharf
Labat, David. Shop Keeper. Hasell St.
Labounde, Fansoia. Gentleman. 171 Meeting St.
Lacoste, Stephen. Merchant. 77 East Bay
Ladson, ——, Mrs. 48 Tradd St.
Ladson, James. Major. 17 Meeting St.
Lahiffe, Elizabeth. Tavern Keeper. 56 King St.
Lamb, Edward. Merchant. 6 Tradd St.
Lamey, Frederick. Grocer. 250 King St.
Lamote & Chisolm. Factors. Vanderhorst's Wharf
Lance, Lambert. Planter.
Langstaff, Ben. Jr. Butcher. 162 Meeting St.
Lanneau, Basil. Tanner. Harleston's Green
Lapenne, Joseph. Grocer. 184 Meeting St.
Larrue, Surcoias. Shop Keeper. 179 Meeting St.
Larry, Robert. Carpenter. 62 Church St.
Latham, Daniel. Distiller. 3 Hasell St.
Latham, Joseph. Distiller. 13 Moore St.
Lathauson, J. W. Queen St., corner Union
Lauderdale & Dowthwaite. Grocers. 106½ Church St.
Laurence, Ettsel. Brick Layer. Liberty St.
Lawrence, ——, Mrs. Widow. 15 Pinckney St.
Lawson, James. Grocer. 138 King St.
Lawton, Winborn. Planter. 5 Lynch's Lane
Leadbetter, William. Ship Carpenter. Liberty St.
Lecat, Rachel. Confectioner. 31 Broad St.
Lee, James. Merchant. East Bay
Lee, John & Co. Merchants. 47 King St.
Lee, Stephen. Factor. Geyer's Wharf
Lee, Thomas. Attorney at Law. 42 Meeting St.
Legar, Elizabeth. Widow. Federal St.
Legare, ——, Mrs. Widow. 101 Church St.
Legare & Burden. Factors. 5 East Bay
Legare, Solomon, Jr. Factor. South Bay
Legge, Edward. Auctioneer. Trott St.
Legge, James. Brick Layer. 198 King St.
Lehre, Mary. Widow. Liberty St.
Lehre, Thomas. Gentleman. 293 King St.
Lehre, William, Dr. Physician. 128 King St.
Lennox, William. Merchant. 26 King St.
Leroux, John. Carpenter. Trott St.
Lessesne, ——, Mrs. Widow. 123 East Bay
Lesugneur, Vincent, Dr. Physician. 5 Tradd St.
Levy, Dennis. Grocer. 301 King St.
Levy, Hart. Shop Keeper. 188 King St.
Levy, Lyon. Clerk. 203 King St.
Levy, Moses. Merchant. 233 King St.
Levy, Nathan. Tobacconist. 171 King St.
Levy, Samuel & Co. Merchants. King St., corner Broad
Levy, Solomon. Merchant. 247 King St.
Lewis, Christiana. Widow. Liberty St.
Lewis, Joseph. 135 East Bay
Lewis, Philip. Merchant. 19 Broad St.

Ley, Francis. Merchant. 20 Elliot St.
Liddle, John. Grocer. South Bay
Lightwood, E. Mantua Maker. 35 Trott St.
Lightwood, Edward. Planter. 266 Meeting St.
Lindal, Johannes. Custom House Office. 96 Meeting St.
Lindsay, Robert. Gentleman. 140 Church St.
Ling, John. Grocer. 17 Hasell St.
Little, Robert. Carpenter. 12 Wragg's Alley
Livingston, Eleanor, Miss. George St.
Lloyd, John, Jr. Merchant. 22 Elliot St.
Lloyd, Joseph. Merchant. 22 Elliot St.
Lockey, George. Merchant. 92 Queen St.
Logan, ——, Mrs. Widow. 32 Tradd St.
Logan, M. John. Carpenter. 60 Church St.
Logan, William. 292 King St.
Logan, William, Jr. Attorney at Law. 32 Tradd St.
Lonam, ——, Mrs. Widow. 112 Church St.
Long, ——, Mrs. 77 Meeting St.
Long, John. Bookkeeper. 42 George St.
Long, Mary. Nurse, Widow. Union St. Continued
Lopez, David. Auctioneer. 2 Champney's Row
Love, John. Fruit Shop. 8 Tradd St.
Loveday, John. Powder Receiver. 10 Moore St.
Lowndes, James. Attorney at Law. 74 Broad St.
Lowndes, Rawlins. Gentleman. 74 Broad St.
Lowndes, Thomas. Attorney at Law. 74 Broad St.
Luther, Giles. Shoemaker. 10 Union St.
Luyten, William. 5 Elliot St.
Lynah, James, Dr. Physician. 55 Meeting St.
Lyon, Mordecai. Tailor. 53 East Bay
M'Bride, James. Shop Keeper. 45 East Bay
M'Call, Esther. Widow. 1 Short St.
M'Call, John. City Treasurer. 110 Church St.
M'Calla, Thomas H., Dr. Physician. 10 Elliot St.
M'Carty, John, Dr. Physisian. 22 Beresford St.
M'Cleery, John. Merchant. 5 Crafts' North Range
M'Clure, William. Merchant. 20 Broad St.
M'Cormic, William. Grocer. 2 Tradd St.
M'Credie, David & Co. Merchants. 8 Broad St.
M'Donald, Christopher. Grocer. 125 Tradd St.
M'Donald, ——, Mrs. Widow. Union St. Continued
M'Dowall, James. Grocer. 58 King St.
M'Dowall, John. Merchant. 151 King St.
M'Evoy, James. Grocer. 4 Tradd St.
M'Ewan, Archibald. 164 King St.
M'Ewan, Samuel. Shoemaker. 156 King St.
M'FarLane, Alexander. Merchant. 11 Broad St.
M'Gann, Patrick. Watch Maker. 3 Coats' Row
M'Ginnis, Patrick. Grocer. 67 King St.
M'Iver, John. Printer. 111 Tradd St.
M'Kay, Malcom. Grocer. 40 King St.
M'Kee, John. Tailor. 5 Pinckney St.
M'Kenzie, Andrew. Grocer. 107 Broad St.
M'Key, Abraham. Clerk. 24 Trott St.
M'Kie, Cobert. Coach Maker. Parsonage Alley
M'Kie, John. Brick Layer. 298 King St.
M'Lean, Evan. Tailor. 229 Meeting St.
M'Lean, Lauchlin. Grocer. 51 Tradd St.
M'Leith & Moss. Brass Founders. 64 Meeting St.
M'Leon, ——. Merchant. South Bay
M'Neil, Archibald. Tide Waiter. 12 Union St. Continued
M'Pherson, ——. Colonel. 102 Meeting St.
M'Pherson, Duncan. 73 King St.
M'Pherson, James. Factor. 101 Meeting St.
M'Shan, William & Co. Merchants. 9 Broad St.
Macaul, Paul. Laborer. 4 King St.

Macaulay, George. Merchant. 17 Broad St.
Macbeth & Rosss. Merchants. 121 Tradd St.
Macdonald, Duncan. Upholsterer. 224 Meeting St.
Macdonald, William. Merchant. 22 East Bay
Mackay, Crafts. Watch Maker. 61 Meeting St.
Magan, James. Carpenter. 23 Church St.
Magwood, Simon. Factor. 5 Amen St.
Main, William. Grocer. 137 Fish Market
Mair & Gordon. Merchants. 23 East Bay
Manan, Cloudy. Tobacconist. 28 Union St.
Manigault, Gabriel. Planter. 89 East Bay
Manigault, Joseph. Planter. Maiden Lane
Mann, ----, Mrs. Widow. 20 King St.
Mann, ----, Mrs. School Mistress. 180 Meeting St.
Mann and Foltz. Merchant. 13 East Bay
Manuel, Abraham. 112 King St.
Marcus, Lazarus. Grocer. 101 King St.
Marie, John. Watch Maker. 34 Church St.
Markley, Abraham. Merchant. 125 King St.
Marks, Humphrey. Shop Keeper. 208 King St.
Marlin, Edward. Custom House Off. Trott St.
Marr, Ann. Widow. 137 Church St.
Marsh & Dabney. Merchants. 134 Tradd St.
Marshall, ----. Shop Keeper, Widow. 39 Pinckney St.
Marshall, John. Cabinet Maker. 219 Meeting St.
Marshall, William. Auctioneer. 6 East Bay
Marshall, William. Captain. 34 Guignard St.
Marshall, William. Attorney at Law. 43 Meeting St.
Martial, ----, Mrs. Boarding House. 38 Union St.
Martin, Charles. Brick Layer. 15 Pinckney St.
Martin, Christian. Tanner. 155 Meeting St.
Martin, Daniel. City Scavenger. 269 King St.
Martin, Elizabeth. Widow. 12 King St.
Martin, Jacob. Clerk S. C. Bank. 214 Meeting St.
Martin, Thomas, Merchant.
    Wentworth St.
Matthews, John, Hon. Chancellor. Montague St.
Mattute, John. Butcher. Magazine St.
Mauger, John. Merchant. 26 Elliot St.
Mauren & Buschman. Grocers. 23 Union St.
Maximin, Clastrier. Starch Manufacturer. 15 Beresford
    St.
Maxwell, Robert. Grocer. 17 Tradd St.
Maxwell, Thomas. Shoemaker. 169 Meeting St.
Mayer, John G. Broker. 5 Union St. Continued
Mayers, Israel. Tide Waiter. Union St. Continued
Mazyck, William. Factor. 75 Broad St.
Merrill, Benjamin. Livery Stable. 46 Church St.
Mey, Charles. Merchant. 40 Pinckney St.
Mickle, John. Shoemaker. 282 King St.
Middleton, ----, Mrs. Widow. 121 East Bay
Middleton, Saul. Tailor. Liberty St.
Middleton, Solomon. Tailor. 130 King St.
Miller, David John. Goldsmith, Jeweller. Market
    Square
Miller, James. Wine Merchant. 64 East Bay St.
Miller, John. Merchant. 186 King St.
Miller, Nicholas. Baker. Wentworth St.
Miller, Robertson & Co. Merchants. East Bay
Miller, William. Factor. 272 Meeting St.
Milligan, John. Lumber Measurer. 118 East Bay
Mitchell, John. Magistrate, Notary Public. 31 East Bay
Moncrief, John. Carpenter. 103 East Bay
Mondeher, ----. Surgeon, Midwife. 252 King St.
Monk, John. Merchant. 25 Church St., corner Tradd.
Monro, John. Watch Maker. 7 Elliot St.
Monroe, ----, Mrs. Midwife. 126 Broad St.
Monroe, William. Grocer. 20 Tradd St.

Monteith, Robert. Grocer. 79 King St.
Mood, Peter. Silversmith. 238 King St.
Moodie, ----. British Consul. Ellery St.
Moore, John. Butcher. George St.
Moore, John. Boarding House. 3 Unity Alley
Moore, Joseph. Doctor. 43 King St.
Moore, Joseph. Drayman. 107 East Bay
Moore, Philip. Cabinet Maker. 246 Meeting St.
Morce, Garner. Carpenter. 72 Meeting St.
Morgan, B. Edward. Carpenter. Liberty St.
Morgan, Charles. Shipwright. 2 Pinckney St.
Morgan, Edward. Cooper. 4 Pinckney St.
Morony, John. Boarding House. Chambers Alley
Morris, Lewis. Colonel. 260 Meeting St.
Morris, Thomas. Merchant. East Bay
Morris, Thomas. Merchant. 114 East Bay
Morrison, ----, Mrs. Widow. 14 Trott St.
Morrison, James. Grocer. 125 Tradd St.
Morrison, John. Carpenter. 55 Tradd St.
Mortimer, Edward & Co. Merchants. 126 Broad St.
Moser, Philip, M.D. Physician. 108 Broad St.
Moses, Abraham. Grocer. 65 East Bay
Moses, Henry. Shop Keeper. 55 East Bay
Moses, Isaac & Co. Auctioneers. 4 Champney's Way
Moses, Lyon. Shop Keeper. 16 East Bay
Moses, Philip. Merchant. 165 Meeting St.
Moses, Solomon. Store Keeper. 203 King St.
Motta, Isaac. Auctioneer. 18 King St.
Motte, ----, Mrs. Widow. 18 Meeting St.
Motte, Esther. Widow. 30 Beaufain St.
Motte, Francis. Merchant. 23 Meeting St.
Motte, L. D. Emanuel. 18 King St.
Moucket, Castonel Simeon. Clerk French Consulate.
    Pinckney St.
Moules, ----, Madam. Coffee House. 96 Church St.
Moultrie, Kirkland & Co. Druggists. 23 Meeting St.
Muir & Boyd. Merchant. 120 Broad St.
Muirhead, James. Merchant. 7 Elliot St.
Muller, ----, Mrs. Widow. Smith St.
Mulligan, Francis. Collector Revenue. 97 Broad St.
Mulligan, Francis. Collector. Revenue. 3 East Bay
Murphy James. Store Keeper. 11 Elliot St.
Murphy, James. Spanish Consul. 283 King St.
Myerers, H. George. Block & Pump Maker. 136 Cost
    Row
Myers, Samuel. Tailor. 83 King St.
Myln, James. Baker. 20 Union St.
Nadough, ----, Mr. 12 Trott St.
Naysor, Philip. Baker. 84 King St.
Neilson, ----, Mrs. Widow. Federal St.
Nelson, Ambrose. Goldsmith. 42 Trott St.
Nelson, Francis. Ship Carpenter. 113 East Bay
Nelson, George. Carpenter. 63 Meeting St.
Nelson, Jane. Nurse. 63 Meeting St.
Neufville, Isaac. Loan Office. 29 Society St.
Neufville, John. Sr. Commission Loan Office. 85
    Queen St.
Neufville, John, Jr. Attorney at Law. 16 King St.
Neufville, William. Doctor. 18 Society St.
Newton, Catharine, Mrs. 3 Church St.
Nicholas, Thomas. Factor. 135 Nichols Wharf
Nichols & Woodward. Merchants. 14 Elliot St.
Nicholson, James. Attorney at Law. 53 Broad St.
Nipper, H. David. Book Binder. 99 King St.
Nobbs, Samuel. Hair Dresser. 17 Pinckney St.
Nobbs, Samuel. Hair Dresser. 118 King St.
Noble, Ezekiel. Store Keeper. 162 King St.
Norris, Andrew. Attorney at Law. Wentworth St.

Norris, James. Painter. 7 Maiden Lane
Norris, Nicholas. Broker. 93 Meeting St.
Norris, White & Co. Factors. 1 Bedon's Alley
Nort, ——, Mrs. 37 Tradd St.
North & Co. Ship Chandlers. 43 East Bay
North, Edward. Ship Chandler. 7 Church St.
Nott, Izabella. Widow. 58 Church St.
O'Elliot, Thomas. Planter. 16 Legare St.
O'Kelley, ——, Mr. Preceptor. 242 Meeting St.
O'Neil, John. Tanner. Maiden Lane
Oats, Charles. Vendue Master. 9 Trott St.
Ogier, Lewis. Grocer. 89 King St.
Ogier, Thomas. Merchant. 31 East Bay St.
Ohland, John. Grocer. 27 Union St.
Ohonlon, Terence. Store Keeper. 156 King St.
Oliver, Stephen. Butcher. 164 Meeting St.
Oliver, William. Captain. 9 Stoll's Alley
Oree, Diana Mrs. Widow. 92 East Bay
Osborn, Henry. School Master. 79 Queen St.
Osborn, Thomas. Planter. South Bay
Otis, Joseph & Co. Merchants. 31 East Bay
Owen, ——, Mr. 27 Tradd St.
Paine & Bridgham. Merchants. 99 Church St.
Paine & Bridgham. Merchants. 1 Crafts' South Range
Palmer, Job. Carpenter. 26 Trott St.
Parisian, Philip. Merchant. 98 Church St.
Park, F. Gabriel. Carpenter. 3 Trott St.
Park, Joseph. Merchant. 1 Crafts' N. Wharf
Parker, ——, Dr. Physician. 145 East Bay
Parker, Isaac. Planter. 11 Legare St.
Parker, John. Attorney at Law. 29 Trott St.
Parker, Martha, Mrs. Butcher. 112 East Bay
Parker, Thomas. Attorney S.C. Dist.
Parks, John. Shoemaker. 26 Union St.
Parson, James. Shoemaker. 200 King St.
Parsons, Susannah. Widow. 20 Church St.
Patton, Alexander. 220 King St.
Paynter, Paul. Mariner. 5 Pinckney St.
Payton, Henry. Captain. 136 East Bay St.
Peace, Isaac. Merchant. 110 Tradd St.
Peak, John. Carter. Harleston's Green
Pearce, Thos. Tavern Keeper. 4 Chambers Alley
Pearse, John. Painter. 8 Elliot St.
Peigne, Lewis. Shop Keeper. 62 East Bay
Pelor, George. Captain. 102 East Bay
Pelsbury, Samuel. Custom House Officer. 20 Guignard St.
Peppin, Joseph & Co. Merchants. 142 Gaillard's Wharf
Peroneau, ——, Mrs. Widow. 6 Church St.
Perry, ——, Mrs. Midwife. 21 Elliot St.
Perry, ——, Mrs. Widow. 25 Broad St.
Perry, Edward. Planter. 34 Pinckney St.
Pesture, Josiah. Shop Keeper. 35 Meeting St.
Petrie, ——, Mrs. Widow. 1 Orange St.
Petrie, Alexander. Gentleman. Federal St.
Philips, Benjamin. Shop Keeper. 194 King St.
Philips, Dorothy. Saddler. 223 Meeting St.
Philips, John. Painter. 36 Meeting St.
Philips, Mary. Widow. Burckmyer's Alley
Philips, R. John. Mazyck St.
Philson, Alexander. 3 Bedon's Alley
Pillans, Robert. Preceptor. 122 Tradd St.
Pincel, Emanuel. Tin Plate Worker. 48 Meeting St.
Pinckney, Charles. Governor. 268 Meeting St.
Pinckney, F. Susannah Mrs. 15 Legare St.
Pinckney, Roger. Planter. 15 Legare St.
Plombard, ——, Mrs. Widow. 106 Church St.

Pole, ——, Mr. Grocer. 239 King St.
Polony, Lewis John, M.D. Physician. 9 Church St.
Pont, Victor du. Consul of France. Anson St., corner George
Ponton, Archibald. Confectioner. 118 Tradd St.
Postell, Edward. Chair Maker. 28 Beaufain St.
Postell, Susanna. Widow. 9 Parsonage Alley
Potter, John. Merchant. 131 Tradd St.
Poulton, Edward. Captain. 120 Church St.
Poyas, Lewis John. Carpenter. 6 Guignard St.
Poys, James. Merchant. 87 Queen St.
Pratt, H. Samuel. Grocer. 37 East Bay
Prentice, John. Coach Maker. 7 Archdale St.
Prestman, William. Merchant. 10 East Bay
Price, John. Merchant. 108 Church St.
Price, Thomas. Planter. 20 Friend St.
Prichard, Paul. Ship Carpenter. 142 East Bay
Prichard, William. Ship Carpenter. 1 Quince St.
Prichard, William. Senior Shipwright. 1 Pinckney St.
Primrose, Catharine. Widow. St. Philip's St.
Prince, Charles. Tin Plate Worker. 266 King St.
Prince, Charles. Pilot. 13 King St.
Pringle, John J. Attorney General. 105 Tradd St.
Prioleau, ——, Mrs. Boarding House. 93 Queen St.
Prioleau, John. Factor. 8 Guignard St.
Prioleau, Samuel. Gentleman. 12 Ellery St.
Purcell, Joseph. Surveyor. 127 King St.
Purse, William. Jeweller. 83 Broad St.
Pyatt, Peter. Planter. St. Philip's St.
Quay, Alexander. Grocer. 147 King St.
Quin, James. 92 Meeting St.
Quinby, James. Carpenter. 4 Pinckney St.
Ragley, Anthony. Merchant. 23 Elliot St.
Ramage, Francis. Merchant. 95 King St.
Ramanssin, Daniel Paul. Gentleman. 10 Beaufain St.
Ramsay, David, M.D. Pres. S.C. Senate. 90 Broad St.
Ramsay, J. John. Physician. 60 King St.
Ramson, J. John. Boarding House. 12 Union St.
Rancier, J. L. Gunsmith. 210 King St.
Ratcliff, ——, Mrs. Widow. George St.
Ratcliff, Thomas. Planter. 6 George St.
Raville, ——, Madam. 12 Broad St.
Read, ——. Doctor. 11 Church St.
Read, B. James. Doctor. 113 Church St.
Rechon, David. Tailor. 110 King St.
Reed, George. Notary Public. 209 Meeting St.
Reed, John. Wheelwright. 212 Meeting St.
Reeves, Enos. Jeweller. 83 Broad St.
Reice, ——, Madam. Cigar Maker. 23 Union St.
Reid & King. Tin Plate Workers. 45 Church St.
Reid, James. Accountant. Wentworth St.
Reid, William. Hatter. 12 Elliot St.
Reot, ——, Mrs. Widow. Wentworth St.
Repon, Barnard. Grocer. 29 Union St.
Reside, William. Cabinet Maker. 114 Tradd St.
Revell, ——. Captain. 2 Quince St.
Reyneau, Charles. Federal St.
Rhind, ——, Mrs. Widow. 304 King St.
Richornme, Gabriel. 95 Tradd St.
Righton, Joseph. Cooper. 10 Stoll's Alley
Rivers, James. Carpenter. 16 Hasell St.
Rivers, Samuel. Ship Carpenter. 4 Water St.
Rivers, Thomas. Planter. 1 Stoll's Alley
Rivers, Thomas. Butcher. 40 Trott St.
Robb, Michael. Shoemaker. 38 King St.
Roberts, ——, Mrs. Widow. 16 Church St.
Roberts, Adam. Ship Capenter. 56 Meeting St.
Roberts, Alexander. Grocer. 40 Church St.

Roberts, John. Tailor. 102 Church St.
Roberts, William. Chair Maker. 80 Queen St.
Robertson, Alexander & Son. Merchants. 155 King St.
Robertson, John. Merchant. 24 King St.
Robiac, ----, Mrs. Wentworth St.
Robinson, ----, Mrs. Widow. 112 Church St. Continued
Robinson, John. Usher. Maiden Lane
Robinson, Peter. Painter. Shevers Alley
Robinson, William. Attorney at Law. 21 Meeting St.
Roche, I. Boarding House. 9 Union St.
Roche, William. Clerk. 5 Queen St.
Rogers & Barker. Merchants. 7 Crafts' Wharf
Rogers, Christopher. Tailor. 25 Tradd St.
Rogers, Lewis. Merchant. 24 Broad St.
Rogers, Samuel. Organist. 10 Church St.
Roper, ----, Mrs. Widow. 4 East Bay
Roper, Joseph. Tanner. 13 Pinckney St.
Roper, Thomas. Major. 75 East Bay
Rose, ----, Mrs. Widow. 5 Smith's Ln.
Rose, Alexander. Gentleman. 2 Church St.
Rosembeaum, ----, Mrs. Widow. 10 Trott St.
Ross, Hugh. Grocer. 118 Meeting St.
Ross, Kenneth. Grocer. 14 Church St.
Ross, Thomas. Captain. Liberty St.
Rosseitte, ----. Portrait Painter. 44 Broad St.
Rou, Michael. Carter. George St.
Roullito, ----, Miss. 259 King St.
Roupel, ----, Mrs. 82 Tradd St.
Rouple, Daniel. Harness, Umbrella Maker. 98 Meeting St.
Rouse, William. Shoemaker. 78 Meeting St.
Rout, George. School Master. 11 Moore St.
Roux & Hills. Grocers. 51 East Bay
Row, Jane. Shop Keeper. 310 King St.
Rowand, ----, Mrs. 2 Friend St.
Rumney, Joseph. Grocer. 98 East Bay
Rush, Mathias. Grocer. 243 King St.
Russell, ----, Mrs. Widow. 14 Trott St.
Russell, ----, Mrs. Widow. 7 Quince St.
Russell, Benjamin. Brick Layer. 31 Guignard St.
Russell, Dinah. Grocer. 7 King St.
Rutledge, Edward. Attorney at Law. 56 Broad St.
Rutledge, Hugh. Judge, Court Equity. 3 Short St.
Rutledge, John. Late Chief Justice. 82 Broad St.
Rutledge, John, Jr. Planter. 56 Meeting St.
Ryan, S. Peter. Merchant. 54 East Bay
Ryckbosch, Francis. Bookkeeper. George St.
Saltus, Yates & Co. Ship Chandlers. 2 Crafts' 4th Range, East Bay
Sampson, Simeon. Gentleman. 106 King St.
Santi, Angelo & Co. Confectioners. 55 King St.
Sarazin, Jonathan. Lumber Merchant. Wentworth St.
Sarzedas, ----. Doctor. 3 Hasell St.
Sasportas, Abraham. Merchant. 12 Tradd St.
Saunders, ----, Mrs. Widow. 121 East Bay
Savage, ----, Mrs. Widow. 68 Broad St.
Savage, George. Grocer. 92 East Bay
Savary, J. Marie. 6 King St.
Schmidt, John H. Merchant. 79 East Bay
Schutt, Casparil. Merchant. 88 Broad St.
Schutt, Casper. Merchant. Crafts' Wharf
Scot, ----, Mrs. Dry Goods Store. 246 King St.
Scot, James. Grocer. 18 King St.
Scott, Guy. Hair Dresser. 6 Union St. Continued
Screven, Thomas. Planter. 117 Church St.
Sebbin, John. Grocer. 224 Meeting St.
Sedgwick, ----, M. D. Physician. 97 Tradd St.

Seixas, Abraham. Broker. 69 Broad St.
Selby, George. Merchant. 192 King St.
Serjeant, ----, Mrs. Shop Keeper. 34 Broad St.
Seymour, ----. Captain, Harbormaster. 6 Orange St.
Shaw, Elizabeth. Widow. Stoll's Alley
Sheed, George. Teacher. 283 King St.
Shepherd, John. Carpenter. 3 King St.
Shephere, ----, Mrs. Shop Keeper. 37 Meeting St.
Sheppard, James. Saddler. 196 King St.
Shirtliff, William. Merchant. St. Philip's St., corner George
Shiry, John. Carpenter. Common St.
Shouldbred, James. Planter. 17 Meeting St.
Shreiner, Nicholas. Keeper Poor House. -
Shrewsbury, Stephen. Clerk S.C. Bank. George St.
Siegar, L. Charles, M.D. Physician. 11 Guignard St.
Simmons & Brown. Merchants. 1 Geyer's Range
Simmons, Francis. Planter. Tradd St.
Simmons, Keating. Factor. 4 Orange St.
Simmons, William. Merchant. 216 Meeting St.
Simons, Thomas. Factor. 124 East Bay
Simpson, ----, Mrs. Widow. 118 Church St.
Sims, John. Shop Keeper. 96 Meeting St.
Sims, White & Co. Factors. 5 Geyer's Wharf
Singleton, Rippleton. Drayman. 4 Trott St.
Sisk, Susannah. Boarding House. Pritchard's Wharf
Sitter, Gabriel. Tanner. 76 Meeting St.
Skirving, Charlotte. Widow. 8 Church St.
Smallwood, Richard. Grocer. 12 Union St.
Smerdon, Elias. Merchant. 125 East Bay
Smith, ----, Mr. Merchant. 87 Broad St.
Smith, ----, Mrs. 15 Broad St.
Smith, ----, Mrs. Widow. 83 Queen St.
Smith, ----, Mrs. Widow. 21 Friend St.
Smith, B. Thomas. 5 Church St.
Smith, Caleb. Mariner. 113 Church St.
Smith, Christian John. Merchant. 52 King St.
Smith, Christopher. Store Keeper. 181 King St.
Smith, Daniel. Conveyancer. 3 Orange St.
Smith, Henry. Ship Carpenter. 7 Guignard St.
Smith, James. Custom House Officer. 112 East Bay
Smith, James. Attorney. King St., corner Lamboll
Smith, John. Captain. 36 Church St.
Smith, John. Upholsterer. 37 King St.
Smith, John. Cabinet Maker. Pinckney St.
Smith, Josiah. Cashier, National Bank. Meeting St.
Smith, Peter. Planter. South Bay
Smith, Robert. Bishop. Wentworth St.
Smith, Roger. 2 Orange St.
Smith, Samuel. Cabinet Maker. 175 Meeting St.
Smith, Sarah. Widow. 30 Church St.
Smith, Whiteford. Grocer. 61 Church St.
Smith, William. Tailor. 215 King St.
Smith, William. Ironmonger. 3 Broad St.
Smyth, John. Painter. 11 Ellery St.
Smyth, John. Merchant. 236 King St.
Snowden, Charles. Merchant. 19 Pinckney St.
Snowden, Charles & Co. Merchants. 128 Broad St.
Snowden, William. & Co. Grocer. 128 Broad St.
Solomon, Joseph. Merchant. 6 Moore St.
Solomon, Joseph. Merchant. 204 King St.
Somersall, William & Son. Merchants. 2 East Bay
Spears, James. Carpenter. 7 Society St.
Speiren, Patrick. Merchant. 212 King St.
Speissenger, ----, Jr. Musical Instrument Maker. 4 Quince St.
Spencer, ----. Doctor. 307 King St.
Spiddle, Everhart. Tanner. Montague St.

Stall & Wait. Coach Makers. 74 Meeting St.
Stedman, James. Carpenter. 31 Trott St.
Steedman, Charles. Carpenter. 167 Meeting St.
Stent, Samuel. Tailor. 42 Church St.
Stephen, William. Merchant. 160 King St.
Stephen, William. Merchant. 124 Tradd St.
Stephens, Daniel. George St.
Summers, ----, Miss. 88 Tradd St.
Swinton, Hugh. Factor.
Taylor, Bennet. Merchant. 18 Broad St.
Teasdale, John. Merchant. 43 Elliot St.
Teasdale, John. Merchant. 38 East Bay
Tew, Thomas. Brick Layer. 110 King St.
Thackman, Thomas. Jailer.
Theus, James. Merchant. 11 East Bay
Theus, Simeon. State Treasurer. 43 King St.
Timothy & Mason. Printers. 44 East Bay
Tolloneer, ----, Mrs. Widow. 105 Church St.
Torrans, H. William. Attorney at Law. 242 Meeting St.
Tragey, Laurence. Brick Layer. St. Philip's St.
Trenholm, William. 109 Church St.
Trescot, Edward. Tax Collector. 82 Meeting St.
Trezevant, Lewis. Attorney at Law. 46 Meeting St.
Trezevant, Peter. Broker. 13 Federal St.
Troop, James. Attorney at Law. 247 Meeting St.
Tunno, ----, Mr. Merchant. George St.
Tunno & Cox. Merchants. 28 East Bay
Tunno, Thomas. Merchant. 16 East Bay
Turner, Thomas. Dancing Master. 94 Queen St.
Turpin, William. Merchant. 28 Trott St.
Tweed, Alexander. Gentleman. 110 East Bay
Vale, John D. Merchant. 42 Broad St.
Vanderhorst & Miller. Factors. 4 Vanderhorst's Wharf
Vanderhorst, Arnoldus. Gentleman. 15 East Bay
Vos & Graves. Merchants. 17 East Bay
Vos, Andrew. Merchant. 32 Beaufain St.
Ward, J. Attorney at Law. 253 Meeting St.
Ward, James M. Attorney at Law. Hasell St.
Ward, John. Attorney at Law. 50 Church St.
Waring, Monon. Factor. 12 Guignard St.
Waring, Thomas. Factor. 40 Meeting St.
Warley, Feliz. Clerk of Senate. 44 Trott St.
Watson, John. Cabinet Maker. 21 King St.
Watson, Samuel. Merchant. 121 Broad St.
Watts, Charles. Cabinet Maker. 47 Church St.
Webb, Benjamin. Planter. 26 Beaufain St.
Webb, John. Merchant. 14 Moore St.
White, John. Factor. 16 Meeting St.
Whitfield & Brown. Merchants. Bedon's Alley
Wilcox, Jeremiah. Painter. Beresford's Alley
Wilke, William. Factor. 8 Meeting St.
Williams, John. Coffee House. 127 Tradd St.
Williamson, John. Merchant. 113 East Bay
Williman, Jacob. Tanner. Montague St.
Williman, Jacob. Druggist. 241 King St.
Wilson, ----. Doctor. 45 Broad St.
Wilson, Robert. Druggist. 97 Church St.
Winthrop, Joseph. Factor. 4 Geyer's Range
Wish, William. Merchant. 114 Broad St.
Wolf, Henry. Merchant. 232 King St.
Woodman, Edward. Captain. 33 Pinckney St.
Wrightman, William. Jeweller. 287 Meeting St.
Yates, Jeremiah. Merchant. 126 Church St.
Young, Sarah. Widow. 270 Meeting St.

CHAPTER 7

THE 1800 CENSUS

The 1800 census has a total of 2229 heads of households. Of these 43 are simply listed as free without names being given for them. This list excludes those and thus contains 2186 entries. This census had 356 more households than did the 1790 one. Of the households 388 were headed by women (18%).

The most popular first names for women were Mary 16%, Eliza and Elizabeth 16%, Ann and Anna 11%, Frances 8%, and Sarah 8%. This reflects little change from 1790.

For men the most used first names were: William 19%, John 17%, Thomas 6%, James 6%, Joseph 4%, and Robert 4%. William had become far more popular than in 1790 when only 9% had this name.

The city of Charleston can be found on pages 74-154 of the original South Carolina census. This includes the parishes of St. Philip's and St. Michael's as well as the Charleston Neck Area, then the district above Boundary (now Calhoun) Street. It is, however, difficult to know where each area begins and ends in the census.

This census has been indexed by by Ronald Vern Jackson as *South Carolina 1800* (North Salt Lake, Utah: Accelerated Indexing Systems International, Inc., 1973). The index is in alphabetical order. A comparison of the original with the index indicates that a number of individuals were omitted from the index while others were included who should not have been. In addition, many errors occurred in the spelling of names. Some are unproofed mistakes such as "Joeph" for "Joseph." Others are misreadings such as "Moultril" for "Moultrie." More serious is the use of the wrong initial letter of a name such as "Peland" for "Oeland" or "Sew" for "Tew."

The number after the name refers to the page of the original census report.

Abendanone, Hiam, 147
Abendanone, Joseph, 137
Abrams, Jacob, 77
Abrams, Moise, 138
Adams, Ezekiel, 89
Addison, Ann, 96
Aertsen, Guilliam, 112
Affigne, Joseph, 108
Aiger, James, 123
Ainger, Edward, 113
Airs, Ann, 84
Airs, George, 143
Akin, Ann, 145
Akin, Eleanor, 88
Akin, Sarah, 83
Alexander, Abraham, 146
Alexander, David, 133
Alexander, Juda, 144
Alexander, Rachael, 92
Alexander, William, 82
Alfred, James, 93
Allen, Samuel, 111
Allen, William, 131
Allison, James, 138
Allmon, Benjamin, 112
Allport, John, 93
Allwright, James, 107
Alston, William, 118
Ancille, John B., 97
Ancrum, William, 87
Anderson, Archibald, 147
Anderson, Jeremiah, 74
Anderson, Robert, 129
Anderson, William, 124
Andrews, James, 138
Andrews, Moses, 130
Annelly, George, 133
Annotto, Benveaux, 125,
Anthony, John, 150
Antichan, ——— , 150
Arms, Sylvanus, 80
Armstong, Rebecca, 94
Armstrong, William, 149
Arnot, John, 109
Ash, Elizabeth, 115
Ash, Hannah, 118
Ash, John, 122
Ashton, Catharine, 86
Atkinson, Mary, 112
Atmar, Ralph, 140
Austin, Catharine, 78
Austin, William, 94
Avenne, Peter, 154
Axon, Jacob, 148
Axson, Mary, Mrs., 117
Axson, William, 113
Azevedo, J. D., 142
Azube, Abraham, 146
Bacot, Henry H., 126
Bacot, Thomas W., 125
Badger, James, 152
Bagshaw, Thomas, 149
Bailey, David, 151
Bailey, G. G., 125

Bailey, Henrey, 132
Baker, Amey, 127
Baker, Frances, 116
Baker, Joseph, 94
Baker, Thomas, 116
Baker, Thomas, 149
Bakman, Adolph, 84
Baldwin, William, 150
Ball, Elizabeth, 126
Ball, Thomas, 128
Bampfield, Rebecca, 140
Bampfield, Sarah A., 100
Banks, Charles, 130
Banks, William, 93
Barber, John, 153
Barker, Joseph J., 150
Barnett, Samuel, 152
Barrett, Esther, 75
Barrett, James, 103
Barrett, James, 103
Barron, Alexander, 104
Barron, Jane E., 104
Barron, John, 130
Barry, David, 114
Barry, Nicholas, 142
Basquen, William, 120
Bass, Thomas, 89
Baxtal, Mary, 120
Bay, E. H., Judge, 124
Beale, John, 133
Beale, Joseph, 126
Beard, Frederick, 103
Beatie, Robert, 114
Beaufort, Charles, 111
Beckman, Elizabeth, 90
Beckman, Samuel, 152
Bee, Eliza, 82
Bee, John S., 140
Bee, Thomas, Jr., 102
Bee, Thomas, Judge, 131
Bee, William, 116
Bell, Daniel, 108
Bell, David, 94
Bellamy, Esther, 129
Belser, Christian, 98
Bennett, Henrey, 130
Bennett, Thomas, Jr., 104
Bennett, Thomas, Sr., 104
Benoist, John, 93
Bentham, James, 133
Benthor, Ebenezer, 82
Berdroit, Joseph, 88
Beresford, Richard, 125
Bering, John, 97
Berney, John, 117
Beslisle, Peter, 89
Besselieu, Mark Anthony, 140
Bessiere, Anthony, 125
Best, William, 147
Bethune, Angus, 133
Bevin, Frances, 82
Bezeuil, Julian, 154
Bigelow, Elizabeth, 90
Billings, Samuel, 148

Bird, Sarah, 139
Bird, William, 140
Black, James, 127
Black, John, 133
Black, Nathaniel, 84
Blacklock, William, 103
Blair, James, 130
Blair, William, 123
Blake, John, 103
Blake, John, 114
Blakeley, Samuel, 124
Blakeley, Seth, 124
Blakely, Robert, 99
Blakey, Elizabeth, 126
Blamyer, William, 88
Bloma, John, 93
Blundell, Benjamin, 83
Bobbs, Elizabeth, 141
Bocquet, Elizabeth, 103
Bold, John, 130
Bolloughs, Elias, 148
Bone, Daniel, 90
Bonetheau, Elizabeth, 83
Bonneau, Frances, 115
Bonsell, Elizabeth, 145
Bonwell, Elenor, 150
Bonwers, Charles, 92
Boomer, Dorah, 142
Booner, Christian, 138
Booth, Benjamin, 95
Borde, Augustus, 150
Bouchonneau, Charles, 109
Bounetheau, Gabriel M., 146
Bourgreau, Constance, 97
Bouyshre, Peter, 109
Bow, James, 150
Bowen, J. B., 137
Bowering, Henrey, 131
Bowers, David, 88
Bowldes, Tobias, 110
Bowman, Dominick, 103
Boyd, Benjamin, 100
Boyer, Jacob, 109
Boyle, Jame, 76
Bracey, Jolly, 126
Bradford, Lydia Ann, 124
Bradford, Thomas, 153
Brailsford, Edward, Dr., 135
Brailsford, Elizabeth, 113
Brailsford, Morton, 126
Braisbane, William, 114
Branden, David, 92
Brandon, David, 111
Braughton, Ann, 120
Braun, Samuel, 105
Brebner, Archibald, 129
Bremar, Frances, 145
Brenan, Richard, 78
Bribner, David, 145
Bridie, Elionere, 121
Broadfoot, Whalley, 130
Brockway, Samuel, 145
Brodie, Robert, 122
Brodie, Thomas, 89

Broiske, Sarah, 134
Bron, John Peter, 105
Bross, John, 149
Brower, Jeremiah, 92
Brown, Ann, 151
Brown, Charles, 86
Brown, Daniel, 119
Brown, Daniel, 129
Brown, Daniel, Capt., 127
Brown, Heriot, 113
Brown, James, 84
Brown, John, 109
Brown, John, 88
Brown, Joshua, 100
Brown, Joshua, 110
Brown, Mariah, 132
Brown, Mary, 90
Brown, William, 86
Brownlee, John, 102
Bruckner, Daniel, 151
Brunett, Joseph, 138
Brunson, John, 106
Bryant, John, 106
Buchannon, Jacob, 153
Buchannon, John, 127
Buckel, Margaret, 115
Buckle, Gert, 81
Budd, Rosanna, 151
Buely, Jacob, 99
Buford, Elizabeth, 129
Buist, George, Rev., 123
Bulen, Catharine, 150
Bulgin, James, 122
Buller, Joseph, 142
Bulow, John, 99
Bunton, William, 114
Burckmyer, John, 104
Burden, Kinsey, 123
Burger, David, 153
Burger, Susanna, 74
Burges, Edward, 110
Burges, James, 151
Burke, E. Judge, 123
Burke, Henrey T., 130
Burke, Walter, 91
Burnes, James, 127
Burns, John, 94
Burns, Michael, 119
Burr, Nathaniel, 82
Burrows, Frederick, 92
Burrows, George, 88
Burrows, William, 130
Butler, C. D., 137
Butterton, Joseph, 96
Byers, Robert, 93
Byke, Peter, 124
Byrnes, Joseph, 95
Byrnes, Patrick, 90
Bythewood, Daniel, 85
Bythewood, Thomas, 85
Cabos, John, 125
Cain, Thomas, 81
Caldwell, Henrey, Sr., 129
Caldwell, Henry, Jr., 126
Caldwell, John, 142
Caldwell, Samuel, 108
Calhoun, Henry, 118
Calhoun, James, 85

Calhoun, William, 115
Callaghan, John, 132
Calvert, Elizabeth, 133
Cambridge, Philip, 116
Cambridge, Tobias, 115
Cameau, Peter, 75
Cameron, Alexander, 142
Cameron, David, 107
Cameron, Lewis, 125
Cameron, Samuel, 82
Campbell, Angus, 87
Campbell, Collin, 131
Campbell, Laurence, 135
Campson, Harman, 109
Cannon, Daniel, 107
Cantor, Emanuel, 112
Cantor, Isaac, 112
Cantor, Jacob, 112
Cantor, Joshua, 115
Capdeville, Peter, 76
Cape, Brian, 79
Cardoza, David, 118
Carey, Joseph, 91
Carmand, Peter, 148
Carn, John, 85
Carnes, Laurence, 106
Carnes, Samuel, 140
Carnes, Thomas W., 95
Carns, Susanna, 95
Carpenter, Joseph, 107
Carr, James, 109
Carr, John, 85
Carr, Richard, 133
Carrell, Daniel, 154
Carrere, Charles, 89
Carroll, Barthomew, 111
Carson, James, 113
Carson, William, 122
Cart, John, 103
Carter, George, Dr., 141
Casey, Benjamin, 151
Castro, John, 144
Cave, Thomas, 111
Caveneau, Mary, 107
Caw, Rachael, 91
Cecat, Frances, 138
Chambers, Gilbert, 140
Chambers, William, 75
Chambers, William, 76
Champey, Edme, 98
Champney, John, 143
Chandler, Isaac, Dr., 116
Chaplin, Darcus, 146
Chapman, Catharine, 121
Charles, Andrew, 102
Charteir, Marian, 101
Chase, James, 85
Chechester, Jonathan, Dr., 124
Cheeves, Alexander, 144
Chinners, John, 124
Chisholm, Alexander, 118
Chisholm, George, 127
Chitty, William K., 94
Chouler, Joseph, 78
Christian, Elizabeth, 93
Christian, William, 98
Christie, Alexander, 153
Chupien, Lewis, 132

Clabrook, Richard, 89
Claret, Joseph, 107
Clark, David, 121
Clark, Elizabeth, 106
Clark, James, 132
Clark, James, 87
Clark, Lucretia, 87
Clark, Robert, 80
Clark, Sarah, 111
Clarkson, William, 94
Clarkson, William Sr, 138
Classtier, ——, 107
Clastrier, John, 119
Cleary, John R., 147
Cleaspors, Charles, 84
Clement, John, 137
Clements, William, 117
Clime, Martin, 100
Clissey, Raymond, 125
Clitheral, James, 94
Club, Alexander, 121
Coates, Thomas, 131
Coates, William, 79
Cobia, Christianna E., 143
Cobia, Nicholas, 110
Cochran, Charles B., 149
Cochran, Margaret, 137
Cochran, Thomas, Jr., 78
Cochran, Thomas, Sr., 78
Coffin, Ebenezer, 104
Cogdell, Mary A., 125
Cohen, Cely, 146
Cohen, Gershon, 137
Cohen, Mordecai, 147
Cohen, Moses, 78
Cohen, Philip, 115
Cohen, Solomon, 99
Colback, Millicent, 122
Colcock, Henrietta, 149
Colford, George, 87
Coller, ——, Mons., 152
Collins, Bartholomew, 94
Collins, J. M., 82
Collins, Mary, 147
Colman, Qusy, 152
Colzy, Charles, 125
Combe, John, 107
Connelly, George, 116
Connely, Elizabeth, 92
Conner, Samuel, 141
Connor, Brian, 77
Conte, Siegnout, 96
Conyers, Elizabeth, 119
Conyers, William, 89
Cook, Eleanor, 78
Cooper, John, 87
Coram, Thomas, 139
Corazzens, Mary, 74
Corbett, Samuel, 150
Corbett, Thomas, Sr., 83
Cordier, Peter, 109
Corker, Thomas, 88
Corman, Frances, 103
Cormick, Thomas, 79
Corre, Charles G., 136
Correl, Alexander, 79
Corrie, Samuel, 106
Cortes, Thomas, 83

Elmore, Jesse, 131
Elstob, Lymon, 81
Elsworth, Theophilus, 77
England, Alexander, 154
Ernest, Jacob, 153
Essues, -----, 138
Evans, John, 89
Evans, William, 105
Everingham, John, 152
Every, Park, 85
Ewing, John, 123
Ewing, Mathew, Dr., 122
Faber, John C., 148
Fabre, Christiana, 105
Fair, William, 103
Fairchild, Aaron, 102
Fairley, Hance, 151
Faisch, Sarah, 137
Farley, James, 124
Farley, Owin, 135
Faroll, James, 119
Farrow, Thomas, 116
Faures, Laurence, 100
Fayzaux, Ann, 113
Feilds, Rebecca, 118
Fell, Thomas, Jr., 124
Fell, Thomas, Sr., 124
Ferguson, Ann, 102
Ferguson, John, 113
Ferrand, Alexander, 99
Fiddy, William, 79
Fields, William B., 86
Fife, James, 134
Findlay, John, 135
Fisher, James, 123
Fisher, John B., 88
Fisher, Peter, 139
Fisk, Edmund, 79
Fisk, Susanna, 79
Fitsberry, John, 83
Fitzpatrick, Nicholas, 114
Fitzsimons, Christopher, 79
Flagg, George, 79
Flagg, George, Jr., 147
Flagg, Rachel, 111
Flagg, Samuel H., 153
Fleming, Robert, 100
Flint, Joseph, 75
Flood, Daniel, 117
Florance, Zachariah, 100
Florin, Lucas, 85
Floto, H. J., 110
Fluvett, Samuel, 137
Fogartie, -----, Miss, 82
Fogartie, James, 97
Folker, John C., 144
Follz, J. F., 129
Folmed, Jonas, 138
Footman, John, 98
Ford, Jacob, 122
Ford, Timothy, 126
Fordham, Richard, 83
Forest, Charity, 90
Forrest, Thomas H., 119
Foster, John, 81
Foster, Robert, 132
Foster, Thomas, 118
Foster, William, 133

Fowler, John, 129
Fowler, Maria, 143
Frances, David, 130
Frances, David, 92
Fraser, Elizabeth, 130
Fraser, James, 106
Fraser John, 87
Fraser, Mary, Mrs., 117
Frederick, John, 121
Freeman, William, 120
Freneau, Peter, 100
Friar, Sarah, 104
Friend, Uldrick, 92
Frierson, John, 86
Frink, Thomas, 131
Frish, Michael, 107
Frisk, Charles, 101
Fritz, Peter, 105
Fronty, Michael, 148
Frost, Thomas, Rev., 140
Fueston, Samuel, 84
Fuller, Oliver, 93
Furman, Richard, Rev., 126
Fyall, Peter, 119
Gabeau, Anthony, 150
Gabriel, Mary, 105
Gadet, John, 93
Gadsden, Christopher, 95
Gadsden, Martha, 96
Gadsden, Philip, 95
Gafkin, William, 89
Gaillard, Theodore, 138
Gaillard, Theodore, Jr., 81
Gairdner, Edwin, 78
Galbraith, Robert, 102
Gallaher, Simon F., 102
Gallaway, Alfred, 87
Gandouin, John, 79
Gappin, William, 102
Garden, Alexander, 79
Gardner, Edward, 142
Gardner, John, 108
Gardner, John, 86
Gardner, William, 150
Garman, John, 149
Garnett, William, 145
Garyon, Laffetal, 105
Gaskins, Henry, 105
Gaspiuses, John B., 108
Gates, Jacob, 106
Gathischat, Mary, 150
Geddes, Henry, 101
Geddes, John, 151
Geddes, Robert, 99
Gedieze, Esvois, 106
Gennerick, John, 98
Gensel, John, 94
George, James, 91
George, Mark, 83
George, Mary, 147
Gerard, Philip, 132
Gerkey, Frederick, 138
Gerley, John, 139
Gervais, Mary, 136
Gessintanner, Lucretia, 103
Geyer, Elizabeth, 140
Geyer, John, 116
Gibbes, William H., 138

Gibbs, George, 132
Gibbs, John, 123
Gibbs, Lewis, 122
Gibbs, Robert, 122
Gibson, James, 115
Gibson, Robert, 136
Gibson, Robert, 148
Gidney, Isaac, 96
Gilbert, John Joseph, 146
Gilbert, Joseph, 128
Gilbert, Sarah, 128
Gilbraith, Jean, 96
Gilchriest, Adam, 126
Giles, Robert, 113
Giles, Thomas, 120
Gill, John, 150
Gillespie, John, 134
Gillon, Ann, 96
Giradon, John, 81
Gist, William, 99
Given, Mary, 99
Gladding, Joseph, 88
Glen, John, 113
Glover, Charles, 100
Glover, Wilson, 122
Godard, Rene, 148
Godfrey, Eliza, 118
Godfrey, John, 117
Goldfinch, Charles, 152
Good, Sarah, 116
Goodtown, Peter, 93
Gordon, Andrew, 152
Gordon, Elizabeth, 86
Gordon, James, 134
Gordon, Patsey, 144
Gordon, Richard, 128
Gordon, Thomas, 79
Gordon, Thomas, 93
Gordon, William, 143
Goultiere, Joseph, 116
Gowdey, Margaret, 147
Gowdy, James, 106
Graddick, Christian, 109
Grade, Marian, 75
Grafton, Benjamin, 78
Graham, James, 110
Graham, Richard, 84
Grand, Lewis, 105
Grannerett, Christopher, 92
Grant, Ann, 87
Grant, Hetty, 93
Graser, Conrod J., 153
Gravenstine, Frederick, 143
Graves, Charles, 113
Graves, Massa, 122
Gray, Alexander, 100
Gray, Caleb, 99
Gray, William R., 127
Greegary, Jonathan, 75
Greehill, Hume, 113
Green, James, 93
Green, William, 74
Green, William A., 109
Greenland, George, 120
Greenwood, William, Sr., 140
Greet, James, 80
Gregorie, James, 116
Gregorie, James, 154

Gregson, Dorothea, 97
Gregson, Thomas, 139
Grey, Christopher, 146
Grey, James, 105
Grierson, James, 79
Griffith, Thomas, 81
Grimbol, John, 122
Grimkie, Jonathan F., 125
Groceman, Mary, 135
Gross, Charles, 109
Grossman, Henry, 103
Gruber, Charles, 139
Gruber, Christian, 143
Gruber, Samuel, 106
Guillon, Samuel, 152
Gunn, William, 77
Hackell, Philip, 131
Hackett, Jane, 136
Hadden, Gardner, 131
Hagan, Richard, 143
Hagarty, Dennis, 75
Hagood, Johnston, 136
Hahnbaum, Catharine, 148
Haig, David, 94
Haig, Robert, 93
Haig, Robert, Dr., 113
Hall, D. A., 141
Hall, Daniel, 138
Hall, Mary Ann, 139
Hall, Sarah, 123
Hall, Thomas D., 145
Hall, Thomas, Esq., 124
Hall, William, 145
Hall, William, Capt., 95
Halsall, William, 86
Ham, Samuel, 81
Ham, Thomas, 97
Ham, William, 141
Hamilton, Anthony, 125
Hamilton, Dudley, 143
Hamilton, James, 101
Hamilton, Marlborough S., 118
Hamilton, Paul, 100
Hamitt, Thomas, 98
Hamlin, Hannah, 84
Handy, Thomas, 84
Hangnard, Oliver, 149
Hans, John, 87
Happoldt, John George, 143
Harbouskie, John, 120
Harby, Solomon, 125
Hare, Frances, 75
Hargraves, Joshua, 111
Hargraves, Jospeh, 133
Harleston, Ann, 146
Harman, Elizabeth, 95
Harper, James, 151
Harper, John, Rev, 135
Harris, Jacob, 101
Harris, Tucker, Dr., 142
Harrison, William, 96
Harriss, Andrew, 79
Harriss, Thomas, 148
Hart, Daniel, 78
Hart, Dorcas, 101
Hart, Sarah, 76
Hart, Simon Moses, 147
Harth, John, 139

Harvey, Archibald, 117
Harvey, Benjamin, 104
Harvey, Elizabeth, 107
Harvey, Elizabeth, 97
Harvey, John, 96
Harvey, Samuel, 85
Haslett, John, 122
Haslett, John, 136
Hatch, Robert, 81
Hatfield, Sarah, 93
Hatter, Elizabeth, 138
Hatture, Henry, 79
Hauser, Elias, 122
Haydon, Mathew, 108
Hayes, Mary, 106
Hayward, Samuel, Capt, 135
Hazlehurst, Robert, 129
Hazlewood, Joseph, 87
Headwright, James, 115
Heary, Dennis, 142
Heath, James, 90
Helsey, John, 97
Hemmett, Charlotte, 131
Henderson, Robert, 81
Hendrickson, B., 109
Hennesey, Catharine, 84
Henning, John F., 134
Henrey, Ann, 132
Henry, Jacob, 147
Henson, Archibald, 96
Here, Henry, 111
Heriot, Anthony, 152
Herrett, Mary, 97
Herron, John, 106
Herron, John, 110
Heward, Hannah, 113
Heyliger, Joseph, 124
Heyward, Thomas, 126
Hiams, David, 101
Hidy, David, 76
Hildreth, Benjamin, 84
Hill, Andrew, 101
Hill, Elizabeth, 81
Hill, Hannah, 121
Hill, Paul, 141
Hilligas, Philip, 104
Himeley, John James, 154
Hinson, Joseph, 122
Hippers, Peter, 89
Hippers, William, 131
Hislop, John B., 83
Hislop, Robert, 80
Hislop, Robert, 83
Hitchborn, Isaac B., 153
Hitchburn, John, 126
Hoffskie, Ann C., 143
Hogarth, William, 96
Hogarth, William, Sr., 74
Hogarty, Charles, 114
Holland, Patrick, 122
Holliday, Hugh, 134
Hollingshead, William, 150
Holmes, Andrew, 91
Holmes, Isaac, 113
Holmes, John B., Esq., 122
Holmes, Sack, 133
Holmes, Thomas, 82
Holmes, William, 103

Honeywood, Elizabeth, 149
Honour, John, 103
Hoodmance, John, 106
Hook, Conrad, 84
Hopkins, John, 126
Hopton, Sarah, 150
Hore, Thomas, 129
Horlbeck, Henry, 148
Horlbeck, John, Jr., 148
Horlbeck, John, Sr., 148
Horry, Elias , 115
Horry, Elias Lynch, 118
Horry, Thomas, 123
Horsey, Thomas, 107
Hoskins, John, 84
Houck, John, 77
Houlton, James, 84
House, Samuel, 80
Houston, James, 92
Houston, Samuel, 84
Howard, Mary, 108
Howard, Robert, 97
Howell, John, 118
Hoyland, Anna M., 137
Hubbert, Mary, 114
Hubert, Charles, 110
Huger, Daniel E., 114
Huger, John, 136
Hughes, Edward, 121
Hughes, James, 82
Hughes, Mary, 92
Hugley, John K., 140
Humback, Jacob, 109
Humbert, Godfrey, 128
Hunter, James, 79
Hunter, James, 92
Hunter, Jane, 134
Hunter, Thomas, 141
Hunter, William, 134
Huntington, Mary, 129
Hurd, Sarah, 93
Hussey, Bryan, 128
Huston, Andrew, 149
Hutchinon, Hugh, 134
Hutchinson, Jeremiah, 144
Hutson, Mary, 116
Hutson, William, 101
Hutton, James, 114
Huxham, Elizabeth, 129
Hyams, Samuel, 78
Hyndman, James, 99
Inglesby, Henry, 153
Inglesby, William, 126
Inglish, Dominick, 114
Ingram, Nathaniel, 118
Ireland, Benjamin, 137
Ireland, Edward, 108
Irving, James, 128
Izard, Charlotte, 83
Izard, Ralph, Jr., 136
Izard, Ralph, Sr., 122
Jacks, James, 153
Jackson, John, 149
Jackson, William, 77
Jacque, Victine, 78
Jahern, Joseph, 111
James, John, 103
Jearden, Lewis, 100

Jeffers, John, 89
Jeffers, Mary, 130
Jefferson, John, 116
Jenkins, Edward, Rev., 115
Jenkins, Elias, 102
Jenkins, Jonathan, Mrs., 122
Jenkins, Michael, 116
Jennings, Elizabeth, 130
Jerrazin, Jonathan, 145
Jessop, Jeremiah, 78
Jewel, Benjamin, 79
Johnson, Alexander, 90
Johnson, Edward, 82
Johnson, Esther, 141
Johnson, Jabez W., 154
Johnson, Jacob, 146
Johnson, John, 99
Johnson, William, 88
Johnston & Dunlap, 133
Johnston & Dunlap, 133
Johnston, Charles, 115
Johnston, Hugh, 137
Johnston, John, 130
Johnston, Sarah, 102
Jones, ----, 125
Jones, Abner, 136
Jones, Alexander, 116
Jones, Alexander S., 127
Jones, Daniel, 151
Jones, Edward, Dr., 115
Jones, Henry, 80
Jones, Jesse, 117
Jones, Joseph, 129
Jones, Nathaniel, 129
Jones, Samuel, 137
Jones, Sarah, 151
Jones, Thomas, 152
Jones, Thomas, 85
Joseph, Isarael, 120
Joseph, Samuel, 150
Josephs, Joseph, 144
Joy, Abraham, 90
Joy, Daniel, 108
Judon, Isaac, 106
Kahnle, John, 98
Kaiser, Jacob J., 99
Keeley, Edmond, 107
Keeley, Mary, 145
Keels, Peter, 104
Keenan, George, 128
Keenan, Thomas, 126
Keith, Isaac, Rev., 118
Keley, Joseph, 151
Kelley, William, 110
Kemp, Alexander, 129
Kempton, Ann, 120
Kempton, George, 121
Kennedy, James, 139
Kennedy, Peter, 146
Kennedy, Susanna, 129
Kennon, Henry, 94
Ker, John, 78
Kern, John F., 146
Kerr, Andrew, 90
Kerr, Eliza, 124
Kerr, Samuel, 138
Kershaw, Charles, 143
Kessick, Frances W., 74

Kevan, Alexander, 100
Kevan, William, 130
King, Benjamin, 97
King, Christopher, 115
King, David S., 144
King, Eleonar, 94
Kingman, Elias, 130
Kingsland, John, 89
Kinmond, David, 128
Kirk, John, 78
Kirkland, Joseph, 150
Kirkwood, John, 91
Kisentaner, Susanna, 140
Knipping & Steinmetz, 117
Knouf, Conrod, 106
Knox, Thomas, 81
Knox, Walter, 147
Kofskie, Ann C., 143
Kreps, Ann, 106
Krietzburgh, Conrod, 107
Labatus, Peter, 144
Laborde, Frances, 100
Labott, David, 146
Lacoste, Stephen, 101
Ladeveze, Joseph, 142
Ladson, Elizabeth, 125
Ladson, James, 122
Lafar, Catharine, 85
Laffitty, Frances, 82
Lafoyge, John, 107
Lahthausen, John W., 93
Lamb, George, 151
Lambert, Joseph, 74
Lambrie, John, 101
Lambrie, John B., 102
Lance, Ann, 136
Lance, Lambert, 136
Lanchester, Henry, 91
Lane, Robert, 115
Lane, Samuel, 94
Lane, William, 139
Lang, J. H., 123
Langlois, Mitchell, 108
Langstaff, Benajmin, 98
Lanneau, Bazil, 111
Lapenne, Joseph, 109
Laporte, ----, Mons., 92
Larry, Robert, 83
Larue, Frances, 150
LaShapelle, Jonathan, 144
Latham, Daniel, 90
Latham, Joseph, 90
Laurance, Elizabeth, 88
Laurence, Peter, 99
Lavasha, ----, Capt, 110
Lawrence, Robert D., 97
Lawton, Winborn, 127
Layer, Stephen, 81
Lazarus, Marks, 144
Leacraft, William, 88
Leadbetter, William, 102
Leaumont, Robert, 143
Leavitt, Joshua, 81
Lee, James, 90
Lee, John, 147
Lee, Stephen, 120
Lee, William, 144
Lee, William, Col., 137

Leefe, Benjamin, 131
Leferve, Stephen, 84
Legare, Solomon, 112
Lege, John M., 152
Leger, Elizabeth, 98
Legge, Edward, 92
Legge, Mary, 108
Lehre, Ann, 144
Lehre, Mary, 102
Lehre, Thomas, 119
Lenoiment, Andrew, 139
Lenox, William, 117
Lenox, William, 83
Leonard, Henrey, 128
Lesesne, Elizabeth, 105
Lessne, Hannah, 91
Levey, J. S., 146
Levey, Nathan, 145
Levy, Emanuel, 78
Levy, Hart, 100
Levy, Lyon, 111
Levy, Moses C., 148
Levy, Rosanna, 150
Levy, Ruben, 74
Levy, Samuel, 101
Lewis, Henry, 151
Lewis, Isaac, 129
Lewis, John, 118
Lewis, John, 143
Lewis, John, 88
Lewis, Joseph, 131
Lewis, Joshua, 88
Lewis, Richard, 88
Ley, Frances, 106
Libben, Joseph, 80
Libben, Lebbi, 126
Libby, Nathaniel, 81
Libby, Robert, 81
Liber, Frances, 101
Liber, John, 99
Lightwood, Elizabeth, 123
Limehouse, Robert, 113
Lindsey, Charles, 89
Ling, John, 90
Lining, Charles, 114
Lionval, Andrew, 116
Little, Robert, 82
Lloyd, John, Jr., 84
Lloyd, Joseph, 148
Lockey, George, 141
Lockwood, Joshua, 122
Logan, Honoria, 121
Long, John, 102
Loper, Daniel, 141
Lopez, Aaron, 140
Lopez, David, 137
Lord, Richard, 136
Lothrop, Seth, 79
Love, Duncan, 126
Loveday, John, 148
Lovely, William, 84
Lovett, William, 115
Lowe, John, 143
Lowndes, Sarah, 136
Lowndes, Thomas, 114
Loyd, John, Orphan House, 110
Lucien, Charles, 144
Luscomb, George, 144

Lynah, James, 149
Lynn, John, 96
Lyon, Mordecai, 78
Mackey, John, 121
Mackie, Ann, 143
Mackie, James, Mrs., 101
Madern, James, 80
Magwood, Simon, 84
Maine, John, 128
Mair, Patrick, 134
Maire, James, 154
Maire, Thomas, 133
Malcolm, Thomas, 83
Malone, James, 119
Manigault, Gabriel, 97
Manigault, Joseph, 89
Mann, Henry W., 120
Mann, Margaret, 89
Mann, Spencer, 145
Manson, George, 96
Manuel, Peter, 111
Mar, Ann, 127
Mar, Joseph E., 150
Markley, Abraham, 101
Marks, Humphrey, 99
Marks, Samuel M., 144
Marlin, Edward, 104
Marlin, Edward, Sr., 86
Marrow, John, 136
Marsh, John, 85
Marshal, Thomas, Dr., 119
Marshall, Eleanor, 96
Marshall, Eliza, 120
Marshall, John, 105
Marshall, Thomas, 108
Marshall, William, 138
Marshall, William, 85
Marshall, William, 95
Marstin, Benjamin, 107
Martin, Brunit, 154
Martin, Charles, 93
Martin, Elizabeth, 144
Martin, Elizabeth, 98
Martin, Frances, 94
Martin, Jacob, 153
Martin, Mary, 119
Martin, Thomas, 113
Mason, Mary, 152
Mason, Susanna, 116
Mason, William, 85
Massicon, Venve, 104
Mathews, George, 104
Mathews, Philip, Rev., 89
Mattuce, John, 104
Maubray, William, 143
Mauger, John, 134
Maverick, Samuel, 99
Maxey, Margaret, 118
Maxwell, John, 140
Mayberry, Thomas, 134
Mayer, Charlotte, 80
Mazyck, Daniel, 104
Mazyck, Nathaniel, 81
Mazycke, William, 139
McAfee, John, 102
McBeth, James, 130
McBlair, William, 139
McBride, James, 78

McBride, John, 129
McCall, Ann, 129
McCall, Elizabeth, 94
McCall, James, 109
McCalla, T. H., Dr., 132
McCan, Edward, 121
McCants, Ann, 112
McCarty, John, 122
McCaulay, George, 133
McCleish, Alexander, 90
McClure, Alexander & Jonathan, 124
McClure, Jonathan, 124
McClury, Sarah, 132
McCorkel, Samuel, 80
McCradie, John, 124
McCredie, David, 133
McCune, Samuel, 106
McDonald, Christopher, 119
McDonald, S. E., 130
McDonell, Alexander, 148
McDow, Robert, 102
McDowall, James, 141
McDowall, John, 99
McDowall, Patrick, 78
McEast, Patrick, 75
McFarlan, Alexander, 125
McGann, Patrick, 134
McGee, John, 119
McGinniss, Patrick, 142
McGuire, Mary, 120
McGuire, William, 75
McGwinn, Daniel, 151
McHaze, Anthony, 152
McIlhany, James, 128
McIntire, Thomas, 132
McIntosh, Simon, 112
McKay, Crafts, 132
McKee, John, 114
McKenzie, Andrew, 153
McKenzie, Kennedy, 109
McKey, Malcom, 116
McKinzie, Elizabeth, 75
McLachlan, Archibald, 129
McLane, Laughlan, 117
McLean, Evan, 150
McLean, Michael, 96
McLean, Watson, 79
McLeod, Catharine, 82
McLeod, William, 118
McMillan, Richard, 106
McNeale, Archibald, 123
McNeil, Catharine, 90
McNiel, Archibald, 142
McPherson, Duncan, 142
McWann, William, 133
Mecomb, Joseph, 99
Meeks, Joseph, 75
Merchant, Peter, 143
Merrell, Benjamin, 151
Merry, Patrick, 81
Meurset, Emelia, 142
Michel, Margaret, 103
Middleton, Ann, 136
Middleton, Mary, 84
Middleton, Mary, 95
Middleton, Solomon, 101
Milhado, Benjamin, 117

Miller, Benjamin, 109
Miller, Frederick, 99
Miller, James, 131
Miller, James, 79
Miller, John, 101
Miller, John, 140
Miller, John, 92
Miller, John, 94
Miller, John J., 148
Miller, Mary, 89
Miller, Nicholas, 145
Miller, William, 123
Miller, William, 77
Milligan, Joseph, 142
Milligan, William, 135
Milligan, William, 89
Mills, John, 110
Mills, Thomas, 107
Mills, William, 80
Mills, William, 91
Milner, George, 83
Minot, Thomas, 130
Minott, William, 118
Mintzing, Mary, 142
Miott, Fanny, 138
Miott, John, 106
Mishaw, John, 87
Mitchel, Elias, 151
Mitchell, Ann, 123
Mitchell, Elizabeth, 80
Mitchell, James, 122
Mitchell, John, 134
Mitchell, John H., 128
Mitchell, William, 136
Moer, William, 111
Moles, James, 91
Moncrief, John, 91
Moncrieffe, John, 129
Monk, James, 133
Monpoy, Henry, 154
Montague, Charles, 81
Montan, Anthony, 124
Mood, Peter, 148
Moodie, Benjamin, 89
Moor, Stephen M., 110
Moore, George, 121
Moore, John, 110
Moore, John, 110
Moore, John, 150
Moore, John E., 145
Moore, Joseph, 91
Moore, Peter Joseph, Dr., 116
Moore, Philip, 124
Moore, Richard, 145
Moore, Samuel, 102
Morales, Jacob, 142
Morcrief, Susanna, 92
Mordecai, Jacob, 152
More, Philip, 80
Moret, Lewis, 154
Morgan, Ann, 102
Morgan, Charles, 91
Morgan, Edward, 136
Morgan, Edward B., 109
Morgan, Henry, 132
Morphy, Don Diego, 119
Morris, Lewis, 123
Morris, Thomas, 92

Purcell, Joseph, 101
Purdy, Joseph, 91
Purse, William, 151
Purvis, William, 105
Pyatt, Elizabeth, 145
Qiblong, Henry, 147
Quash, Robert, 136
Quenan, Dennis, 89
Query, John, 154
Quider, Frances, 153
Quiggin, David, 80
Quigly, Esther, 146
Quin, James, 75
Quinby, Joseph, 87
Rachel, Nathaniel, 92
Radcliff, Thomas, 100
Ralph, John, 152
Ramadge, Frances, 151
Rambert, Charlotte, 136
Ramos, Manuel, 148
Ramsey, David, Dr., 137
Ramsey, George, 75
Ramsey, Jonathan, Dr., 138
Ramsey, Joseph, Dr., 121
Ramsey, Thomas, 143
Randal, Elizabeth, 102
Randall, Esther, 102
Rankins, James, 148
Rannie, George, 115
Rasdale, David, 107
Ravenell, Stephen, 106
Read, James, 104
Read, William, Dr., 127
Redhimer, Peter, 108
Redlich, William, 129
Redman, James, 140
Reed, John, 151
Reeves, Enos, 139
Reid, George, 130
Reid, John, 153
Reiley, Robert, 98
Reiley, Terrence, 135
Reiley, Thomas, 80
Remley, Barbara, 103
Remoussin, Daniel, 140
Renando, Peter, 125
Renauld, John, 121
Rennie, John, 132
Rennier, Mary, 93
Repon, Bernard, 75
Reposk, Joseph, 76
Reside, William, 125
Revell, Hannah, 97
Reynolds, Elizabeth, 141
Ricardo, Benjamin, 143
Richardo, David, 144
Richards, Samuel, 142
Richardson, James, 151
Richardson, John, 132
Richardson, Thomas, 149
Rigaud, Peter, 95
Righton, Joseph, 128
Righton, McCally, 128
Rilber, Elizabeth, 128
Riley, James, 106
Rivers, Gracia, 135
Rivers, James, 145
Rivers, Samuel, 127

Rivers, Thomas, 93
Rivers, Thomas, Sr., 130
Roach, John, 96
Roach, William, 95
Roberts, Adam, 86
Roberts, Ann, 126
Roberts, George, 150
Roberts, John, 125
Roberts, William, 141
Robertson, Alexander, 99
Robertson, John, 131
Robertson, Mary, 138
Robertson, Rachael, 108
Robinet, Frances, 78
Robinson, John, 101
Robinson, John, 99
Robinson, Pamelia, 87
Rodmond, Thomas, 80
Rodrigues, Abraham, 152
Rogers, Christopher, 126
Rogers, Sarah, 128
Rogly, Anthony, 93
Rolaine, Catharine, 136
Roper, Thomas, 79
Roper, William, 130
Rose, Alexander, 127
Rose, Jeremiah, 88
Rose, John S., 147
Roske, John, 74
Ross, George, 75
Ross, Jane, 132
Ross, Thomas, 149
Rosseau, Peter, 86
Roulain, Robert, 97
Roullit, Mary, 152
Rouse, William, 149
Rout, George, 141
Row, George D., 101
Row, Michael, 103
Rowand, Mary, 113
Rowell, Richard, 118
Royal, James, 80
Ruben, ——, 125
Ruberry, John, 130
Ruberry, Mary, 103
Ruger, Elizabeth, 86
Russell, Benjamin, 85
Russell, Daniel, 85
Russell, Mary, 123
Russell, Nathaniel, 129
Rutledge, Frederick, 113
Rutledge, Henry, 95
Rutledge, Hugh, Judge, 135
Rutledge, John, 145
Rutledge, Mary, 115
Ryans, Elizabeth, 78
Ryckbosh, ——, Mrs., 146
Saixas, Michael & Isaac, 112
Samory, Claude, 152
Sante, Angelo, 137
Sargeant, Elizabeth, 151
Sass, Jacob, 138
Saunders, Elizabeth, 100
Saunders, John, 109
Savage, Martha, 112
Schauner, Nicholas, 103
Scheppler, L. C. A., 87
Schmidt, John, 80

Schreiner, Nicholas, 103
Schroler, Jonathan, 137
Schroler, Jonathan Jacob, 109
Schutt, Casper C., 137
Scott, Ann, 148
Scott, Eliza, 91
Scott, James, 134
Scottow, Susanna, 100
Scrimzcour, J. & C., 131
Scriven, Thomas, 128
Seabrook Benjamin, 126
Seamore, Isaac, 118
Seamore, Stephen, 115
Seawars, Abraham, 87
Secrets, Martin, 82
Seiler, Daniel, 103
Seiler, Michael, 105
Selby, George, 101
Self, Samuel, 107
Serjant, Mary, 131
Serrem, Joseph, 134
Serzmour, Bartholemew, 75
Setler, Daniel, 103
Seymour, Joseph, 103
Shackleford, Nathan, 81
Shand, Robert, 153
Shannon, Elizabeth, 93
Sharp, John, 87
Shaw, Richard, 123
Shela, Alexander, 98
Shepherd, James, 103
Shepherd, Thomas R., 108
Sherer, John, 103
Sherman, Simon T., 99
Shievely, George, 98
Shilling, Samuel, 103
Shirer, John, 103
Shirtliff, William, 95
Shitterling, Mary, 140
Shollbred, James, 115
Shrewsbury, Maryann, 86
Shrewsbury, Stephen, 83
Shulblick, Thomas, 110
Shwartz, John, 152
Silberg, Nicolas, 95
Simmons, Benjamin, 82
Simmons, William, 103
Simmons, William, 106
Simons, Frances, 122
Simons, James, 140
Simons, Keating, 115
Simpson, John, 79
Simpson, Margaret, 128
Sims, William, 106
Singletary, Joseph, 105
Singleton, Mary, 92
Singleton, Sarah, 105
Sire, Delalon, 102
Skirving, Charlotte, 127
Skirving, William, 113
Slow, Richard R., 94
Slowman, Henry, 89
Smallwood, Richard, 88
Smart & Evans, 120
Smerdon, Elias, 133
Smith, Agnes, 125
Smith, Agnes, 132
Smith, Amos, 75

Smith, Ann, 121
Smith, Ann, 92
Smith, Archibald, Jr., 92
Smith, Caleb, 83
Smith, Daniel, 94
Smith, Frederick, 151
Smith, George, 95
Smith, Hannah, 78
Smith, Henry, 96
Smith, James, 88
Smith, John, 108
Smith, John, 135
Smith, John, 143
Smith, John, 83
Smith, John, 96
Smith, John C., 137
Smith, Jonathan, Mrs., 113
Smith, Josiah, 137
Smith, Latitia, 85
Smith, Margaret, 145
Smith, O'Brian, 126
Smith, Peter, 135
Smith, Peter, Esq., 114
Smith, Rebecca, 139
Smith, Robert, 145
Smith, Robert, 75
Smith, Rodger, Sr., 102
Smith, Samuel, 120
Smith, Samuel, 128
Smith, Samuel, 78
Smith, Samuel, Dr., 120
Smith, Sarah, 125
Smith, Thomas, 111
Smith, Thomas, 94
Smith, Thomas B., 95
Smith, Thomas R., 113
Smith, Whiteford, 83
Smith, Will S., 120
Smith, William, 100
Smith, William, 132
Smith, William, 90
Smith, William, 91
Smith, William, 96
Smylie, Andrew, 133
Smylie, Susanna, 114
Smyth, John, 101
Smyth, John, 111
Snetter, Charles, 124
Snipes, Benjamin, 96
Snowden, Charles, 79
Soane, Joseph, 108
Solle, John, 117
Solomon, Joseph, 146
Sommarsall, William, 130
Sommarssall, Thomas, 130
Sparks, Thomas, 138
Sparrow, James, 107
Spears, James, 94
Speiren, Patrick, 101
Spencer, Sebastian, 84
Spereck, Thomas, 110
Spidell, Aberhart, 142
Spidell, George, 143
Spinler, Jacob, 152
Spring, John, 99
Spussegger, John, 90
Stablier, Joseph, 75
Stafford, Theodore, 138

Steadman, Charles, 145
Steinmeir, George, 98
Stent, Mary, 124
Stephens, Daniel, 111
Stephens, William, 94
Stephens, William, 98
Stevens, Jerves H., 113
Stevens, Thomas, 150
Stevens, William S., Dr., 118
Stevenson, Jane, 116
Stewart, Alexander, 119
Stewart, Ann, 149
Stewart, Charles, 112
Stewart, Henry, 144
Stewart, John, 147
Stewart, Martha, 130
Stewart, Robert, 147
Stewart, Thomas, 133
Stoll, Jacob, 147
Stoll, Jesse, 144
Stoll, Sarah, 142
Stone, Eliza, 116
Stone, Isabella, 85
Stoney, John, 90
Stoops, Benjamin, 110
Strobel, Daniel, 98
Strobhart, Susanna, 114
Stroble, Jacob, 144
Stroble, John, 104
Stroecher, Catharine, 95
Strohecker, John, 87
Stromer, Henry M., 131
Stroub, Jacob, 99
Struges, Josiah, 127
Stuker, Christopher, 109
Suarres, Jacob, 142
Sutherland, Frances, 77
Sutliffe, Eli, 142
Sutton, Mary, 89
Suwnres, Jacob, Jr, 120
Swain, Joseph, 91
Swain, Luke, 130
Swinton, Hugh, 150
Switzer, John R., 148
Symonds, Frances, 132
Symonds, James, 94
Symons, Sampson, 144
Symons, Samuel, 143
Tabor, Simon, 93
Tagart, Mary, 122
Tair, Robert, 143
Tarver, John, 142
Tate, James, Capt., 132
Taylor, Alexander, 92
Taylor, Joseph, 88
Taylor, Joseph G., 97
Taylor, Margaret, 112
Taylor, Paul, 107
Taylor, Paul, 110
Taylor, William, 110
Teasdale, John, 130
Teraff, Philip, 93
Tew, Charles, 145
Theus, Rosanna, 149
Theus, Simeon, 137
Theuvenin, Peter, 149
Theyer, Ebenezer, 114
Thomas, Frances, 141

Thomas, John, 131
Thomas, John, 145
Thomas, John, 74
Thomas, Mary Lamboll, 118
Thomas, Sarah, 91
Thomas, Stephen, 132
Thompson, Alexander, 138
Thompson, Daniel, 114
Thompson, James, 134
Thompson, John, 107
Thompson, William, 144
Thomson, Margaret, 79
Thomson, Thomas, 83
Thorn, Jacob, 149
Thornby, Hannah, 147
Thorne, John George, 131
Thorney, James, 107
Thron, John, 118
Thron, John, 149
Thuring, David, 87
Thurtle, William, 81
Timmons, Lewis, 138
Timmons, William, 101
Timothy, Benjamin F., 133
Tims, Hannah, 110
Tironguilamb, -----, Madam, 84
Tobias, Joseph, 147
Tobin, Peter, 141
Tofel, John, 141
Tonge, S., Mrs., 127
Toole, John, 132
Toomer, Anthony, Mrs., 114
Torrans, James, 84
Torrans, William H., 102
Tores, Abraham, 142
Tossin, Esther, 120
Toushier, Margaret, 127
Towey, Henry, 87
Treadcraft, Bethel, 137
Trenholm, William, 127
Trescot, Edward, 150
Tresvant, Peter, 130
Trezvant, Theodore, 153
Troup, James, 125
Truckelut, Joseph, 77
Tucker, Ann, 106
Tucker, Sarah, 129
Tunno, Adam, 134
Tunno, Thomas, 127
Tunno, William, 81
Turk, Mary, 82
Turnbull, Gavin, 141
Turnbull, Robert J., 124
Turner, Daniel W., 118
Turner, Joseph, 140
Turner, Thomas , 144
Turner, Thomas, 152
Turner, William, 106
Turpin, Hanna, 132
Turpin, William, 98
Twedell, Mathew, 153
Tweed, Alexander, 91
Tyler, John, 108
Ummensetter, John, 139
Uter, Lewis, 144
Vale, John D., 153
Valencia, Moses, 116
Valk, Ann, 127

71

CHAPTER 8

THE 1801 DIRECTORY

The 1801 directory was published by John Nixon Nelson as *Nelson's Charleston Directory, and Strangers Guide, for 1801* (Charleston: John Nixon Nelson, 1801). In addition to the listing of people, it contains information on the following: Wharfage, Mint, Almanac, Courts, U.S. Towns, Post-Office, Stamps, Duties, Navy's, and Bank of South Carolina. It contains 1978 entries.

The locations of people listed in the directory varied little from that of 1796. King Street still had the greatest number with 15%, while Meeting Street had 10%, Tradd Street 7%, Broad Street 7%, East Bay Street 7%, and Queen Street 6%.

The number for each street was: Amen Street 15, Anson Street 5, Archdale Street 19, Bay Street 1, Beale's Wharf 6, Beaufain Street 25, Bedon's Alley 12, Beresford's Alley 2, Beresford Street 20, Blackbird's Alley 3, Blake's Wharf 8, Boundary Street 19, Broad Street 122, Bull Street 10, Cannon Street 4, Chamber's Alley 11, Champney Street 13, Champney's Alley 1, Champney's Row 3, Champney's Wharf 1, Charles Street 6, Charleston College 2, Church Alley 1, Church Street 108, Church St. Continued 14, Clifford's Alley 8, Coat's Row 2, Cochran's Wharf 2, Coming Street 16, Craft's North Wharf 2, Craft's Range 1, Craft's Row 4, Craft's South Row, Craft's South Wharf 4, Craft's Wharf 6, Cumberland Street 11, Custom House 1, Dutch Church Alley 3, East Bay 120, East Bay Continued 12, Ellery Street 15, Elliot Street 47, Exchange 3, Exchange Alley 1, Exchange Square 1, Federal Street 11, Fort Mechanic 1, Friend Street 13, Frink's Wharf 1, Front Street 4, Gaillard's Wharf 6, George Street 19, Geyer's Front Range 1, Geyer's New Range 2, Geyer's Range 1, Geyer's Wharf 11, Gibbes Street 2, Gibbes Wharf 1, Gillon Street 4, Goodby's Alley 1, Governor's Bridge 1, Guignard Street 31, Ham Street 1, Ham's Wharf 1, Harleston's Green 1, Hasell Street 30, Hopton's Alley 1, Hopton's Lane 5, Horlbeck Alley 1, King Street 276, King Street Road 8, Kinlock Court 3, Kinney Street 1, Lamboll Street 1, Legare Street 18, Liberty Street 9, Lodge Alley 4, Lombard Lane 1, Longitude Lane 2, Lynch's Lane 6, Magazine Street 5, Maiden Lane 11, Market Square 3, May's Wharf 1, Mazyck Street 14, Mazyckborough Creek 1, Meeting Street 181, Middle Street 7, Minority Street 2, Montagu Street 4, Moore Street 12, Nicholl's Wharf 4, Orange Street 7, Pinckney Street 30, Pitt Street 8, Prioleau's Wharf 3, Pritchard's Wharf, Queen Street 113, Quince Street 14, Quince's Alley 1, Rhett's Lane 4, Roper's Wharf 4, Scarborough Street 8, Short Street 2, Smith Street 2, Smith's Lane 4, Society Street 9, South Bay 14, St. Michael's Alley 5, St. Philip's Street 17, State House Square 2, Stoll's Alley 11, Tradd Street 125, Trott Street 30, Union Shop 1, Union Street 43, Union Street Continued 28, Unity Alley 7, Vanderhorst's Alley 1, Vanderhorst's Row 1, Vanderhorst's Wharf 4, Wall Street 9, Water Street 9, Wentworth Street 21, West Street 2, and Wyatt's Lot 7.

The professions most often listed are: merchant 15%, grocer 7%, carpenter 4%, shop keeper 4%, planter 3%, mariner 3%, factor 3%, tailor 2%, physician 2%, attorney 2%, and boarding house 2%. Even added together the grocery stores, the shops, and the stores amount only to 12% which is less than that for the merchants. Apparently the term merchant does not mean as much as it previously had. Also the economy of the city had become more diversified and people are often given more specific professions than simply shop or store. By this time the city has more physicians than lawyers. Only one man is listed as a common laborer. This results from the fact that blacks made up a majority of the population of Charleston and most labor was performed by free persons of color or slaves.

The following is the listing for each profession or status: accountant 1, apothecary 3, attorney 38, auctioneer 6, baker 20, bapt. 1, barber 7, blacksmith 13, block maker 9, boarding house 32, boarding school 1, book shop 1, bookkeeper 3, bookseller 2, boot maker 1, brass founder 1, brewer 1, brick layer 19, brick maker 1, British consul 1, broker 6, butcher 32, cabinet maker 24, cake shop 1, captain 2, carpenter 79, carter 3, cashier , chair maker 7, chancellor 1, city marshall 1, city sheriff 1, city treasurer 1, clerk 15, coach maker 8, collect. Super. Off 1, commission vendue master 1, confectioner 7, constable 1, cook 1, cooper 15, coroner 1, cotton factor 1, cotton gin maker 1, counting house 1, currier 1, custom house officer 1, deputy high constable 1, dancing master 3, dentist 3, deputy collector 1, deputy naval officer, deputy sheriff 3, deputy surveyor 1, distiller 4, district sheriff 1, drayman 7, druggist 6, dry nurse 1, engraver 3, exchange broker 1, factor 51, federal marshall 2, fencing master 1, fiddle maker 1, fire worker 1, founder 1, French teacher 2, fruit shot 8, gardener 2, general 1, goldsmith 10, governor 1, grocer 133, gauger 1, gunsmith 3, H.M. 1, hair dresser 8, harness maker 2, hatter 4, Hebrew minister 1, horse dealer 1, hotel 1, house carpenter 1, import inspector 2, inn keeper 4, inspector 3, instrument maker 1, insurance broker 1, insurance office 1, intendant 1, interpreter 1, ironmonger, jeweller 4, joiner 1, judge 6, justice of peace 3, justice of quorum 1, keeper of jail 1, keeper of poor house 1, laborer 1, land surveyor 2, lieutenant in navy 1, limner 1, livery stables 2, lumber cutter 1, lumber measurer 2, lumber merchant 2, music instrument maker 1, major 1, mantua maker 3, mariner 55, master of poor house 1, merchant 274, midwife 2, milliner 5, millwright 1, minister 8, music shop 1, musician 5, naval officer 1, notary public 2, nurse 2, O.D.C. Bank 1, ordinary for Charleston 1, painter 10, pastry cook 1, physician 40, pilot 3, planter 57, plasterer 1, port collector 1, post master 1, printer 9, prothonator 1, rigger 8, rope maker 1, saddler 7, sailor 1, sailmaker 3, sausage maker 1, school 2, school master 6, school mistress 12, scrivener 2, seamstress 9, sheriff 1, ship carpenter 7, ship changer 5, ship joiner 2, shipwright 6, shoe maker 16, shoe shop 1, shoe store 16, shop keeper 68, silk dyer 1, slop shop 8, Spanish consul 1, stables 1, stage office 1, stamping officer 1, state treasurer 1, stay maker 1, stewart 1, stone cutter 4, store keeper 6, supervisor 1, tailor 43, tallow chandler 2, tanner 8, tax collector 1, teacher of drawing 1, tin plate worker 1, tin man 4, tobacconist 9, trunk maker 1, turner 2, upholsterer 3, vendue cryer 1, vendue master 22, w. washer 1, w.c. 3, washer 1, watchmaker 8, weigher 1, wharfinger, wheelwright 1, widow 109, Windsor chair maker 1, wine merchant 2, wine store 1.

Women constitute 309 of the total entries or 16%. Of these only 103 have professions listed. As usual the greatest number operated shops (21%), ran boarding houses (16%), or taught (13%).

The status of women who have some profession after their names include: baker 1, boarding house 17, boarding school 1, butcher 1, confectioner 4, cook 1, dry nurse 1, fruit shop 1, grocer 11, inn keeper 1, mantua maker 3, merchant 1, midwife 2, milliner 5, nurse 2, pastry cook 1, saddler 1, school 1, school mistress 12, seamstress 9, shop keeper 17, slop shop 2, store keeper 3, tallow chandler 1, teacher of drawing 1, W.C. 3, and washer 1.

Abendenone, Joseph. Merchant. 263 King St.
Abrahams, Jacob. Merchant. 5 Queen St.
Abrahams, Moses. Vendue Master. 41 Queen St.
Abroise, Michael. Fire Worker. Church St.
Adams, Ezekiel. Carpenter. 7 Maiden Lane
Aertsen & Co. Auctioneers. Exchange. North Side
Acrtscn, Guilliam. 15 Friend St.
Aiken, Ann. Boarding School. King St., corner Wentworth
Ainger, Edward. Broker. 78 Tradd St.
Air, George. Carpenter. 91 King St.
Akeen, Elenora. Grocer. 25 Pinckney St.
Alexander & M'Clure. 22 Broad St.
Alexander, Abraham. Shop Keeper. 214 King St.
Alexander, David. Merchant. 9 Broad St.
Alexander, Judah. Grocer. 148 King St.
Alexander, Rachael. Widow. 46 Trott St.
Allen, George. Rigger. 32 Union St.
Allen, Huldah. Kinloch Court
Allen, Mason & Ewing. Merchants. 125 Tradd St.
Almand, Joseph. 17 Friend St.
Alston, John. 9 King St.
Ancrum, William. 13 Ellery St.
Anderson, Ann. W.C. Middle St., corner Minority
Anderson, Archibald. Plasterer. 26 Hasell St.
Anderson, Robert. Merchant. 19 Tradd St.
Anderson, William. Stay Maker. 148 Meeting St.
Andrews, Moses. Mariner. Stoll's Alley
Anger, Edward. Broker. 16 East Bay
Annelly & Lewis. Merchants. 103 Church St.
Anthony, ----. Baker. Union St.
Anthony, John. Harness Maker. 234 Magazine St.
Ash, John. Planter. South Bay
Askew, Ann. Widow. 23 Archdale St.
Aspray, John F. Mariner. Church St. Continued
Atkinson, ----. Widow. 17 Amen St.
Atmore, Ralph. Goldsmith. 98 Broad St.
Austin, Catharine. Slop Shop. 50 East Bay
Avellie, John. Bapt. East End of Boundary St.
Axson, Jacob. O.D.C. Bank. Horlbeck Alley
Axson, Samuel. Carpenter. 17 King St.
Axson, William. Carpenter. 61 Tradd St.
Azaby, Abraham. Hebrew Minister. 130 Hasell St.
Azevedo, Isaac. Commission Vendue Master. Champney's Row
Baas, Thomas. Block Maker. Gillon St.
Bacot, Henry. 26 Tradd St.
Bacot, Thomas. Post Master. 112 Tradd St.
Badger, James. Painter & Glazier. 135 East Bay
Bailey & Waller. Book Shop. 104 Broad St.
Bailey, Henry. Attorney. 22 Elliot St.
Baker, Amery. 10 Church St., corner
Baker, Francis. Brick Layer. 33 King St.
Baker, Joseph. Carpenter. 6 South Bay
Baker, Thomas. Insurance Broker. 103 Queen St.
Bald & Blade. Merchants. 13 East Bay
Baldwin, Robert. Carpenter. 22 Beaufain St.
Baldwin, William. Hatter. Queen St.
Ball, Archibald. 16 George St.
Ball, Elizabeth. Widow. 16 Church St.
Ball, Thomas. Factor. Roper's Wharf
Ballon, Andrew. Hair Dresser. 103 Queen St.
Bampfield, Rebecca. 87 Queen St.

Bandroit, Joseph. Scrivener. 5 Rhett's Lane
Banks & Lockwood. Merchants. 139 Tradd St.
Banks, John. Merchant. 139 Tradd St.
Barker, Joseph. Merchant. 93 Meeting St.
Barn & Throm. Grocers. 159 Meeting St.
Barnes, James. Cabinet Maker. 132 Church St. Continued
Barnet, Alexander. Physician. Wentworth St., corner Smith
Barnet, Samuel. 94 Church St.
Barrie, David. Grocer. 6 King St.
Barron & Wilson. Physicians. 252 Meeting St.
Barron, John. Merchant. 11 East Bay
Barrot, Esther. Boarding House. Chamber's Alley
Bay, Elihu H. Judge. Meeting St., corner St. Michael's
Beale, John. 33 East Bay
Beale, Joseph. Clerk. 8 Tradd St.
Beard, Catharine. W.C. Montagu St., corner Cumming
Beard, Eliza. Widow. 88 Broad St.
Beath, Robert. Store Keeper. 27 Broad St.
Beatie, Edward. Merchant. 45 East Bay
Beauderot, Joseph. Scrivener. Rhett's Lane
Bee, Eliza. 15 Amen St.
Bee, Thomas. Judge. 100 Church St.
Bee, Thomas, Jr. Charleston College
Bee, William. 49 Kinney St.
Beekman, ----, Mrs. East Bay, corner Hasell
Beekman, Adolphus. Painter & Glazier. 133 Meeting St.
Beekman, Samuel. Block Maker. East Bay
Beleaud, John. King St.
Bell, David. Clerk. 175 Meeting St.
Bell, William. Grocer. 248 King St.
Bell, William. Bull St.
Bellamy, ----, Mrs. Widow. Longitude Lane
Bellanton, Filete. 3 Maiden Lane
Belleurgey, Claude. Fencing Master. 244 Meeting St.
Bellings, George. Physician. Mazyck St.
Bellisle, Pierre. Baker. 8 Maiden Lane
Belser, Christian. Butcher. 43 Meeting St.
Belser, Jacob. Butcher. 41 Meeting St.
Belzon, ----. Painter. St. Michael's Alley
Benfield, George. 3 George St.
Bennet & Son. Lumber Measurers. Harleston's Green
Bennet, Joseph. Tin Plate Worker. 46 Meeting St.
Benoist & Blome. Bakers. 171 Meeting St.
Benoit, Theresa. Fruit Shop. 34 Church St.
Benthall, Ebenezer. Mariner. 9 Wyatt's Lot
Bentham, James. Justice of Quorum, Notary Public.
Bering, Jno. Goldsmith, Jeweller. 125 Broad St.
Bernard, Jacob. Merchant. 16 Queen St.
Bernard, Richard. St. Michael's Alley
Berney, John. Merchant. 23 King St.
Besselleau, Mark Anthony. Mariner. Beaufain St.
Bessiere, Anthony. 35 Church St.
Best, William. A. M. 206 King St.
Bethune, Angus. Merchant. 11 Broad St.
Bevin, Francis. Carpenter. 15 Union St. Continued
Bigelow, Elizabeth. Widow. 6 Queen St.
Billy, Anthony. Shoemaker. Unity Alley
Bizeuil, Julian. Fruit Store. 42 Union St.
Black & Yates. Coopers. Beale's Wharf
Black, John. Ironmonger. 12 Broad St.

Blackford, Edward. Merchant. 21 East Bay
Blackledge, Thomas & Co. 181 Union St. Continued
Blair, James. Vendue Master. Stoll's Alley
Blair, John & Co. 85 Church St.
Blair, William. Carpenter. 257 Meeting St.
Blake, Elizabeth. Widow. Church St.
Blake, John. Bull St.
Blake, John. Factor. South Bay
Blakeley, Samuel. Store Keeper. 28 Broad St.
Blakeley, Samuel & Co. Merchants. 193 King St.
Blamyer, William. Weigher. Guignard St.
Blondet, Benjamin. Tailor. 29 Union St.
Blondet, ——, Mons. Shop Keeper. 157 Meeting St.
Blume, Andrew. Butcher. Bull St.
Bob, Elizabeth. Widow. Clifford's Alley
Bocquet, E., Mrs. W.C. St. Philip's St., corner
　Boundary
Boisegerard, Fiabe. Anson St., corner George
Boisgerard, Constant. Anson St., corner George
Bollough, Elias. Shoe and Boot Maker. Wentworth St.
Bonetheau, Elizabeth. 87 Church St.
Bonetheau, G. M. Clerk City Council
Bonneau, Francis. Carpenter. 60 Broad St.
Bonsell, Elizabeth. Widow. 5 Wentworth St.
Booker, Anthony. Boot Maker. 33 Broad St.
Boone, Thomas. Carpenter. Ellery St.
Booner, Christian. Grocer. 33 Queen St.
Booth, B. & Co. Merchants. East Bay
Boothwright, Jabez. Grocer. 11 Archdale St.
Borde, ——. Engraver. 95 Church St.
Borman, Angel. Sailmaker. Blake's Wharf
Bourgneuf, Jean. 7 Society St.
Bournonvivier, G. Pierre. Beresford's Alley
Bouwens, Charles. Grocer. Quince St., corner Trott
Bow, James. Mariner. 18 Meeting St.
Bowen, T. B. Printer. 240 King St.
Bowering, Henry. Merchant. Elliot St., corner Church
Bowers, David. Mariner. Charles St.
Boyd, Benjamin. Merchant. 139 King St.
Boyd, William. Merchant. Geyer's Wharf
Boyle, James. 28 Union St.
Bracey & Lee. Craft's North Wharf
Bradford, ——, Mrs. Milliner. 30 Broad St.
Bradford, Thomas. Music Shop. 84 Church St.
Brady, Robert. Carpenter. Smith's Lane
Brailsford, ——, Mrs. 1 Friend St.
Brailsford, Edward. Physician. Mazyck St.
Brailsford, John & Robert. Factors. 3 East Bay
Brailsford, Morton. Merchant. 223 Tradd St.
Brandon, David. Distiller. Boundary St., corner
　Meeting
Brant, Stephen. 22 Union St. Continued
Brass, John. Grocer. 98 Queen St.
Brebner, Archibald. Tailor. 12 Tradd St.
Brennan, Matthew & R. Grocers. 130 Broad St.
Brian, David. 24 King St.
Bridie, ——, Mons. Meeting St.
Brisbane, William. Planter. Legare St.
Bromigan, John. Grocer. 5 Champney St.
Bron, J. P. Cotton Gin Maker. Meeting St. North
Brown & Burrow. Merchants. 103 Broad St.
Brown & Franklin. 17 Chamber's Alley
Brown, Daniel. Mariner. 131 Church St. Continued
Brown, Daniel. Cabinet Maker. King St.
Brown, Harriot. 57 Tradd St.
Brown, James. City Marshall. 201 Meeting St.
Brown, John. Rigger. Quince St.
Brown, Mariah. Confectioner. 42 Elliot St.

Brown, Moses. Barber. 41 King St.
Brown, William. Mariner. 2 Maiden Lane
Browney, Roger. 22 Pinckney St.
Brownlee, John. 208 King St.
Browson, John. Carpenter. Boundary St.
Bruckner, Daniel. 43 Church St.
Brudieu, John. 87 Meeting St.
Bryant, John. Import Inspector.
Bryant, Perey. Shoe Store. 56 King St.
Buchanon, John. Water St.
Buckle, Margaret. Widow. 56 Broad St.
Budd, ——, Mrs. Boarding House. 48 Church St.
Buford, Ann & Eliza. Milliners. 13 Tradd St.
Builey, H. B. 34 Church St.
Builey, Jacob. Shop Keeper. 271 King St.
Buist, George, Rev. Minister. Church St. Continued
Bulger, John. Deputy Naval Officer
Bulgin, James. Merchant. 3 Craft's Row
Bulkley, Stephen. Merchant. 24 East Bay
Bulow, John and Charles. Merchants. 173 King St.
Bunton, William. Shoemaker. 6 King St.
Burden, Kinsey. Factor. Craft's South Wharf
Burgen, Philip. Boarding House. 6 Union St.
Burger, David. Inn Keeper. 106 Queen St.
Burgess, James. 4 Bedon's Alley
Burke, Aedanus. Judge. 38 Church St.
Burke, Henry & Co. 6 East Bay
Burke, Patrick. Cabinet Maker. 43 Queen St.
Burkmyer, John. Butcher Stall 8. Home, 8 Wentworth
　St.
Burr, Nehemiah. Mariner. 9 Wyatt's Lot
Burrows & Dickenson. Merchants. 134 Tradd St.
Butler, Charles. Goldsmith. 255 King St.
Butler, Joseph. Shop Keeper. 19 Union St.
Butler, Robert. Mariner. 19 Union St.
Butterton, Joseph. Mariner. Rhett's Lane
Byckwood, ——. 12 Coming St.
Byrnes, Joseph. Merchant. Blake's Wharf
Byrnes, Patrick. 37 Hasell St.
Cabos, John. Merchant. 115 Tradd St.
Caitey, Ann. Widow. 26 Maiden Lane
Calder, Alexander. Cabinet Maker. 123 Queen St.
Caldwell, Henry. Merchant. 106 Church St.
Callaghan, John. Grocer. 5 Elliot St.
Calligan, Peter. Inn Keeper. Chamber's Alley
Calvert, Elizabeth. Boarding House. 15 Broad St.
Cambridge, Eliza. Boarding House. King St.
Cambridge, Tobias. Vendue Master. Beale's Wharf
Cameau, Henrietta. 10 Wentworth St.
Cameron, Alexander. Drayman. 80 King St.
Cameron, David. Butcher Stall 15. Home, Cannon St.
Cameron, Lewis. 31 Church St.
Cameron, Samuel. Mariner. Stoll's Alley
Campbell, Angus. Shop Keeper. 39 Pinckney St.
Campbell, Donald. 3 Bedon's Alley
Campbell, M'Lauchlan & Co. Merchants. Craft's
　Wharf
Campbell, M'Millan. Grocer. 128 Queen St.
Camps, ——. W. Washer. 15 Clifford's Alley
Canly, George. Carpenter. 2 King St.
Cannon, Daniel. Carpenter. 23 Queen St.
Canter, Joshua. Limner. 61 Broad St.
Cantey, Anna, Mrs. 7 Guignard St.
Cantey, Henry & Co. Merchants. Craft's Row
Cape, Brian. Notary Public. 80 East Bay
Cape, Brian & Co. Inspector, Insurance Broker.
Cape de Vielle, Peter. Grocer. Queen St., corner
　Union

75

Cardoza, David. Lumber Measurer. 13 King St.
Carew, Thomas. Ship Carpenter. 6 Charles St.
Carmand, Peter. Tailor. 243 King St.
Carn, Lawrance. King St.
Carne, T. William. 11 Pinckney St.
Carnes, Samuel. Rope Maker. 28 Beaufain St.
Carpenter, Joseph. Butcher Stall 15. Home, Cannon St.
Carrell, Daniel. Goldsmith. 124 Broad St.
Carrere, Charles. French Teacher. 13 Hasell St.
Carrol, Bartholomew. Planter. West End of Boundary St.
Carson, James. 20 Friend St.
Carson, William. Planter. 9 Meeting St.
Cart, John. Factor. Bull St.
Cart, Sarah. Queen St., corner Kinloch Court
Carter, George. Physician. 29 Archdale St.
Casey, Benjamin. Coach Maker. 107 Broad St.
Cattel, Frances. Seamstress. 6 Beresford St.
Caught, Thomas. Ship Carpenter. 112 East Bay
Cave, Thomas. Merchant. Mazyckborough Creek
Chalabre, J. D. & Co. Merchants. 217 King St.
Chalmers, Gilbert. Carpenter. 18 Beaufain St.
Champney, John. Planter. 94 King St.
Champy, Edme. Merchant. Meeting St., corner Society
Chanler, Isaac. Physician. 55 Broad St.
Channer, Esther. Grocer. 10 Middle St.
Charlemagne, Colzy. Tailor. 27 Church St.
Charles, Andrew. Merchant. 16 Liberty St.
Chartier, Jean J., Mrs. Widow. 17 Federal St.
Cheves, Alexander. Shop Keeper. 96 King St.
Cheves, Langdon. Attorney. 96 King St.
Cheves, Richard H. Drayman. 98 East Bay
Chicester, John. Physician. 107 Tradd St.
Chisholm, Alexander. 307 King St.
Chisholm, George. Factor. Vanderhorst's Wharf
Chitley, J. W. Grocer. 174 Meeting St.
Chomont, ----, Mons. 169 King St.
Chouler, Joseph. Apothecary. East Bay, corner Broad St.
Christian, Elizabeth. Widow. 15 Quince St.
Chupein, Lewis. Hair Dresser. 7 Elliot St.
Clark, David. Watch Maker. 123 Broad St.
Clark, James. Coach Maker. 189 Meeting St.
Clark, James. Tailor. 12 Elliot St.
Clark, Jeremiah. Clerk Market. 38 Church St.
Clark, Lucretia. Widow. 9 Pinckney St.
Clark, Robert. Grocer. Queen St., corner Union
Clarkson & Co, William, Jr. Merchants. 7 Champney St.
Clarkson, William. Planter. 52 Meeting St.
Clastrier, John. 277 King St.
Claybrook, Richard. Carpenter. 20 Pinckney St.
Cleary, John R. School Master. 23 Hasell St.
Clements, William. Attorney. 84 Tradd St.
Clethral, James, Dr. Physician. 56 Meeting St.
Clime, Geer. Carpenter. 125 King St.
Clitheral, George. Planter. 100 Meeting St.
Club, Alexander. Grocer. 26 Meeting St.
Club, Alexander. Grocer. 8 Tradd St.
Coanary, Samuel. Tobacconist. 13 Clifford's Alley
Coats, Thomas. Mariner. 128 Tradd St.
Cobia, Daniel. Butcher Stall 34. Home, 12 Beresford St.
Cobia, Frances. Widow. 12 Beresford St.
Coburn, John. 6 St. Philip's St.
Cobwen, Seth. 44 Meeting St.
Cochran, Charles. Federal Marshall. 75 Meeting St.

Cochran, Margaret. Widow. 262 King St.
Cochran, Robert. 75 Meeting St.
Cochran, Robert. Attorney. 75 Meeting St.
Cochran, Thomas, Jr. Grocer. 58 East Bay
Cochran, Thomas, Sr. Merchant. Cochran's Wharf
Coffin, E. Merchant. 14 Tradd St.
Cogdell, M. E. School. 1 St. Michael's Alley
Cohen, ----, Mrs. Shop Keeper. 199 King St.
Cohen, Gershom. Merchant. 259 King St.
Cohen, Jacob. Vendue Master. 266 King St.
Cohen, Mordecay. Shop Keeper. 244 King St.
Cohen, Moses. 52 East Bay
Cohen, Philip. Auctioneer. 9 Orange St.
Cohen, Solomon. Shop Keeper. 171 King St.
Colas & Cournand. Bakers. 1 Trott St.
Colcock, Henrietta. 61 Meeting St.
Cole, Ira. Sailer. 205 King St.
Coles, S. Widow, Nurse. 11 Quince St.
Colford, Joseph. Boarding House. 8 Pinckney St.
Colhoun, James. Merchant. 123 Tradd St.
Colhoun, William. Merchant. Craft's Wharf
Collins, Mary. 20 Hasell St.
Collins, William. 15 Mazyck St.
Colwell, Henry. 22 Church St.
Connoly, Elizabeth. Widow. 15 Quince St.
Connoly, James. 21 Meeting St.
Connor, Brian. Grocer. 132 Queen St.
Conte, ----, Seignoretta. Widow. 16 Wall St.
Conyers & Co. Vendue Masters. Exchange
Conyers, Elizabeth. Widow. 285 King St.
Conyers, William. Mariner. 15 Pinckney St.
Cook, Eleonor. Merchant. 57 East Bay
Cooper, Sarah. Seamstress. Archdale St.
Cooper, William. Shoe Store. 238 Meeting St.
Coram, Francis. Factor. 26 George St.
Coram, Thomas. Engraver. 81 Queen St.
Corbett, Samuel. Inn Keeper. 233 Meeting St.
Corbett, Thomas. Planter. 13 Ellery St.
Corbett, Thomas. Merchant. 11 Cumberland St.
Corker, Thomas. Grocer. Pinckney St.
Cornier, Charles. Carpenter. 12 Wall St.
Corr, Charles. Tailor. King St.
Corre, Charles G. Merchant. 49 King St.
Corrie, Alexander. Cotton Factor. 13 East Bay
Coskray, Charles. Grocer. 13 Union St.
Cosnay, John. Deputy Surveyor. 1 Archdale St.
Cosse, Margaret. Widow. 17 Pinckney St.
Coste, Amee. Widow. 37 Trott St.
Cotton, James. Carver & Gilder. 71 Meeting St.
Cournand, Pierre. Baker. 2 Trott St.
Courson, Delilah. Shop Keeper. 6 King St.
Courtin, John. Merchant. 5 Magazine St.
Courtney, Edward. Merchant. 46 East Bay
Courtney, H. Merchant. 42 Meeting St.
Courtney, James. Merchant. 44 Meeting St.
Courtney, John. Boarding House. 32 Union St.
Coveney, Thomas. Grocer. Pinckney St.
Cowen, John. Rigger. Governor's Bridge
Cowen, John. Boarding House. 7 Union St.
Cox and Sheppard. Printer. 137 Tradd St.
Cox, Elizabeth. 302 King St.
Cox, James. Merchant. Church St.
Cox, John. Brick Layer. 4 Federal St.
Craft, Samuel. Merchant. Hasell St.
Crafts, W. & E. Merchants. Craft's South Wharf
Craig, Thomas. Hair Dresser. 4 Elliot St.
Crawford, Alexander. Painter. 258 Meeting St.
Crawford, James. Grocer. 56 Queen St.

Crawford, John. Grocer. 19 King St.
Crawford, Joseph. East Bay
Crawford, William. Grocer. 91 East Bay
Creighton, Edwards. Hair Dresser. 20 Union St. Continued
Creighton, S. Hair Dresser. 18 Union St. Continued
Crips, John S. Merchant. 61 Meeting St.
Cristie, Alexander. Baker. 104 Queen St.
Crocker & Hichburn. Merchants. Crafts' Wharf
Croft, Edward. 38 Tradd St.
Crombee, Joseph. Merchant. 94 Church St.
Cromwell, Oliver. 34 Tradd St.
Cross, George. East Bay Continued
Cross, James. Silk Dyer. 1 Beresford Alley
Cross, M. William. Brick Layer. Kinloch Court
Cross, Susannah. Widow. 7 Pitt St.
Crovat, Peter. Grocer. 21 Union St.
Crow & Query. Booksellers. 123 Broad St.
Crowie, Elizabeth. Shop Keeper. 97 Church St.
Crowley, Charles. Merchant. 46 Broad St.
Cruckshanks, Daniel. Shoemaker. 126 Queen St.
Cruger, David. Factor. 38 Meeting St.
Cruger, Elizabeth. Widow. 9 Guignard St.
Cruger, Nicholas. 4 Anson St.
Cudworth, Benjamin. 17 Beaufain St.
Cudworth, Nathaniel. 2 Amen St.
Cunningham, Charles. Merchant. 161 King St.
Cunningham, John. Merchant. 144 King St.
Cunnington, William. Justice of Peace. 39 East Bay
Currie, John. Grocer. 40 Tradd St.
Curry, Samuel. Shoe Store. 60 King St.
Custer, James. Factor. 13 Guignard St.
Cyples, Margaret. 32 Guignard St.
D'Oyley, Daniel. State Treasurer. 2 St. Philip's St.
Dacauety, John B. Grocer. 6 Moore St.
DaCosta & Co. Tobacconists. 117 King St.
DaCosta, Isaac. Merchant. 13 Beresford St.
DaCosta, Joseph. Tobacconist. Wentworth St.
Dady, Mary. Widow. 2 Wall St.
Dailey, Henrietta. School Mistress. 36 Tradd St.
Dalcho & Auld. Apothecaries. 132 East Bay
Dalton, Grace. Widow. Stoll's Alley
Darby, John. Goldsmith. 10 Beaufain St.
Darrell, ----, Mrs. 81 Tradd St.
Darrell, Edward, Jr. Attorney. 84 Broad St.
Darrell, Hezekiah. Widow. 1 Water St.
Dart, Benjamin. Factor. 28 Tradd St.
Dart, Isaac M. 32 Hasell St.
Dastas & Guerard. Grocers. 6 Elliot St.
Dastas, M. Grocer. 9 Queen St.
Dastas, Machew. Merchant. 53 Queen St.
Dastas, Marue. Barber. Queen St.
Davis, Eliza. 8 Wentworth St.
Davis, Harmon. Captain City Guard. Quince St.
Davis, Israel. Shop Keeper. 112 King St.
Davis, John & C. Insurance Brokers. 23 East Bay
Dawson, John, Jr. Merchant. 7 Broad St.
Dawson, John, Sr. East Bay. Above Bridge
Day, George. Jeweller. 215 Meeting St.
Deas, ----, Mrs. 103 East Bay Continued
Deas, David. Attorney. 75 Tradd St.
Deas, Henry. Attorney. 106 Tradd St.
Debesse & Co. Ship Chandlers. 135 East Bay
Debesse, Frederic. 239 King St.
Debruhl, M. S. Watch Maker. 137 Queen St.
Debuis, C. L. Grocer. 40 Church St.
DeGrass, Augustus. 9 Federal St.
DeLaHogue, Jean B. Federal St.

Delaire, James & Co. Merchants. Nicholl's Wharf
Delamotte, Emanuel. 48 Tradd St.
Delany, Daniel. Carpenter. 15 Boundary St.
Delarue, Rene. Merchant. 100 Meeting St.
Deleon, Jacob. Vendue Master. 90 Tradd St.
Delieben, Israel. Vendue Master. 51 East Bay
Delorme, J. T. Upholsterer. 44 Broad St.
Demiliers, Ann. Teacher of Drawing. 50 Broad St.
Denner, George. Tanner. 21 Mazyck St.
Denner, George. Tanner. 130 King St.
Dennis, Richard. Merchant. 11 Hasell St.
Dennison, James. Mariner. 38 Elliot St.
Denoon, David. Insurance Broker. 38 East Bay
Denton, James. Carpenter. 8 St. Philip's St.
Depass, Ralph. Vendue Master. 35 Trott St.
Depeyster, Horatio. Planter. 20 Coming St.
Derkham, Meyer. Grocer. 8 Queen St.
Derson, Bernard. Grocer. 5 Union St.
Desaussure & Ford. Attornies. 29 Tradd St.
Desaussure, H. W. Attorney. 24 Meeting St.
Desbeaux, John. Cooper. 3 Cumberland St.
Desell, Charles. Cabinet Maker. 51 Broad St.
Devago, Moses. Shop Keeper. 61 King St.
Devies, Caty. Boarding House. Champney's Alley
Devillier, ----, Mons. 279 King St.
Diamond, John. Land Surveyor. 22 Trott St.
Dickenson, Francis. 50 Church St.
Dickenson, Joseph. Inspector Exports.
Dickeson, Joseph. Fort Mechanic
Dickinson, Joseph. Grocer. Archdale St.
Dickinson, Samuel. Vendue Master. Champney St.
Dickson, Samuel. School Master. 150 King St.
Dill, Susana. Widow. 299 King St.
Doliver, Henry. Mariner. 131 Church St.
Donald, Margaret. 115 Church St.
Donaldson, James. Carpenter. 116 Tradd St.
Doughty, Thomas. Factor. 59 Meeting St.
Doughty, William. Smith St.
Douglas, John. Cabinet Maker. 138 Meeting St.
Douglas, Nathaniel. Merchant. 19 Broad St.
Drake, John. Block Maker. 7 Qunice St.
Drayton, Jacob. Prothonator. 109 Tradd St.
Drayton, John. Governor. 84 Broad St.
Drennis, George. Baker. Beaufain St.
Drexler, John. Grocer. Smith's Lane
Drummond, Anna. 24 Guignard St.
Drummond, James. Shoemaker. 115 Queen St.
Drummond, John. Shoemaker. 2 Broad St.
Dubois, Peter. Carpenter. 28 St. Philip's St.
Duckham, John. Water St.
Duddle, James. Cabinet Maker. 251 Meeting St.
Duffus, John. 17 Elliot St.
Duffus, John. Merchant. 113 Broad St.
Duffy, Patience. Grocer. 19 East Bay
Dulles, Joseph. Merchant. 34 East Bay
Dumont, William. Physician. 170 King St.
Duncan, Archibald. Blacksmith. 113 Queen St.
Duncan, John. 47 Tradd St.
Dunn, Alexander. Carpenter. 19 Federal St.
Dunn, John. Merchant. Champney St.
Dunsee, J. A. Physician. 24 Beresford St.
Dupont, ----, Mons. 169 King St.
Dupre, Benjamin. Tailor. 78 East Bay
Dupuis, Claude. 9 Society St.
Durkham, William. Chair Maker. 24 Hasell St.
DuRousseau, Pierre. Guignard St.
Dutrejey, ----, Mrs. 14 Boundary St.
Duval, Catharine. 143 Church St.

77

Dwight, O. D. Merchant. 92 Church St.
Dyre, Kindall. Grocer. 27 Elliot St.
Eberly, Barbara. Guignard St.
Eckhard, Jacob. Musician. 47 Tradd St.
Eder, Joshua. Chair Maker. Church St.
Edgar, James. 150 Meeting St.
Edson, Timothy A. Grocer. 70 East Bay
Edson, Timothy A. Grocer. 22 Union St. Continued
Edwards, Alex. Attorney. St. Michael's Alley
Edwards, Isaac. Merchant. 10 Society St.
Edwards, James. Factor. 24 George St.
Ehlers, Weets. Grocer. 36 Elliot St.
Ehney & Chiner. Tailors. 4 Elliot St.
Ehney, William F. Clerk. 11 Magazine St.
Ehrick, John. Merchant. 91 Broad St.
Elfe, Thomas. 2 West St.
Ellevy, Levy. Slop Shop. 48 East Bay
Elliot, Ann, Mrs. 6 Wentworth St.
Elliot, Bernard. Planter. St. Philip's St.
Elliot, Mary. Legare St.
Elliot, Thomas. Planter. Gibbes St.
Ellis, Thomas. 6 Scarborough St.
Ellison & Mulligan. Grocers. Coats' Row
Ellison, Henry. Counting House. Beale's Wharf
Ellison, John. Shop Keeper. 232 King St.
Ellison, Stephen H. Turner. 99 Tradd St.
Ellison, William. Grocer. 57 King St.
Elmore, Jesse. Tailor. 99 Church St.
Elsworth, Theophilus. Gauger. 135 Queen St.
England, Alexander. Baker. 49 Union St.
Enguchard, Oliver. Grocer. 99 Queen St.
Ernest, Jacob. Tailor. 26 Queen St.
Eschautts, William. 51 Meeting St.
Eston, Susannah. 8 Montagu St.
Evans, John J. Printer. 23 Maiden Lane
Ewing, John M. 259 Meeting St.
Byuley, ——. Deputy Sheriff. 207 King St.
Fair & Fairley. Shoe Store. 26 Broad St.
Fair, Robert. Shoe Store. 93 King St.
Fair, William. Tanner. Pitt St.
Fair, William. Shoe Shop. King St.
Fairchild, Aaron. Blacksmith. Ham's Wharf
Faisson, ——, Mrs. Boarding House. 100 Tradd St.
Farbaut, ——, Chevelier. 10 Coming St.
Farrow, Thomas. Shoemaker. 35 King St.
Fash, Sarah. Widow. 266 King St.
Faures, Laurent. Merchant. George St.
Fayolle, Peter. Dancing Master. 281 King St.
Fell, Eliza. Milliner. 22 Broad St.
Fell, Thomas, Jr. Merchant. 22 Broad St.
Fell, Thomas, Sr. Merchant. 22 Broad St.
Ferguson, ——, Mrs. 5 Liberty St.
Fiddy, William. Merchant. Gillon St.
Fields, William B. 11 Guignard St.
Fife, James. Cooper. 3 Champney St.
Filly, John. Merchant. 6 Tradd St.
Findley, John. 2 Mazyck St.
Fitzpatrick Nicholas. Grocer. 1 King St.
Fitzsimmons, Christopher. Merchant. 76 East Bay
Flagg, George. 228 King St.
Flagg, Samuel. Dentist. 30 Queen St.
Flemming, Robert. Merchant. 141 King St.
Flint, Joseph. Merchant. Union St. Continued
Floran, Lucan. 35 Guignard St.
Florance, Zachariah. Dentist. 178 Meeting St.
Fluet, Samuel. Merchant. 264 King St.
Fogartie, James. Factor. 7 Scarborough St.
Fogarty, James. Factor. 14 Guignard St.

Folker, John C. 34 Beaufain St.
Folmes, Jonas. Tailor. 51 Meeting St.
Footman, John. Clerk. 153 Meeting St.
Ford, Jacob. Attorney. 25 Meeting St.
Ford, Timothy. Attorney. 30 Tradd St.
Forest, Aberdeen. Cooper. 17 Boundary St.
Forrest, ——, Mrs. 4 Hasell St.
Forrest, Thomas H. Cooper. 281 King St.
Forsyth, Walter. Merchant. 1 Craft's Row
Fossin, ——, Mrs. Boarding House. 100 Tradd St.
Foster, Robert. 35 Elliot St.
Foster, Thomas. 306 King St.
Foster, William. Merchant. 96 Church St.
Foults, Jacob. Merchant. Vanderhorst's Alley
Fountain, Jane. Inn Keeper. 14 Chamber's Alley
Fowler, John. Carpenter. Longitude Lane
Fowler, Maria. School Mistress. 4 Beresford St.
Francis, David. Block Maker. 15 Quince St.
Frase, Peter. King St.
Fraser, Elizabeth. Boarding House. 4 Stoll's Alley
Fraser, John. Carpenter. 10 Pinckney St.
Fraser, Mary. Widow. 22 King St.
Fresere, ——, Mrs. Pitt St., corner Wentworth
Freeman, William. 102 Tradd St.
Freneau, Peter. 13 George St.
Friend, Ulric. Baker. 113 East Bay
Frierson, John. Carpenter. 12 Guignard St.
Frink, Thomas. 7 Bedon's Alley
Frish, Charles. Shop Keeper. 188 King St.
Frish, Michael. Butcher Stall 24. Home, Cannon St.
Fronty, William, Dr. Physician. Moore St.
Frost, Thomas, Rev. Minister. 10 Archdale St.
Gabeau, Anthony. Tailor. 222 Meeting St.
Gadsden, Christopher. East Bay Continued
Gadsden, James. Planter. 82 Queen St.
Gadsden, Philip. Factor, Wharfinger. East Bay Continued
Gadsden, Thomas, Mrs. Widow. East Bay Continued
Gailagher, S. F., D. D. Minister. Charleston College
Gaillard & Co. Merchants. Gaillard's Wharf
Gaillard & Mazyck. Factor. Gaillard's Wharf
Gaillard, Bartholomew. 82 Society St.
Gaillard, Theodore. Planter. 81 East Bay
Gairdner Edwin & Co. Merchants. 75 East Bay
Galbraith, Robert. Carpenter. 16 George St.
Galloway, Alfred. Pilot. Rhett's Lane
Galluchat, Maria. Confectioner. 92 Meeting St.
Gandouin, John. Hatter. 61 East Bay
Gantt, Hannah. School Mistress. 40 Trott St.
Gapin, William. Chair Maker. 9 Liberty St.
Garden, Adam. Shoemaker. 22 Beaufain St.
Gardiner, Ruth. Widow. 13 Quince St.
Gardner, Alexander, Dr. Druggist. East Bay
Gardner, John. Blacksmith. 5 Maiden Lane
Gaultier, Joseph. Vendue Master. 91 Tradd St.
Geddes, Henry. Merchant. 183 King St.
Geddes, John. Attorney. 104 Broad St.
Geddes, Robert. Merchant. 165 King St.
Gee, Hannah. 8 Union St. Continued
Gefken, Henry. Butcher Stall 22. Home, Coming St.
Gell, John. Tanner. Market Square
Gennerick, J. F. Shop Keeper. 158 King St.
Gennery, Christopher. Merchant. 112 East Bay
Gensell, John. Grocer. 8 Society St.
George, James. Shipwright. 124 East Bay
George, Mary. Shop Keeper. 215 King St.
Gerard, Philip. Grocer. 6 Elliot St.
Gerk, Frederick. Cake Shop. 42 King St.

Gerley, John. Keeper Poor House.
Gervis, Mary. Widow. 71 Broad St.
Geyer, Elizabeth. Widow. 24 Mazyck St.
Geyer, John. Merchant. 1 King St.
Gibbs, George. Baker. 28 Elliot St.
Gibbs, Mary. Boarding House. 11 Union St.
Gibbs, R., Mrs. Widow. 19 Meeting St.
Gibson, ----. Blacksmith. 62 Queen St.
Gibson, James. Coach Maker. 57 Broad St.
Gibson, Patrick. Merchant. 34 Elliot St.
Gibson, Robert. Shop Keeper. 249 King St.
Gibson, Robert. Blacksmith. South Bay
Gidnay, Isaac. Carpenter. 16 Minority St.
Gilbert, Elizabeth. 125 Church St.
Gilbert, Eugene. 3 Pitt St.
Gilbert, J. J. Saddler. 28 Hasell St.
Gilbert, Joseph. Brick Layer. 125 Church St.
Gilbert, Seth. Wharfinger. 125 Church St.
Gilchrist, Adam. Merchant. 21 Church St.
Giles, Robert. Planter. 63 Tradd St.
Gillespie & Mackay. 31 East Bay
Gissendaher, Lucretia. Nurse. Bull St.
Gist, William. Merchant. 154 King St.
Given, Robert. Stone Cutter. 158 King St.
Gividon, ----, Mons. Grocer. 14 Union St. Continued
Glaan, Barnard. Instrument Maker. 199 Meeting St.
Glen, John. Planter. 52 Tradd St.
Glover, Charles. 176 King St.
Godard, John. Grocer. 169 Meeting St.
Godard, Rene. French Tutor. 2 Moore St.
Godfrey, Eliza. Widow. 304 King St.
Gomez & Sister. Shop Keepers. 84 King St.
Good, Sarah. School Mistress. 37 King St.
Goodwin, Mary. Seamstress. 18 Trott St.
Gordon & Barber. Grocers. Meeting St., corner Quince
Gordon, Andrew. Brick Layer. 111 Queen St.
Gordon, Elizabeth. Widow. 24 Guignard St.
Gordon, James. 26 East Bay
Gordon, John. Brick Layer. 92 Tradd St.
Gordon, Martha. 3 Hopton's Alley
Gordon, Thomas. Cashier.
Gordon, Thomas. Grocer. 71 East Bay
Gordon, Thomas. 39 Trott St.
Gordon, William. Grocer. 87 King St.
Goring, Francis. Import Inspector.
Goring, Frederick. Ellery St.
Gouton, Peter. Mariner. 170 Meeting St.
Gow, Andrew & Co. Merchants. 116 Broad St.
Gowdy, James. Gunsmith. King St., North End
Gowdy, Margaret. Widow. 23 Guignard St.
Gowdy, William. Gunsmith. Queen St.
Graat, James. Rigger. 33 Union St.
Graddock, Christian. Butcher Stall 6. Home, King St. Road
Grado, Maraino. Boarding House. Unity Alley
Graft, Peter G. 4 Liberty St.
Graham, John J. 14 Elliot St.
Graser, C. J. Merchant. 110 Queen St.
Gravenstein, Frederick. 2 Beresford St.
Graves & Swinton. Factors. Geyer's Wharf
Graves, Charles. Factor. 53 Tradd St.
Gray, Alexander. Merchant. King St., corner Liberty
Gray, Benjamin. Planter. 3 Anson St.
Gray, Caleb. Tailor. 170 Church St. Continued
Gray, R. William. Brick Layer. Church St. Continued
Gray, William. Inspector Customs. 57 Church St.
Green, James C. Grocer. 13 Trott St.

Green, William. Boarding House. 8 Union St.
Greenhill, Hume. 62 Tradd St.
Greenwood, William. Merchant. 19 Beaufain St.
Greenwood, William. 2 Ellery St.
Gregoire, J. & C., Jr. Merchants. 117 Broad St.
Gregoire, James, Sr. 117 Broad St.
Gregson, ----. Widow. 114 East Bay Continued
Gregson, Thomas. Brewer. 1 Magazine St.
Grierson, James. Grocer. 68 East Bay
Grimball, John. South Bay
Grimke, John F. Judge. 29 Church St.
Groning, Lewis & R. Merchants. Vanderhorst's Row
Groscol, A. Fiddle Maker. 10 Chamber's Alley
Gruber, Charles. 80 Queen St.
Gruber, Christian. Butcher. 18 Beresford St.
Gruber, Martin. Cooper. King St.
Gun, William. Gunsmith. 6 Queen St.
Guy, Christopher. Joiner. 29 Trott St.
Guy, James. Tailor. 18 Boundary St.
Gyles, Thomas. Clerk in Court House. 39 Broad St.
Hackett, ----, Mrs. 10 Friend St.
Hadden, Gardner. Tailor. 102 Church St.
Hagar, Richard. Fruit Shop. 85 King St.
Hagarty, Charles. South Bay
Haggetee, Dinis. Chamber's Alley
Hagood, Hanna. Widow. Legare St.
Hagood, Johnson. Attorney. 47 King St.
Hague, Robert. Carpenter. 38 Trott St.
Hahnbaum, G., Mrs. 7 Moore St.
Haig, ----. Physician. Legare St.
Haig, David. Cooper. 160 Meeting St.
Hains, William. Planter. Smith St.
Hall, ----, Miss. 261 Meeting St.
Hall, ----, Mrs. Widow. 12 Magazine St.
Hall & Quay. Merchants. 147 King St.
Hall, Daniel. Factor. 2 State House Square
Hall, Dom. A. Attorney. 66 King St.
Hall, Thomas. Clerk Federal Court. 32 Broad St.
Hall, William. Mariner. Front St. Federal Green
Hall, William H. Carpenter. 3 Wentworth St.
Halsall, William. Butcher Stall 39. Home, Guignard St.
Ham, Samuel S. Carpenter. 14 Amen St.
Ham, Thomas. Factor. Pritchard's Wharf
Ham, Thomas. Grocer. Anson St., corner Pitt
Ham, William. Mariner. 89 Queen St.
Hamilton, Anthony. Tailor. 19 Tradd St.
Hamilton, David. Merchant. Guignard St.
Hamilton, David. Bookkeeper. Blake's Wharf
Hamilton, Dudley. Brick Layer. 8 Beresford St.
Hamilton, Malboroug. 10 King St.
Hamlin, Hannah. 206 Meeting St.
Hammet, Charlotte. Widow. 13 Elliot St.
Hammett, Thomas. Chair Maker. Meeting St.
Hampton, William. Cabinet Maker. 63 Queen St.
Hanahan, John. Merchant. Champney St.
Handy, Thomas. Grocer. 201 Meeting St.
Happoldt, J. G. Butcher Stall 44. Home, 20 Beresford St.
Harabowski, J. S. Planter. 46 Broad St.
Harby, Soloman. Auctioneer. 119 Tradd St.
Hare, Francis. Slop Shop. 19 Union St.
Hargreaves, J. & J. Merchants. 23 Broad St.
Harleston, ----, Mrs. Widow. Hasell St., corner Meeting
Harleston, Elizabeth, Mrs. Widow. 107 Tradd St.
Harleston, Nicholas. Planter. 99 Meeting St.
Harman, Elzabeth. Widow. 7 Middle St.

79

Harper, John, Rev. Minister. 3 Broad St.
Harris, Andrew. Merchant. 61 East Bay
Harris, J. & H. Merchants. 190 King St.
Harris, Thomas. Shop Keeper. 237 King St.
Harris, Tucker. Physician. 70 King St.
Harrison, W. P. Stamping Officer. Geyer's New Range
Hart, Daniel. Vendue Master. 56 East Bay
Hart, Dorcas. School Mistress. 16 Federal St.
Hart, Simon M. Vendue Master. 223 King St.
Harth, John. Planter. 1 Archdale St.
Harvey, Archibald. Deputy Sheriff. 27 King St.
Harvey, Benjamin. Brick Layer. Wentworth St.
Harvey, John S. 4 Wall St.
Harvey, Samuel. Mariner. Guignard St.
Haslet, John. Merchant. Blake's Wharf
Hatch, Robert. Mariner. Union St. Continued
Hatter, Elizabeth. Widow. 38 Queen St.
Hattier, ----, Mrs. Grocer. 20 Tradd St.
Hattier and Ricard. Grocer. East Bay
Hauck, John. Grocer. 124 Queen St.
Hayward, ----, Mrs. Legare St.
Hayward, Nathaniel. Planter. East Bay Continued
Hayward, Samuel. Lieutenant Navy. Mazyck St.
Hazlehurst, Robert. Merchant. 13 East Bay
Hazlewood, Joseph. Painter. 39 Pinckney St.
Henderson, Robert. Stage Office. 88 East Bay
Henry, Alexander. Merchant. 139 King St.
Henry, Ann, Mrs. Milliner. 21 Elliot St.
Henry, Jacob. Shop Keeper. 211 King St.
Henson, Archibald. Carpenter. 21 Minority St.
Herriot, G. & R. Merchants. 7 Craft's South Wharf
Herron, John. Merchant. King St., North End
Heslit, John. Painter. Queen St.
Heyden, David. Boarding House. 27 Union St.
Heylinger, Joseph. Engraver. 244 Meeting St.
Hichborn & Crocker. Merchants. 24 Tradd St.
Highland, Nicholas. Grocer. King St. N. End
Hildreth, Benjamin. Sailmaker. 2 Champney St.
Hill, Andrew. Carpenter. 150 Meeting St.
Hill, Paul. 27 Archdale St.
Hillegas, Philip. Distiller. 21 Coming St.
Hilson, Sarah. Seamstress. 150 Meeting St.
Himley, John J. Merchant. 119 Broad St.
Hinchman, John. Grocer. 26 Elliot St.
Hinds, Thomas. Attorney. 24 Broad St.
Hinson, Joseph. 11 Meeting St.
Hipper, Peter. Grocer. 178 Meeting St.
Hislop, John. Carpenter. 63 Church St. Continued
Hislop, Robert. Tailor. 6 Church St.
Hislop, Robert. Lumber Merchant. 5 Union St.
    Continued
Hodgon, Mary. Boarding House. 366 King St.
Hodgson, John. Carpenter. 20 Amen St.
Hogarth, William. Shoemaker. 38 Union St.
Hogarth, William. Shoemaker. 9 Wall St.
Holliday, Hugh. Cooper. 9 Champney St.
Hollinshead, William, Rev. Minister. 94 Meeting St.
Holmes, Andrew. 3 Pinckney St.
Holmes, Isaac. Legare St.
Holmes, Thomas. 4 Wyatt's Lot
Holmes, William. Vendue Master. Boundary St.
Holmes, William & Co. Vendue Masters. Exchange
    Square
Honour, John. Saddler. 15 Coming St.
Honywood, Elizabeth, Mrs. 67 Meeting St.
Hook, Conrad. Carpenter. Ellery St.
Hooper, Mary. Widow. 51 Tradd St.
Hopkins & Charles. Merchants. Craft's South Wharf

Hopkins, Benjamin. 4 Lodge Alley
Hopton, ----, Mrs. 11 Meeting St.
Horeare, Thomas. Grocer. 3 Tradd St.
Horlbeck, Henry. Brick Layer. 3 Moore St.
Horlbeck, John. Brick Layer. 8 Moore St.
Horlbeck, John, Jr. Brick Layer. 8 Moore St.
Hornby, Hannah. 214 King St.
Horry, Elias. 18 Church St.
Horry, Harriot. Widow. 51 Tradd St.
Horry, Linch E. Planter. 211 King St.
Horry, Thomas. Planter. 273 Meeting St.
Hosmer & Haslet. Merchants. 1 Frink's Wharf
Houlton, James. 4 Cumberland St.
House, Samuel. Justice of Peace. Union St. Continued
Houser, Elias. Clerk Hay Market.
Howard, Richard. Cooper. Blake's Wharf
Howard, Robert. 3 George St.
Hoyland, Anna Maria. 86 Broad St.
Hudson, ----. Grocer. 129 Church St.
Hudson, William. Millwright. 8 Federal St.
Huger, Daniel. Planter. Legare St.
Huger, John. Planter. 73 Broad St.
Huger, Rosannah. 6 Union St. Continued
Hughes, Mary. Boarding House. Trott St.
Hughs, Edward. 55 Tradd St.
Hughes, Thomas. Factor. East Bay Continued
Humes, John. Planter. Montagu St.
Hunter, James. Grocer. 69 East Bay
Hunter, James. Mariner. 112 East Bay
Hunter, Thomas. 78 Church St.
Huntington, Mary. Widow. 105 Church St.
Hurst, Charles. Tailor. 49 Church St.
Hussey, Bryan. Pilot. Water St.
Huston, James. Merchant. 5 Cumberland St.
Hutchins, Hugh. Mariner. 3 Champney St.
Hutchinson, Elizabeth. 106 Meeting St.
Hutton, James. Factor. South Bay
Huxham, Elizabeth. 14 Tradd St.
Hyams, David. Shop Keeper. 189 King St.
Hyams, Samuel. Merchant. 55 East Bay
Hyer, Henry. Drayman. Boundary St. West End
Hyndman, James. Shop Keeper. 168 King St.
Icarden, Lewis. Mariner. 12 Trott St.
Ingles, Henry. Merchant, Tailor. 25 Tradd St.
Ingles, Thomas. Barber. 48 Meeting St.
Inglesby, William. Merchant. 110 Broad St.
Inglish, Dominick. Merchant. 6 Meeting St.
Ingraham, Nat. Merchant. 5 East Bay
Irland, Benjamin. Carpenter. 55 Queen St.
Irvine, Mathew. Physician. 7 Meeting St.
Ivans, Leacraft. Carpenter. 7 Wyatt's Lot
Izard, Charlotte. 1 Cumberland St.
Izard, Henry. Planter. Bull St.
Izard, Ralph. 1 Meeting St.
Jacks, James. Jeweller. 109 Broad St.
Jackson, William. Shoe Store. 182 Meeting St.
Jackson, William. Shoe Store. 135 Queen St.
Jacobs, Elizabeth. 95 Queen St.
Jahan, Joseph. Meeting St. Above Bound.
James, John. Carpenter. 19 Archdale St.
Jarman, John. Livery Stables. 73 Meeting St.
Jeffe, Sarah, Mrs. 50 Broad St.
Jeffers, John. 10 Pinckney St.
Jefferson, John. Turner. 43 King St.
Jeffreys, Mary. Dry Nurse. 78 King St.
Jenkins, Edward, Rev. Minister. Lamboll St.
Jenkins, Elias. Brick Layer. 15 Liberty St.
Jenkins, Mica. Planter. 86 Tradd St.

Jessop, Jeremiah. 12 King St.
Jewel, Benjamin. Slop Shop. 62 East Bay
John, Anthony. Shop Keeper. 18 Broad St.
Johnson & Dunlop. Druggists. 5 Broad St.
Johnson, Hugh. Grocer. King St., corner Queen
Johnson, Jacob. Carpenter. 36 Trott St.
Johnson, John. Cooper. 3 Lodge Alley
Johnson, John. Blacksmith. Gillon St.
Johnson, John. Justice of Peace. 167 King St.
Johnson, W. Jabez. Watch Maker. 122 Broad St.
Johnson, William. Blacksmith. Charles St.
Johnson, William, Jr. Judge. 80 Church St.
Johnson, William P. Merchant. 167 King St.
Johnston, ——. Seamstress. Clifford's Alley
Johnston, Alexander. Printer. 40 Hasell St.
Johnston, Edward. Rigger. 19 Amen St.
Johnston, James. Merchant. 149 King St.
Johnston, William. 10 Liberty St.
Jones, Abner. Tailor. 45 King St.
Jones, Alexander. Merchant. 88 Tradd St.
Jones, Alexander. Grocer. Church St. Continued
Jones, Charles. Merchant. 26 Church St.
Jones, E. Currier. 25 King St.
Jones, Edward. Physician. 5 Orange St.
Jones, Henry. Ship Carpenter. 5 Lodge Alley
Jones, Iris. Tailor. 51 Church St.
Jones, Jehu. Tailor. 97 Broad St.
Jones, Joseph. Shop Keeper. 104 King St.
Jones, Joshua. Grocer. 68 Meeting St.
Jones, Nathaniel. Grocer. 9 Tradd St.
Jones, Samuel. Merchant. 268 King St.
Jones, Thomas. 4 Guignard St.
Joseph, Joseph. Shop Keeper. 105 King St.
Joseph, Samuel. Shop Keeper. 246 King St.
Josseaume, Mathew. 34 Union St. Continued
Joy, Abraham. Ship Joiner. Quince St.
Kahnle, John H. 14 Boundary St.
Kaiser, John J. Butcher. Blackbird's Alley
Kay, Alexander. Merchant. 16 Tradd St.
Keels, Peter. Carpenter. Wentworth St.
Keen, Thomas. Mariner. Union St. Continued
Keenen, George. Shop Keeper. 123 Church St.
Keenen, Thomas. Merchant. Water St.
Keirnan, James. Grocer. 100 Queen St.
Keith, Isaac S., Rev. Minister. 305 King St.
Keith, Sylvanus & Co. Merchants. 136 East Bay
Kelly, Mary. Shop Keeper. 114 King St.
Kelly, Michael. Merchant. 18 Tradd St.
Kelly, William. Butcher Stall 6. Home, Ham St.
Kelsey, William. 6 Boundary St.
Kempton, Anna. Shop Keeper. 26 Meeting St.
Kempton, George. Roper's Wharf
Kennedy, James. Planter. 20 Mazyck St.
Kennedy, Peter. Grocer. 98 Meeting St.
Kenoff, C. Butcher Stall 14. Home, King St. Road.
Ker, Andrew. Merchant. 106 East Bay
Ker, Eliza. Store Keeper. 25 Broad St.
Ker, John. Hatter. 49 East Bay
Ker, Samuel. Attorney. 50 Meeting St.
Kern, John F. Merchant. 193 King St.
Kershaw, Charles. Factor. 95 King St.
Kevan, William. Merchant. 136 Tradd St.
Kin, Eleanor. Shop Keeper. 175 King St.
King, Benjamin. Carpenter. 9 Wentworth St.
King, Christian. Tailor. Lombard Lane
Kingman, Elias. Shoe Store. 133 Tradd St.
Kinloch, Francis. 2 Short St.
Kinmont, David. Blacksmith. East Bay

Kirk, John. Merchant. 58 East Bay
Kirkland, Joseph. Apothecary. 237 Meeting St.
Kirkpatrick, John. Merchant. 98 Church St.
Kirkwood, John. Blacksmith. 97 East Bay
Kissick, Francis. Mariner. 146 Meeting St.
Knipping & Steinmetz. Merchants. Gaillard's Wharf
Knox, Matthew. Grocer. 10 Queen St.
Knox, Thomas. Grocer. 21 Amen St.
Knox, Walter. Carpenter. 26 Hasell St.
Koffskey, Ann. Grocer. 88 King St.
Kohne, Frederick. Merchant. 29 East Bay
Kreds, Ann. Baker. King St.
Krietsburg, Conrad. Butcher Stall 42.
Lane, Robert. 10 Orange St.
Lane, Samuel. Carpenter. 5 Society St.
Lane, William. Blacksmith. Ellery St.
Labat, David. Shop Keeper. 16 Hasell St.
Laborde, Francis. Shop Keeper. 133 King St.
Ladeveze, Joseph. Shop Keeper. 85 King St.
Ladson, Eliza. Boarding House. 39 Church St.
Ladson, James. Planter. 13 Meeting St.
Lafer, David. Vendue Master. Champney's Row
Laffer, Catharine. Widow. 39 Guignard St.
LaFrenk, Peter F. Merchant. Queen St.
Lambert, Joseph. Boarding House. 10 Union St.
Lamdry, John B. Grocer. 122 King St.
Lance, Ann. Widow. 12 Friend St.
Lance, Lambert. Attorney. 11 Friend St.
Lang, J. H & Co. Merchants. Geyer's Range
Lang, T. H. Merchant. Church St. Continued
Langstaff & Frink. Grocers. Beale's Wharf
Langstaff, Benjamin. 157 Meeting St.
Lanneau, Basil. Tanner. Beaufain St.
Larey, Robert. Carpenter. 62 Church St.
Laroche, Isaac. 26 Beaufain St.
Lartigue, ——, Mons. Pitt St.
Larue, Francis. Shop Keeper. 97 Meeting St.
Latham, Daniel. Distiller. 2 Hasell St.
Latham, Joseph. Distiller. 8 Hasell St.
Laurans, Peter. Grocer. 174 King St.
Lawrence, R. & T. Factors. Roper's Wharf
Lawrence, Robert D. Factor. 23 George St.
Lawton, Winborn. Planter. Lynch's Lane
Lazarus, Marks. 100 King St.
Leaumont, Robert. Musician. 22 Beresford St.
Leavitt, Joshua. Grocer. 83 East Bay
Lebby, Nathaniel. Block Maker. 14 Amen St.
Lebby, Robert. Block Maker. 60 Church St.
Lecat, Francis. Musician. 47 Meeting St.
Lee & Theus. Factors. Geyer's Wharf
Lee and Brescey. Merchant. 22 Tradd St.
Lee, James. Merchant. 1 Craft's Row
Lee, John & Co. Merchants. 218 King St.
Lee, Stephen. Factor. 42 Broad St.
Lee, William. Merchant. 2 Hopton's Lane
Lee, William, Col. Watch Maker. 50 King St.
Leese, Benjamin. Merchant. 127 Tradd St.
Lefevre, Stephen. Cumberland St., corner Meeting
Legare, Edward. Accountant. 47 Trott St.
Legare, Solomon. Planter. 13 Friend St.
Legare, Thomas. Gibbes St.
Legare, Thomas, Jr. Planter. 50 Tradd St.
Leger, ——. Dancing Master. 114 Queen St.
Leger, Elizabeth. 106 Meeting St.
Legge, Edward B. Attorney. 47 Trott St.
Lehere, ——, Mrs. Widow. 14 Liberty St.
Lehre, Thomas. District Sheriff. 297 King St.
Lenormant, Andrew. Goldsmith. 44 Queen St.

Lenox, William. Clerk. Church St.
Lenox, William. Merchant. 26 King St.
LeSeigneur, Vincent. Physician. 2 Hopton's Lane
Leuder, Frances. Confectioner. 31 Queen St.
Levrier, Peter. School Master. 411 Meeting St.
Levy, Hart. Shop Keeper. 138 King St.
Levy, Lyon. Clerk Treasurer's Office.
Levy, Moses C. Shop Keeper. 233 King St.
Levy, Nathan. Shop Keeper. 210 King St.
Levy, Rose. Shop Keeper. 250 King St.
Levy, Samuel. Shop Keeper. 128 King St.
Levy, Samuel. Merchant. 85 Broad St.
Levy, Samuel S. Shop Keeper. 194 King St.
Lewis, Alexander & Co. 2 Tradd St.
Lewis, Isaac & Alexander. Merchants. 11 Tradd St.
Lewis, John. Carpenter. 7 Beresford St.
Lewis, John. Grocer. 309 King St.
Lewis, John. Merchant. 17 Church St.
Lewis, Joseph. Merchant. 124 Tradd St.
Ley, Francis. Grocer. King St. N. End
Liber, Elizabeth. Grocer. 166 King St.
Liblong, Henry. Shoemaker. 25 Hasell St.
Lightwood, Edward. Planter. 266 Meeting St.
Limehouse, Robert. 63 Tradd St.
Linch, Margaret. Grocer. 4 Union St. Continued
Ling, John. Grocer. 38 Hasell St.
Lining, C. Ordinary for Charleston. Legare St.
Little, Robert. Carpenter. 21 Union St. Continued
Lloyd, John. Planter. 83 Tradd St.
Lloyd, John, Jr. Merchant. 202 Meeting St.
Lloyd, John, Jr. Factor. 3 Vanderhorst's Wharf
Lloyd, Joseph. Store Keeper. 242 King St.
Lockey & Naylor. Merchants. Prioleau's Wharf
Lockey, George. Factor. 90 Queen St.
Lockwood, Joshua. 1 Smith's Lane
Lockwood, Joshua, Jr. Planter. 206 Meeting St.
Logan, George. Carpenter. 20 Union St. Continued
Logan, Honoria, Mrs. 32 Tradd St.
Logan, William. Merchant. 296 King St.
Logan, William, Jr. Attorney. 10 Moore St.
Loker, Daniel. Shoemaker. 12 Clifford's Alley
Long, John. Bookkeeper. 23 George St.
Lopez, David. Auctioneer. 256 King St.
Lopez, Sarah. Widow. 5 Dutch Church Alley
Lord, Richard. Factor. 58 Queen St.
Love, Duncan. Grocer. 15 Church St.
Loveday, John. 10 Moore St.
Lovely, William. Grocer. Ellery St.
Lowe, John. 105 Church St.
Lowndes, James. Attorney. 216 Meeting St.
Lowndes, Sarah, Mrs. Widow. 74 Broad St.
Lowndes, Thomas. Planter. Legare St.
Lunt, Mary. Tallow Chandler. 8 Maiden Lane
Lyburn, Francis. Mariner. 15 Federal St.
Lynah, James. Physician. 14 Moore St.
Lynn & Weyman. Merchants. 15 Broad St.
Lynn, John. Merchant. Front St.
Lyon, Mordecai. Slop Shop. 53 East Bay
M'Affee, John. Carpenter. 11 St. Philip's St.
M'Alpin, Angus. Merchant. 5 Tradd St.
M'Beth, Henry & Co. Merchants. 132 Tradd St.
M'Blair, William. Vendue Master. 10 Mazyck St.
M'Bride, James. Merchant. 60 East Bay
M'Bride, John. Grocer. 107 Church St.
M'Call, ----, Mrs. Widow. 101 Meeting St.
M'Call, Ann. Widow. 110 Church St.
M'Call, James. Planter. King St. Rd.
M'Calla, Thomas H. Physician. 10 Elliot St.

M'Candish, Anthony. Merchant. 14 Tradd St.
M'Carty, John. Constable. 3 Meeting St.
M'Cleish, Alexander. Brass Founder. 64 Meeting St.
M'Clure, A. & J. Merchants. 22 Broad St.
M'Cormick, William. Merchant. 127 Queen St.
M'Credie, David & Co. 8 Broad St.
M'Donald, ----, Mrs. Grocer. 138 Tradd St.
M'Donald, C. Shop Keeper. 294 King St.
M'Donald, Susannah. 22 East Bay
M'Dowall & Co. Merchants. 176 King St.
M'Dowell, Alexander. Saddler. 236 King St.
M'Dowell, James. Merchant. 59 King St.
M'Dowell, John. Merchant. 151 King St.
M'Enery, John. Slop Shop. 35 Union St.
M'Farlane & Player. Merchants. 4 Broad St.
M'Farlane, Alexander. 120 Church St.
M'Gann, Patrick. 3 Coat's Row
M'Ginnes, Patrick. Grocer. 67 King St.
M'Gowen, Dennis. Merchant. 9 Champney St.
M'Guire, Mary. Shop Keeper. 38 Meeting St.
M'Intire, Thomas. 29 Elliot St.
M'Intosh, Simon. Attorney. 18 Tradd St.
M'Iver, John. Printer. 47 East Bay
M'Kee, Ann. 3 Beresford St.
M'Kee, John. Brick Layer. 301 King St.
M'Kenna, Charles. Druggist. 120 Queen St.
M'Kenzie, Andrew. Grocer. 107 Broad St.
M'Kenzie, Elizabeth. Unity Alley
M'Kinfuss, Henry. Brick Layer. Wentworth St.
M'Kinfuss, M. Cabinet Maker. 48 King St.
M'Lachlan, Archibald. Merchant. 7 Tradd St.
M'Lean, L. Grocer. 52 Tradd St.
M'Hugo, Anthony. 28 Queen St.
Macadam, James & Co. Merchants. 11 Broad St.
Macaulay, George. Merchant. 17 Broad St.
Macaulay, George & Son. 20 Elliot St.
Makay, C. Watch Maker. 41 Elliot St.
Makkay, John. Carpenter. 33 Tradd St.
Marshall, John. Meeting St. N. end
Mauran, J. R. Grocer. 129 Queen St.
Maverick, Samuel. Merchant. 127 King St.
Maxwell & Ogier. Merchants. Craft's Wharf
Maxwell, John. Shoemaker. 101 King St.
Mayer, Charlotte. 7 Union St. Continued
Mayhew, Joseph. Carpenter. South Bay
Mazyck, Hannah. 57 Queen St.
Mazyck, Nathaniel. Factor. 65 Meeting St.
Mazyck, William. 6 Archdale St.
McCrady, John. Attorney. 33 Broad St.
Mecomb, Joseph. Merchant. 146 King St.
Meeks, Joseph. Grocer. 15 Union St.
Meguire, William. Church Alley
Melhada, Benjamin. 45 Tradd St.
Menville & Coats. Grocers. Prioleau's Wharf
Merrell, Benjamin. Stables. 45 Church St.
Merry, Patrick. Mariner. 12 Union St. Continued
Meurset, Amelia. 79 King St.
Mey, F. Charles. 44 Pinckney St.
Middleton, Ann. 81 Broad St.
Middleton, Frost, Mrs. Front St. Fed. Green
Middleton, Solomon. Tailor. 89 King St.
Miers, Francis. Tobacconist. 113 Meeting St.
Miller & Robertson. Merchants. Geyer's Wharf
Miller, Frederick. Butcher. Blackbird's Alley
Miller, James. Wine Merchant. 64 East Bay
Miller, James. Merchant. 101 Church St.
Miller, John. Merchant. King St., corner Federal
Miller, John. Drayman. 102 Meeting St.

Miller, John T. Carpenter. 23 Beaufain St.
Miller, Mary. 174 Meeting St.
Miller, Morrison & Co. Merchants. 91 Church St.
Miller, Nicholas. Baker. 4 Wentworth St.
Miller, William. Tailor. 3 Queen St.
Miller, William. Factor. South Bay
Milligan, John. Lumber Merchant. Kinloch Court
Milligan, Joseph. Shop Keeper. 72 King St.
Milligan, William. 1 Craft's Range
Milligan, William. Grocer. Maiden Lane
Mills and Shaw. Merchant. 121 Tradd St.
Mills, Thomas. Merchant. 105 Church St.
Mills, William. East Bay Continued
Milner, George. Blacksmith. 86 Church St.
Mincon, Mary. 77 King St.
Minot, John. Planter. Stoll's Alley
Minott, Thomas. Carpenter. Stoll's Alley
Miott, Frances. 54 Meeting St.
Mishaw, John. Grocer. Pinckney St., corner East Bay
Mitchell, Ann. 246 Meeting St.
Mitchell, Dennison & Co. Vanderhorst's Wharf
Mitchell, James. Cooper. 22 Meeting St.
Mitchell, James. Carpenter. 4 West St.
Mitchell, John H. 11 Lynch's Lane
Mitchell, Margaret. 14 Coming St.
Moderen, Jame. Union St., corner Lodge Alley
Moles, James. Blacksmith. 12 Pinckney St.
Molony, ——. Fruit Shop. 272 King St.
Moncrief, John. Carpenter. 101 East Bay
Moncrief, John & Co. 110 Church St.
Moncrief, Susannah. Widow. 38 Hasell St.
Monk, James. Jeweller Shop. 20 Broad St.
Monpoy, Honore. 44 Union St.
Mood, Peter. Goldsmith. 238 King St.
Moodie, Benjamin. British Consul. 12 Hasell St.
Mooney, Patrick. Grocer. 131 Queen St.
Moore, Elias. 34 Trott St.
Moore, George. Grocer. 308 King St.
Moore, John. Grocer. 238 Meeting St.
Moore, John. Butcher Stall 40. Home, King St. Road
Moore, Joseph. Drayman. 100 East Bay Continued
Moore, P. J., Dr. Dentist. 42 King St.
Moore, Philip. Cabinet Maker. 247 Meeting St.
Moralles, Jacob. Shop Keeper. 72 King St.
Moret, Lewis. Confectioner. 121 Broad St.
Morgan, Anna. 11 Liberty St.
Morgan, Charles. Ship Carpenter. 2 Pinckney St.
Morgan, David. Carpenter. Blake's Wharf
Morgan, Henry. 30 Elliot St.
Morphy, Don Diego. Spanish Consul. 282 King St.
Morre, ——, Mrs. Widow. 263 Meeting St.
Morris, A. B. Widow. 10 Bedon's Alley
Morris, George. Factor. 14 Archdale St.
Morris, Lewis. Planter. 260 Meeting St.
Morris, Thomas. Factor. Bay, corner Trott
Morrison, Spencer. Grocer. 1 Scarborough St.
Mortimer, Edward. Merchant. 13 Broad St.
Morton, Edward. Tailor. Stoll's Alley
Morton, Joseph. Drayman. 3 Pitt St.
Moser, Philip. Druggist. 108 Broad St.
Moses, Abraham. Shop Keeper. 65 East Bay
Moses, Henry. Slop Shop. 54 East Bay
Moses, Isaiah. Grocer. 206 King St.
Moses, Lyon. Broker. Archdale St.
Moses, Philip. Shop Keeper. 26 Union St.
Moses, Solomon. Shop Keeper. 200 King St.
Moses, Stewart & Co. 4 Champney's Row
Motta, J. & C. Auctioneer. Exchange Alley

Motte, ——, Mrs. Widow. 263 Meeting St.
Motte, ——, Mrs. Widow. 18 Meeting St.
Motte, Abraham. Planter. 118 East Bay
Motte, Francis. Merchant. 31 East Bay St.
Mouatt, ——. Merchant. 15 King St.
Moubray, Martha. Baker. 90 King St.
Moultrie, ——, Mrs. Widow. Bull St.
Moultrie, Ann. 9 Wentworth St.
Moultrie, James. Physician. 2 Cumberland St.
Muir & Boyd. Merchants. Geyer's Wharf
Muir, William. Merchant. 56 Meeting St.
Muirhead & Smilie. Merchants. 14 Broad St.
Mulin, Roze. Widow. 32 Trott St.
Mullen, Peter. 7 King St.
Mulligan, Francis. Collect. Super. Office
Munro, Catherine. Midwife. 21 Tradd St.
Munro, John. Watch Maker. 8 Elliot St.
Munro, Sarah. Mantua Maker. 5 Guignard St.
Murphy, Eliza. Boarding House. 6 Tradd St.
Myers, George H. Block Maker. 5 Quince St.
Myers, Izrael. 5 Beresford St.
Myers, Michael. Vendue Cryer. 9 Hopton's Lane
Myers, Samuel. Tailor. 222 King St.
Mylne, James. Baker. 20 Union St.
Naggle, Susannah. Widow. Stoll's Alley
Napier, A. T. & Co. Merchants. Craft's Wharf
Nathan, David. Merchant. 245 King St.
Nathan, S. Shop Keeper. 245 King St.
Nebuhr, John D. Mariner. 199 King St.
Negrin, John J. 9 Archdale St.
Neil, Peter. 174 Meeting St.
Nelson, Ambrose. Merchant. 42 Trott St.
Nelson, Francis. Ship Carpenter. 113 East Bay
Nelson, John Dixon. Printer. 3 Broad St.
Neufville, Anna. Widow. Ellery St.
Neufville, Isaac. Bookeeeper. Wentworth St.
Neufville, J. J. 85 Queen St.
Neunes, Peter. Tailor. 15 Beaufain St.
Neville, James. Cabinet Maker. Broad St.
Neville, Joshua. Cabinet Maker. 11 Clifford's Alley
Newser, Harman. Baker. 27 Beaufain St.
Newton, Sarah. Washer. 12 Meeting St.
Newton, William. Butcher Stall 37. Home, Cannon St.
Neyle, Philip. Physician. 61 Tradd St.
Nicholls, George. Mariner. 3 Scarborough St.
Nicholls, Thomas. Factor. 82 East Bay
Nicholson, James. Attorney. Broad St.
Nobbs, Samuel. 89 Meeting St.
Noble, Ezekiel. Merchant. 162 King St.
Noble, John. Physician. 162 King St.
Norris, Andrew. Attorney. Wentworth St.
Norris, James. Windsor Chair Maker. 97 King St.
Norroy, John. Tobacconist. Meeting St. North end
North, Edward. Merchant. 43 East Bay
North, Edward William. 7 Church St. Continued
North, Gersholm. Shop Keeper. 207 King St.
North, Susannah. Widow. 37 Tradd St.
Nott, Isabella. Widow. 38 East Bay
Nowel, Edward B. Broker. 108 Queen St.
Nowel, John. 36 Trott St.
O'Harra, Daniel. Merchant. 128 Broad St.
O'Harra, Henry. Merchant. 128 Broad St.
O'Harra, James. 128 Church St. Continued
O'Mitchell, William. Carpenter. Queen St.
Odanna, Peter. 236 Meeting St.
Oeland, John. Grocer. 9 Union St. Continued
Ogier, Lewis. Factor. 85 Tradd St.
Ogier, Thomas. Merchant. Blake's Wharf

Ogier, Thomas. Merchant. 22 Tradd St.
Ogilvic, Alexander. Planter. 20 George St.
Oliphant, David. Painter. 58 Broad St.
Oliver, James. Brick Layer. 115 East Bay Continued
Oliver, James. Butcher Stall 31. Home, King Street Road.
Oliver, Stephen. Butcher Stall 25. Home, King St. Road
Oliver, William. Mariner. 1 Tradd St.
Olman, ----, Mrs. Confectioner. 133 Queen St.
Ormond, William. Mariner. 102 East Bay
Osborne, Henry. 3 Mazyck St.
Osborne, Thomas. Sheriff. Legare St.
Otis, Joseph. 131 Trad St.
Ovrin, George. Founder. Market Square
Pain,----. Mariner. 92 Tradd St.
Paine, Seth. Printer. 111 Tradd St.
Paine, Thomas. Mariner. 92 Tradd St.
Palmer, Job. House Carpenter. 33 Guignard St.
Park, Gabriel. 5 Boundary St.
Parker & Noble. Physicians. King St.
Parker, Catherine. Mantua Maker. 72 Meeting St.
Parker, Elizabeth. Widow. 25 Mazyck St.
Parker, Florida. Widow. Goodby's Alley
Parker, George. Brickmaker. 87 East Bay
Parker, Isaac. Planter. Legare St.
Parker, John, Jr. Planter. 36 Trott St.
Parker, Martha. Butcher Stall 32. Home, Coming St.
Parker, Sarah. Widow. Legare St.
Parker, Thomas. Attorney. 141 Meeting St.
Parker, Thomas. Shoe Store. 123 Queen St.
Parker, William. Physician. 15 George St.
Parks, John. Shoemaker. 26 Union St.
Parks, Samuel. Shoe Store. 91 King St.
Parmitary, Philipina. Widow. 16 Coming St.
Passer, Emanuel. 45 Meeting St.
Patcot, ----, Mrs. School Mistress. 122 King St.
Patterson, Hugh. Factor. 121 Queen St.
Payne, James. Mariner. 44 Tradd St.
Payne, William. Merchant. 115 Broad St.
Payne, William R. Stone Cutter. 48 Broad St.
Peak, John. Carter. Pitt St.
Pearce & Carter. Shoe Store. 9 Bedon's Alley
Pearce, Elizabeth. Mantua Maker. 101 Broad St.
Pearce, Joseph. Attorney. State House Square
Pearce, William. Watch Maker. 101 Broad St.
Pearson, Benjamin. Mariner. 14 Scarborough St.
Pearson, Francis. Mariner. 14 Elliot St.
Pelletant, John A. Grocer. 136 Queen St.
Pelor, Joseph. Butcher. Beresford St.
Pendleton, Oliver. 15 Lynch's Lane
Pepoon, Benjamin. 14 Queen St.
Pepoon, Joseph. Grocer. 29 Union St.
Peppin & Co. Merchants. Geyer's Wharf
Peppin, Joseph. Merchant. 109 Church St.
Perdriau, ----. Carpenter. 6 Smith's Lane
Peronneau, Ann. 49 Broad St.
Peronneau, William. 8 George St.
Perry, ----, Mrs. Widow. 16 Coming St.
Perry, Izabella,. Midwife. 62 Meeting St.
Perth, Creighton. Barber. 17 Guignard St.
Petrie, Alexander. Factor. Orange St.
Petrie, John. 278 King St.
Petrie, ----, Mrs. 120 Queen St.
Peyster, John. Laborer. 249 Meeting St.
Phelon, Edmond M. Grocer. 225 Meeting St.
Philips, Dorothy. Saddler. 219 Meeting St.
Philips, Ebenezer. Shoe Store. 24 Queen St.

Philips, Thomas. Keeper of Jail. Mazyck St.
Phillips, John M. Painter & Glazier. 47 Broad St.
Phillips, Timothy. Coach Maker. 59 Broad St.
Philson, Alexander. Merchant. 4 Bedon's Alley
Phol, ----, Mons. Shop Keeper. 240 King St.
Pickton, Charles. Carpenter. 20 Amen St.
Pickton, Ruth. School Mistress. Amen St.
Pickton, Thomas. Carpenter. 20 Amen St.
Pillans, ----, Mrs. Widow. 122 Tradd St.
Pilsbury, Amos. School Master. Guignard St.
Pilsbury, Samuel. King St.
Pinckney Charles. 267 Meeting St.
Pinckney, Charles C. General. 92 East Bay
Pinckney, Frances, Mrs. Legare St.
Pinckney, Thomas. Major. 21 George St.
Piot, Edward. 35 St. Philip's St.
Platt, Ebenezer. Merchant. 208 Meeting St.
Poincignon, ----. Tin Man. 2 Queen St.
Poinsett, Elisha. Physician. 312 King St.
Pollock, Solomon. Horse Dealer. Bull St.
Polony, John L. Physician. 9 Church St.
Pool, Isaac. Mariner. 238 King St.
Pooser, W. & H. Tailors. 11 Meeting St.
Porter, Benjamin. Cabinet Maker. 217 Meeting St.
Porter, William. 34 Union St.
Postell, Edwards. Chair Maker. 10 George St.
Potter, John. Merchant. 18 Broad St.
Poulton, Edward. 120 Church St.
Poyas, John. Physician. 35 Meeting St.
Poyas, John L. Carpenter. 12 Ellery St.
Poymot, Anthony. 34 King St.
Pratt, John. Mariner. 14 Elliot St.
Pratt, Samuel H. Grocer. 37 East Bay
Prentice, John. Coach Maker. 7 Archdale St.
Pressley, William. Grocer. 36 Queen St.
Pressley, William. 16 King St.
Prestman, William. Wine Store. 18 Queen St.
Prevot, Mary J. 125 Queen St.
Price, John. Merchant. Geyer's Wharf
Price, Thomas. Planter. 109 Meeting St.
Primrose, ----, Mrs. Widow. 27 St. Philip's St.
Primrose, James. Mariner. 11 Beresford St.
Prince, Charles. Ellery St.
Prince, Charles. Tin Man. 266 King St.
Pring, James. Barber. 7 Queen St.
Pringle, John S. Attorney. 105 Tradd St.
Pringle, Mary. Widow. Quince's Alley
Pringle, Robert. Physician. 9 Friend St.
Prioleau, ----. Physician. 57 Meeting St.
Prioleau, Alice Edith. 93 Queen St.
Prioleau, Jane B. School Mistress. 22 Maiden Lane
Prioleau, John C. Factor. 86 Queen St.
Prioleau, Samuel. 12 Ellery St.
Pritchall, Paul. Shipwright. Pritchard's Wharf
Pritchard, William, Jr. Shipwright. 3 Charles St.
Pritchard, William, Sr. Shipwright. 1 Pinckney St.
Provost, Elizabeth. 19 Beresford St.
Purcell, Henry, Rev. 1 Legare St.
Purcell, Joseph. Land Surveyor. 127 King St.
Purdy, Joseph. Rigger. 18 Hasell St.
Quash, Robert. Planter. 76 Broad St.
Quigley, Esther. Widow. 15 Hasell St.
Quigyn, David. Mariner. 6 Lodge Alley
Quin, James. Boarding House. Unity Alley
Quinby, Joseph. Carpenter. 4 Pinckney St.
Quince, Susanna. East Bay
Radcliff, Thomas, Sr. 6 George St.
Raine, Thomas. Clerk. 237 King St.

Ralph, John. Boarding House. 52 Church St.

Ramage, Frances, Mrs. 229 Meeting St.

Ramondo, Peter. Fruit Shop. 28 Church St.

Ramsay, David. Physician. 90 Broad St.

Ramsay, George. Merchant. Chamber's Alley

Ramsay, John. Physician. 45 Meeting St.

Ramsay, Joseph H. Physician. 31 Tradd St.

Ramsay, Thomas. Baker. 92 King St.

Randall, ----, Mrs. 14 St. Philip's St.

Randall, Esther. School Mistress. 11 Liberty St.

Rankin, James. Grocer. King St., corner Queen

Raustorne, Elizabeth. 6 Cumberland St.

Ravenel, Elizabeth. 70 Meeting St.

Ravenel, Stephen. West End of Boundary St.

Raymond, Cliffey. Saddler. 31 Church St.

Read, John. Tin Man. 44 Church St.

Read, William. Physician. 11 Church St. Continued

Rechon, David. Tailor. 100 King St.

Redlich, William. Clerk. 5 Tradd St.

Redman, Jemes. Rigger. Beaufain St.

Reed, James. 34 Coming St.

Reeves, Enos. Goldsmith. 99 Broad St.

Reid, George. Notary Public. 12 East Bay

Reid, John. Wheelwright. 208 Meeting St.

Reigne, John. Baker. 9 Elliot St.

Remlay, Barbara. Widow. Coming St.

Remlay, Michael. Carpenter. Wentworth St.

Remoussin, Daniel. 29 Beaufain St.

Renauld, John. Fruit Shop. 53 Tradd St.

Rennio, George. Stone Cutter. 57 Broad St.

Repon, Bernard. 12 Chamber's Alley

Reside, William C. 221 Meeting St.

Revel, Ann. Shop Keeper. 89 King St.

Reynolds, Elizabeth. 93 Queen St.

Ricard, Benjamin. Shop Keeper. 89 King St.

Richards, Samuel. Broker. 8 Dutch Church Alley

Richardson, John. 26 Elliot St.

Richardson, John S. Attorney. 69 Meeting St.

Richardson, Thomas. Attorney. 41 Church St.

Rigaud, Peter. Grocer. 6 Middle St.

Right, Joseph. Cooper. East Bay

Righton, Joseph. Cooper. Water St.

Righton, M'Cully. Cooper. Water St.

Riley, James. Physician. 7 Union St. Continued

Ritfield, ----, Mrs. Widow. 10 Clifford's Alley

Rivers, Gracia. 1 Short St.

Rivers, James. Carpenter. 261 King St.

Rivers, Samuel. Ship Carpenter. 4 Water St.

Rivers, Thomas. Butcher Stall 1. Home, Trott St.

Rivers, Thomas. Planter. Stoll's Alley

Roach, William. City Treasurer. 12 Quince St.

Roberts, Aaron. Mariner. 5 Charles St.

Roberts, Ann. Widow. 16 Church St.

Roberts, John. Mariner. 118 Tradd St.

Roberts, John. Tailor. 19 Elliot St.

Roberts, William. Chair Maker. 88 Queen St.

Robertson, A. & Sons. Merchants. 155 King St.

Robertson, Francis. Factor, Vendue Master. 8 Elliot St.

Robertson, John. Merchant. 103 Church St.

Robertson, John & Co. Merchants. 131 Tradd St.

Robertson, Peter. Painter. 8 Hopton's Lane

Robinet, Francis. Cooper. Blake's Wharf

Robinson & Lang. Merchants. 142 King St.

Robinson & Pendal. Merchant. 187 King St.

Robinson, William. Shoe Store. 3 Champney St.

Robinson, William. 51 King St.

Robiou, Elizabeth. 10 Bull St.

Roche, John. Grocer. 9 Union St.

Rodgers, Samuel. Musician. 10 Church St.

Rodman, Thomas. 23 Union St.

Rodrigues, Abraham. Merchant. 16 Queen St.

Rogers, Christopher. Tailor. 25 Tradd St.

Rogley, Anthony. Grocer. 163 Meeting St.

Rolain, Rhett. 57 Queen St.

Ronpek, ----, Mrs. Widow. 83 Tradd St.

Roper, Thomas. Intendant. 75 East Bay

Rose & Ehney. Tailors. 40 Church St.

Rose, Alexander. Merchant. Church St. Continued

Rose, Jeremiah. Tailor. 14 Pinckney St.

Rose, John, Sr. 19 Hasell St.

Ross, Elizabeth. Shop Keeper. 43 Queen St.

Ross, Jane. Store Keeper. 24 Elliot St.

Ross, Thomas. Mariner. 102 Queen St.

Rossignol, Nanette. Widow. 10 Wall St.

Rote, Mary. Seamstress. 18 Middle St.

Roullit, Mary. Shop Keeper. 117 Queen St.

Rouse, William. Tanner. 78 Meeting St.

Rout, George. School Master. 15 Archdale St.

Roux, Lewis. 56 Broad St.

Row, Daniel. Cabinet Maker. 11 Federal St.

Row, Michael. Carter. 26 George St.

Rowand, Mary. 2 Tradd St.

Rowter, Lewis. Tailor. 98 King St.

Royr, Leah. Seamstress. 5 Wyatt's Lot

Rubel, ----, Mrs. 10 Pinckney St.

Ruberry & Co. Shoe Store. 108 Church St.

Rugan, William & Co. Merchant. 6 Broad St.

Russell, Benjamin. Brick Layer. 31 Guignard St.

Russell, Daniel. Carpenter. 3 Ellery St.

Russell, Nathaniel. 16 East Bay

Rutledge, Henry M. Front St.

Rutledge, Hugh. Chancellor. 15 St. Philip's St.

Ryal, James. 30 Union St. Continued

Ryan, Elizabeth. Slop Shop. 55 East Bay

Saltus & Yates. Ship Chandlers. Craft's Wharf

Samory, Claude. Grocer. 24 Queen St.

Sanders, John. 177 King St.

Santi, Angelo. Confectioner. 55 King St.

Sasa, Jacob. Cabinet Maker. 40 Queen St.

Savage, Martha. Widow. Broad St. W. end

Sayre, Steven. Ship Joiner. 22 Amen St.

Scheppler, L. C. A. Merchant. 38 Pinckney St.

Schmidt, John F. Merchant. 79 East Bay

Schutt, Caspar C. Merchant. 87 Broad St.

Scott, Ann, Mrs. Shop Keeper. 246 King St.

Scott, Campbell & Co. Auctioneers. Champney St.

Scott, Ely. Grocer. May's Wharf, corner East Bay

Scrimzeour, James & Charles. Merchants. 122 Tradd St.

Scriven, Thomas, Col. 117 Church St.

Seaver, Abraham. Carpenter. 37 Pinckney St.

Secress, Martin. Mariner. Union St. Continued

Seixas, J. M. Master Work House.

Selby, George & Co. Merchants. 191 King St.

Serjeant, Elizabeth. Grocer. 229 Meeting St.

Serjeant, Mary. Shop Keeper. 104 Church St.

Seyler, D. Butcher Stall 9. Home, Coming St.

Seymour, Isaac. Captain. 16 King St.

Seymour, Stephen. H. M. Orange St.

Shackleford, Nathan. Factor. Nicholl's Wharf

Shackleford, Nathan. Factor. 7 Cumberland St.

Shands, Robert. Custom House Officer. 97 Tradd St.

Sharp, John. Block Maker. 7 Pinckney St.

Shaw, Richard. Tailor. 150 Meeting St.

Shaw, Samuel. Merchant. 121 Tradd St.

Sheperd, James. Harness Maker. 17 Coming St.
Sherman & M'Neil. Merchants. 164 King St.
Shields, Margaret. School Mistress. Dutch Church Alley
Shievely, George. Grocer. 148 Meeting St.
Shirer, John. Carpenter. 10 Coming St.
Shirras, Alexander. Merchant. 17 Elliot Strett
Shirtiff, William. Merchant. Wall St.
Shoolbred, James. Legare St.
Shrewsbury, Edward. Ship Carpenter. 12 Guignard St.
Shrewsbury, Jeremiah. 12 Guignard St.
Shriner, Nicholas & Co. Grocers. George St.
Shrusbury, Stephen. 8 Cumberland St.
Shutterlee, Mary. Widow. 27 Beaufain St.
Sibbin, Siblee. Grocer. 24 Church St.
Sibley, Joseph. Wine Merchant. 10 Union St.
Silberg, Nicholas. Cabinet Maker. 13 Middle St.
Silbert, Lewis. Sausage Maker. Unity Alley
Simmons, William. Carpenter. North End of King St.
Simond, B. Fruit Shop. 14 Union Shop
Simons, James. Port Collector. 2 Beaufain St.
Simons, Keating. 3 Orange St.
Simons, Keating & Son. 1 Geyer's Front Range
Simons, Sampson. Shop Keeper. 103 King St.
Simons, Samuel. Merchant. 23 Beresford St.
Simons, Thomas. Merchant. 123 East Bay
Simons, Thomas. Merchant. Gaillard's Wharf
Simons, William. Tailor. 1 Bull St.
Simpson, John. Ship Chandler. Nicholl's Wharf
Simpson, Margaret. Widow. 118 Church St.
Singleton, ——, Mrs. Widow. 16 Boundary St.
Singleton, Lucy. Seamstress. 18 Trott St.
Singleton, Mary. Widow. 4 Trott St.
Sisk, Susannah. Boarding House. 77 East Bay
Skirving, Charlotte, Mrs. Widow. 8 Legare St.
Skirving, William, Jr. Legare St.
Slann, Ann Catharine. 7 Wentworth St.
Slowman, Henry. Tailor. 34 Hasell St.
Smallwood, Richard. 17 Pinckney St.
Smerdon, Elias. Insurance Office. 40 East Bay
Smiser, Anna. 56 Church St.
Smith, Agnes. Widow. 34 Elliot St.
Smith, Agnes. Milliner. 46 Church St.
Smith, Ann. Grocer. 25 Meeting St.
Smith, Archibald. 16 Quince St.
Smith, Bryan. 20 Church St.
Smith, Caleb. 85 Church St.
Smith, Christopher. Grocer. 136 King St.
Smith, Daniel. 4 Society St.
Smith, George. Shoe Store. 5 East Bay
Smith, Henry. Shipwright. 4 Maiden Lane
Smith, James. Carpenter. 16 Pinckney St.
Smith, Jane. Widow. 21 Tradd St.
Smith, John. Rigger. Ellery St., corner
Smith, John. Upholsterer. 7 Wall St.
Smith, John. School Master. 80 Broad St.
Smith, John C. Merchant. 52 King St.
Smith, Josiah. Cashier, National Bank. 92 Broad St.
Smith, Margaret. Shop Keeper. 198 King St.
Smith, Mary Ann. School Mistress. 83 Church St.
Smith, Peter. Planter. South Bay
Smith, Robert. Planter. 12 Boundary St.
Smith, Robert. Chamber's Alley
Smith, Robert, Bishop. Minister. Wentworth St.
Smith, Roger. 25 St. Philip's St.
Smith, Samuel. Factor. 41 Broad St.
Smith, Samuel. Shop Keeper. 126 Broad St.
Smith, Sarah. Widow. 30 Church St.

Smith, Susanna. Boarding House. 273 King St.
Smith, Thomas Rhett. Attorney. 54 Tradd St.
Smith, Whiteford. Grocer. 61 Church St.
Smith, William. Attorney. 40 Broad St.
Smith, William. Tailor. 179 King St.
Smith, William. Merchant. 7 Tradd St.
Smith, William & Co. Merchants. Beale's Wharf
Smith, William, Jr. Carpenter. 108 East Bay
Smyth, John. Planter. Ellery St.
Smyth, John & Co. Merchants. 185 King St.
Snelling, Abey. Pastry Cook. 37 Broad St.
Snowden, Charles. Merchant. 63 East Bay
Snyder, John Paul. Carpenter. 7 Federal St.
Solley, John. 46 Tradd St.
Solomon, Chapman. Shop Keeper. 129 King St.
Solomon, Hyams & Co. Vendue Masters. Champney St.
Solomon, Joseph. Shop Keeper. 194 King St.
Solomons, Nathan. Grocer. 130 Queen St.
Somarsall, William. Merchant. 2 East Bay
Somarsall, William & Son. Merchants. 10 East Bay
Sowarris, Judith. Shop Keeper. 91 King St.
Spark, Thomas. Saddler. 43 Queen St.
Sparrow, James. Butcher Stall 16. 16 Coming St.
Spears, James. Carpenter. 9 Society St.
Speissegger, John. Music Instrument Maker. Hasell St.
Spencer, Sebastian. 204 Meeting St.
Spidel, John G. Carpenter. 10 Beresford St.
Spierin, Patrick. Merchant. 184 King St.
Spinler, Jacob. Hair Dresser. 118 Queen St.
Squires, Andrew. Hatter. 175 King St.
St. Cellery, Peter. Hair Dresser. 2 Elliot St.
St. Mary, Francis. Hotel. 17 Queen St.
Stafford, Theodore. Chair Maker. 98 Tradd St.
Starkey, Susannah. Shop Keeper. 197 King St.
Stedman, Charles. Carpenter. 161 Meeting St.
Steel, James. Merchant. Craft's North Wharf
Steinmeyer, George. Baker. Boundary St.
Stent, Mary C. Widow. 42 Church St.
Stephens, Thomas. Vendue Master. Market Square
Stephens, William. Merchant. 160 King St.
Stern, Caleb. Boarding House. 16 Union St.
Stevens & Ramsay. Physicians. 47 East Bay
Stevens, Daniel. Supervisor. Geyer's New Range
Stevens, J. H. City Sheriff. 77 Meeting St.
Stevens, S. William. Physician. 11 King St.
Stevens, William. Factor. Cochran's Wharf
Stevenson, Jane. Widow. 85 King St.
Stewart, ——, Miss. School. 66 Meeting St.
Stewart, Alexander. Carpenter. 296 King St.
Stewart, Catherine. 39 St. Philip's St.
Stewart, Charles. Cabinet Maker. 62 Broad St.
Stewart, John. Vendue Master. 22 Hasell St.
Stewart, Martha. Widow. Bedon's Alley
Stewart, Robert. Merchant. 212 King St.
Stewart, Robert. Ship Chandler. 30 East Bay
Stewart, Thomas. Merchant. 32 East Bay
Stoll, Jacob. Tin Man. 209 King St.
Stoll, Justinius. Brick Layer. 13 Wyatt's Lot
Stoll, Thomas D. Coach Maker. 30 Trott St.
Stone, Elizabeth. 11 Orange St.
Stowe, Richard R. Mariner. 11 Society St.
Strobel, Daniel. Tanner. 149 Meeting St.
Strobel, Jacob. Butcher. 102 King St.
Strobel, Jacob. Butcher Stall 26. Home, King St. Road
Strobel, John. Butcher Stall 29. Home, Wentworth St.
Strohecker, John. Blacksmith. 186 Meeting St.
Stromer, H. M. Merchant. 18 Elliot St.

Sturgis, Josiah. 136 Church St.
Sturgis, Josiah. Merchant. 4 Craft's South Row
Suau, L. Faures & Co. Merchants. Gaillard's Wharf
Suau, Peter. Merchant. 123 King St.
Sutcliffe, Ely. Carpenter. Geyer's Wharf
Sutherland, Francis. Shoe Store. 4 Queen St.
Sutton, Mary. Grocer. 176 Meeting St.
Swain, J. Clerk. Geyer's Wharf
Swain, Joseph. Pilot. 115 East Bay
Swaine, Luke. Mariner. Stoll's Alley
Sweeney, James. Vendue Master. Exchange
Swinton, Hugh. Planter. 86 Meeting St.
Switzer, J. Rodolph. Saddler. 234 King St.
Sykes, Thomas. 257 King St.
Symonds, Francis. 20 Elliot St.
Taggart, Mary. Widow. 21 Meeting St.
Tarver, John. 73 King St.
Tash, Ann. Widow. 29 Union St.
Tate, James. Mariner. 3 Elliot St.
Taylor, Alexander. Mariner. 10 Quince St.
Taylor, Jane. Store Keeper. 230 King St.
Taylor, Joseph. Mariner. 4 Charles St.
Taylor, Joseph G. Broker. 11 Scarborough St.
Taylor, ----Mrs. 15 Friend St.
Teasdale, Isaac. Merchant. 122 Queen St.
Teasdale, John. Merchant. 38 East Bay
Teasdale, John. Merchant. 1 East Bay
Tew, Charles. Coroner. 43 Elliot St.
Thackman, James. Gardener. 21 Beaufain St.
Thayer, E. Exchange Broker. 43 Elliot St.
Theus, Simon. Factor. 258 King St.
Theus, Thomas. Planter. 102 Queen St.
Thevenin, Pierre. 77 Meeting St.
Thirtle, William. Grocer. 13 Union St. Continued
Thom & Quackinbush. 76 Meeting St.
Thomas, E. S. Bookseller. 130 Tradd St.
Thomas, Francis. Clerk. 94 Queen St.
Thomas, Jean Jacques. Merchant. 31 Trott St.
Thomas, John. Hair Dresser. 11 Bedon's Alley
Thomas, John. Boarding House. 36 Union St.
Thomas, John. Shop Keeper. 116 East Bay
Thomas, Mary L. Widow. 8 King St.
Thomas, Stephen. Tailor. 32 Elliot St.
Thompson, Ann. Chamber's Alley
Thompson, Daniel. Shop Keeper. South Bay
Thompson, James. Boarding House. Champney's Wharf
Thompson, Margaret. 66 East Bay
Thompson, William. 97 King St.
Thorn, John G. Sailmaker. 6 Bedon's Alley
Thorney, Jane. Widow. King St. Rd.
Thornhill, John. Merchant. Tradd St., corner Church
Threadcraft, Bethel. Watch Maker. 258 King St.
Timme, Henry. Shoemaker. 33 Queen St.
Timmons, Lewis. Vendue Master. 101 Queen St.
Timmons, William. Merchant. 6 Federal St.
Timothy, B. F. Printer. 43 East Bay
Tobias, Joseph. Merchant. 213 King St.
Tobin, Peter. Tobacconist. 8 Clifford's Alley
Toby, Henry. Block Maker. 19 Guignard St.
Tofel, John. Confectioner. 65 Queen St.
Tool, John. Tailor. 11 Elliot St.
Toomer, Ann. Widow. Legare St.
Torrans, H. William. Attorney. 26 St. Philip's St.
Touissiger, Margaret. Widow. 12 Water St.
Tourrette, Thomas. Fruiterer. 14 Queen St.
Tradwell, Hannah. 10 Friend St.
Trench, William. Tobacconist. Beaufain St.

Trenclague, ----, Madame. 203 Meeting St.
Trescot, Edward. Tax Collector. 82 Meeting St.
Trezvant, Lewis. Judge. 107 Queen St.
Trezvant, Peter. 22 Mazyck St.
Trezvant, Theodore. Tailor. 107 Queen St.
Troup, James. Attorney. 110 Tradd St.
Truchelut, Joseph. Baker. 133 Queen St.
Truelle, Jacques. Tailor. 14 Wyatt's Lot
Tucker, Sarah. 114 Church St.
Tunno & Cox. Merchants. 27 East Bay
Tunno & Price. Merchants. Geyer's Wharf
Tunno, William. Planter. 84 East Bay
Turnbull, James. Gibbes Wharf
Turnbull, Robert J. 248 Meeting St.
Turner, Thomas. Dancing Master. 7 Hopton's Lane
Turner, Watson. Deputy High Constable. 13 King St.
Turner, William. Shop Keeper. King St. North end
Turpin, ----, Mrs. Boarding House. 26 Elliot St.
Turpin, William. Merchant. 157 King St.
Tweed, Alexander. 3 Pinckney St.
Ummensetter, John. 31 Beaufain St.
Upham, Amos. Trunk Maker. 21 Amen St.
Valbrune, Leonard. Tobacconist. 32 Union St.
Vale, John D. Merchant. 111 Broad St.
Valentine, Antionette. Cook. 27 King St.
Valk, Ann. Widow. Church St. Continued
VanArden, John. 40 Union St.
Vanderhorst & Miller. Factors. Vanderhorst's Wharf
Vanderhorst, Arnoldus. Factor. East Bay
Vandernerchen, Andrew. Tailor. 38 Church St.
Vandeuvre, John. 6 Cumberland St.
VanRhyne, A. E. Merchant. 118 Broad St.
Vardell, Elizabeth. Widow. 20 King St.
Vaughn, Jesse. 53 Church St.
Veissay, Cato. Barber. Unity Alley
Veitch, William. Brick Layer. 29 St. Philip's St.
Verony, William. Livery Stables. 172 Meeting St.
Verree & Blair. Vendue Masters. Gillon St., corner
Verree, ----, Captain. Attorney. 19 Queen St.
Verree, Mary. Widow. 14 Church St.
Vesey, Joseph. Merchant. 20 Queen St.
Vessel, Catharine. 25 Union St. Continued
Viegra, Joseph. Interpreter. 264 King St.
Vigier, Anthony. 14 Beresford St.
Villaneuve, John B. Merchant. Nicholl's Wharf
Villars, Philip. Musician. 95 Church St.
Vinyard, John. Cabinet Maker. 181 Meeting St.
Vionnet, ----, Miss. 274 King St.
Vos, Andrew. Merchant. 30 Beaufain St.
Wadsworth, Joel. 113 King St.
Wagner, Christopher. Drayman. 7 Trott St.
Wagner, George. Merchant. 85 Broad St.
Waite, William. Coach Maker. 74 Meeting St.
Wales, Horatio. Grocer. Prioleau's Wharf
Walker & Evans. Stone Cutters. 26 Trott St.
Walker, David. Grocer. 273 King St.
Walker, Robert. Cabinet Maker. 57 Broad St.
Walker, William. Cabinet Maker. 29 Hasell St.
Wall, Mary. Widow. 35 Elliot St.
Wall, R. Boarding House. 30 Union St.
Wallis, James. Deputy Sheriff. 271 Meeting St.
Wallis, Thomas. Cabinet Maker. 22 Queen St.
Ward, James M. Attorney. 87 Tradd St.
Ward, John. Attorney. 55 Church St.
Ward, Joshua. Attorney. 252 Meeting St.
Warham, Mary. 82 Queen St.
Waring and Smith. Factor. Roper's Wharf
Waring, Daniel. 5 Scarborough St.

Waring, Morton. Factor. 298 King St.
Waring, Thomas. 40 Meeting St.
Waring, Thomas, Sr. Naval Officer. Custom House
Warley, Catharine, Mrs. 25 Beaufain St.
Warley, Elizabeth, Mrs. Beaufain St.
Warley, Felix. Planter. 9 Trott St.
Warner, Penelope. Widow. 246 Meeting St.
Warnock, Joseph. Stewart Orphan House
Washburn, Eleazor. Mariner. 26 Guignard St.
Washington, William. South Bay
Watson, ——, Mrs. Widow. 4 Friend St.
Watson, ——, Mrs. Seamstress. 34 St. Philip's St.
Watson, Alexander. Factor. 107 East Bay
Watson, John. Cabinet Maker. 21 King St.
Watson, M'Lean & Co. Grocers. 72 East Bay
Watson, William. Shop Keeper. 84 Meeting St.
Watts, Charles. Cabinet Maker. 67 Church St.
Watts, James. Grocer. 129 Church St.
Watts, Robert. Grocer. 12 Friend St.
Webb, John. Merchant. 14 Moore St.
Webb, William. Deputy Collector. 14 Moore St.
Weckrlee, John. Gardener. 20 St. Philip's St.
Weissinger, John. Baker. 181 King St.
Well, Edward. Boarding House. 120 East Bay St.
Wells, Edgar, Mrs. Widow. 25 George St.
Welsh, Anthony. Grocer. Unity Alley
Welsh, Edmond. Beale's Wharf
Welsh, George. 19 Boundary St.
Welsh, John. Tobacconist. 27 Pinckney St.
Wershing, Catharine. Blackbird's Alley
Wesh, Mary. 12 Amen St.
West, Catharine. Widow. 10 Guignard St.
West, James. Physician. 49 Tradd St.
West, Simeon. Mariner. 8 Wall St.
West, Thomas. Mariner. 21 Amen St.
Westermeyer, Andrew. Goldsmith. 22 Union St.
Weston, Plowden. Planter. 37 Queen St.
Weyman & Lynn. Merchants. 15 Broad St.
Weyman, Edward. 6 Pitt St.
Whalley & Bradfoot. Merchants. 135 Tradd St.
Wheeler & Warren. Merchant. 6 Bedon's Alley
White & Norris. Merchants. 1 Bedon's Alley
White, James. Grocer. 134 Queen St.
White, John. Butcher Stall 20.
White, John. Factor. 2 Geyer's Wharf
Whitfield & Brown. Merchants. 2 Bedon's Alley
Whitman, William. Jeweller. 227 Meeting St.
Whittemore, R. Carpenter. 181 Meeting St.
Wilcox & Flagg. Painters. 133 East Bay
Wilder, Carr R. Merchant. 42 East Bay
Wilkie, William. 147 Meeting St.
Wilkinson, John. 3 Union St. Continued
Will, Mathew. Cabinet Maker. 205 Meeting St.
Will, Philip. Federal Marshall. 11 Middle St.
Williams, Abner. Coach Maker. Archdale St.
Williams, Ann. Boarding House. 16 Elliot St.
Williams, Charles. 150 Meeting St.
Williams, Isham. East Bay Continued
Williams, James. 43 Tradd St.
Williams, James. 31 Union St. Continued
Williams, Nicholas & Co. 222 King St.
Williamson & Stoney. Merchant. Gaillard's Wharf
Williamson, A. Tallow Chandler. 5 Union St.
Williamson, Emelia. 22 Guignard St.
Williman, Jacob. Physician. 241 King St.
Williman, Jacob, Sr. Tanner. 1 Montagu St.
Willis, William. Mariner. 10 Boundary St.
Wilson, Gabriel. Barber. Chamber's Alley

Wilson, Glover. Planter. 2 Meeting St.
Wilson, John. Merchant. 157 King St.
Wilson, John. 156 Meeting St.
Wilson, R. & Sons. Druggists. 97 Church St.
Wilson, R. T., Dr. Physician. 75 Broad St.
Wilson, Robert. Physician. 72 Broad St.
Wilson, Robert. Mariner. 9 Hasell St.
Wilson, Robert, Sr. Druggist. 27 Church St.
Wilson, Samuel. Physician. 45 Broad St.
Win, James. Grocer. King St., corner Queen
Winkin, John. 39 Union St.
Winn, Joseph. Merchant. 12 Tradd St.
Winthrop, Joseph. Merchant. 4 East Bay
Wish & Bryan. Merchants. 114 Broad St.
Wish, John. Carpenter. 61 Queen St.
Wittick, Charles. Goldsmith. 29 Broad St.
Wogan, James. 4 King St.
Wolfe, Mathias. 38 Broad St.
Wolfe, Mathias. Dwelling House. 17 Mazyck St.
Wolfe, Rachael. Widow. 280 King St.
Wood, William. Archdale St.
Woodill, John Anthony. Lynch's Lane
Woodrop, John. Merchant. 9 East Bay
Woodrop, John. Merchant. 112 Church St.
Woodruff, E. L. Merchant. 93 Church St.
Woodward, Warham & Co. Merchants. 129 Broad St.
Worthing, Joseph. Upholsterer. St. Michael's Alley
Wright, John Izard. Planter. 4 Scarborough St.
Wright, Rebecca. Widow. 43 Tradd St.
Wurdeman, J. G. Grocer. 18 Union St.
Wyatt, Peter. Lumber Cutter. 1 Lynch's Lane
Wyatt, Richard. Carpenter. 60 Church St.
Wyatt, Violetta. 79 Church St.
Wyllie, Samuel. Merchant. 112 Broad St.
Yates, D. School Mistress. 1 South Bay
Yates, Jeremiah. Merchant. 1 South Bay
Yates, Seth. Shipwright. 12 Lynch's Lane
Yeldon, Richard. 14 King St.
Yoer, Jacob. Shoemaker. 218 Meeting St.
You, John. Merchant. 31 Archdale St.
Young, John. Merchant. 28 Guignard St.
Young, Sarah. Widow. 20 Meeting St.
Young, William P. Printer. 43 Broad St.
Zealy, Joseph. Grocer. 6 King St.
Zealy, Joseph. Butcher. 8 King St.
Zylstra, Peter. Ship Chandler. 67 East Bay

CHAPTER 9

THE 1802 DIRECTORY

The 1802 Directory was compiled by J. J. Negrin as *New Charleston Directory and Stranger's Guide of the Year 1802* (Charleston: John A. Dacqueny, 1802). In addition to the listing of people it contained information on Regulations and Members of the Different Banks in Charleston, Societies and Clubs, Staff of the Militia of this State, City of Charleston City Council, Custom House Officers, Parishes, Churches, Table of the Streets, Alleys, Courts, Squares and Wharves, Public Notaries, Barristers or Attorneys at Law, Physicians, Belles Letres, and Gardener's Calendar. It has 2506 entries.

The locations with the greatest number of entries were King Street and King Street Road 13%, Meeting Street and Meeting Street Continued 9%, Church Street and Church Street Continued 8%, East Bay Street and East Bay Street Continued 7%, Queen Street 5%, Broad Street 5%, and Tradd Street 5%. This showed no significant change from the previous year.

The locations were: Amen Street 12, Anson Street 10, Archdale Street 24, Beale's Wharf 3, Beaufain Street 24, Bedon's Alley 11, Beresford Street 19, Beresford's Alley 14, Blake's Wharf 5, Bottle Alley 8, Boundary Street 19, Broad Street 128, Bull Street 15, Cannon Street 1, Chalmer's Alley 5, Champney's Street 15, Champney's Wharf 4, Charles Street 11, Church Street 118, Church Street Continued 30, Clifford Street 8, Coates' Row 1, Cochran's Wharf 2, Cock Lane 7, Coming Street 14, Craft's North Range 6, Craft's North Wharf 3, Craft's Range 1, Craft's South Range 2, Craft's Wharf 10, Cumberland Street 10, Custom House 1, E. B. Blake's Wharf 1, East Bay Street 156, East Day Street Continued 31, Ellery Street 21, Elliot Street 39, Elliot Street Continued 6, Exchange 3, Exchange Square 14, Federal Street 17, Fort Mechanic 1, French Consulate 1, Friend Street 18, Front Street 12, Gadsden's Wharf 2, Gaillard's Wharf 9, Garden of French Republic 1, George Street 34, Geyer's North Range 4, Geyer's Wharf 14, Gibbes Street 2, Gillon Street 6, Guignard Street 30, Ham & Smith's Wharf 3, Harleston Green 3, Hasell Street 43, King Street 334, King Street Road 7, Kinloch's Court 5, Lamboll Street 13, Legare Street 14, Liberty Street 12, Lightwood's Alley 3, Linguard Street 9, Lodge Alley 5, Longitude Lane 4, Lynch's Lane 13, Magazine Street 9, Maiden Lane 12, Market Street 1, Market Wharf, N. E. 1, Mazyck Street 15, Mazyckborough 11, Meeting Street 217, Meeting Street Continued 10, Middle Street 14, Minority Street 6, Montagu Street 8, Moore Street 14, National Bank Square 6, Newton 1, Nicholl's Wharf 7, Orange Street 11, Over Cannon's Bridge 2, Parsonage Lane 10, Pinckney Street 44, Pitt Street 3, Port Street 3, Price's Alley 11, Prioleau's Fourth Range 1, Prioleau's North Range 3, Prioleau's Wharf 5, Pritchard's Wharf 2, Queen Street 132, Quince Street 20, Roper's Wharf 6, Savage Street 3, Scarborough Street 16, Short Street 3, Smith Street 1, Smith's Lane 4, Smith's Wharf 1, Society Street 12, South Bay 17, St. Michael's Alley 7, St. Philip's Street 22, State Bank 1, State House 4, State House Square 4, Stoll's Alley 12, T & C Counting House 1, Tradd Street 125, Trott Street 70, Union Street 51, Union Street Continued 25, Unity Alley 1, Vanderhorst's Row 1, Vanderhorst's Wharf 2, Wall Street 19, Water Street 7, Wentworth Street 33, West Street 4, Wharves 1, Whim's Court 4.

Where professions are given for people the greatest numbers are for merchants 13%, planters 6%, shop and stores 6%, grocers 5%, various types of carpenters 4%, factors 2%, boarding houses 2%, tailors 2%, physicians 2%, and lawyers 2%.

This directory has far more planters than the previous one (147 to 57), more physicians (45 to 40), more boarding houses (52 to 32), but fewer butchers (14 to 32). Obviously some groups are undercounted by each compiler. The percentage of factors in the city, however, remained fairly constant over the years.

The listings are as follows: academy 7, accountant 2, agent French Republic 1, architect 2, assistant clerk 3, assistant St. Mary's Hotel 1, associate judge 1, attorney 30, attorney general 1, auctioneer 4, baker 25, barber 7, barrister 14, bell & lock smith 1, bell handler & founder 1, biscuit maker 1, bishop obitt. 1, black & white smith 1, blacksmith 11, block maker 4, boarding academy 1, boarding house 52, boarding school 13, boat builder 1, bookbinder 1, bookkeeper 13, bookseller 2, boot & shoe maker 3, boot & shoe store 3, boot & shoe warehouse 1, botanist 1, bottle merchant 1, brass founder 2, brewer 2, brick layer 21, British consul 1, broker 14, butcher 15, cabinet maker 27, cake seller 2, cake shop 3, captain 90, carpenter 23, carter 2, cartman 2, carver 4, cashier 4, chair maker 11, chancellor 1, Charleston Theatre manager 1, city guard 3, city marshall 1, city sheriff 1, city theatre 1, city treasurer 1, clear starcher 1, clerk 11, coach maker 10, coffee house 1, collector 4, colonel 1, comm. of loans 1, commission merchant 2, commission store 1, confectioner 8, constable 3, consul 3, cook 1, cookshop 1, cooper 19, cotton gin maker 4, counsellor 1, counting house 6, currier 1, custom house 2, custom house inspector 6, dancing master 2, dentist 2, deputy collector 1, deputy collector custom house 1, deputy naval officer 1, deputy sheriff 5, deputy supervisor 1, deputy surveyor 1, deputy surveyor general 1, deputy weigher customs 1, director of Charleston Theatre 1, director of National Bank 6, director of S.C. Bank 6, discount clerk 1, distiller 10, district sheriff 1, drawing master 1, dray keeper 2, drayman 5, druggist 2, dyer 1, editor 2, engineer 2, engraver 1, esquire 25, export inspector 1, F.& W. office 1, F.M. 1, factor 55, federal marshall 2, fencing master 1, fish market clerk 1, fisherman 4, French school 1, French teacher 4, French tutor 1, fruit shop 3, gardener 2, gauger 1, general 2, gold & silver smith 4, governor 1, grand negociant 1, grocer 120, hair dresser 12, harbor master 2, hardware & jewellery store 1, harness maker 2, hat & shoe shop 1, hatter 3, horse dealer 1, hotel 1, house builder 2, house carpenter 68, import inspector 2, inn keeper 1, inspector 4, insurance broker 2, intendant 1, interpreter 2, ironmaker 1, ironmonger 2, jeweller 12, judge 8, junior deputy surveyor 1, justice of peace 1, keeper of jail 1, kolfbaan keeper 1, lady of late governor 1, land surveyor 2, late distiller 1, late intendant 1, librarian 1, lieutenant of city guard 1, limner 2, livery stable 5, lodging house 1, lumber measurer 1, lumber merchant 4, M.C.C.C. 1, major 1, major general 2, mantua maker 11, marble cutter 1, marble mason 1, marine insurance 2, mariner 10, market woman 2, mast, pump and block maker 3, master in equity 1, master poor house 1, master work house 1, mattress maker 1, merchant 297, mesne conveyancer 1, midwife 2, milliner 11, miniature painter 1, minister 7, music and instrument maker 1, music master 1, music store 1, musician 1, National Bank discount clerk 1, National Bank guard 1, naval commander 1, naval officer 1, negotiant 1, newspaper carrier 1, notary public 6, nurse 4, oakum maker 1, optician 1, ordinary office 1, organist 2, outdoor clerk 1, painter 16, pastor 3, pastry cook 2, perfumer 3, physician 45, pilot 8, planter 147, porter 2, portrait painter 1, postmaster 1, power inspector 1, president, National Bank 1, president Santee Canal Co. 1, president, South Carolina Bank 1, print seller, printer 5, private boarding house 1, professor of music 3, professor of pianoforte 2, prothonotary 1, pump maker 3, Q.U. office 1, Ravaudeuse 1, recorder 1, representative 1, rigger 7, rope maker 1, S.C. Bank 1, saddler 10, sail maker 8, school 5, school master 5, school mistress 3, scrivener 3, seamstress 34, sergeant, city guard 1, sheriff 3, ship builder 1, ship carpenter 1, ship chandler 4, ship master 4, shipwright 24, shoe & boot maker 2, shoe & boot store 2, shoe store 3, shoe warehouse 2, shoemaker 18, shop keeper 101, silversmith 1, societies housek. 1, SOH, orphan house 1, spinster 2, SSTD of Roman Church 1, stable yard 1, stage office 1, stamp master 1, starch manufacturer 1, state constable 1, state treasurer 1, stationery store 1, stay maker 1, store 44, supervisor 1, surgeon 1, surveyor 1, tailor 50, tallow chandler 2, tanner 7, tavern keeper 4, teacher Assoc. Academy 1, teacher of mathematics 1, teller 5, tin plate worker 6, tobacconist 11, trader 4, translator 1, turner 2, turnkey at Jail 1, tutor 1, U.S. Envoy to Spain 1, umbrella maker 1, upholder 1, upholsterer 1, vendue cryer 1, vendue master 29, veston to synagogue 1, warehouse 1, washer 19, watch maker 14, weigh master 1, wharffiller 1, wharfinger 6, wheelwright 2, white & blacksmith 2, wholesale store 1, widow 73, Windsor chair maker 2, wine merchant 6, wood measurer 1, young masters school 1, young misses boarding school 1.

Women who have actual occupations listed for them worked as seamstresses and mantua makers 22%, shop and store keepers 19%, operators of boarding houses 12%, teachers or operators of schools 11%, and as planters 10%.

This is suprisingly different from previous directories. Women who sewed for a living are represented in earlier years but nothing like the numbers show here (54 in 1802 to 12 in 1801). Also, women rarely had been noted as operating plantations while 24 of them were doing this in 1802. Two women are shown as physicians; however, in both cases their husbands had worked in these fields. Also, Mrs. and Miss Roullit who are listed as merchants can probably be identified with Mary Roullit who was a shop keeper in 1801.

The listings for all women who have some profession or status after their names are: academy 1, baker 1, boarding academy 1, boarding house 30, boarding school 13, cake seller 2, cake shop 3, clear starcher 1, coffee house 1, confectioner 2, French school 1, French teacher 1, fruit shop keeper, grocer 6, jewellery store 1, lady of late governor 1, mantua maker 15, market woman 2, merchant 1, midwife 2, milliner 11, nurse 4, pastry cook 2, physician 2, planter 24, private boarding house 1, ravaudeuse 1, saddleshop 1, school 5, school mistress 4, seamstress 39, shop keeper 39, spinster 2, store keeper 8, tailor 1, tavern keeper 1, umbrella maker 1, wagon yard 1, washer 17, widow 85.

Abbot, William. Merchant. 4 Bedon's Alley

Abendanone, Haim. Shop Keeper. 195 King St.

Abendanone, Joseph. Shop Keeper. 244 King St.

Abrahams, ——, Mrs. Shop Keeper. 185 King St.

Abrahams, Jacob. Shop Keeper. 4 Queen St.

Abrahams, Judah, Mrs. Widow. 10 Beresford St.

Abrahams, Moise. Vendue Master. 36 Queen St.

Adam, Mary, Miss. Mantua Maker. 20 Scarborough St.

Adams, Ezekiel. House Carpenter. 6 Maiden Lane

Adams, John S. & Co. Distillers. 6 Quince St.

Aertson, Guilliam. Dwelling House. 16 Friend St.

Aertson, Guilliam & Co. Vendue Masters. Exchange, N. Side

Ainger & Shaw. Insurance Broker. 16 East Bay St.

Airs, George. House Carpenter. 92 King St.

Aiton, Thomas & Co. Merchants. 15 Elliot St.

Akeen, Helena. Shop Keeper, Widow. 32 Pinckney St.

Akin, Ann, Mrs. Boarding Academy. King St., corner Wentworth

Akin, Thomas. Physician. 117 King St.

Alain, Hulda. Boarding House. 9 Union St. Continued

Alexander & Sons (Judah, Moses). Merchants. 109 King St.

Alexander, Abraham. Shop Keeper. 183 King St.

Alexander, Abraham. Clerk Custom House. 75 Meeting St.

Alexander, Alexander. Captain Mariner. 56 Trott St.

Alexander, Rachel, Mrs. Widow. 56 Trott St.

Alexander, William. Factor. 12 Amen St.

Alix, Lucient. Confectioner. 20 Church St.

Allan, Mason & Ewing. Merchants. 113 Tradd St.

Allan, William. Merchant. 5 Federal St.

Allemand, Robert. Merchant.

Allen, John. Grocer. 110 King St.

Allison & Fife. Coopers. Champney's St.

Allison, James. Cooper. 20 Queen St.

Allport, John. Blacksmith & Farrier. 113 King St.

Alston, Joshua. Esquire. 93 Church St.

Alston, William. Planter. 13 King St.

Ancrum, James. Planter. 30 Hasell St.

Ancrum, William. Planter. 22 Ellery St.

Anderson, Ann. Widow. Minority St.

Anderson, John. Grocer. 11 Ellery St.

Anderson, Robert. Store Keeper. 18 Tradd St.

Ann, Mary. Seamstress. 20 Trott St.

Annely & Lewis. Merchants. 96 Church St.

Anone & Co. Print Sellers. 28 Elliot St.

Anthony, John. Harness Maker. 192 Meeting St.

Arms, Sylvester. House Carpenter. 44 Trott St.

Armstrong, Rebecca. Widow. Minority St.

Ash, Elizabeth, Mrs. Widow. 5 Lamboll St.

Ash, Hannah. Widow. 19 King St.

Ash, John, Sr. Planter. 17 South Bay

Ashton, Catharine. Widow. 1 Ellery St., corner Maiden

Askew, Ann. Widow. 24 Archdale St.

Aspray, John F. Mariner. 73 Church St.

Atkinson, Mary, Mrs. Widow. 4 Friend St.

Atmar, Ralph. Gold & Silver Smith. 20 Beaufain St.

Austen, Catherine. Shop Keeper. 47 East Bay St.

Austin, William. Merchant. 90 Meeting St.

Aveilhe, John B. Architect. Boundary St., East End

Avene, John. Distiller and Confectioner. 5 King St. Road

Avery, Park. Store Keeper. 96 King St.

Axson, Jacob. Clerk, South Carolina Bank. 91 Queen St.

Axson, Samuel. House Carpenter. 22 King St.

Ayrault, Peter. Merchant. 126 East Bay St.

Baas, Thomas. Block Maker. Gillon St.

Bacot, Henry. Attorney. 26 Tradd St.

Bacot, T. W. Postmaster. 99 Tradd St.

Bacot, Thomas. Cashier South Carolina Bank, PM. 99 Tradd St.

Badger, James. Painter & Glazier. 108 East Bay St.

Badia, Alexander. Engineer. 109 King St.

Bagneres, B. Distiller. 29 King St.

Bailey & Waller. Merchants & Booksellers. 121 Broad St.

Bailey, George. Commission Store. 26 Church St.

Bailey, H. B. Lodging House. 26 Church St.

Bailey, Henry. Attorney. 42 Church St.

Bain, Archibald. Merchant. 12 Broad St.

Baker, Francis. Brick Layer. 37 King St.

Baker, Joseph. House Carpenter. 7 Society St.

Baker, Thomas. Brick Layer. 38 King St.

Ball, Elizabeth. Widow. 5 Church St.

Ball, John. Planter. 31 Hasell St.

Ball, Thomas. Factor. Roper's Wharf

Ball, Thomas. Dwelling House. Lynch's Lane

Ballon, Andrew. Grocer. 132 Queen St.

Bampfield, Maria. Seamstress. 11 Society St.

Bampfield, Rebecca. Widow. 77 Queen St.

Bampfield, Sarah, Mrs. Widow. 8 George St.

Banks & Lockwood. Merchants. 116 Tradd St.

Baring, John. Jewellery Store. 141 Broad St.

Baring, John. Dwelling House. 117 Meeting St.

Barker, Joseph S. Merchant. 117 East Bay St.

Barker, Joseph S. Merchant. 78 Meeting St.

Barnett, Samuel. Planter. 46 Church St.

Barnett, Woolf. Watch Maker. 207 King St.

Baron, Alexander, Dr. Dwelling House. Wentworth St.

Baron, Alexander, Dr. Physician. 211 Meeting St.

Barre, Catharine. Shop Keeper. 2 King St.

Barret, James. Gardener. Bull St., West End

Barrett, G. L. Fencing Master. Savage St.

Barrett, James. Blacksmith. 23 Hasell St.

Barron, James. Merchant. Geyer's N. Range

Barron, John. Wine Merchant. 11 East Bay St.

Barton, Elizabeth. Widow & Mantua Maker. 17 Hasell St.

Bay, Elihu H. Judge. 197 Meeting St.

Beale, John E. 32 East Bay St.

Beard, ——, Mrs. Widow. 104 Broad St.

Beard, Frederick. Teller, S.C. Bank. Montagu St., corner Cumming

Beattie, Edward. Merchant. 43 East Bay St.

Beatty, Robert. Merchant. 28 Broad St.

Beauford, ——, Miss. Milliner. 30 Church St.

Beckman, Adolph. Painter & Glazier. 161 Meeting St.

Bedman, Edward. Pump & Block Maker. Quince St.

Bedman, Isaac. Pump & Block Maker. 28 Quince St.

Bee, Eliza. Widow. 11 Amen St.

Bee, John. House Carpenter. 16 Mazyck St.

Bee, Thomas. Judge. 4 Short St.

Beeckman, Samuel. Pump Maker. East Bay St.

Beeckman, Samuel. Dwelling House. 102 Queen St.

Beleurgey, Claudius. F.M. 200 Meeting St.

Bell, David. Clerk & Bookkeeper. Middle St.

Bellanton, Fillette & Emilie. Seamstress. 139 Meeting St.

Bellinger, George, Dr. Planter. 24 Mazyck St.

Bellisle, Peter. Baker. 5 Maiden Lane

Belser, Christian. Butcher. 123 Meeting St.

Benlist, Jean-Baptiste. Baker. 138 Meeting St.

Bennett, ——, Mrs. Boarding House. Chalmer's Alley

Bennett, Henry. Custom House. 9 Liberty St.

Bennett, Thomas & Son. Lumber Merchants. Bull St., West End

Benoit, Therese. Fruit Shop Keeper. 25 Church St.

Bentham, James. Notary Public & Q. U. 39 East Bay St.

Bernard, R. Physician. 39 King St.

Bernard, Rene. Perfumer. 4 Tradd St.

Berney, John. Merchant. 28 King St.

Berresford, Richard. 2 St. Michael's Alley

Besselen, Marc Anthony. 24 Beaufain St.

Bessiere, Anthony. Tailor. 24 Church St.

Best, William, Rev. A. M. Academy. 193 King St.

Bethune, Angus. Merchant. 11 Broad St.

Bevin, Francis. House Carpenter. 16 Union St.

Bieller, Joseph. Butcher. 23 Archdale St.

Billeaud, John. Broker. 108 King St.

Billing, J. Livery Stable. 214 King St.

Bitewood, Daniel. Captain Mariner. Coming St.

Bixby, J. Merchant. 120 Tradd St.

Bize, Daniel. House Carpenter. 33 Hasell St.

Bizeuil, Julien. Shop Keeper. 39 Union St.

Black & Yates. Coopers. Beale's Wharf

Black, Ann. Boarding House. Union St.

Black, James. Shipwright. 92 East Bay St.

Black, Johanna. Widow. 12 Ellery St.

Black, John. Ironmonger. 13 Broad St.

Blackledge, Thomas. Shop Keeper. 141 King St.

Blacklock, William. Merchant. Craft's Wharf

Blacklock, William. Dwelling House. Bull St., corner Coming

Blackwood, Thomas. Merchant. East Bay St.

Blackwood, Thomas. Dwelling House. 1 Longitude Lane

Blaikia, Elizabeth. Widow. 4 Church St.

Blair, James. Vendue Master. Exchange Square

Blair, James. Dwelling House. 2 Stoll's Alley

Blair, William. Shipwright. 212 Church St.

Blake & Magwood. Factors. Blake's Wharf

Blake, John. Captain & Wharfinger. 5 South Bay

Blakeley, Samuel & Co. Merchants. 154 King St.

Blakeley, Samuel & Co. Merchants. 29 Broad St.

Blamyer, William. Weigh Master Custom House. 13 Pinckney St.

Blancan, Peter. Turner. 195 King St.

Bleakley, Seth. Tailor. 69 Queen St.

Blome, John. Baker. Beresford's Alley

Blonbery, Peter. Tobacconist. 23 Guignard St.

Blount, Mary, Miss. Milliner. 23 King St.

Blume, Andrew. Butcher. Harleston Green

Bocquet, Elizabeth, Jr. Widow. 12 St. Philip's St.

Bocquet, Elizabeth, Sr. Widow. 12 St. Philip's St.

Boiel, James. Boarding House. 32 Union St.

Boisgerard, Constant & Fidelle. Merchants. 7 Anson St.

Bold & Rhodes. Factors. 13 East Bay St.

Bollough, E. Shoemaker. 88 Queen St.

Bonham, James. 112 East Bay St.

Bonneau, Francis. Carpenter. 58 Broad St.

Bonsall, Elizabeth, Mrs. Widow. 5 Wentworth St.

Boone, Thomas. House Carpenter. 17 Ellery St.

Booner, Christian. Grocer. 33 Queen St.

Booth, Benjamin. Merchant. 18 Front St.

Boothwroyd, Tabez. Grocer. 13 Archdale St.

Borde, Augustus. Engraver. 98 King St.

Borman, Angel. Sailmaker. Blake's Wharf

Borrows, George. Captain. 19 Amen St.

Bosley, Joshua. 162 King St.

Bostick, Lucretia. Widow & Washer. West St.

Bouchanneau, Charles. Porter, National Bank.

Bounetheau, Edward. House Carpenter. 69 Church St.

Bounetheau, Elizabeth. Widow. 69 Church St.

Bounetheau, Gabriel. M.C.C.C. 3 Quince St.

Bourgeois, Alex. French Consulate

Bourgeois, Mary, Mrs. Milliner. 107 Tradd St.

Bouwens, Charles. Grocer. 50 Tradd St.

Bouyssou, Peter. Captain Gendarmerie. 5 King St. Road

Bow, Ann. Shop Keeper. 76 Meeting St.

Bowering, Henry. Merchant. 12 Tradd St.

Bowers, David. Ship Master. 9 Charles St.

Bowmen, ——. City Guard. 21 George St.

Bowmen, T. B. Printer. 3 Broad St.

Boyd, Benjamin. Merchant. 134 King St.

Bracey & Lee. Merchants. Craft's Wharf

Bradford, Lydia, Mrs. Milliner. 31 Broad St.

Bradford, Thomas. Music Store. 76 Church St.

Bradley, M. Planter. 28 Elliot St.

Brailsford, ——, Mrs. Widow. 1 Friend St.

Brailsford, John & Robert. Factors. 4 East Bay St.

Brailsford, Morton. Esquire. 22 Tradd St.

Brandon, David. Distiller. Meeting St. Continued cr

Brandt, James. Wine Merchant. 43 East Bay St.

Branford, Mary, Mrs. 17 Legare St.

Brebner & Huston. Merchant Tailors. 11 Tradd St.

Bredner, David. Biscuit Baker. 100 Tradd St.

Bremar, Francis. Esquire. 6 Wentworth St.

Brenan, Matthew & Richard. Merchant. 146 Broad St.

Bride, ——, Miss. Mantua Maker. 149 Church St.

Bride, E., Mrs. Grocer & Umbrella Maker. 183 Meeting St.

Bride, John. Merchant. 183 Meeting St.

Bridie, Eleonora, Mrs. Boarding House. 25 Meeting St.

Brisbane, William. Planter. Legare St.

Broaders, Sarah. Boarding School. 34 Union St.

Brockway, Martha. Widow. 173 King St.

Brockway, Samuel. House Carpenter. 27 Trott St.

Brodie, Robert. House Carpenter. 3 Smith's Lane

Bron, J. Peter. Cotton Gin Maker. Meeting St. Continued

Brooks & Potter. Merchants. Craft's N. Range

Broskie, ——, Mrs. Boarding House. Champney's St.

Bross, John. Blacksmith. 30 Union St. Continued

Broughton, Ann, Miss. 92 Tradd St.

Brower, Jeremiah. 23 Quince St.

Brown, ——. Widow. 13 East Bay St. Continued

Brown & Borrow. Merchants. 16 Broad St.

Brown, Charles. Brick Layer. 14 Maiden Lane

Brown, Daniel. Grocer. 100 Church St.

Brown, Daniel. 31 Church St.

Brown, Harriet, Mrs. 58 Tradd St.

Brown, John. Pilot. Kinloch's Court

Brown, Joshua. Broker. St. Philip's Court

Brown, Moris. Shoemaker. 50 King St.

Brown, Moses. Hair Dresser. 50 King St.

Brown, Sarah. Shop Keeper. 247 King St.

Brown, William. Captain Sav. Pac. 2 Maiden Lane

Brown, William. Boarding House. Union St. Continued
Brown, William. 14 Ellery St.
Brown, William. 4 Linguard St.
Browne, James. City Marshall and Keeper of Exchange. 164 Meeting St.
Brownlee, John. Merchant. 14 St. Philip's St.
Bruckner, Daniel. Porter, S.C. Bank. 35 Church St.
Brunet, Joseph. Tin Plate Worker. 38 Meeting St.
Bryan, John. Planter. 85 East Bay St.
Bryant, Perez. Shoestore. 61 King St.
Buchanan, Archibald. Brass Founder. 99 King St.
Buckle, George. Shipwright. 29 Pinckney St.
Budd, ----, Mrs. Boarding House. 40 Church St.
Buik, Peter. Bottle Merchant. 199 Meeting St.
Buist, G., Rev. Dr. Minister Scotch Presbyterian Church. 3 Church St. Continued
Bulger, John. Deputy Naval Officer.
Bulgin, James. Merchant. Craft's N. Wharf
Bulgin, James. Dwelling. 18 South Bay
Bulit, Catherine. Widow & Shop Keeper. 102 King St.
Bulkley, Stephen. Ship Chandler. 24 East Bay St.
Bull, John. Planter. 34 Pinckney St.
Bull, Thomas. Shoemaker. Chalmer's Alley
Bulow, John & Charles. Merchants. 166 King St.
Buntine, William. Shoemaker. 5 Meeting St.
Burch, Henry J. & Co. Merchants. 7 East Bay St.
Burd, William. Silversmith. 8 Archdale St.
Burden, Kinsey. Dwelling House. 224 Meeting St.
Burden, Kinsey. Factor. Craft's Wharf
Burger, David. Societies Housek. 97 Queen St.
Burgess, James. Merchant. 41 Church St.
Burk, Patrick. Cabinet Maker. 40 Queen St.
Burk, Walter. 12 Pinckney St.
Burke, Aedanus. Judge in Equity. 47 Church St. Continued
Burkmeyer, John. Butcher Stall 8. Wentworth St., West End (home)
Burn, John. Grocer. 131 Meeting St.
Burnes, James. Counting House. Blake's Wharf
Burnet, Andrew. Planter. Gibbes St.
Burns, James. Cabinet Maker. 39 Church St. Continued
Burr, N. Captain Mariner. Linguard St.
Burrows & Dickinson. Grocers. 121 Tradd St.
Burrows, Frederick. Pilot. 5 Tradd St.
Butler, Benedict A. Shop Keeper. 10 Queen St.
Butler, Charles P. Jeweller. 136 King St.
Butler, Joseph. Grocer. 66 Broad St.
Butler, R. Captain Mariner. 54 Trott St.
Butler, William. Major General.
Butterton, Martha. Widow. 16 Scarborough St.
Byers, Robert. Tailor. 10 Trott St.
Byrne, Patrick. Sailmaker. 38 Hasell St.
Byrnes, Joseph. Merchant. 101 Tradd St.
Cabage, Clister. Trader. King St. Road
Cabos, ----- Madame. Boarding House. 16 Broad St.
Calder, Alexander. Cabinet Maker. 113 Queen St.
Caldwell, John. House Carpenter. 1 Clifford St.
Calhoun, William. Dwelling House. 9 Lamboll St.
Calhoun, William. Merchant. Craft's Wharf
Callaghan, John. Merchant. 5 Elliot St.
Calwell, Henry. Merchant. 99 Church St.
Calwell, Sarah, Mrs. Lynch's Lane
Cambridge, Eliza. Widow & Boarding House. 45 King St.
Cambridge, Tobias. Vendue Master. Elliot St. Continued
Cambridge, Tobias. Dwelling House. 6 Orange St.

Cameau, Henriette, Mlle. 160 King St.
Cameron, Alexander. Dray Keeper. 81 King St.
Cameron, Lewis. Merchant. 23 Church St.
Cameron, Samuel. Captain Mariner. Linguard St.
Cameron, Samuel. Boarding House. Union St.
Campbell, Alice. Widow & Seamstress. 14 Hasell St.
Campbell, Archibald. Merchant. 92 Church St.
Campbell, Colin. Merchant. 3 Bedon's Alley
Campbell, Laurence. Broker. 11 St. Philip's St.
Campbell, M'Millan. Grocer. 122 Queen St.
Canary, Samuel. Bottle Alley
Cannon, D. 18 Queen St.
Canter, D. Merchant. 6 Moore St.
Canter, Joshua. Limner. 60 Broad St.
Cantor, E. & J. Merchants. Champney's St.
Cantor, Jacob. Bookkeeper & Interpreter. 49 Broad St.
Capdevielle, Mary. Widow & Grocer. 8 Queen St.
Cape, Brian. Notary Public. 77 East Bay St.
Cape, Brian & Co. Inspector & Insurance Brokers. 77 East Bay St.
Cardozo, David. Lumber Measurer. 17 King St.
Carew & Co. Mast, Pump & Block Makers. 4 Ellery St.
Carmand, Peter. Tailor. 228 King St.
Carne, Thomas William. Bookkeeper. 4 Anson St.
Carnes, Samuel. Rope Maker. 27 Beaufain St.
Carns, Susannah. Widow & Planter. 24 Hasell St.
Carpenter, Joseph. Butcher Stall 15. 15 Cannon St.
Carr, R. W. Ironmaker. 40 East Bay St.
Carrere, Charles. French Teacher. 13 Hasell St.
Carroll, Bartholomew. Planter. Boundary St.
Carson, James. Dwelling House. 20 Friend St.
Carson, James. Merchant. 10 Broad St.
Carson, William. Planter. 9 Meeting St.
Cart, John. Factor. Cochran's Wharf
Cart, John. Dwelling House. Bull St., West End
Cart, Sarah. Widow. Kinloch's Court
Carter, George. Physician.
Carter, Mary. Cake Seller. 10 Trott St.
Casey, Benjamin. Coach Maker. 116 Broad St.
Castens, J. M. Watch Maker. 91 King St.
Castro, Jacob. Tobacconist. 199 King St.
Catovesica, -----. Barber. 186 King St.
Cattle, Catharine. Mantua Maker. Whim's Court
Caught, Thomas. Ship Builder. 21 East Bay St.
Cave, Thomas. Distiller. Mazyckborough
Caw, Rachel, Mrs. Planter. 74 Tradd St.
Chadirac, Genis Madame. Wall St.
Chalmers, Gilbert. House Carpenter. 16 Beaufain St.
Chamber, William. Boarding House. 23 Union St.
Chambers, William. Captain Mariner. 21 Union St.
Champneys, John. Planter. 95 King St.
Champovy, Joseph. Merchant. Wall St.
Champy, Edme. Merchant. 130 Meeting St.
Chancognie, Simon-Jude. Agent French Republic. 5 Charles St.
Chandler, Isaac. Physician. 52 Broad St.
Charles, Andrew. Merchant. Craft's N. Wharf
Charles, Andrew. Dwelling House. 14 Liberty St.
Chateauvieux, Thomas. Grocer. 89 Queen St.
Chatelain, -----. Widow. 4 Trott St.
Chazal, F., Madame. Middle St.
Cheves & Peace Langdon. Barristers. State House Square
Cheves, Susannah, Mrs. Widow & Store Keeper. 97 King St.
Chichester, John. Physician. 205 Meeting St.
Chion, Caty. Washer & Ironer. 5 Water St.

Chion, J. F. Merchant. 17 East Bay St.
Chisolm, Alexander. Planter. 287 King St.
Chisolm, George. Factor. 141 East Bay St.
Chisolm, George. Dwelling House. 30 Church St.
Chistian, William. Shipwright. 18 Federal St.
Chittey, William. Bookkeeper & Vendue Master. 46 Trott St.
Chollit, Alexander. Distiller. 2 Coming St.
Chouler, Joseph, Dr. Apothecary. 147 Broad St.
Christian, Elizabeth. 20 Trott St.
Christopher, Charles. Shop Keeper. 14 Friend St.
Chupein, Lewis. Perfumer. 7 Elliot St.
Claims, Mary. Widow. 130 King St.
Clarckson, William. Planter. 44 Meeting St.
Clarckson, William. Merchant. Champney's St.
Claret, Joseph. Merchant. 104 King St.
Clark, David. Watch Maker. 3 Price's Alley
Clark, David. Watch Maker. 141 Broad St.
Clark, Felix. House Carpenter. 18 Magazine St.
Clark, James. Coach Maker. 156 Meeting St.
Clark, James. Tailor. 12 Elliot St.
Clark, Jermiah. Clerk East Beef Market. 50 Church St.
Clark, Robert. Grocer. Champney's Wharf
Clarke, Lucretia. Widow & School Mistress. 10 Pinckney St.
Clastrier, John. Captain Mariner. 256 King St.
Clastrier, Maximin. Starch Manufacturer. 22 Quince St.
Clayton, Morris. Broker. Champney's St.
Cleapor, Charles. Dwelling House. Ellery St.
Cleapor, Charles. Sail Maker Loft 5. Nicholl's Wharf
Cleary, John R. School Master. 20 Hasell St.
Clement, John P. 44 Queen St.
Clement, Sarah. Widow. 44 Queen St.
Clement, William. Attorney. 77 Tradd St.
Cliffey, Raimond. Coach & Harness Maker. 24 Church St.
Clitherell, Elizabeth. Planter. 33 East Bay St.
Club, Alexander. Merchant. 7 Tradd St.
Club, Alexander. Dwelling House. 21 Meeting St.
Coates, ——, Mrs. Coffee House. 115 Tradd St.
Coates, Thomas. Captain Mariner. 115 Tradd St.
Coates, William. Grocer. 2 Prioleau's North Range
Cobia, Daniel. Butcher Stall 34. 14 Beresford St. (home)
Cobia, Frances. Widow. 14 Beresford St.
Cochran, Charles B. Federal Marshall. 20 Federal St.
Cochran, Margaret. Widow & Store Keeper. 243 King St.
Cochran, Robert. Captain. 67 Meeting St.
Cochran, Robert E. Barrister. 67 Meeting St.
Cochran, Thomas, Jr. Grocer. 122 East Bay St.
Cochran, Thomas, Sr. Planter. 120 East Bay St.
Coffin, Eben. Merchant. 4 Crafts Wharf
Coffin, Eben. Dwelling House. Bull St.
Coffskey, Ann Catherine. Widow & Shop Keeper. 8 King St.
Cogdell, M. Ann E., Mrs. Boarding School. St. Michael's Alley
Cohen, Jacob & Co. Vendue Masters & Store. Exchange Square
Cohen, Joseph. Veston to Synagogue. 149 King St.
Cohen, Mordecai. Merchant. 210 King St.
Cohen, Moses. Store Keeper. 49 East Bay St.
Cohen, Philip. Vendue Master. Exchange Square
Cohen, Philip. Dwelling House. 7 Orange St.
Cohen, Rebecca, Mrs. Shop Keeper. 240 King St.
Cohen, Solomon. Shop Keeper. 164 King St.

Coils, Marguerite. Widow & Seamstress. 19 Pinckney St.
Colas & Cournand. Bakers. 1 Trott St.
Colcock, Henrietta, Mrs. Boarding School. 53 Meeting St.
Colcock, Mellisscent, Mrs. Boarding School. 6 Lamboll St.
Coleman, Lucy. Widow. 13 Friend St.
Colford, Joseph. Rigger. 9 Pinckney St.
Colhoun, John. Broker. Wall St.
Collin, Daniel. Inn Keeper. Chalmer's Alley
Collins, Ann, Mrs. Planter. 9 Federal St.
Collins, Mary. Widow & Mantua Maker. 18 Hasell St.
Colzy, Charlemagne. Tailor. 9 Church St.
Conly, George. House Carpenter. 36 King St.
Connoir, Brian. Grocer. 126 Queen St.
Connoly, Thomas. Captain Mariner. 24 Quince St.
Connonltry, John. Captain Mariner. 17 Meeting St.
Conte, Ann, Mrs. Wall St.
Conyers, Elizabeth, Mrs. Boarding School. 264 King St.
Conyers, John & Co. Vendue Masters. Exchange Square
Conyers, William. Captain Mariner. 27 Pinckney St.
Cook, Elender. Store Keeper. 55 East Bay St.
Cooper, John. Dwelling House. 5 Pinckney St.
Cooper, John. Blacksmith. Ham & Smith's Wharf
Cooper, Sarah. Clear Starcher. 22 Archdale St.
Coram, Francis. Factor. Prioleau's Wharf
Coram, Francis. Dwelling House. 20 George St.
Coram, Thomas. Painter & Engraver. 70 Queen St.
Corbett, Catharine. Tailor. 5 Linguard St.
Corbett, Samuel. Tavern Keeper. 191 Meeting St.
Corbett, Thomas M. Planter. 10 Cumberland St.
Cordes, ——, Mrs. Widow. 13 Society St.
Cordes, Elizabeth, Miss. 17 Guignard St.
Cordier, Peter. Grocer. King St. Road
Corker, Thomas. Shipwright. 29 Pinckney St.
Cormick, Thomas. Grocer. 70 East Bay St.
Corr, Charles. Tailor. 50 King St.
Corree, Charles G. Merchant. 54 King St.
Corrie, A. & J. Dwelling House. 6 Charles St.
Corrie, A. & J. Factors. 112 East Bay St.
Cosnay, John. Physician & Deputy Surveyor. 40 Trott St.
Cotton, James W. Carver & Guilder. 63 Meeting St.
Couie, John. Grocer. 41 Tradd St.
Courdougnier, Magdelaine. 43 Tradd St.
Cournand, Chadirac. Shop Keeper. 96 Queen St.
Cournand, Pierre. Baker. 2 Trott St.
Courtney, Edward. Wine Merchant. 1 Moore St.
Courtney, Humphrey. Merchant. 34 Meeting St.
Courtney, James. Merchant Tailor. 36 Meeting St.
Courtois, M., Madame. 7 Queen St.
Courty, John. Shop Keeper. 29 Union St.
Cousin, E., Mrs. Boarding House. 27 Broad St.
Coveney, Thomas. Grocer. 3 Prioleau's North Range
Cox & Sheppard. Printers. 124 Tradd St.
Cox, John. Tailor. 36 East Bay St. Continued
Cox, John. Brick Layer. 2 Federal St.
Cox, Joseph D. House Carpenter. 127 Meeting St.
Crafts, Abel. Merchant. 21 Tradd St.
Crafts, W. & E. Merchants. Wharves
Crafts, William. Director National Bank.
Craig & Monnar. Perfumers & Hairdressers. 23 Queen St.
Crane, Joseph. Shoe Store. 63 King St.

Crawford, Alexander. Painter & Glazier. 213 Meeting St.

Crawford, James. Grocer. 68 Queen St.

Crawford, John. Grocer. 23 King St.

Crawford, William. Grocer. 88 East Bay St.

Creighton, Edward. Barber. Union St. Continued

Creighton, James. Hair Dresser. Wentworth St., West End

Creighton, Pearce. Barber. 16 Guignard St.

Creighton, Peter. Barber. 11 Trott St.

Creighton, William. Barber. 39 Pinckney St.

Cripps, John S. Merchant. 52 Meeting St.

Cristie, Alexander. Baker. 96 Queen St.

Crocker & Hichborn. Merchants. 23 Trott St.

Crocker & Hichborn. Merchants. Crafts's N. Range

Croft, Edward. Barrister. 39 Tradd St.

Crombie, Joseph. Merchant. 85 Church St.

Croper, Elizabeth. Mantua Maker. 33 King St.

Crosby, Josiah. Captain Mariner. 23 Scarborough St.

Cross & Baker. Brick Layers. Kinloch's Court

Cross, George. U.S. Navy, Commander James Adams Frigate. 19 East Bay St. Continued

Cross, James. Dyer & Scourer. 1 Beresford St.

Cross, John. House Carpenter. Pitt St., corner Short

Crovat, Peter. Grocer. 18 Union St.

Crow & Query. Booksellers. 139 Broad St.

Crowley, Elizabeth. Store Keeper. 90 Church St.

Crowly, Charles. Merchant. 105 Broad St.

Cruckshanks, Daniel. Boot & Shoe Maker. 120 Queen St.

Cruckshanks, William. Boot & Shoe Maker. 40 Elliot St.

Cruger, Elizabeth. Widow. 7 Guignard St.

Cruger, F. Davis. Factor. Cochran's Wharf

Cruger, F. Davis. Dwelling House. 30 Meeting St.

Cruger, Nicholas. Esquire. 6 Anson St.

Cudworth, Benjamin. Deputy Supervisor. 15 Beaufain St.

Cudworth, Nathaniel. Export Inspector. 21 Trott St.

Cuhun, Henry. Custom House Import Inspector. 77 King St.

Culliatt, James S. Coach Maker. 7 Clifford St.

Cummings, John & Co. Merchants. 4 Broad St.

Cunningham, Charles. Merchant. 152 King St.

Cunningham, John. Merchant. 138 King St.

Cunningham, John. Merchant. 148 King St.

Cunnington, William. Q.U. Office. 37 East Bay St.

Curry, Samuel. Boot & Shoe Store. 65 King St.

Curtis, Francis. Saddler. Montagu St.

Custer, James. Factor. Prioleau's Wharf

Custer, James. Dwelling House. 13 Guignard St.

Cutter, Robert. Captain Mariner. 213 Meeting St.

D'Oyley, Daniel. State Treasurer. 1 St. Philip's St.

D'Oyley, Daniel E. 1 St. Philip's St.

Dabney, William. Merchant. 12 Tradd St.

DaCosta, Isaac. Planter. 241 King St.

DaCosta, Joseph. Broker. 1 Trott St.

DaCosta, Joseph. Broker. 115 King St.

Dacqueny, John. Printer. 46 King St.

Dacqueyn, John. Printer. 1 Broad St.

Dalton, James, Dr. Apothecary. 179 Meeting St.

Daly, Henriette. Boarding School. 37 Tradd St.

Daniel, -----, Mrs. Pastry Cook & Boarding House. 109 Church St.

Danton, James. Carter. 5 St. Philip's St.

Darby, Artemias B. Deputy Surveyor General. 29 Wentworth St.

Darby, John. Gold & Silver Smith. 3 Beaufain St.

Darby, Margaret. Widow & Mantua Maker. 11 Maiden Lane

Darby, Robert. Tailor. 26 Union St.

Darrell, -----, Mrs. Widow. 3 Water St.

Darrell, E., Mrs. Widow. 100 Broad St.

Dart, I. M. Attorney. 25 Hasell St.

Dastas & Gerard, M. Grocers. 30 Pinckney St.

Dastas, Aine. 21 Queen St.

Dastas, Mathew, John & Marc. Merchants 58 King St.

Datty, J., Miss. French Teacher. 29 Hasell St.

Datty, -----, Mr. French Teacher. 29 Hasell St.

Davago, Moses. Shop Keeper. 66 King St.

Davidson, G. Merchant. 17 Broad St.

Davidson, J. Librarian, Charleston. 5 Society St.

Davis, Harman. Captain City Guard. 7 Cock Lane

Davis, Israel. Store Keeper. 112 King St.

Davis, John & Co. Marine Insurance. 23 East Bay St.

Davis, Sally. Seamstress. 3 Anson St.

Davis, Thomas. Shop Keeper. 85 Tradd St.

Dawson, John. Planter. 2 East Bay St. Continued

Dawson, John & William. Merchants. 7 Broad St.

Dawson, John, Jr. Merchant. 28 Hasell St.

Day, George. Jeweller. 175 Meeting St.

Dayton, -----. Shipwright. Over Cannon's Bridge

Dazivedo, Isaac. Store Keeper. 76 King St.

Deal, Anthony. Shoemaker. 3 King St.

Deas, -----, Mrs. Widow. 12 East Bay St.

Deas, Davis. Barrister. 66 Tradd St.

Deas, Henry. Attorney. 67 Tradd St.

Deas, Robert. Physician. 57 Queen St.

Deas, William A. Merchant. 1 Meeting St.

Debesse, J. J. & Co. Ship Chandlers. 106 East Bay St.

Debesse, J. J. & Co. Dwelling House. 215 King St.

Debow, William. Physician. 37 East Bay St.

Debruhl, M. S. Watch Maker. 131 King St.

Degrant, -----, Mr. Esquire. Middle St.

Deirson, Bernard. Grocer. 3 Union St.

Delahogue, J. B. 8 Federal St.

Delaire, James & Co. Merchants. Nicholl's Wharf

Delaire, James & Co. Dwelling House. 171 King St.

Delajonchere, -----. Planter. Bull St.

Delany, Michael. Pilot. Lynch's Lane

Delarue, R. Merchant. 5 Gaillard's Wharf

Delarue, R. Dwelling House. 86 Meeting St.

DeLeon, Jacob. Dwelling House. 80 Tradd St.

DeLeon, Jacob. Vendue Master. Exchange Square

DeLieben, Israel. Shop Keeper. 48 East Bay St.

Delorme, John F. Upholsterer. 42 Broad St.

Demilliere, Auguste. Limner. Newton

Dener, George. Tanner & Currier. 9 Mazyck St.

Dener, George. Dwelling House. 127 King St.

Denis, Thomas. Physician. 33 Church St.

Dennison, James. Captain Mariner. 38 Elliot St.

Denniss, Richard. Merchant. 11 Hasell St.

Denoon, David. Dwelling House. 38 Trott St.

Denoon, David. Commission Merchant. 36 East Bay St.

Depass, Abraham. Auctioneer. 7 Wentworth St.

Depass, Ralph. Vendue Master. Champney's St.

Depass, Ralph. Dwelling House. 35 Trott St.

Depau & Toutain. Merchants. 95 East Bay St.

Depestre, Hector. Planter. 3 Coming St.

Desaussure, H. W. Dwelling House. 206 Meeting St.

Desbeaux, John. Dwelling House. 3 Cumberland St.

Desbeaux, John. Cooper. Gaillard's Wharf

Desil, Charles. Cabinet Maker. 50 Broad St.

Despisole, Mathew. Shop Keeper. 257 King St.

Desportes, P. 93 Queen St.

Desrivaux, Melanie. Cake Shop. 252 King St.
Dessaussure & Ford. Barristers. 29 Tradd St.
Deveaux, Jacob. Esquire. 23 Meeting St.
Devillers, L. Professor Music. 258 King St.
Dewar, Robert. S.C. Bank, Director 82 Tradd St.
Dewees, William. Factor. Prioleau's Wharf
Dewees, William. Dwelling House. Mazyckborough
Diamond, John. Land Surveyor. 22 Trott St.
Dickinson, Francis. Attorney. 7 Cumberland St.
Dickinson, Joseph. House Carpenter. 203 Meeting St.
Dickinson, Joseph. Captain Inspector Exports. Fort Mechanic
Dickinson, Samuel. Vendue Master and Commission Merchant. Champney's St.
Dickson, Samuel. School Master. 143 King St.
Dill, Jane E. Widow. 9 Price's Alley
Dill, Susannah. Widow. 274 King St.
Dollas, Joseph. Merchant. 7 Church St. Continued
Domec, ——. 6 St. Michael's Alley
Don, Alexander. House Carpenter. 21 Federal St.
Donaldson, James. House Carpenter. 103 Tradd St.
Donaldson, Sophie. Seamstress. 35 Hasell St.
Dorrell, Robert. Factor. 8 Boundary St., West End
Dougherty, John. Grocer. 32 Hasell St.
Doughty, Thomas. Factor. 2 Gaillard's Wharf
Doughty, Thomas. Dwelling House. 51 Meeting St.
Doughty, William. Harleston Green
Douglas, James. Stationery & Shoe Store. 98 Church St.
Douglass, Alexander. Tailor. 105 Tradd St.
Douglass, John. Cabinet Maker. 186 Meeting St.
Douthwarti, A. & Co. Wine Merchants. Union St. Continued
Draiton, Lucia. Kinloch's Court
Draiton, Sally. School. 16 Trott St.
Drake, John. Block Maker. 28 Pinckney St.
Drayton, Jacob. Prothonotary. State House
Drayton, Jacob. Dwelling House. 96 Tradd St.
Drayton, John. Governor & Commander in Chief. 74 Queen St.
Drennis, George. Baker. 34 Beaufain St.
Dresdel, Betsy. Washer & Ironer. 36 Union St. Continued
Drouillard, James. 37 Trott St.
Drummond, James. Shoe & Boot Maker. 105 Queen St.
Drummond, John. Shoe & Boot Maker. 2 Broad St.
Dubois, L. Grocer. 32 Church St.
Dubois, Peter. House Carpenter. 22 St. Philip's St.
Dubuard, Peter F. Hair Dresser. 84 Tradd St.
Duddell, James. Cabinet Maker. 209 Meeting St.
Dueston, Stephen. Lieutenant of City Guard.
Duffus, John. Merchant. 129 Broad St.
Duffy, Patrick. Grocer. 70 East Bay St.
Dulles, Joseph. Merchant. 83 East Bay St.
Dumoutet, John B. Jeweller. 120 Broad St.
Duncan, ——. Tallow Chandler. Over Cannon's Bridge
Duncan, Archibald. Dwelling House. 103 Queen St.
Duncan, Archibald. Blacksmith. 118 Queen St.
Duncan, John. Merchant. 46 Tradd St.
Dunn, John. Store Keeper. Champney's St.
Dunseeth, James Alexander. Physician. 2 Longitude Lane
Dupont, Nancy. Seamstress. 2 Parsonage Lane
Dupont-Delorme. Wall St., corner Pitt
Dupre, Benjamin. Tailor. 75 East Bay St.
Dupuis, Claudius. Esquire. 175 King St.
Durousseau, Peter. Tobacconist. Maiden Lane

Dwight, O. D. Merchant. 83 Church St.
Dyre, Kendall. Grocer. 31 Church St.
Eason, William. Block & Pump Maker. 21 Quince St.
Easterbey, ——, Mrs. Seamstress. 3 Cock Lane
Eastern, Susannah. Widow & Seamstress. Mongagu St.
Eberly, Barbara. Widow. 18 Guignard St.
Eckhard, Jacob. Organist German Church. 47 Tradd St.
Eden, Joshua. Chair Maker. 62 Church St.
Edwards, Alexander. Recorder. 3 St. Michael's Alley
Edwards, Alexander. S.C. Bank Director & Barrister. 3 St. Michael's Alley
Edwards, George. Planter. 90 Tradd St.
Edwards, Isaac. Factor. Prioleau's Wharf
Edwards, Isaac. Dwelling House. 4 Society St.
Edwards, James. Geyer's Wharf
Egleston, John. Grocer. 67 East Bay St.
Ehlers & Weets. Shop Keepers. 33 Union St.
Ehney, Jacob. Brick Layer. 30 Guignard St.
Ehney, Peter. Tailor. 32 Church St.
Ehney, William F. Dwelling House. 18 Magazine St.
Ehney, William F. Clerk. T & C Counting House
Ehrich, John M. Merchant. 107 Broad St.
Elf, ——. Cartman. Mazyckborough
Elfe, Thomas. House Carpenter. 17 Wentworth St.
Elford, James. Captain Mariner. 88 Meeting St.
Eliezer, Eliza. Shop Keeper. 194 King St.
Elliot, Barnet. Planter. 29 George St.
Elliot, C. R. Painter. 13 Queen St.
Elliot, Mary. Widow. 75 Legare St.
Elliot, Thomas. Planter. 29 Gibbes St.
Ellis, Thomas. Wood Measurer. 14 Scarborough St.
Ellison & Sweeney. Counting House. E. B. Blake's Wharf
Ellison, Henry. Dwelling House. Mazyckborough
Ellison, Henry. Grocer. 125 East Bay St.
Ellison, John. Store Keeper. 216 King St.
Ellison, William. Grocer. 62 King St.
Elmore, J. Tailor. 93 Church St.
Elstob, Simon. Painter. 89 East Bay St.
Elsworth, Theophilus. Gauger.
England, Alexander. Baker. 40 Union St.
England, James. Jeweller. 196 Meeting St.
English, Ann. Shop Keeper. 7 King St.
Enguehard, Oliver. Grocer. 3 Tradd St.
Ernest, Jacob. Tailor. 22 Queen St.
Eschausse, William. Mattress Maker. 42 Meeting St.
Esnard, Peter J. Planter. 17 George St.
Ewing, John. Merchant. 214 Meeting St.
Eyre, Daniel. Pilot. 20 Amen St.
Faber, John C., Rev. Minister German C. 12 Moore St.
Faber, —— Mr. Merchant. 29 East Bay St.
Fair, Richard. Shoemaker. 107 King St.
Fair, Robert. Boot & Shoe Store. 94 King St.
Fair, William. Tanner. Bull St., corner Pitt
Fairchild, Aga P. Bottle Alley
Fairchild, Aron. Black & White Smith. 15 George St.
Fairchild, Morris. Butcher. 38 Church St.
Fairley, Hance. Cabinet Maker. 28 Queen St.
Fanning, Maria, Mrs. Mantua Maker. 241 King St.
Farley, James. Shoemaker. 27 Broad St.
Farr, Thomas, Mrs. Widow. 11 Church St. Continued
Farreley, James. House Carpenter. 34 East Bay St. Continued
Farrow, Thomas. Shoemaker. 255 King St.
Faures, F. Merchant. 15 Society St.
Faures, Laurent. Merchant. 33 George St.

Fayolle, Peter. Dancing Master. 260 King St.
Fell, Eliza. Milliner. 24 Broad St.
Fell, Thomas, Jr. Merchant. 26 Broad St.
Ferguson & Gunter. Merchants. 87 Church St.
Ferguson, Ann. Widow. 3 Liberty St.
Ferreau, M. 160 King St.
Ferret, Marie-Louise. Seamstress. 22 Hasell St.
Feuilloley, J. W. 85 King St.
Fiddy, William. Merchant. Gillon St.
Fields, William B. Tobacconist & Clerk of St. Philip's Church. 11 Ellery St.
Fife, James. Cooper. Champney's St.
Findley, Jacob. Brick Layer. 1 Mazyck St.
Fisher, James. Esquire. 16 South Bay
Fisher, John. Captain Mariner. 40 Pinckney St.
Fisher, Peter. Merchant. 11 Magazine St.
Fitzpatrick, Helena, Mrs. Grocer. 1 King St.
Fitzsimmons, Christopher. Merchant & Director, South Carolina Bank. 73 East Bay St.
Flagg, George, Sr. Esquire. 212 King St.
Flagg, Rachel, Mrs. 3 Parsonage Lane
Flagg, Samuel. Dentist. 26 Queen St.
Flemming, R. Merchant. 135 King St.
Fletcher, Thomas. Merchant. 7 Crafts's Wharf
Flinn, Margaret. Shop Keeper. 9 King St.
Flint, Joseph & Co. Dwelling House. 31 Union St.
Flint, Joseph & Co. Grocers. 33 King St.
Florance, Zacharia. Dentist. 126 King St.
Florin, Lucas. 32 Guignard St.
Fogartie, James. Dwelling House. 15 Scarborough St.
Fogartie, James. Factor. Prioleau's Wharf
Foissir, Esther, Mrs. Widow. 89 Tradd St.
Folker, John. 38 Beaufain St.
Folmer, J. Tailor, Ladies Wear. 106 Tradd St.
Foltz, F. Jacob. S.C. Bank Director & Merchant. 3 Longitude Lane
Forbes, J. G. Merchant. 23 East Bay St.
Ford, Jacob. Attorney. 19 Meeting St.
Ford, John. Mariner. 23 Pinckney St.
Ford, Timothy. Barrister. 29 Tradd St.
Fordham, Richard. Shipwright. 59 Church St.
Forest, Thomas H. Cooper. 262 King St.
Forgasse, Sarah. 68 Church St.
Forrest, Charity. Widow. 2 Hasell St.
Foster, Nathan. Grocer. 13 Elliot St.
Foster, Robert. Merchant. 24 Elliot St.
Foster, Thomas. Outdoor Clerk, National Bank. 285 King St.
Foucard, ----. Musician. 256 King St.
Fowler, ----, Mrs. Boarding House. 38 East Bay St. Continued
Fowler, John. House Carpenter. 4 Longitude Lane
Francis, Amelia, Mrs. Boarding House. 8 Stoll's Alley
Francis, Davis. Mariner. 8 Stoll's Alley
Fraser, James. Planter. 1 East Bay St.
Fraser, John M. House Carpenter. 26 Trott St.
Fraser, Mary, Mrs. Widow & Planter. 27 King St.
Frederic, John. National Bank Guard. 1 Price's Alley
Freeman, William. Teller National Bank. 71 Tradd St.
Freneau & Williams. Editors, Gazette. 44 East Bay St.
Freneau, Peter. 35 George St.
Friend, Ulric. Baker. 22 East Bay St. Continued
Frink & Langstaff. Merchants. Beale's Wharf
Frish, Charles. Merchant. 181 King St.
Frits, Peter. State Constable. 17 St. Philip's St.
Fronty, Michael. Physician. 11 Moore St.
Frost, Thomas, Rev. Dr. Minister St. Phillip's. 9 Archdale St.

Fuller, Oliver. Captain. 39 Trott St.
Funck, John C. Grocer. 10 Anson St.
Furman, Richard, Rev. Minister Baptist Church. 10 Church St.
Futerell, James. Teller, S.C. Bank.
Gabeau, A. Tailor. 190 Meeting St.
Gadsden & Co. Merchants. Gadsden's Wharf
Gadsden, Christopher. General. 16 Front St.
Gadsden, M., Mrs. Widow. 19 Front St.
Gadsden, Philip. Wharfinger. 8 Front St.
Gaillard & Mazyck. Factors. 93 East Bay St.
Gaillard, Bartholomew. Merchant. 94 East Bay St.
Gaillard, Bartholomew. Dwelling House. 1 Anson St.
Gaillard, Theodore. Barrister, Speaker House Representatives. 45 Meeting St.
Gaillard, Theodore, Jr. Factor. 93 East Bay St.
Gaillard, Theodore, Sr. Esquire. Montagu St.
Gaillard, Theodore, Sr. Esquire. 78 East Bay St.
Gairdner & Co. Merchants. 114 East Bay St.
Gairdner, Edwin. Director National Bank. 72 East Bay St.
Gallagher, ----, Rev. SSTD of Roman Church. 28 Wentworth St.
Gallaway, Alford. Pilot. 8 Church St.
Galluchat, Mary. Widow & Shop Keeper. 77 Meeting St.
Gandouin, John. Hat & Shoe Shop. 58 East Bay St.
Gantt, Esther. School Mistress. 45 Trott St.
Gappin, William. Chair Maker. 8 Liberty St.
Garden, Alexander. Physician. 121 East Bay St.
Gardener, Samuel. Tailor. National Bank Square
Gardiner, Ruth. Widow. 163 Meeting St.
Garrick, Frederick. Confectioner. 37 Queen St.
Gary, Benjamin. Planter. 10 Wentworth St.
Gaultiere, Joseph. Vendue Master. 81 Tradd St.
Gavin, Charlotte. Cake Seller. Scarborough St.
Gayle, Samuel. Deputy Surveyor. Custom House
Geddes, Henry. Store Keeper. 176 King St.
Geddes, John. Attorney. 104 Broad St.
Geddes, Robert. Merchant. 156 King St.
Gee, Ann. Widow. 7 Union St.
Gefferys, Mary, Mrs. 5 Stoll's Alley
Gennerick, John F. Merchant. 150 King St.
Gensel, John. Keeper of Jail.
George, James. Shipwright. 32 East Bay St. Continued
George, M., Mrs. Shop Keeper. 204 King St.
Gerard, Philip. Grocer. 30 Pinckney St.
Gere, Greenman. Shipmaster. 8 Beresford St.
Gerley, John. Master Poor House. Resigned.
Geyer, Elizabesth. Widow & Seamstress. 11 Mazyck St.
Geyer, John. Capt. Merchant and Counting House. Geyer's Wharf
Geyer, John W. Factor. Geyer's Wharf
Geyer, John W. Dwelling House. 35 King St.
Gibbes, John. Planter. Church St. Continued
Gibbes, William Hasell. Master In Equity. State House Square
Gibbs, ----, Mrs. Widow. 14 Meeting St.
Gibbs, George. Baker. 29 Elliot St.
Gibbs, Lewis. Planter. 8 South Bay
Gibbs, Robert. Planter. 8 Meeting St.
Gibson & Broadfoot. Merchants. Geyer's Wharf
Gibson, James. Coach Maker. 55 Broad St.
Gibson, Patrick. Merchant. 36 Elliot St.
Gibson, Robert. Store Keeper. 232 King St.
Gidney, Isaac. Captain Mariner. Minority St.
Gilbert, Elizabeth, Mrs. Widow. 25 Church St.
Gilbert, J. J. Saddler & Harness Maker. 21 Hasell St.

Gilbert, P. Brewer. 1 Magazine St.
Gilbraith, Robert. House Carpenter. 14 George St.
Gilchrist, Adam. President, Santee Canal Co.
Gilchrist, Adam. President, National Bank. 12 Church St.
Gillespie & Mackay. Merchants. 30 East Bay St.
Gillon, Ann Purcel, Mrs. Widow. Wall St.
Gills, ——. Livery Stable. National Bank Square
Girardon, Antoine. Shop Keeper. 14 Union St.
Gist, William. Merchant. 146 King St.
Given, Mary. Widow & Wagon Yard. 159 King St.
Glading, Joseph. House Carpenter. 20 Pinckney St.
Glen, John. Planter. 54 Tradd St.
Glover, Charles, Jr. Physician. 168 King St.
Glover, Charles, Sr. Planter. 168 King St.
Glover, Moses. Planter. 11 Liberty St.
Godard, Rene. French Tutor. 2 Moore St.
Godet, John. Grocer. 134 Meeting St.
Godfrey, Elizabeth, Mrs. 281 King St.
Godfrey, John. Tailor. 25 King St.
Goldfinch, Charles. Boarding House. Chalmer's Alley
Goldsmith, Abraham. Shop Keeper. 126 King St.
Gomez, ——. Turnkey at Jail.
Gomez, P. H. Shop Keeper. 126 King St.
Good, Sarah. School Mistress. 42 King St.
Goodtown, Peter. Captain Mariner. 136 Meeting St.
Gordon & Miller. Merchants. 26 East Bay St.
Gordon, A. Brick Layer. 101 Queen St.
Gordon, John. Grocer. 181 Meeting St.
Gordon, Martha. Widow. 4 Parsonage Lane
Gordon, Thomas. Cashier, Custom House. 8 Orange St.
Gordon, Thomas & Co. Grocers. 68 King St.
Gordon, William. Grocer. 87 King St.
Gow, Andrew & Co. Merchants. 132 Broad St.
Gowen, Sarah. Washer & Ironer. 25 Trott St.
Grado, Mariano. Boarding House. 17 Union St.
Grafstein, Frederick. Shop Keeper. 2 Beresford St.
Graham, Phebe. Washer & Ironer. Lynch's Lane
Grainger, James. Painter & Glazier. 32 Pinckney St.
Grantt, James. Planter. 38 George St.
Graves & Swinton. Factors. Geyer's Wharf
Graves, Charles. Factor. Roper's Wharf
Graves, Charles. Dwelling House. 55 Tradd St.
Gray, Alexander. Custom House. 125 King St.
Gray, Caleb. Tailor. 140 King St.
Gray, William. Customs Inspector. 6 Mazyck St.
Gray, William. Brick Layer. 42 Church St. Continued
Green, James C. Grocery Store. 14 Trott St.
Green, Richard. Boarding House. 35 Union St.
Green, William J. Grocer. 6 Union St.
Greenhill, Hume. Carpenter. 63 Tradd St.
Greenland, George. Factor. 31 Meeting St.
Greenwood, William, Jr. Merchant. 1 Charles St.
Greenwood, William, Sr. S.C. Bank Director 7 Beaufain St.
Gregorie, James, Jr. Dwelling House. 10 Orange St.
Gregorie, James, Jr. & Colby. Merchants. 133 Broad St.
Gregory, Aga. Washer & Ironer. 1 Scarborough St.
Gregson, Thomas. Brewer. 18 Magazine St.
Grierson, James. Tavern Keeper. 65 East Bay St.
Griffin, Lewis. Saddler. 8 Clifford St.
Griffiths & Manciee. Merchants. 118 East Bay St.
Grimball, John. Planter. 21 South Bay
Grimke, John F. Associate Judge. 21 Church St.
Grio, Paul. Captain Mariner. 35 Hasell St.
Groafman, Henry. Wharffiller. Coming St.

Groafman, Mary. Widow. 2 Mazyck St.
Grochan, John. Captain Mariner. 175 King St.
Groefer, Conrad Jacob. Merchant. 100 Queen St.
Groning, Lewis & R. Store & House. 128 East Bay St.
Gruber, Catharine. Widow. Wentworth St., West End
Gruber, Charles. 79 Queen St.
Gruber, Christian. Butcher. 15 Beresford St.
Gruber, Martin. Cooper. 249 King St.
Gruber, Samuel. Cooper. 70 Tradd St.
Guilbert, Eugene. Professor of Pianoforte. Wall St., corner Pitt
Guilou, Samuel. Tailor. 109 Queen St.
Gunn, William. Blacksmith. 5 Queen St.
Gunter, Philis. Seamstress. 8 Clifford St.
Gyles, Rosina, Mrs. Milliner. 37 Broad St.
Hackell & Oswald. Tailors. 20 Elliot St.
Hacket, ——, Mrs. Boarding House. 8 Friend St.
Hadden & Lonry. Gardeners. 95 Church St.
Hagen, Richard. Grocer. 88 King St.
Hagens, Esther. Seamstress. 49 Trott St.
Haig, Robert. House Carpenter. 43 Trott St.
Hall, ——, Misses. 216 Meeting St.
Hall, Daniel. Factor. State House Square
Hall, Marshall. Carpenter. 12 Lamboll St.
Hall, Mary Ann, Mrs. Widow. 19 Magazine St.
Hall, Thomas. Clerk of Court. 33 Broad St.
Hall, William. House Carpenter. 3 Wentworth St.
Hall, William. Captain. 5 Front St.
Hall, William & Co. Merchants. 17 Broad St.
Halliday, Hugh. Cooper. Champney's St.
Halsall, William. Butcher Stall 30. 18 Guignard St.
Ham, Samuel. Shipwright. Ham & Smith's Wharf
Ham, Samuel. Dwelling House. 10 Amen St.
Hamett, Charlotte. Widow. 14 Elliot St.
Hamilton, Dudly. Brick Layer. 7 Bedon's Alley
Hamilton, ——, Mr. City Theatre. 14 King St.
Hamilton, Paul. Esquire. 11 George St.
Hammett, Thomas. Chair Maker. 112 Meeting St.
Hanahan, John. Merchant. 1 Tradd St.
Hanahan, John. Dwelling House. 281 King St.
Hanahan, Maria. Seamstress. 1 Short St.
Hands, John. Captain. 3 East Bay St. Continued
Happoldt, John George. 17 Beresford St.
Harabowski, John S. Planter. 45 Broad St.
Harby, Solomon. Auctioneer. Exchange Square
Hare, Francis. Shop Keeper. 16 Union St.
Hargreaves, J. & J. Merchants. 22 Broad St.
Hargreaves, Joshua. Distiller. Mazyckborough
Hariott, Roger. Dwelling House. 26 Wentworth St.
Hariott, Roger. Merchant. Crafts's Wharf
Harleston, Ann. Widow & Planter. 83 Meeting St.
Harleston, Elizabeth. Widow & Planter. 94 Tradd St.
Harleston, Nicholas. Planter. 4 Boundary St., West End
Harleston, William. Planter. 90 Broad St.
Harman, Elizabeth. Seamstress. 13 Mazyckborough
Harper, James. Baker. 43 Tradd St.
Harper, John. Merchant. 43 East Bay St.
Harris, J. & H. Merchants. 20 Tradd St.
Harris, Nancy. Seamstress. Middle St.
Harris, Thomas. Shop Keeper. 221 King St.
Harris, Tucker. Physician. 71 King St.
Harrison, J. Rigger. Lodge Alley
Harrison, William Primrose. Stamp Master. Middle St.
Hart, Daniel. Vendue Master. 54 East Bay St.
Hart, Dorcas. School Mistress. 17 Federal St.
Hart, Samuel. Store Keeper. 190 King St.
Hart, Sarah. Shop Keeper. 5 Queen St.

Hart, Stewart & Co. Vendue Masters. Exchange Square

Harth, John. Lumber Merchant. 1 South Bay, West End

Harvey, Archibald. Deputy Sheriff. 31 King St.

Harvey, Benjamin. Captain 28 Regiment. Boundary St., West End

Harvey, Elizabeth. Widow. 120 Meeting St.

Harvey, Elizabeth. Widow. 13 Moore St.

Harvey, John Smith. Ordinary Office. 36 George St.

Harvey, Samuel. Captain. 27 Guignard St.

Harvey, Thomas. Sailmaker. 33 Pinckney St.

Haslett, John. Counting House. Blake's Wharf

Haslett, John. Dwelling House. 94 Church St.

Hatch, R. Captain. 15 Union St. Continued

Hatfield, Sarah. Widow. 41 Trott St.

Hatter, E. Widow. 32 Queen St.

Hattier, ——, Mrs. Grocery Store. 16 Church St.

Hattier & Richard. Grocers. Prioleau's 4th Range

Hattier & Richard. Grocers. 117 East Bay St.

Hauck, John. Grocer. 133 Queen St.

Haup, Philip. City Guard. Boundary St., West End

Havey, Dennis. Tailor. 220 King St.

Hayne, William. Captain & Planter. 12 Scarborough St.

Hayward, Nathan. Planter. 25 East Bay St. Continued

Hayward, Samuel. Captain. 21 Mazyck St.

Hazlehurst, Robert. Director National Bank.

Hazlehurst, Robert & Co. Merchants. 14 East Bay St.

Hazlewood, Joseph. Painter. 35 Pinckney St.

Heath, James. Sail Maker. 37 Hasell St.

Hedderly, William. Bell Hanger & Founder. 44 Trott St.

Henderson, D. Bell & Lock Smith. 24 Queen St.

Henderson, Robert. Stage Office. National Bank Square

Henderson, Robert. Dwelling House. 24 Queen St.

Henderson, William. Stay Maker. 204 Meeting St.

Henrey, J. Cabinet Maker. 39 Church St.

Henry, Ann, Mrs. Millinery Store. 22 Elliot St.

Henry, Jacob. Store Keeper. 200 King St.

Henson, Archibald. House Carpenter. Minority St.

Herriot, G. & R. Merchants. Crafts's 4th Wharf

Herron, John. Merchant. 145 King St.

Heydd, David. Grocer. 163 Meeting St.

Heyliger, Joseph. Deputy Sheriff. 200 Meeting St.

Heyward, ——, Mrs. Widow & Planter. 10 Legare St.

Heyward, Thomas. Planter. 9 Church St.

Hichborn, ——. Captain. 47 Trott St.

Hier, ——, Mrs. 38 Queen St.

Hig, David. Cooper. 132 Meeting St.

Hig, David. Cooper. Crafts's Wharf

Hildreth, Benjamin. Sailmaker Loft. Champney's St.

Hill, Andrew. Shipwright. 22 Trott St.

Hill, Hannah, Miss. School. 24 Meeting St.

Hill, Paul. Distiller, Clerk of German Church. 28 Archdale St.

Hillegas, Philip. Late Distiller. 22 George St.

Himely, J. J. Merchant, Watch and Clock Maker. 135 Broad St.

Hinds, Thomas. Barrister. 24 Broad St.

Hingle, Thomas. Hair Dresser. 40 Meeting St.

Hinson, Sarah. Seamstress. 7 Price's Alley

Hippers, Peter. Shop Keeper. 146 Meeting St.

Hippius, ——. Captain Mariner. 6 East Bay St. Continued

Hislop, John. Carpenter. 61 Church St. Continued

Hislop, Robert. Tailor. 58 Church St.

Hislop, Robert. 3 Union St. Continued

Hodge, Helena. Widow. 25 Guignard St.

Hodgson, Mary. Widow. 41 King St.

Hogarth, William, Jr. Shoemaker Shop. Wall St.

Hogarth, William, Jr. Shoemaker Shop. 41 East Bay St. Continued

Hogarth, William, Sr. Shoemaker. 7 Union St.

Holland, Diana. Seamstress. 8 Price's Alley

Hollinshead, William, Rev. Dr. Pastor Independent Church. 79 Meeting St.

Holmes & Co. Vendue Masters. 129 East Bay St.

Holmes, Andrew. Merchant. 4 Pinckney St.

Holmes, John Bee. Barrister. 6 Meeting St.

Holmes, William. Dwelling House. Coming St., West End & Boundary

Honeywood, Elizabeth. Shop Keeper. 59 Meeting St.

Honour, John. Saddler. Coming St.

Hook, ——, Mrs. Boarding House. 2 Linguard St.

Hook, Conrad. House Carpenter. Ellery St.

Hook, Susannah. 8 Pinckney St.

Hopper, Joseph. Butcher Stall 48. Trott St.

Hoppins & Charles. Merchants. Crafts S. Range

Hopson, Morris. Shoestore. 245 King St.

Hora, Saul. Clerk. 31 Archdale St.

Horiot, Anthony. Blacksmith. Beresford's Alley

Horlbeck, Henry. Brick Layer. 3 Moore St.

Horlbeck, John, Jr. Brick Layer. 9 Moore St.

Horlbeck, John, Sr. Brick Layer. 8 Moore St.

Hornby, Hannah, Mrs. Boarding School. 203 King St.

Horry, E. Lynch. Planter. 69 Broad St.

Horry, Elias. Planter. 13 Lamboll St.

Horry, Harriot, Mrs. 50 Tradd St.

Horry, Jonah. Planter. Mazyckborough

Horry, Thomas. Planter. 225 Meeting St.

Hosmer & Haslet. Painters & Glaziers. 1 Elliot St. Continued

Houlton, James. Broker. 4 Cumberland St.

House, Samuel. Justice of Peace & Clerk of Control Office. Wentworth St.

Houser, ——. Clerk Hay Market. 5 Smith's Lane

Houset, ——, Mr. Shop Keeper. 128 King St.

Howard, George. Dwelling House. 1 George St.

Howard, Richard. Cooper. Gillon St.

Howard, Richard. Cooper. Gillon St.

Hoyland, Ann M., Mrs. Boarding School. 102 Broad St.

Hudson, Rebecca, Miss. 82 Queen St.

Huger, ——, Misses. 85 Meeting St. From the Northward.

Huger, Carlos. Tailor. Union St. Continued

Huger, Daniel E. Planter. 12 Legare St.

Huger, John. Planter. 88 Broad St.

Hughes, Edward. Teacher Associate Academy. 36 Tradd St. (house)

Hughes, Mary, Mrs. Boarding House. 7 Trott St.

Humber, Godfrey. House Carpenter. 3 Lynch's Lane

Hume, John. Planter. Montagu St.

Humeston, Joy. Windsor Chair Maker. 135 Meeting St.

Humphreys, Betsey. Seamstress. 11 King St.

Hunter, J., Mrs. Store Keeper. 41 Meeting St.

Hunter, James. Store Keeper. 66 East Bay St.

Hunter, James. Shipwright. 30 East Bay St. Continued

Hunter, James. Captain Mariner. 64 Church St.

Hunter, Jane. Shop Keeper. 33 Church St. Continued

Hunter, John. Hair Dresser. 39 Meeting St.

Hunter, William. Tailor. 7 Elliot St. Continued

Huntington, Mary, Mrs. 3 Lightwood's Alley

Hussey, Brian. Pilot. 13 Water St.

Hutchinson, Hugh. Captain. Champney's St.
Hutchinson, Jeremiah. Chair Maker. 5 Archdale St.
Hutson, James. Merchant. 5 Cumberland St.
Hutson, James H. Carpenter. 52 Trott St.
Hutson, William. Cotton Machine Maker. 155 Meeting St.
Hutton, James. Factor. 12 South Bay
Huxham, ——, Misses. Milliner. 13 Tradd St.
Hyams, David. Shop Keeper. 183 King St.
Hyams, Samuel. Shop Keeper. 53 East Bay St.
Hyams, Solomon & Co. Vendue Masters. Exchange Square
Hyer, Henry. Drayman. Boundary St., West End
Hyndman, James. Shop Keeper. 159 King St.
Hyslop, Christiana, Mrs. Shop Keeper. 3 Union St.
Iadon, Isaac. Tailor. 3 Maiden Lane
Icarden, Lewis. Grocer. 13 Trott St.
Ingelsby, Henry and Co. Merchant. 126 Broad St.
Ingraham, Nathaniel. Captain. 292 King St.
Ingram, Grace. Seamstress. Boundary St., East End
Ireland, Benjamin. Carpenter. 42 Queen St.
Irvine, Matthew. Physician. 7 Meeting St.
Izard, Henry. Esquire. Bull St.
Izard, Ralph, Jr. Planter. 99 Broad St.
Izard, Ralph, Sr. Representative. 1 Meeting St.
Jack, J. Fisherman. 52 Church St.
Jacks, James. Merchant Jeweller. 125 Broad St.
Jackson, Ann. Boarding House. 20 Union St.
Jackson, John. Watch Maker With Mr. M'Gann. 132 East Bay.
Jackson, John. Dwelling House. 66 Meeting St.
Jackson, William. Shoe & Boot Store. 130 Queen St.
Jackson, William. Dwelling House. 153 Meeting St.
Jacobs, Abraham. Cartman. 6 Front St.
Jacobs, B. Shop Keeper. 13 Queen St.
Jacobs, Eliza. Widow. 86 Queen St.
Jacques, M. Fisher. 123 East Bay St.
Jahan, Joseph. Architect Builder. 2 Meeting St. Continued
James, John. House Carpenter. 21 Archdale St.
Jamieson, George. Hair Dresser. 38 Church St.
Jamieson, Samuel. Tailor. National Bank Square
Jarman, John. Livery Stable. 65 Meeting St.
Jarvis, Saint Clair. Attorney. 85 Broad St.
Jeanneret, C. Collection Clerk, Bookkeeper. State Bank
Jeffe, Sarah. Spinster. King St. Southeast, corner Broad
Jefferson, John. Turner. 150 Meeting St.
Jeffords, John. Tailor. 21 Pinckney St.
Jenkins, ——, Mrs. Planter. 20 South Bay
Jenkins Edward, Rev. Dr. Minister St. Michael's. 10 Lamboll St.
Jenkins, Elias. Brick Layer. 13 Liberty St.
Jenkins, Micah. Planter. 76 Tradd St.
Jennings, Elizabeth, Mrs. 9 East Bay St.
Jenny, John. Baker. 2 Beresford's Alley
Jessop, J. Hotel. 127 East Bay St.
Jewell, Benjamin. Shop Keeper. 59 East Bay St.
John, Alexander J. Grocer. 36 Church St. Continued
John, Jabez W. Watch Maker. 138 Broad St.
John, Signor. Fisherman. 54 Church St.
Johnson & Dunlop. Druggist & Physician. 5 Broad St.
Johnson, Barbara. Widow. 22 Trott St.
Johnson, Benjamin. Carpenter. 60 Church St.
Johnson, Clarissa. Market Woman. 49 Church St.
Johnson, Esther & Daughter. 1 Bottle Alley
Johnson, John. Judge of Peace. 158 King St.

Johnson, John. Hair Dresser. 16 Ellery St.
Johnson, John. Blacksmith. Gillon St.
Johnson, John. Boarding House. 8 Union St.
Johnson, John. Dwelling House. 6 East Bay St.
Johnson, John, Jr. 87 East Bay St.
Johnson, Sarah, Mrs. 8 Liberty St.
Johnson, William. Judge. 66 Church St.
Johnson, William P. Store Keeper. 158 King St.
Johnson, William, Sr. 10 Charles St.
Johnston, Charles, Jr. Planter. 11 South Bay
Johnston, Charles, Sr. Planter. 1 Lamboll St.
Johnston, David. Deputy Collector Custom House. 44 Queen St.
Johnston, Edward. Shop Keeper. 15 Amen St.
Johnston, Eleanor, Mrs. Grocer. 234 King St.
Jones, Abner. Tailor. 9 Beresford's Alley
Jones, Alexander. 78 Tradd St.
Jones, Daniel. Tailor. 9 Beresford's Alley
Jones, Edward. Physician. 4 Orange St.
Jones, Henry. Merchant. 18 Church St.
Jones, Jehu. Tailor. 110 Broad St.
Jones, Joseph. Shop Keeper. 14 Tradd St.
Jones, Margaret. Widow. 29 King St.
Jones, Nathaniel. Merchant. 8 Tradd St.
Jones, Samuel. Shop Keeper. 248 King St.
Jones, Samuel B. S.C. Bank. 1 Charles St.
Jones, Sarah. Widow & Seamstress. 16 Beresford's Alley
Jones, Sarah. Boarding School. 2 Anson St.
Jones, Thomas. Tailor. 43 Church St.
Jones, Thomas. President of S.C. Bank. 1 Guignard St.
Jose, Michael. F.& W. Office. 44 East Bay St.
Joseph, Israel. Broker. 44 Broad St.
Joseph, Joseph. Shop Keeper. 6 Queen St.
Joseph, Lazarus. Shop Keeper. 133 King St.
Joseph, Samuel. Shop Keeper. 230 King St.
Joy, Abraham. House Carpenter. 2 Quince St.
Judah, Jacob. Grocer. 124 Queen St.
Kaiser, John J. Butcher.
Kamps, ——, Mrs. Bottle Alley
Keen, Thomas. Captain Mariner. 25 Union St. Continued
Keenan, George. Shop Keeper. 23 Church St. Continued
Keenan, Thomas. Grocer. 1 Church St. Continued
Keisey, William. Invalid. Boundary St., East End
Keith, Isaac, Rev. Pastor Independent Church. 50 Tradd St.
Keith, Silvanus & Co. Merchants. 109 East Bay St.
Kelly, Martha. Shop Keeper. 3 Scarborough St.
Kelly, Mary. Shop Keeper. 114 King St.
Kelly, Michael. Merchant. 17 Tradd St.
Kemp, Alexander. Merchant. 9 Tradd St.
Kempton, Ann. Shop Keeper. 29 Meeting St.
Kempton, George. Factor. 26 Meeting St.
Kennedy, James. Planter. 8 Mazyck St.
Kennedy, P. Grocer. 82 Meeting St.
Kennedy, Susannah, Mrs. Tavern Keeper. 20 East Bay St.
Ker, Eliza. Milliner. 26 Broad St.
Ker, John. Hatter. 46 East Bay St.
Ker, Samuel. Attorney. 41 Meeting St.
Kern, John F. Merchant. 185 King St.
Kern, John F. Dwelling House. 2 Gaillard's Wharf
Kershaw, Charles. Factor. 97 Tradd St.
King, Benjamin. House Carpenter. 16 Scarborough St.
King, David. Tailor. 24 Queen St.
King, Eleanora, Mrs. 142 Meeting St.

Kinsey & Burden. Factors. 5 Craft's S. Range
Kinsland, John. House Carpenter. 114 Meeting St.
Kirby & Myles. Merchants. 92 Church St.
Kirk & Lukens. Merchants. 56 East Bay St.
Kirkland, Joseph. Physician. 194 Meeting St.
Kirkpatrick, John. Merchant. 89 Church St.
Kirkwood, Jessy. Widow & Shop Keeper. Wall St.
Knight, Andrew. Captain. 2 Whim's Court
Knipping & Steinmetz. Store & Counting House. 52 Tradd St.
Knipping & Steinmetz. Store & Counting House. Geyer's Wharf
Knox, Thomas. Grocer. 18 Amen St.
Knox, Walter. House Carpenter. Wall St.
Kohne, Frederick. Merchant. 28 East Bay St.
Koster, Henry. Grocer. 2 Smith's Lane
Kugley, George. Tailor. 14 Mazyck St.
Kugley, John. House Carpenter. 14 Mazyck St.
Labatt, David. Shop Keeper. 119 Queen St.
Labattut, Peter. Drawing Master. 37 Beaufain St.
Laborde, Francis. Merchant and Public Chairs Keeper. 133 King St.
Lacombe, -----. Tobacconist. 224 King St.
Lacoste, Stephen. Merchant. 76 Queen St.
Lacy, Thomas. House Carpenter. 29 King St.
Ladeveze, Joseph. Merchant. 85 King St.
Ladson, Eliza, Mrs. Boarding House. 114 Queen St.
Lafar, Catherine. Widow. 31 Guignard St.
Lafilly, Francis. Scrivener. 14 Guignard St.
Lafrantz, Peter. Merchant. Vanderhorst's Wharf
Lahthausen, J. W. Grocer. 24 Trott St.
Laidler, William. Captain Mariner. 142 Meeting St.
Laissac, John & C. Grocers. 90 Queen St.
Lambol, Diana. Washer. 4 King St.
Lance, Ann, Mrs. 10 Friend St.
Lance, Lambert. Attorney. 10 Friend St.
Landry, John B. Grocer. 118 King St.
Lane & Mushett (William & John). Blacksmith Shop. 10 Ellery St.
Lane & Mushett (William and John). Dwelling House. 9 Magazine St.
Lane, Samuel. House Carpenter. 6 Society St.
Lange, J. 1 Church St. Continued (home)
Lange, J. H. & Co. Merchants. 146 East Bay St.
Langstaff, Benjamin. Merchant. 128 Meeting St.
Langstaff, William. Grocer. 152 Meeting St.
Lanneau, Bazile. Tanner & Currier. 1 Pitt St.
Lanter, Catharine. Washer. 13 Quince St.
Laporte, R. 55 Trott St.
Laroch, Elizabeth. Widow. 29 Beaufain St.
Larrey, Robert. Carpenter. 57 Church St.
Larue, Francis. Cabinet Maker. 81 Meeting St.
Larue, Mad. Shop Keeper. 81 Meeting St.
Latham, Daniel. Distiller. 1 Hasell St.
Latham, Joseph. Distiller. 6 Hasell St.
Latirue, Robertjot. Planter. 19 Federal St.
Latoache, Isaac. Tailor. 162 Meeting St.
Laurans, Peter. Grocer. 167 King St.
Laurens, Henry. Planter. 28 East Bay St. Continued
Lavaudan, -----, Mr. Trader. 256 King St.
Lawrence, Elizabeth. Widow. 17 Pinckney St.
Lawrence, Robert & Thomas. Factors. Roper's Wharf
Lawrence, Robert Daniel. Factor. Roper's Wharf
Lawrence, Robert Daniel. Dwelling. 44 George St.
Lawton, Winborn. Planter. 1 Lightwood's Alley
Lazrus, Marks. Store Keeper. 101 King St.
Leacraft, William. House Carpenter. 25 Pinckney St.
Leadbetter, William. Shipwright. 10 Liberty St.

Leaumont, R. Professor of Music. 19 Beresford's Alley
Leavitt, Joshua. Grocer. 80 East Bay St.
Lebby, Nathaniel & Co. Dwelling House. 10 Amen St.
Lebby, Nathaniel & Co. Block, Mast & Pump Makers. 90 East Bay.
Leblong, Henry. Shoemaker. 7 Liberty St.
Lecat, -----, Mrs. Confectioner. 39 Meeting St.
Lecat, F. Professor of Music. 39 Meeting St.
Lee & Theus. Factors. Geyer's Wharf
Lee, James. Store & Counting House. Geyer's Wharf
Lee, James. Merchant. 11 East Bay St. Continued
Lee, John & Co. Merchants. 206 King St.
Lee, Stephen. Planter. 40 Broad St.
Lee, Timothy. Factor. Crafts' N. Range
Lee, William. Merchant. 1 Archdale St.
Lee, William, Jr. Attorney. 55 King St.
Lee, William, Sr. Watch Maker. 55 King St.
Leese, Benjamin. Merchant. 127 Broad St.
Lefevre, Stephen. Store & Counting House. Nicholl's Wharf
Lefevre, Stephen. Merchant. 171 Meeting St.
Lefoie, Mary. Widow. 85 Queen St.
Legare, James. Planter. 2 Church St.
Legare, Joseph. Planter & Factor. Cochran's Wharf
Legare, Joseph. Dwelling House. Boundary St., East End
Legare, Mary, Mrs. 283 King St.
Legare, Solomon. Planter. 19 Friend St.
Lege, J. M. Dancing Master. 104 Queen St.
Leger, Elizabeth, Mrs. 4 Federal St.
Legge, Edward. Accountant. 57 Trott St.
Legge, Edward B. Attorney. 57 Trott St.
Legoux, J. Francis. Watch Maker. 10 Queen St.
Lehre, Ann, Mrs. 27 St. Philip's St.
Lehre, Mary, Mrs. 12 Liberty St.
Lehre, Thomas. District Sheriff. 127 King St.
Lehre, Thomas. State Sheriff. State House
Lennox, William. Merchant. 30 King St.
Lenormant, Andrew. 41 Queen St.
Lenox, William. Store Keeper. 6 Cumberland St.
Leonhard, Henry. Grocer. 27 Church St. Continued
Lepoole, Peter. Kinloch's Court
LeSeigneur, Vincent. Physician. Parsonage Lane
Lesesne, Eliza, Mrs. 3 Meeting St. Continued
Lesesne, Hannah, Mrs. 43 East Bay St. Continued
Lesesne, Peter & Thomas. Planters. 42 Pinckney St.
Lester, Johanna. Seamstress. 10 Guignard St.
Leuder, F. Confectioner. 27 Queen St.
Leve, Nathan. Shop Keeper. 115 King St.
Leve, Samuel. Merchant. 124 King St.
Levey, Hart, Mrs. Shop Keeper. 131 King St.
Levrier, Peter. French Teacher. 42 Meeting St.
Levy, Eliza. Umbrella Maker. 37 Union St.
Levy, Emanuel & Co. Store Keepers. 45 East Bay St.
Levy, Moses C. Shop Keeper. 217 King St.
Levy, R., Mrs. Shop Keeper. 233 King St.
Levy, Simon. Shop Keeper. 115 King St.
Lewis, -----. Merchant, Co Partner of Annely. 7 Church St.
Lewis & You. Merchants. 112 Tradd St.
Lewis, Charles J. & Co. Merchant. 10 Broad St.
Lewis, Henry. Deputy Sheriff. 9 Beresford's Alley
Lewis, Isaac & Alexander. Merchants. 20 Broad St.
Lewis, John. Carpenter. 6 Beresford St.
Lewis, John. Shop Keeper. 209 King St.
Lewis, Maria. Widow. 20 Union St. Continued
Lewis, Richard. Captain. 41 Pinckney St.
Liber, Elizabeth. Shop Keeper. 157 King St.

Lightbourn, Francis. Captain. 239 King St.
Lightwood, Edward. Barrister. 220 Meeting St.
Lightwood, Eliza. Seamstress. 18 Trott St.
Lightwood, Elizabeth, Mrs. 220 Meeting St.
Limehouse, Robert. 64 Tradd St.
Linguard, ——, Mrs. 65 Church St.
Lining, Charles. Attorney & Ordinary for Charleston District. 8 Legare St.
Linning, Robert. Shoe & Boot Store. 105 Queen St.
Little, Robert. House Carpenter. 22 Union St. Continued
Livingston, Robert Young. Bookkeeper. 57 Trott St.
Livingston, William. Captain. 14 Pinckney St.
Lloyd & Snyder. Grocers. 227 King St.
Lloyd, Daniel, Sr. Esquire. Bull St.
Lloyd, John. Carpenter. Middle St.
Lloyd, John, Jr. Factor. 166 Meeting St.
Lockey & Naylor. Merchant. 105 East Bay St.
Lockey, George. Merchant. 81 Queen St.
Lockwood, Joshua. Planter. 170 Meeting St.
Logan, Honoria, Mrs. 31 Tradd St.
Logan, William. Attorney. 13 Moore St.
Logan, William, Sr. Esquire. 271 King St.
Long, ——, Mrs. Nurse. Coming St.
Long, John. Bookkeeper. 31 George St.
Longerman, F. Widow & Boarding House. Bottle Alley
Lopez, David. Store. 237 King St.
Lopez, David. Vendue Master. Exchange Square
Lopez, David. Dwelling House. 33 Beaufain St.
Lord, Richard. Merchant. Gillon St.
Lord, Richard. Dwelling House. 56 Queen St.
Loughride, David. Grocer. 24 Pinckney St.
Loveday, John. Power Inspector. 10 Moore St.
Lovely, William. Boarding House. Beresford's Alley
Lovett, William. Carpenter. 3 Lamboll St.
Lowe, John. Merchant. 5 Bedon's Alley
Lowndes, Jane, Mrs. Planter. 45 Tradd St.
Lowndes, Mary, Miss. 45 Tradd St.
Lowndes, William. 89 Broad St.
Luckins, John. Merchant. 98 Tradd St.
Luntt, Mary. Shop Keeper. 27 Union St.
Luscombe, Eliza, Mrs. 9 Wentworth St.
Luscombe, George. Captain Mariner. 9 Wentworth St.
Lynah, James. Physician and S.C. Bank Director. 47 Meeting St.
Lynn & Weyman. Merchants. 107 East Bay St.
Lynn, John. Merchant. 2 Front St.
Lyon, Mordecai. Shop Keeper. 50 East Bay St.
M'Adam, James & Co. Merchants. 145 East Bay St. House & Store
M'Affee, John. Carpenter. 7 St. Philip's St.
M'Alla, Thomas Harrison. Physician. Elliot St.
M'Alpin, Angus. Merchant. 21 East Bay St.
M'Aulay, George. Merchant. 18 Broad St.
M'Aulay, George & Sons. Merchants. 111 Tradd St.
M'Blair, William. Vendue Master. 19 Pinckney St.
M'Bride, Samuel. Shop Keeper. 57 East Bay St.
M'Call, ——, Mrs. 105 Church St.
M'Call, Elizabeth. Widow. 14 Meeting St.
M'Call, Paul. 5 King St.
M'Can, Edward. Clerk of Fish Market. 6 Price's Alley
M'Candish, A. Merchant. 6 Geyer's N. Range
M'Cants, William. Esquire. Montagu St.
M'Carty, John. Constable. 16 Hasell St.
M'Clallan, John. Captain at Ft. Moultrie.
M'Cleish, Alexander. Dwelling House. 9 St. Philip's St.

M'Cleish, Alexander. Brass Founder. 56 Meeting St.
M'Clure, Alexander & John. Merchants. 23 Broad St.
M'Cormick, William. Grocer. 121 Queen St.
M'Credie & Cogdell. Barristers.
M'Credie, David. Merchant. 8 Broad St.
M'Donald, J. E., Mrs. Store. 136 King St. Northwest corner George
M'Donald, J. E., Mrs. 22 East Bay St.
M'Donnald, Christopher. Grocer. 269 King St.
M'Dowall, Ann. Washer & Ironer. 16 Trott St.
M'Dowall, James. Store. 169 King St.
M'Dowall, Patrick & A. & Co. Merchants. 143 Broad St.
M'Dowell, A. Saddler. 221 King St.
M'Dowell, James. Merchant. 64 King St.
M'Dowell, John. Merchant. 144 King St.
M'Eneny, Duncan & Co. Merchants. 192 King St.
M'FarLane & Player. Merchant. 7 Gaillard's Wharf
M'Gann, Patrick. Watch Maker. 132 East Bay St.
M'Ginness, P. Grocer. 70 King St.
M'Gown, William. House Carpenter. 42 Queen St.
M'Ilhenny, James. Pilot. Lynch's Lane
M'Intire, Thomas. Captain Mariner. 9 Stoll's Alley
M'Intosh, Samuel. Attorney. 18 Friend St.
M'Inzey, Ann, Mrs. Lynch's Lane
M''verin, Daniel. Carpenter. National Bank Square
M'Jure, William. Boarding House. 14 Union St.
M'Kay, Ann, Mrs. Physician. 3 Beresford St.
M'Kay, Crafts. Watch Maker. 41 Elliot St.
M'Kay, Malcolm. Grocer. 44 King St.
M'Kee, ——, Mrs. Shop Keeper. 277 King St.
M'Kee, John. Brick Layer. 277 King St.
M'Kee, Mary, Mrs. Boarding House. 44 Church St.
M'Kenna, Charles. Druggist. 110 Queen St.
M'Kenzie, Andrew. Grocer. 123 Broad St.
M'Keven, Rebecca. Shop Keeper. 280 King St.
M'Kie, Robert. 6 Parsonage Lane
M'Kinfull, Henry. Brick Layer. 31 Wentworth St.
M'Kinlay, D. Merchant. Craft's N. Range
M'Lachlan, Campbell & Co. Merchants. 6 Tradd St.
M'Lane, Evan. Store. 188 Meeting St.
M'Lane, L. Grocer. 53 Tradd St.
M'Lean, Edward. Fish Market Clerk.
M'Lean, Watsen. Grocer. 69 East Bay St.
M'Leod, William. Planter. 286 King St.
M'Man, ——. Captain Mariner. 39 King St.
M'Millan, Richard. Stables & Wagon Yard. 3 King St. Continued
M'Neal, Archibald. Hatter. 29 Beaufain St.
M'Neal, Catherine. Shop Keeper. 36 Hasell St.
M'Phelon, Edward. Grocer & Liquor Store. 182 Meeting St.
M'Pherson, Duncan. Store. 72 King St.
M'Pherson, John. Planter. 97 Broad St.
M'Taggart, David. Merchant. 139 East Bay St.
M'Whann & Nephew. Merchants. 9 Broad St.
Macbeth, Henry & Co. Warehouse. 138 East Bay St.
Macbeth, Henry & Co. Merchants. 119 Tradd St.
Magee, James. Merchant. 18 Elliot St.
Mail, Sarah L. Seamstress. 4 Church St. Continued
Maine, John. Commission Merchant. Lynch's Lane
Mair & Means. Merchants. 136 Broad St.
Mair, James. Merchant. 10 Meeting St.
Mair, Patrick. Merchant. 25 East Bay St.
Mair, Thomas. Merchant. Craft's Range
Mair, Thomas & Co. Merchants. 34 East Bay St.
Malcolm, Thomas & Co. Merchants. 4 Nicholl's Wharf

103

Malone, James. Teacher of Mathematics. 75 Meeting St.

Malone, Mary, Mrs. Boarding House. 165 Meeting St.

Manigault, Gabriel. Planter. 122 Meeting St.

Manigault, Joseph. Planter. 7 Maiden Lane

Mann & Foltz. Merchants. Geyer's N. Range

Mann, Henry W. Grocer. 27 Wentworth St.

Mann, Marguerite. Boarding School. 148 Meeting St.

Mann, Spencer. Merchant. 25 Wentworth St.

Manson, George. Boat Builder. Wall St.

Manuel, Philip. Tailor. 59 King St.

Marc, George. Grocer. 63 Church St.

Marchal, Francis. Professor of Pianoforte. 21 Queen St.

Marchgaff, ——. Shoemaker. 249 King St.

Markley, Abraham. Merchant. 122 King St.

Marks, Humphrey. Shop Keeper. 137 King St.

Marks, S. M, & Joseph. Shop Keepers.

Marler, Francis. Tailor. 1 Elliot St.

Marlin, Edward. Tailor. Bull St., West End

Marlin, Edward, Sr. Import Inspector. 6 Guignard St.

Marr, Ann, Mrs. 43 Church St. Continued

Marsh, James. Shipwright. 24 Guignard St.

Marshall, Elizabeth, Miss. 86 Tradd St.

Marshall, Helena. Widow. Wall St.

Marshall, John. Planter. 12 Meeting St. Continued

Marshall, Mary S., Mrs. 251 King St.

Marshall, William. Vendue Master. Exchange Square.

Marshall, William. Dwelling House. Middle St.

Marshall, William. Captain. 33 Guignard St.

Marshall, William. Chancellor. 55 Meeting St.

Marshbourn, Nicholas. Carpenter. 5 George St.

Martin, Charles. Brick Layer. 17 Scarborough St.

Martin, Charlotte, Mrs. 72 Tradd St.

Martin, Elizabeth. Widow. 26 St. Philip's St.

Martin, George. Currier. 22 Beaufain St.

Martin, Henry. Oakum Maker. 10 Meeting St. Continued

Martin, Jacob. S.C. Bank, Medium Bookk. 174 Meeting St.

Martin, John. Assistant Clerk, National Bank.

Martin, John C. Livery Stable. 214 King St.

Martin, Lewis. Barber. 38 Union St.

Martin, Mary, Mrs. Seamstress. 249 King St.

Martin, Thomas. Merchant. 72 Tradd St.

Masias, S. H. Translator. 7 Clifford St.

Maslin, William. Trader. 19 Amen St.

Mason, Susanna. Widow. 50 Broad St.

Mason, William. Young Masters School. 27 Quince St.

Mason, William A. M. Academy. 19 Ellery St.

Mathew, Philip, Rev. Minister Trinity Church. 9 Maiden Lane

Mathews, George. Vendue Master, Holmes and Co. Wentworth St., corner Bull

Mathews, John. Judge. Wentworth St., West End

Mathews, Mary, Mrs. Planter. 71 Tradd St.

Mathews, Thomas. Planter. 8 Church St. Continued

Mattuce, Mary. Boarding House. Bottle Alley

Maubant, P. & Co. Merchants. 88 Tradd St.

Maurant, John R. Grocer. 123 Queen St.

Maure, Lucie. Seamstress. 8 King St.

Mauroy, Leopold L. Engineer and Major, French Republic. 204 Queen St.

Maverick, Samuel. Merchant. 165 King St.

Mayas, Francis. Tobacconist. 114 King St.

Mazyck, Elizabeth C. Widow. 57 Meeting St.

Mazyck, Stephen. Planter. 3 Boundary St., West End

Mazyck, William. Factor, Gaillard and Mazyck. 3 Archdale St.

Mecomb, Joseph. Merchant. 139 King St.

Meeks, Joseph. Grocer. 4 St. Philip's St.

Melhado, Benjamin. Grocer. 8 Wentworth St.

Melic, Dusac. Barber. 41 Queen St.

Mener, Mathew. Shipmaster. 1 Trott St.

Merchant, Peter. Esquire. 15 Broad St.

Mercier, Lewis. Baker. 93 King St.

Merrell, Benjamin. Livery Stable. 37 & 38 Church St.

Merry, Patrick H. Captain, Mariner. 22 Guignard St.

Meurset, Amelia. Shop Keeper. 80 King St.

Mey, Florain C. Merchant. 43 Pinckney St.

Michaux, Francis D. Garden of French Republic

Michel, Els. Cookshop. Beresford's Alley

Michel, Veuve, Madame. Coming St.

Middleton, A., Mrs. 6 Front St.

Middleton, Dido. Seamstress. 8 Scarborough St.

Middleton, F., Mrs. 95 Broad St.

Middleton, Joseph. Carpenter. 17 Trott St.

Millar, Morrison & Co. Merchants. 82 Church St.

Millar, William. Tailor. 12 Queen St.

Miller & Robertson. Merchant. Geyer's Wharf

Miller, James. Shop Keeper. 2 Tradd St.

Miller, James. Wine Merchant. 61 East Bay St.

Miller, James, Jr. House Carpenter. Wentworth St., West End

Miller, John. Tavern Keeper. 179 King St.

Miller, John. Carpenter. 23 Beaufain St.

Miller, John. Dray Keeper. 87 Meeting St.

Miller, John D. 51 Trott St.

Miller, John David. Gold & Silver Smith and Jeweller. 111 Broad St.

Miller, Mary. Widow. 13 Ellery St.

Miller, Nicholas. 16 George St.

Miller, Nicholas. Baker. 4 Wentworth St.

Miller, William. Tailor. 1 Union St. Continued

Miller, William. Factor. 226 Meeting St.

Milligan, Joseph. Store Keeper. 73 King St.

Milligan, William. Director National Bank, Merchant. Craft's North Wharf

Milligan, William. Dwelling House. 11 Meeting St.

Mills, Thomas. Merchant. 108 Tradd St.

Mills, William. Esquire. 45 East Bay St. Continued

Milner, George. White & Blacksmith. 72 Church St. also home

Minchin, Male & Co. Wharfingers & Factors. Champney's Wharf

Minott, Thomas. Carpenter. 11 Stoll's Alley

Miot, ——, Mrs. Boarding House. Champney's St.

Mishaw, John. Grocer. 4 East Bay St. Continued

Mitchell, Ann, Mrs. 118 Meeting St.

Mitchell, James. Cooper. Vanderhorst's Wharf

Mitchell, James. Dwelling House. 18 Meeting St.

Mitchell, James. Carpenter. West St.

Mitchell, John, Col. Notary Public. 29 East Bay St.

Mitchell, John H. Notary Public. 2 Coates' Row.

Mitchell, John H. Dwelling House. 134 Lynch's Lane

Mitchell, Maria. Nurse. Lodge Alley

Mitchell, N. Carpenter. 55 Queen St.

Moan, John. Shipwright. 1 Lamboll St.

Moderen, James. Boarding House. Lodge Alley

Moer, William. Cooper. Mazyckborough

Moles, James. Dwelling House. 15 Pinckney St.

Moles, James. Blacksmith. Champney's Wharf

Moncrieff & Co. Merchants. 104 Church St.

Monk, James. Gold & Silver Smith. 21 Broad St.

Monpoey, Honore. Grocer. 41 Union St.

Montmain, Lewis-Claudius-Henry de. Planter. 85 King St.

Mood, Peter. Jeweller. 222 King St.

Moodie, Benjamin. British Consul. 12 Hasell St.

Moon, D. Chair Maker. 42 Queen St.

Mooney, Patrick. Grocery Store. 125 Queen St.

Moore & Meevers. Draymen. 8 East Bay St. Continued

Moore, George. Grocer. 40 Tradd St.

Moore, John. Grocer. 196 Meeting St.

Moore, John E. Planter. 33 Trott St.

Moore, Philip. Cabinet Maker. 28 Meeting St.

Moore, Richard. Painter. 11 Wentworth St.

Morales, Jacob. Store Keeper. 74 King St.

More, P. J., Dr. Surgeon, Dentist, Midwife. 47 King St.

Moret, Lewis. Confectioner. 137 Broad St.

Morgan, Charles. Shipwright. 2 Pinckney St.

Morgan, Henry. Boarding House. 31 Elliot St.

Morphy, Don Diego. Spanish Consul. 261 King St.

Morris, George. House Carpenter. 16 Archdale St.

Morris, Lewis, Col. Planter. 215 Meeting St.

Morris, Thomas. Captain. 58 Trott St.

Morrison, ——, Capt. Mariner. 37 George St.

Morrison, A. B., Mrs. 10 Bedon's Alley

Mortimer & Heron. Merchants. 14 Broad St.

Mortimer, William. 9 Meeting St. Continued

Morton, Alexander. Grocer. 231 King St.

Moser, Philip. Physician. 124 Broad St.

Moses, Abraham. Shop Keeper. 62 East Bay St.

Moses, Henry. Shop Keeper. 51 East Bay St.

Moses, Isaac. Store Keeper. 78 King St.

Moses, Isaiah. Store Keeper. 179 King St.

Moses, Joseph. Shop Keeper. 225 King St.

Moses, Lyon. Merchant. 18 Archdale St.

Moses, Philip. Shop Keeper. 268 King St.

Moses, Solomon. Constable. 188 King St.

Motta, E. D. L. Vendue Master. 48 Tradd St.

Motta, I. & E. Auctioneers. Exchange Square

Motte, Abraham. Planter. 39 East Bay St. Continued

Motte, Isaac, Mrs. 217 Meeting St.

Motte, Jacob. Merchant. 2 Cock Lane

Mouatt, John A. Clerk of S. C. Bank.

Moubray, Martha. Baker. 90 King St.

Moulin, Pierre. Mariner. 11 King St.

Moultrie, Alexander. Counsellor & Advocate. 2 Cumberland St.

Moultrie, Ann, Mrs. Planter. 62 Tradd St.

Moultrie, James. Physician. 48 Broad St.

Muckenfuss, Michael. Cabinet Maker. 53 King St.

Muir & Boyd. Merchants. Geyer's Wharf

Muir, William. Merchant & Director National Bank. 48 Meeting St.

Mulin, Rose. Widow. 31 Trott St.

Mulligan, Francis. Dwelling House. Mazyckborough

Mulligan, Francis. Collector of Excise. 133 East Bay.

Mulligan, John. Grocer. 131 East Bay St.

Muncreeff, John. House Carpenter. 9 East Bay St. Continued

Muncreeff, John, Jr. House Carpenter. 16 Federal Street

Muncreeff, Susannah, Mrs. 34 Hasell St.

Munds, Israel, Rev. Minister, Trinity Church. 6 Union St.

Munro, Amelia. Widow & Mantua Maker. 2 Guignard St.

Munro, Catharine, Mrs. Midwife. 19 Tradd St.

Munro, George. Captain Mariner. 63 Queen St.

Munro, John. Jewellery Store. 8 Elliot St.

Myer, Michael. Vendue Master's Cryer. 9 Parsonage Lane

Myers, Israel. Inspector Custom House & G. L. Tyler. Beresford St.

Myers, Samuel. Tailor. 208 King St.

Myers, Sarah. Widow. 5 Quince St.

Mylne, James. Baker. 17 Union St.

Naar, Moise. Tobacconist. 43 King St.

Naar, Mordecai. Trader. 12 Lamboll St.

Nailer, Robert. Merchant. 23 Lamboll St.

Napier, A. T. & Co. Merchants. Craft's Wharf

Nasar, Philip. Baker. 84 King St.

Nathan, Solomon. Shop Keeper. 229 King St.

Naylor, Thomas. Dwelling House. Minority St.

Naylor, Thomas. Store. 105 East Bay.

Nebuhr, J. David. Shop Keeper. 188 King St.

Negrin, J. J. Interpreter & Teacher of French and English Languages. 49 Church

Nelson, Ambrose. Captain Mariner. 53 Trott St.

Nelson, Francis. Shipwright. 24 East Bay St. Continued

Nelson, James. Attorney. 49 Broad St.

Nelson, John Dixon. Merchant. 73 Church St.

Neufville, Ann, Mrs. 125 King St.

Neufville, Isaac. Bookkeeper National Bank. Wentworth St., West End

Neufville, John. Comm. of Loans. 75 Queen St.

Neufville, Judy. Washer & Ironer. 48 Queen St.

Nevile, Joshua. Cabinet Maker. 43 Queen St.

Newman, ——, Miss. 6 Front St.

Newton, Sarah. Washer. 12 Meeting St.

Nicholls, George. Captain Mariner. 21 Scarborough St.

Nicholls, Thomas. Esquire. 79 East Bay St.

Nicholson, James. Attorney.

Niel, P. Planter of St. Domingo. 141 Meeting St.

Nipper, David. Bookbinder. 100 King St.

Nobbs, Samuel. Inspector of Custom House. 76 Meeting St.

Noble, Ezekiel. Merchant. 153 King St.

Noble, John. Physician. 189 King St.

Noble, Paul. Carpenter. 70 Tradd St.

Norris, Andrew. Attorney. 2 Wentworth St.

Norris, James. Chair Maker. 80 Meeting St.

Norris, Stephen. Shipwright. 163 King St.

Norroy, J. C. Francis. Tobacconist. 4 Meeting St. Continued

North, Richard B. Merchant. 15 Church St. Continued

North, Susannah. Widow. 38 Tradd St.

Norville, G. Mariner. Pinckney St.

Notts, E., Mrs. Boarding House. 44 Elliot Street

Nowell, E., Mrs. 99 Queen St.

Nowell, John. South Carolina Bank Director. 34 Trott St.

Nowell, Thomas S. Assistant Clerk of South Carolina Bank.

Nugent & Ward. Academy. 42 Broad St.

Nugent, Mary & Daughters. 13 Lamboll St.

Nunes, Elizabeth. Seamstress. 29 Beaufain St.

Nusser, Harmon. Baker. 29 Beaufain St.

O'Brien, M. Isabella, Miss. Jewellery Store. 120 Broad St.

O'Dino, ——. Grocer. 134 Meeting St.

O'Hara, Charles. Merchant. 9 Smith's Lane

O'Hara, Daniel & Sons. Merchants. 144 Broad St.

O'Hweiller, M. Baker. 9 Beresford St.

O'Kear, James. Accountant. 28 Church St. Continued

O'Kelley John. Tutor. Inquire at Translator's Office.

O'Kelley, Laurens. Grocer. 5 East Bay St. Continued

O'Neal, Charles. Negotiant. 138 King St.
O'Neal, Elizabeth. Nurse. 3 Clifford St.
Oeland, John. Shop Keeper. 8 Union St. Continued
Ogier & M'Kinney. Merchants. 113 East Bay St.
Ogier, & Maxwill. Dwelling House. 75 Tradd St.
Ogier & Maxwill. Factor. Crafts's N. Range
Ogilvie, John Alexander. Planter. 41 George St.
Oliphant, David. Painter. 9 Ellery St.
Oliver, James. Brick Layer. Wall St.
Olivier, Antonio. Hair Dresser. 12 Union St.
Olman, -----, Madame. Confectioner. 127 Queen St.
Ormond, William. Captain Mariner. 10 East Bay St. Continued
Orth, George. Baker. Boundary St., West End
Osborne, Henry. Academy. 65 Queen St.
Osborne, Thomas. Planter. 6 South Bay
Oston, Elizabeth. Seamstress. 8 King St.
Otto, John. Drayman. 105 Meeting St.
Owen, John. Dwelling House. Bull St
Owen, John. Merchant. 27 Tradd St.
Paine & Collier, William. Merchants. 131 Broad St.
Paine, James. Captain, Mariner. 34 King St.
Paine, Thomas. Captain Mariner. 265 King St.
Palmatry, Philepina. Seamstress. Bull St., corner Coming
Palmer, Job. House Carpenter and Clerk of Independent Church. 32 Trott St.
Palmer, John. Sergeant City Guard. 4 Price's Alley
Paque, F. Gabriel. House Carpenter. Boundary St., East End
Parker, Catherine. Milliner. 64 Meeting St.
Parker, Elizabeth, Mrs. 64 Queen St.
Parker, Florida. Widow. 26 Guignard St.
Parker, George. Planter. 83 East Bay St.
Parker, Isaac. Planter. 9 Legare St.
Parker, John. Attorney. 4 St. Michael's Alley
Parker, John, Jr. Planter. 36 Trott St.
Parker, Thomas. Attorney. 33 Meeting St.
Parker, Thomas C. Store. 6 Broad St. House Same
Parker, William. Physician Poor, Orphan House
Parker, William. Physician. 39 Hasell St.
Parks, John. 6 St. Philip's St.
Parks, John. Shoemaker. 23 Union St.
Parks, Samuel. Shoe Warehouse. 92 King St.
Patch, Francis. Captain Mariner. Bottle Alley
Paterson, Hugh. Insurance Broker, Mut. Co. 3 Broad St.
Patiot, Francoise, Madame. French School. 109 King St.
Paton, John. Bookkeeper. 22 Hasell St.
Paul, D. Shop Keeper. 224 King St.
Payne, William. Marble Mason. 209 King St.
Peace, Joseph. Attorney. State House Square
Pearce, Reuben & Co. Shoe Warehouse. 28 Church St.
Peaxton, Henry. Bookkeeper. 4 Beresford St.
Pebarte, Jean. Planter. 17 George St.
Peigne, L. 195 Meeting St.
Pelam, Charles. City Guard. 114 Meeting St.
Pelletant, J. A. Grocery Store. 131 Queen St.
Pellisson, William. Clerk of Roman Church. 145 Meeting St.
Penge, -----, Mrs. Mantua Maker. 195 Meeting St.
Pennall, James. Merchant. 180 King St.
Pepoon, Benjamin. Grocery Store. 10 Queen St.
Peppin, Joseph & Co. Merchants. Geyer's Wharf
Peppin, Joseph & Co. Dwelling House. 103 Church St.
Perdriau, Peter. House Carpenter. 1 Linguard St.

Perinchief, James. Captain Mariner. 49 Church St.
Peronne, Cesar. Captain & Grocer. Wall St.
Peronneau, -----, Mrs. 41 Church St. Continued
Peronneau, William. Esquire. 9 George St.
Peronner, Hagen. Washer. 2 Lightwood's Alley
Perrie, Isabella, Mrs. Midwife. 54 Meeting St.
Perry, Samuel. Tin Plate Worker. 113 Broad St.
Petrie, Alexander. Factor. Geyer's Wharf
Petrie, Alexnader. Dwelling House. 1 Orange St.
Petrie, George. School Master. 9 Federal St.
Peyton, -----. Captain Mariner. Champney's St.
Phelps, Anson G. Saddler & Harness Maker. 111 King St.
Philips, David. Broker. 200 Meeting St.
Philips, Dorothea. Widow & Saddlershop. 180 Meeting St.
Philis, Thomas. Mariner. 4 Ellery St.
Phillips, E. & B. Boot & Shoe Store. 27 Elliot St.
Phillips, J. Watch Maker. 15 Trott St.
Phillips, John. Painter & Glazier. 46 Broad St.
Philson, Alexander. Merchant. 196 King St.
Pickton, Charles & Thomas. House Carpenters. 8 Anson St.
Pilotte, John. Grocer. King St. Road
Pilotte, Onesime. Grocer. 6 Elliot St
Pilsbury, Samuel. Custom House Export Inspector. 4 Charles St.
Pinckney, Charles. U. S. Envoy to Spain. 222 Meeting St.
Pinckney, Charles Coatesworth. General. 1 East Bay St. Continued
Pinckney, Maria & Harriot. 59 Tradd St.
Pinckney, Roger, Mrs. 14 Legare St.
Pinckney, Thomas. Planter. 2 Price's Alley
Pinckney, Thomas, Major. Planter. 42 George St.
Pinsan, Charles. Hardware & Jewellery Store. 93 Queen St.
Piot, Elizabeth P., Mrs. Planter. 25 St. Philip's St.
Placide, Alexander. Charleston Theatre Manager and Dancing Master. 93 Broad St.
Plissonneau, John. Sailmaker. 49 Broad St.
Plumet, John, Dr. Physician. 255 King St.
Poincignon, P. A. Tin Plate Worker. 2 Queen St.
Poinsett, Eliza. Physician & South Carolina Bank Director. 294 King St.
Poissenot, Joseph. Shop Keeper. Beresford's Alley
Pollock, Solomon. Horse Dealer. Bull St.
Polony, Jean-Louis. Physician. 17 Church St.
Pool, Isaac. Shop Keeper. 223 King St.
Porter & Watson. Vendue Masters. Exchange Square
Porter, Benjamin. Cabinet Maker. 177 Meeting St.
Porter Peter. Blacksmith. 245 King St.
Porter, William. Boarding House. 13 Union St.
Porter, William. Vendue Master. 39 Elliot St.
Postel, -----, Mrs. Meeting St. Continued
Postell, Edward. Chair Maker. 12 George St.
Potter, Isaac. Vendue Master. Savage St.
Potter, John. Merchant. 19 Broad St.
Poulson, Edward. Mariner. 20 Church St.
Power, Thomas. Shop Keeper. Minority St.
Poyas, John Honest. Planter. 29 Meeting St.
Poyas, John Lewis. House Carpenter. 1 Cumberland St.
Pratt, Samuel H. Merchant. 35 East Bay St.
Prendergast, Cloe. Boundary St., East End
Prendergast, P. E. School Master. National Bank Square
Prentice, John. Chair Maker. 30 Archdale St.

106

Prentice, John. Chair Maker. 4 Archdale St.
Presley, William. Merchant. 86 King St.
Prestman & Co. Merchants. 115 East Bay St.
Presvot, E., Mrs. Planter. 16 Beresford St.
Presvot, Maria J. Mantua Maker.
Price, John. Counting House. 15 Guignard St.
Price, John. Counting House. Geyer's Wharf
Price, Thomas. Planter. 7 Boundary St., West End
Price, William. Planter. Orange St.
Primrose, Amelia. Mantua Maker. 11 Beresford St.
Primrose, Catherine. 21 St. Philip's St.
Prince, Charles. Captain Mariner. 15 Ellery St.
Prince, Charles. Tin Plate Worker. 246 King St.
Pringle, ——, Mrs. Seamstress. 4 Cock Lane
Pringle, John J. Attorney General. 93 Tradd St.
Pringle, Robert, Dr. Physician. 7 Friend St.
Prioleau, Isaac. Factor. 49 Meeting St.
Prioleau, Jane B., Mrs. Maiden Lane
Prioleau, John Cordes. Captain Merchant. 7 Front St.
Prioleau, Philip Gendron. Physician. 49 Meeting St.
Prioleau, Philip, Mrs. 32 Queen St.
Prioleau, Rose. Washer. 52 Queen St.
Prioleau, Samuel. Esquire. 49 Meeting St.
Pritchard, George. Planter (Christ Church). Linguard St.
Pritchard, Joseph. Wharfinger. Gadsden's Wharf
Pritchard, W., Jr. Shipwright. 2 Charles St.
Pritchard, William, Sr. Dwelling House. 1 Pinckney St.
Pritchard, William, Sr. Shipwright. Pritchard's Wharf
Provand, Baird & M'Murrich. Merchants. 16 Elliot St.
Purcel, Joseph. Land Surveyor. 123 King St.
Purcell, Henry, Rev. Dr. Pastor St. Michael's. 1 Legare St.
Purse, F., Mrs. Mantua Maker. 117 Broad St.
Purse, William. Jeweller & Watchmaker. 117 Broad St.
Purvis, William. Merchant. 8 Meeting St. Continued
Quackinbush, Laurence. Cabinet Maker. 9 Guignard St.
Quanan, Dennis. Tobacconist. 26 Hasell St.
Quash, Robert. Planter. 91 Broad St.
Quigin, David. Boarding House. Lodge Alley
Quigly, Esther, Mrs. 15 Hasell St.
Quinby, Joseph. House Carpenter & Shop. 6 & 7 Pinckney St.
Radcliffe, Thomas, Sr. Planter. 6 George St.
Radcliffe, Thomas, Sr. Planter. 43 George St.
Radman, James. Rigger. 25 Beaufain St.
Radman, Samuel. Painter. 8 Beresford St.
Ragg, Squash. Wheelwright. Middle St.
Raine, Thomas. Scrivener. 221 King St.
Ralph, ——, Mrs. Boarding House. 44 Church St.
Ralston & Co. Merchants. 4 Elliot St. Continued
Ramage, F., Mrs. Boarding House. 187 Meeting St.
Ramely, Barbara. Washer & Ironer. Coming St.
Ramsay, David. Physician. 106 Broad St.
Ramsay, George. Shop Keeper. Chalmer's Alley
Ramsay, John. Physician. 37 Meeting St.
Ramsay, Joseph. Physician. 30 Tradd St.
Randale, Hannah, Mrs. 11 Legare St.
Randle, Esther. Boarding School. 9 Federal St.
Rankin & Co. Grocers. 233 King St.
Ravenel, Daniel, Esquire. Planter. 81 Broad St.
Ravenel, Daniel, Jr. 115 Broad St.
Ravenel, Elizabeth, Mrs. Planter. 62 Meeting St.
Ravenel, Stephen. Mesne Conveyancer. 2 Boundary St., West End
Read, William. Physician. 19 Church St. Continued
Recard, Peter. Cook. 10 Amen St.

Rechon, David. Tailor. 110 King St.
Reeves, Enos. Dwelling House. West St.
Reeves, Enos. Jeweller. 112 Broad St.
Reid, George. Notary Public. 12 East Bay St.
Reid, James. Assistant Clerk National Bank. 1 Coming St.
Reid, John. Tin Plate Worker. 36 Church St.
Reid, John. Wheelwright. 173 Meeting St.
Reigne, John. Baker. 9 Elliot St.
Reilly, R. Hatter. 59 Queen St.
Reilly, Thomas. Physician. 4 Union St. Continued
Reinoldes, Elizabeth, Mrs. 84 Queen St.
Remondo, Peter. Shop Keeper. 30 Elliot St.
Remouissin, Daniel. Planter. 7 Legare St.
Remouissin, M. P. D. Planter. 30 Beaufain St.
Renauld, John. Fruit Shop. 34 Tradd St.
Reside, William. Cabinet Maker. 189 Meeting St.
Revel, ——, Mr. Merchant. 6 Elliot St. Continued
Rhind, Elizabeth, Mrs. Wentworth St., West End
Rhodes, ——. Factor, Bold and Rhodes. 13 East Bay St.
Ricardo, Benjamin. Store Keeper. 89 King St.
Richard, Samuel. Broker. 21 East Bay St. Continued
Richards, ——. Captain Mariner. 14 East Bay St. Continued
Richardson, James. Captain Mariner. 7 Beresford's Alley
Richardson, Thomas. Merchant. 61 Meeting St.
Richer, Felix. 47 Broad St.
Rigalle, Benjamin. Cotton Gin Maker and Razor Grinder. 137 Meeting St.
Rigaud, Peter. Grocer. Middle St.
Righton, Joseph. Cooper. 1 Water St.
Righton, M'Cully. Cooper. 1 Water St.
Rivers, Samuel. Shipwright. 6 Water St.
Rivers, Thomas. Planter. 1 Stoll's Alley
Rivers, Thomas, Jr. 48 Trott St.
Rivers, Tobia. Fisherman. Lynch's Lane
Riviere, Mary Louisa. Cake Shop. 108 King St.
Roach, William. City Treasurer. 15 Quince St.
Roberts, Adam. Captain Mariner. 4 Maiden Lane
Roberts, Ann, Mrs. 7 Church St.
Roberts, John. Captain Mariner. Wall St.
Roberts, Susannah, Mrs. Private Boarding House. Amen St., corner 24 Union
Roberts, William. Chair Maker. 78 Queen St.
Robertson & Co. Merchants. 118 Tradd St.
Robertson & Sons. Merchant. 147 King St.
Robertson, Peter. Painter. 8 Parsonage Lane
Robertson, William. Attorney. 56 King St.
Robinet, Francis. Cooper. 123 East Bay.
Robinet, Francis. Dwelling house. Wentworth St., West End
Robinson, Francis, Miss. Seamstress. 5 Whim's Court
Robinson, John. Merchant. 142 King St.
Robinson, Mary, Mrs. 38 Queen St.
Robinson, William. Assistant St. Mary's Hotel.
Robiou, N. C. Planter of St. Domingo. 6 Federal St.
Roche, John. Grocer. 10 Union St. Continued
Rodgers, Samuel. Organist St. Michael's. 18 Church St. Continued
Rodick, Thomas & Co. Merchants. 5 Tradd St.
Rodman, Mary. Boarding House. 33 Union St. Continued
Rodrigues, Abraham. Merchant. 106 Queen St.
Rogers, Christopher. 25 Tradd St.
Rogers, Samson. Rigger. 115 Meeting St.
Rogers, Sarah, Mrs. Planter. 26 Church St. Continued

Rolain, Catherine, Miss. 54 Queen St.
Roper, Thomas. Late Intendant. 71 East Bay St.
Roper, William. Planter. 5 East Bay St.
Ross, E. Shop Keeper. 69 King St.
Ross, Jeremiah, Mrs. 71 Meeting St.
Ross, Thomas. Captain Mariner. 21 Ellery St.
Rossignol, ----, Madame. 71 Meeting St.
Rou, M. Jr. Cabinet Maker. 22 George St.
Rou, M., Sr. Carter. 22 George St.
Roulain, Robert. Brick Layer. 43 George St.
Roullit, ----, Mrs. & Miss. Merchant. 107 Queen St.
Roupell, E., Mrs. Planter. 73 Tradd St.
Rouse, William. Tanner & Leather Manuf. 43 Meeting St.
Rout, George. Young Misses Boarding School. 17 Archdale St.
Roux, Lewis. Merchant. 54 Broad St.
Rowand, ----, Mrs. 2 Friend St.
Roworth, George. Saddler. 1 Market St.
Royall, James. Mariner. 34 Union St. Continued
Royer, Leah. School. 3 Linguard St.
Royer, Maire Magdelaine. Cake Shop. 167 King St.
Ruberry, John. Carpenter. Stoll's Alley
Rugan, John. Merchant. Craft's N. Range
Russel, Benjamin. Brick Layer. 29 Guignard St.
Russel, Daniel. House Carpenter. 2 Charles St.
Russel, Nathaniel. Director National Bank.
Russel, William & Co. Merchants. 29 Church St.
Rutledge, Frederic. Planter. 59 Tradd St.
Rutledge, H. Planter. 6 Front St.
Rutledge, Hugh. Judge Court Equity. 15 St. Philip's St.
Rutledge, Mary. Lady of late Gov. Obiit. 53 Broad St.
Ryan, Elizabeth. Shop Keeper. 52 East Bay St.
Ryan, James. State House
Ryckbosch, Temperance, Mrs. 70 Church St.
Sage, William. House Carpenter. 144 Meeting St.
Saint Cellery, Peter. Hair Dresser. 2 Elliot Street
Saltus & Yates. Ship Chandlers. 41 East Bay St. & Craft's Range
Samory, Claudius. Grocery Store. 19 Queen St.
Sanders, John. Dwelling House. 170 King St.
Sanders, John. Factor. Roper's Wharf
Sanders, Lindart. Washer. West St.
Santi, Angelo. Confectioner. 60 King St.
Sarrazin, Catherine & Mary. Spinsters. 12 Wentworth St.
Sartoris, P. Merchant. 2 Society St.
Sass, Jacob. Cabinet Maker. 34 & 35 Queen St.
Savage, Martha, Mrs. Broad St., Southwest End
Scanty, Ann, Mrs. 4 Guignard St.
Schem, J. F. Watch Maker, See Himeley. 135 Broad St.
Schepeler, L. C. A. Merchant. 37 Pinckeny St.
Schepeler, L. C. A. Store & Counting House. 5 Nicholl's Wharf
Schmidt, John F. Merchant. 205 King St.
Schmidt, John F. Merchant. 116 East Bay St.
Schutt, Caspar C. Merchant. 103 Broad St.
Schutt, Caspar C. Stores & Counting House. 8 East Bay St.
Scoffery, John. Merchant of St. Domingo. 10 Society St.
Scott, Alexander. Drayman. 20 Scarborough St.
Scott, Ann. Shop Keeper. 230 King St.
Scott, Campell & Co. Vendue Masters. Exchange Square, corner Champney's
Scott, James. Vendue Master. Champney's St.

Scrimzeour, J. & C. Merchants. 110 Tradd St.
Scriven, Thomas, Col. Planter. Mazyckborough
Seagraft, Peter. Esquire. 2 Liberty St.
Sears, Louisa. Boarding House. 11 Union St.
Seaver, Abraham. House Carpenter. 36 Pinckney St.
Sebbe, Sebben. Grocer. 14 and 15 Church St.
Sebrook, Benjamin. Planter. 86 Broad St.
Seecreets, Martin. Captain Mariner. 16 Amen St.
Seixas, J. M. Master Work House. Savage St.
Serjant, Mary. Store. 97 Church St. also house
Seyle & Schultze. Saddle & Harness Makers. 100 King St.
Seyler, Daniel. Butcher Stall 9. Bull St., corner Coming
Seymour, Isaac. Harbor Master. 5 Orange St.
Seymour, Stephen. Harbor Master. 5 Orange St.
Shackleford & Dupre. Factors. 4 Gaillard's Wharf
Shackleford, Nathan. Merchant. 23 Union St. Continued
Shand, Robert. Custom House Inspector. 178 Meeting St.
Sharp, John. Mast, Pump & Block Maker. 100 East Bay.
Sharp, John. Dwelling House. 8 Pinckney St.
Shaw, James. Factor. Blake's Wharf
Shaw, Richard. Tailor. 147 Meeting St.
Shepherd, James. Harness Maker. Coming St.
Shepphard, Samuel. Carver & Guilder. 186 Meeting St.
Sher, John. House Builder. Coming St.
Sherer, John. Captain Mariner. 25 Quince St.
Sherman & Macneill. Merchants. 155 King St.
Shievely, George. Grocer. 116 Meeting St.
Shilling, Samuel. Tailor. Coming St.
Shirras, Alexander. Merchant & Director, S.C. Bank. Elliot St.
Shirtliff, William & Co. Factors. 1 Prioleau's North Range
Shoolbred, James. Planter. 7 Lamboll St.
Shreiner, N. & Co. Grocers. George St., corner Coming
Shrewbury, Mary Ann. Widow. 12 Guignard St.
Shrewbury, Stephen. Collection Clerk, S.C. Bank. 8 Cumberland St.
Shrockmorton, Richard. Grocer. 106 King St.
Shumway, Alpheus. Saddler. King St.
Shutterlane, Mary. Widow. 27 Beaufain St.
Sibley, Joseph. Wine Merchant. 10 Union St. Continued
Silbery, Nicholas. Cabinet Maker & Undertaker. 9 Front St., corner Middle
Simmons, Francis. Planter. 19 Legare St.
Simmons, William. Planter. 16 Meeting St.
Simon, Bartholemy. Tailor. 12 Union St.
Simon, Simpson. Shop Keeper. 105 King St.
Simons, James. Collector Custom House. 18 Beaufain St.
Simons, Keating. Factor & Director, South Carolina Bank. 3 Orange St.
Simons, Keating & Son. Factors. 150 East Bay St.
Simons, Samuel. Broker. 20 Beresford St.
Simons, Sarah R., Mrs. Planter. 58 Tradd St.
Simons, Thomas. Merchant & Director National Bank. 2 Gaillard's Wharf
Simons, Thomas. Dwelling House. 44 East Bay St.
Simpson, John. Ship Chandler & Grocer. 104 East Bay St.
Simpson, M., Mrs. 111 Church St.
Sinclair, Alexander & Co. Merchants. 17 Elliot St.
Singleton, Jane, Miss. Milliner. 107 Tradd St.

Singleton, Mary, Mrs. 3 Trott St.
Singleton, Tobitha. Seamstress. 19 Trott St.
Sisk, Susanna, Mrs. Boarding House. 74 East Bay St.
Skirving, Charlotte, Mrs. 16 Church St. Continued
Slann, Ann. Seamstress. 18 Trott St.
Sleedman, Charles. House Carpenter. 133 Meeting St.
Slowcock, Caty. Washer & Ironer. 11 Guignard St.
Smallwood, Richard. Deputy Weigher Customs. 22 Pinckney St.
Smart & Evans. Boot & Shoe Makers. 36 Broad St.
Smerdon, Elias. Marine Insurance & Ship Broker. 38 East Bay St.
Smerdon, Henry. Vendue Master. 38 East Bay St.
Smille, Susannah, Mrs. 7 South Bay
Smiser, Hannah, Mrs. 48 Church St.
Smith, ----. Deputy Sheriff. 5 Boundary St., West End
Smith, Amos. Shoemaker. 26 Union St.
Smith, Angus, Mrs. Planter. 10 Mazyck St.
Smith, Ann. Shop Keeper. 20 Meeting St.
Smith, Archibald. Esquire. 20 Quince St.
Smith, B., Mrs. Planter. 73 Queen St.
Smith, Benjamin Burgh. Attorney. 103 Tradd St.
Smith, Caleb. Custom House Inspector. 71 Church St.
Smith, Christopher F. Kolfbaan Keeper. 132 King St.
Smith, Daniel. Bookkeeper. 5 Society St.
Smith, Frederick. Grocer. 183 Meeting St.
Smith, George. Scrivener. 8 Guignard St.
Smith, George. House Carpenter. Middle St.
Smith, Henry. Shipwright. 6 Maiden Lane
Smith, James. Rigger. 6 Cock Lane
Smith, John, L. L. D. Academy. 82 Broad St.
Smith, John R. Planter. Short St.
Smith, Josiah. Cashier, National Bank.
Smith, Margaret. Shop Keeper. 187 King St.
Smith, Mary Ann. School. 69 Church St.
Smith, Mary J. C., Mrs. Planter. 57 King St.
Smith, Obrien. Planter. 11 Church St.
Smith, Peter. Planter. 2 South Bay
Smith, Peter. Wharfinger. 4 South Bay
Smith, Peter. Captain. South Bay.
Smith, Peter. 23 Mazyck Lane
Smith, Phibus. Washer. 63 Queen St.
Smith, Robert. Planter. Boundary St., East End
Smith, Robert. Bishop Obitt. 23 Wentworth St.
Smith, Roger, Jr. Planter. Mazyckborough
Smith, Roger, Sr. Esquire. 19 St. Philip's St.
Smith, Samuel. Shop Keeper. 142 Broad St.
Smith, Samuel. Miniature Painter. 27 Hasell St.
Smith, Samuel. Factor. 39 Broad St.
Smith, Sarah, Mrs. 22 Church St.
Smith, T., Mrs. 21 Friend St.
Smith, Thomas Rhett. Planter. 56 Tradd St.
Smith, Whiteford. Grocer. 56 Church St.
Smith, William. Shipwright. 3 Charles St.
Smith, William. Merchant. 42 East Bay St. Continued
Smith, William. Wharfinger. Smith's Wharf
Smith, William. Shipwright. 16 Union St.
Smith, William. Ironmonger. 21 Elliot St.
Smith, William. Captain Mariner. 10 Stoll's Alley
Smith, William. House Carpenter. Wall St.
Smith, William S. Barrister. 38 Broad St.
Smithers, Mary. Shop Keeper. 4 Beresford's Alley
Smylie, Andrew. Merchant. 15 Broad St.
Smylie, Andrew. Dwelling House. 17 East Bay St. Continued
Smyth, John. Planter. 20 Ellery St.
Smyth, John & Co. Merchants. 178 King St.
Snelling, Abey. Pastry Cook. 35 Broad St.

Snipes & Sanders. Factors. 6 East Bay St.
Snowden, Charles. Merchant. 60 East Bay St.
Snyder, Ann. Seamstress. Middle St.
Sollee, John. Broker. 15 Federal St.
Solomon, Alexander. Shop Keeper. 188 King St.
Solomon, Chapman. Shop Keeper. 185 King St.
Solomon, Joseph. Shop Keeper. 186 King St.
Somarsall, Thomas. Merchant. 10 East Bay St.
Somarsall, William. Merchant & Director, S.C. Bank. 3 East Bay St.
Sparks, Thomas. Harness Maker. 39 Queen St.
Spears, James. House Carpenter. 3 Society St.
Speissegger, John, Jr. Music & Instrument Maker. 4 Hasell St.
Spencer, Joseph. Captain Mariner. 16 Queen St.
Spencer, Sebastian. 168 Meeting St.
Spidle, John G. House Builder. 24 Archdale St.
Spierin, Patrick. Merchant. 177 King St.
Spierin, Thomas P. Planter. 266 King St.
Spinler, Jacob. Hair Dresser. 108 Queen St.
Stafford, Theodore. Chair Maker. 42 Queen St.
Stall, Thomas D. Coach Maker. 28 Trott St.
Stank, Christopher. Shop Keeper. 25 Trott St.
Stent, ----, Mrs. Widow. King St.
Stent, Mary C., Mrs. 34 Church St.
Stephen, Hannah. Nurse. 4 Smith St.
Stephen, Thomas. Vendue Master & Commercial Broker. 102 Tradd St.
Stephen, William. Merchant. 151 King St.
Stephens, William. Factor. Nicholl's Wharf
Stephens, William. Dwelling House. 17 Friend St.
Stevens & Ramsay. Physicians. 44 East Bay St.
Stevens, Daniel. Supervisor, Custom House. 30 George St.
Stevens, J. H. Sheriff, City. Exchange
Stevens, Jarvis H. City Sheriff. 68 Tradd St.
Stevens, William S. Physician. 15 King St.
Stevenson, Mary, Mrs. 40 King St.
Stewart, Alexander. House Carpenter. 275 King St.
Stewart, Charles. Barrister. State House
Stewart, Henry. House Carpenter. 28 St. Phillip St.
Stewart, John. Vendue Master. 19 Hasell St.
Stewart, Lambold. Newspaper Carrier. 278 King St.
Stewart, M., Miss. Boarding School. 58 Meeting St.
Stewart, M., Mrs. 14 Bedon's Alley
Stewart, Mary. Washer. 12 Quince St.
Stewart, R. Merchant & Ship Chandler. 201 King St.
Stewart, R. Merchant & Ship Chandler. 29 East Bay St.
Stewart, Thomas. Merchant. 31 East Bay St.
Stewart, William. School Master. 4 Price's Alley
Still, Jacob. Shop Keeper. 164 King St.
Stock, Margaret, Mrs. Planter. 6 Legare St.
Stoll, Jacob. Tin Plate Worker. 198 King St.
Stone, F., Mrs. Coming St.
Stoney, John. Merchant, Williamson and Stoney. 8 Hasell St.
Stowe, Richard R. Captain Mariner. 52 King St.
Striker, Catharine. Seamstress. Middle St.
Strobel, John. Butcher Stall 29. Bull St., corner Wentworth
Stroble, Daniel, Sr. Tanner & Currier. 118 Meeting St.
Stroble, Jacob. Butcher at New Market. 10 Magazine St.
Strohecker, J. White & Blacksmith. 154 Meeting St.
Stromer, H. M. Merchant. 19 Elliot St.
Stul, Sarah. Widow. Clifford St.

Sturgis, Josiah. Merchant. 4 Craft's Wharf

Sturgis, Josiah. Dwelling House. 40 Church St. Continued

Suares, Jacob & David. Merchants. 83 Tradd St.

Suau, Peter & Co. Merchants. Gaillard's Wharf

Suau, Peter & Co. Dwelling House. 120 King St.

Sutcliffe, Ely. House Carpenter. 26 Archdale St.

Sutherland & Carmichael. Merchants. 86 Church St.

Sutherland, F. Boot & Shoe Warehouse. 3 Queen St.

Sutton, Mary, Mrs. 145 Meeting St.

Swain, Joseph. Pilot. 35 East Bay St.

Swain, Rebecca, Mrs. 3 Stoll's Alley

Swaine, John. Printer. 25 Quince St.

Sweeney, James & Co. Vendue Masters. Exchange, Under South East Corner

Sweeny & Atkinson. Grocers. 40 East Bay St.

Sweet, ——, Mrs. Store Keeper. 3 Elliot St.

Swinton, Hugh. Planter. 74 Meeting St.

Switzer, John R. Saddler. 218 King St.

Symonds, ——, Mrs. Boarding House. 12 Church St. Continued

Symonds, Francis. Inspector Custom House. 12 Church St. Continued

Symonds, James. Cotton Gin & Mill Maker. 89 Meeting St.

Tabor, Elizabeth. Boarding House. 20 Trott St.

Taggart, Mary, Mrs. 17 Meeting St.

Tarver, John. Merchant. Tradd St.

Tate, James. Captain Mariner. 3 Elliot St.

Taylor, Benjamin. Tailor. 5 St. Philips St.

Taylor, Diana. Washer. 5 Anson St.

Taylor, J. G. Dwelling House. 19 Quince St.

Taylor, J. G. Grocery Store. Market Wharf, N.E.

Taylor, Joseph. Captain Mariner. 3 Charles St.

Taylor Margarite. Mantua Maker. 140 Meeting St.

Taylor, Sarah. Widow. 10 Quince St.

Teasdale, Isaac. Merchant. 112 Queen St.

Teasdale, John. Planter. 2 East Bay St.

Teraf, Philip. Rigger. 81 Meeting St.

Tew, Charles. Notary Public & Q. U. 43 Elliot St.

Tew, Charles. Dwelling House. 30 Wentworth St.

Thackam, Thomas. Planter. Boundary St., East End

Ther, Ebenezer. Broker. 79 Tradd St.

Therrel, Mary, Miss. Shop Keeper. 130 King St.

Theus, Rosanna, Mrs. 94 Queen St.

Theus, Simeon. Cashier of State Bank. 239 King St.

Thevenin, Peter. Planter in St. Domingo. 69 Meeting St.

Thirtle, William. Grocer. 13 Union St. Continued

Thom & Quackinbush. Cabinet Makers. 68 Meeting St.

Thomas, E. S. Bookkeeper & Stationer. 117 Tradd St.

Thomas, Francis. National Bank Discount Clerk. 29 Archdale St.

Thomas, J. R. Planter in St. Domingo. 6 Federal St.

Thomas, Jean Jacquer. Bookkeeper. 30 Trott St.

Thomas, John. Hair Dresser. 11 Bedon's Alley

Thomas, John. Captain Mariner. 41 East Bay St. Continued

Thomas, John. Grocer. 31 Union St.

Thomas, John D. 22 Union St.

Thomas, Joseph. Coach Makers, Wing and Thomas. 15 Hasell St.

Thomas, Mary Lamboll, Mrs. 12 King St.

Thomas, Stephen. Tailor. 34 Elliot St.

Thompson, Alexander. Brick Layer. 30 Queen St.

Thompson, Daniel. Shop Keeper. 13 South Bay

Thompson, James. Captain, Boarding Off. Champney's Wharf

Thompson, Margarite. Widow & Shop Keeper. 21 Beaufain St.

Thompson, Margarite. Widow & Boarding House. 63 East Bay St.

Thompson, Thomas. Boarding House. Lodge Alley

Thompson, William. Windsor Chair Maker. 138 Meeting St.

Thomson, S., Mrs. School. 40 Meeting St.

Thorne & Byrne. Sail Maker's Loft. Pritchard's Wharf

Thorne, J. Gardner. 3 Guignard St.

Thornhill, Wallis & Co. Merchants. 109 Tradd St.

Thornhill, Wallis & Co. Merchants. 17 Church St.

Threadcraft, Bethel. Watch & Clock Maker. 235 King St.

Thron, John. Grocer. 60 Meeting St.

Thwing & Hamell (Edward & Alexander). Carpenters. 4 Guignard St.

Timmons, William. Store. 143 East Bay St. & house

Timothy, Benjamin Franklin. Editor State Gazette. 32 East Bay St.

Tobias, Isaac. Store Keeper. 202 King St.

Tofel, John. Confectioner. 68 King St.

Toomer, Ann, Mrs. 7 Legare St.

Torrance, ——, Miss. 32 Queen St.

Torrance, James. Grocer. 157 Meeting St.

Torrans, Williams H. Attorney. 20 Trott St.

Torres, Abraham. Shop Keeper. 84 King St.

Torrey, William. Captain Mariner. 15 Ellery St.

Torry & Co. Opticians. 114 Tradd St.

Tourette, Thomas. Fruit Shop. 11 Queen St.

Toussiger, Marguerite. 4 Water St.

Tovey & Sharp. Mast, Pump & Block Makers. 100 East Bay St.

Trajetta, Fil. Music Master. 19 Beresford St.

Tran, William. Tobacconist. 12 Mazyck St.

Trenholm, William. Merchant. 149 East Bay.

Trenholm, William. Dwelling House. 14 Church St. Continued

Trescot, Edward. Planter. 72 Meeting St.

Trezevant, Lewis. Judge. 98 Queen St.

Trezevant, Peter. Discount Clerk State Bank. 2 Stoll's Alley

Triquelague, ——, Madame. 167 Meeting St.

Troup, James. Attorney & J. P. 104 Tradd St.

Truchelut, Joseph. Baker. 128 Queen St.

Truelle, James. Tailor. 38 Union St. Continued

Tucker, Mary, Mrs. 49 Church St.

Tucker, Sarah, Mrs. Academy. 108 Church St.

Tunno & Cox. Merchants. 27 East Bay St.

Tunno & Price. Merchants. Geyer's Wharf

Tunno, Adam. Director, National Bank.

Tunno, William. Merchant. 81 East Bay St.

Turci, Mary. Mantua Maker. 6 Linguard St.

Turnbull, James. Lumber Merchant. South Bay, West End

Turnbull, James. Dwelling House. 4 Lynch's Lane

Turnbull, James. Boarding House. 29 Union St. Continued

Turnbull, Robert J. Barrister. 198 Meeting St.

Turner, D. W. Deputy Sheriff. 6 Whim's Court

Turner, T. Boarding Hosue. 35 Union St.

Turner, Thomas. Captain & Dancing Master. 7 Parsonage Lane

Turpin, William. Junior Deputy Surveyor. 149 King St.

Turpin, William. Store Keeper. 149 King St.

Tush, ——, Mrs. 12 Friend St.

Tweddell, ——. Shoemaker. 29 Queen St.
Tweed, Alexander. Esquire. 3 Pinckney St.
Uglou, James. Baker. 17 Union St.
Ummensetter, John. Tanner & Currier. 27 Archdale St.
Unon, B. Merchant. Broad St.
Valbrune, Leonard. Tobacconist. 37 Union St. Continued
Vale, J. D. Planter. Harleston Green
Valentine, ——, Mrs. 32 King St.
Valk, Jacob Robert. Captain Mariner. 10 Stoll's Alley
Van Rhyn, A. E., Miss. Store. 134 Broad St. & house
Vanderherchen, Andrew. Tailor. 209 King St.
Vanderhorst & Miller. Merchants. Vanderhorst's Row
Vanderhorst, Arnoldus. Planter. 16 East Bay St.
Vardel, Elizabeth, Mrs. 24 King St.
Vaughn, Jesse. Shop Keeper. 45 Church St.
Vernon & Co. Jewellers. Union St., corner Broad
Verree & Blair. Auctioneer. Exchange Square
Verree, Mary, Mrs. 3 Church St.
Verree, Robert. Merchant. 15 Tradd St.
Vesey, ——, Capt. Merchant. King St. Road
Vesey, Charles M. Bookkeeper. 5 Parsonage Lane
Viannay, ——, Miss. Ravaudeuse. 254 King St.
Viegra, Joseph. Interpreter. 153 King St.
Vigie, Anthony. Grand Negociant en figares. 20 Archdale St.
Villaneavue, John B. Merchant. 6 Nicholl's Wharf
Villaneavue, John B. Dwelling House. Society St.
Vincendiere, La, Mr. King St. Road
Vincent, ——, Mrs. Boarding House. 5 Tradd St.
Virgent, Elizabeth, Mrs. 3 King St.
Vos, Andrew. Merchant. 31 Beaufain St.
Waggoner, Christopher. Drayman. 6 Trott St.
Wagner, George. Planter. 101 Broad St.
Waite, William. Coach Maker. 66 Meeting St.
Walker & Evans. Marble Cutters. 24 Trott St.
Walker, David. Grocer. 255 King St.
Walker, Robert. House Carpenter. Middle St.
Walker, William. Cabinet Maker. 23 Hasell St.
Wall, Richard. Boarding House.
Wallace, Alexander. Grocer. 14 Beresford's Alley
Wallace, Alexander. Grocer. 89 Meeting St.
Wallace, James. Sheriff. 223 Meeting St.
Wallace, James. Painter. 208 Meeting St.
Wallace, Moses. Merchant. 83 Tradd St.
Wallace, Thomas. Cabinet Maker. 25 Queen St.
Waller, Bayfield. Merchant & Bookseller, Bailey and Waller. 13 Magazine St.
Walsh, Edmond. Boarding House. 2 Elliot St. Continued
Ward, James M. Attorney. 176 Meeting St.
Ward, John. Intendant & Director, National Bank. 47 Church St.
Ward, Joshua. Planter. 210 Meeting St.
Warham, Mary, Mrs. Planter. 72 Queen St.
Warham, Woodward & Co. Factors. 145 Broad St.
Waring & Smith. Factor. Roper's Wharf
Waring, Daniel. Attorney. 13 Scarborough St.
Waring, Mary J., Mrs. 32 Wentworth St.
Waring, Morton. Factor. 273 King St.
Waring, Thomas, Sr. Naval Officer. 32 Meeting St.
Warley, Christiana & Daughters. 26 Beaufain St.
Warley, Elizabeth, Mrs. 6 Parsonage Lane
Warley, Felix. Planter. 8 Trott St.
Warner, Peneloppe, Mrs. Widow. 202 Meeting St.
Warnock, Joseph. S.O.H. Orphan House.
Warnock, Joseph. House Carpenter. 10 Liberty St.

Washbourn, Eleazar. Captain. 16 King St.
Washington, William. Colonel. Port St., corner South Bay
Wassinger, John. Baker. 174 King St.
Watson & Wodill. Cabinet Makers & Upholsterers. 5 Price's Alley
Watson & Wodill. Cabinet Makers and Upholsterers. 26 King St.
Watson, Alexander. Factor. 15 East Bay St. Continued
Watson, Lydia. Washer. 5 Friend St.
Watson, W. Grocer. 73 Meeting St.
Watt, James. Grocer. 29 Church St. Continued
Watts & Walker. Cabinet Makers. 39 Church St.
Watts, Robert. Grocer. 51 Queen St.
Weatherby, Daniel. Botanist. 11 Ellery St.
Weatherly, Statira, Mrs. 44 Tradd St.
Weathers, Thomas. Shipwright. 5 Cock Lane
Webb, John. Merchant. 14 Moore St.
Webb, W. Teller State Bank. 14 Moore St.
Webb, William. Deputy Collector. 14 Moore St.
Weets & Daker. Grocers. 24 Union St.
Weever, Mary. Seamstress. 2 Clifford St.
Welch, ——. Captain Mariner. 143 Meeting St.
Welch, Thomas G. Carver & Guilder. 16 Hasell St.
Weidman, ——, Mrs. Shop Keeper. 125 King St.
Wells, David. Tallow Chandler. Montagu St.
Wells, Edgar, Mrs. 19 George St.
Wells, Samuel. Mariner. 11 Pinckney St.
Welsh, Anthony. Grocer. Unity Alley
West, James. Physician. 49 Tradd St.
West, Simeon. Captain Mariner. Wall St.
Westerburg, John. Shipwright. 1 Cock Lane
Westermeyer, Andrew. Merchant & Gold & Silversmith. 19 Union St.
Weston, Plowden. Planter. 31 Queen St.
Weyman, Edward. Surveyor Custom house. Pitt St.
Whaley & Booadfoot. Merchants. 122 Tradd St.
Whaley, Thomas. Planter. 293 King St.
Wheeler & Parmele. Merchants. 101 Church St.
Wheeler & Warren. Merchants. 6 Bedon's Alley
White & Co. Merchant. 1 Bedon's Alley
White, James. Grocer. 129 Queen St.
White, John. Factor & Counting House. Geyer's N. Range
White, John. Dwelling House. 124 Meeting St.
Whitfield & Brown. Counting House & Stores. 13 Bedon's Alley
Whitfield & Brown. Merchants. 2 Bedon's Alley & house
Whitley & Co. Grocer. 10 East Bay St.
Whitney, Thomas H. Carver & Frame Maker. 196 Meeting St.
Whittimore, Retire. House Carpenter. 151 Meeting St.
Wigfall, Thomas. Planter. 46 George St.
Wightman, William. Jewellery Store. 186 Meeting St.
Wilcox & Flagg. Painters & Glaziers. 103 East Bay St.
Wilkenson, John. Boarding House. 2 Union St. Continued
Wilkenson, Samuel. Tailor. 15 Trott St.
Wilkey, William. Major. 116 Meeting St.
Wilkins, William. Constable. 6 Beresford St.
Wilkinson, Richard. Shoemaker. 9 Pinckney St.
Wilkinson, William. Captain Mariner. 49 Church St.
Will & Marlin. Cabinet Makers. 169 Meeting St.
Will, Philip. Federal Marshall. Middle St.
Williams, ——. Portrait Painter. 95 Queen St.
Williams, Abner. Coach Maker. 22 Archdale St.
Williams, David R. A. M. Planter. 110 Church St.

Williams, Isham. Wharfinger. Ham & Smith's Wharf
Williams, James. Import Inspector. 85 Union St.
Williams, John. Boarding House. 28 Union St.
Williams, Joseph. Hair Dresser. 5 Queen St.
Williams, Thomas. Tailor. 6 King St.
Williamson & Stoney. Factors. 3 Gaillard's Wharf
Williamson, Emilia. 103 King St.
Williamson, John. Director of Charleston Theatre. 4 Cumberland St.
Williamson, John. Director, S.C. Bank.
Williman, J. Physician. 226 King St.
Williman, Jacob. Tanner & Currier. Montagu St.
Williman, Jonathan. Planter. 15 Meeting St.
Willis & Millar. Bakers. 102 East Bay St.
Willis, Mary, Mrs. 19 George St.
Wilson, ——, Dr. Academy. 186 Meeting St.
Wilson, Elizabeth. 22 Mazyck St.
Wilson, Gover. Planter. 2 Meeting St.
Wilson, James. House Carpenter. 14 Quince St.
Wilson, James. Merchant. 18 Elliot St.
Wilson, John. Cabinet Maker. 126 Meeting St.
Wilson, Margaret. Seamstress. 267 King St.
Wilson, R. & Son. Physicians. 88 Church St.
Wilson, Robert. Captain Mariner. 2 Anson St.
Wilson, Robert, Jr. Physician. 211 Meeting St.
Wilson, Robert, Sr. Physician. 87 Broad St.
Wilson, Samuel. Physician. 43 Broad St.
Wilson, Thomas. Planter. 1 Federal St.
Windsor, Thomas. Captain Mariner. Wall St.
Wing & Thomas. Coach Makers. 23 Hasell St.
Winken, John H. Boarding House. 36 Union St.
Winn, Richard. Major General, 2d Div.
Winstanley, Thomas. Attorney. 86 East Bay St.
Winthrop, Joseph. Consul of Sweden, Merchant. 8 East Bay St.
Winthrop, Joseph. Consul of Sweden, Merchant. 147 East Bay St.
Winthrop, Joseph. Dwelling House. 57 Tradd St.
Wish & Bryan. Merchants. 148 Broad St.
Wish, Catherine. Widow. 58 Queen St.
Wissmann & Lorent. Merchants.
Wittich, Charles. Merchant, Gold & Silversmith & Jewellery Store. 30 Broad St.
Woddrop, John. Merchant & Director, National Bank. 9 East Bay St.
Woddrop, John. Merchant & Director, National Bank. 106 Church St.
Wolf, George. Grocer. 5 Hasell St.
Wolf, Rachel, Mrs. 259 King St.
Wolfe, John. Grocer. 182 King St.
Wood, William. Custom House Inspector. 15 Archdale St.
Wood, William. Rigger. Bottle Alley
Woodill, John A. Cabinet Maker & Upholsterer, Watson & Woddill 3 Price's Alley
Woodrouffe, E. L. Wholesale Store. 84 Church St.
Woodrouffe, E. L. Merchant. 84 Church St.
Woolf, Marguerite. Widow & Grocer. 5 Hasell St.
Worthington, Joseph. Upholder. 5 St. Michael's St.
Wragg, Samuel. Planter. Wall St.
Wragg, William. Planter. 82 East Bay St.
Wramch, Richard. Boarding House. 242 King St.
Wright, Elizabeth, Miss. 9 Orange St.
Wurdeman, J. C. Grocery Store. 9 Queen St.
Wyatt, ——, Mrs. 65 Church St.
Wyatt, Peter. Lumber Merchant. Lynch's Lane, Southwest End
Wyatt, Richard. Carpenter. 55 Church St.

Wylie, David. Merchant. 98 Church St.
Wyllie, Samuel. Merchant. 35 Elliot St.
Yates, D., Mrs. Boarding School. Port St.
Yates, Jeremiah. Merchant. Port St.
Yates, Joseph. Cooper. Beale's Wharf
Yates, Joseph. Dwelling House. 26 Church St. Continued
Yates, Seth. Ship Carpenter. Lynch's Lane.
Yeadon, Richard. Teller National Bank. 18 King St.
Yeadon, William. Attorney. 71 Queen St.
Yoer, Jacob. Shoemaker. 92 Queen St.
Youait, Susannah. Market Woman. 4 Scarborough St.
Young, Jane, Miss. Shop Keeper. 289 King St.
Young, John & Co. Merchants. 32 Broad St.
Young, Thomas. Boarding House. 25 Union St.
Young, Thomas, Mrs. 21 Friend St.
Young, William P. Bookseller & Printer. 41 Broad St.
Zealy, Joseph. Butcher. 263 King St.
Zeylstra, Peter. Merchant & Ship Chandler. 64 East Bay St.